Praise for *Roger Williams and the Creation of the American Soul*

"John Barry's *Roger Williams and the Creation of the American Soul* establishes Williams as a brave thinker and also a deft political actor. . . . Mr. Barry puts Williams squarely among our great political thinkers, crediting him with bringing liberal democracy to the American colonies."
—*The Wall Street Journal*

"Barry now turns his meticulous hand to the origins of two fundamental and perpetual American fixations: the conflict between church and state and that between the power of the state and the conscience of the citizen. . . . Present-day implications of an elemental clash of ideas may hover over every page, yet the vital drama of Barry's story emblazons two competing visions of American destiny: John Winthrop's 'city on a hill' vs. Williams's community of conscience. As Barry shows well and often prophetically, the national soul formed out of that drama remains a troubled, and occasionally tortured, one." —*The Washington Post*

"To call it a biography sells it short. What it is, really, is the history of an idea—about the critical importance of separating church from state. So revolutionary was this idea that it caused Williams to be banished from Massachusetts. . . . Williams created the first place in the Western world where people could believe in any God they wished—or no God at all—without fear of retribution."
—Joe Nocera, *The New York Times*

"In *Roger Williams and the Creation of the American Soul*, New York Times bestselling author John M. Barry tells the story with passion and an eye for fine detail. . . . If the story were not compelling enough, Barry's dramatic first chapter of conflict, confrontation, and banishment into the wilderness is worth the price of admission alone. . . . As Barry notes, the dispute 'opened a fissure in America, a fault line which would rive America all the way to the present.' John Barry deserves our thanks for illuminating this critical and timely chapter of American history."
—*The Seattle Times*

"There's a recurring theme among the religiously political/politically religious that the United States was founded as a Christian nation and that in this modern era we have somehow strayed from God and from our roots. John M. Barry's new book *Roger Williams and the Creation of the American Soul: Church, State, and the Birth of Liberty* is a counter-argument and it is a significant reminder of whence, exactly, this little experiment in democracy of ours came. . . . Absorbing."

—*Los Angeles Times*

"This biography should be read with today's headlines in mind. . . . Thoroughly researched and accessibly written . . . This is an important book because it brings back an important founding point in the development of the American character. But it also is a timely reminder that the issues that drove Williams into exile in Rhode Island are very much alive and just as perilous today."　—*The Washington Times*

"Fascinating . . . a swath of history Barry brings to urgent life with the same focused intelligence which distinguished *The Great Influenza*."

—*Booklist*

"A commanding history . . . masterly."　—*Library Journal*

"Absorbing narrative . . . This rich work by a master historian enlightens every page."　—*BookPage*

PENGUIN BOOKS

## ROGER WILLIAMS AND THE CREATION
## OF THE AMERICAN SOUL

John M. Barry is a prize-winning and *New York Times* bestselling author whose books have won more than twenty awards, including the National Academies of Science's Keck Award for the year's best book on science or medicine for *The Great Influenza,* and the Society of American Historians' Francis Parkman Prize for *Rising Tide: The Great Mississippi Flood of 1927 and How It Changed America,* named that year's best book on American history. He lives in New Orleans.

# ROGER WILLIAMS

## and

# THE CREATION

## *of the*

# AMERICAN SOUL

*Church, State, and the Birth of Liberty*

## JOHN M. BARRY

PENGUIN BOOKS

PENGUIN BOOKS

Published by the Penguin Group

Penguin Group (USA) Inc., 375 Hudson Street, New York, New York 10014, USA • Penguin Group (Canada), 90 Eglinton Avenue East, Suite 700, Toronto, Ontario M4P 2Y3, Canada (a division of Pearson Penguin Canada Inc.) • Penguin Books Ltd, 80 Strand, London WC2R 0RL, England • Penguin Ireland, 25 St Stephen's Green, Dublin 2, Ireland (a division of Penguin Books Ltd) • Penguin Group (Australia), 707 Collins Street, Melbourne, Victoria 3008, Australia (a division of Pearson Australia Group Pty Ltd) • Penguin Books India Pvt Ltd, 11 Community Centre, Panchsheel Park, New Delhi – 110 017, India • Penguin Group (NZ), 67 Apollo Drive, Rosedale, Auckland 0632, New Zealand (a division of Pearson New Zealand Ltd) • Penguin Books, Rosebank Office Park, 181 Jan Smuts Avenue, Parktown North 2193, South Africa • Penguin China, B7 Jaiming Center, 27 East Third Ring Road North, Chaoyang District, Beijing 100020, China

Penguin Books Ltd, Registered Offices: 80 Strand, London WC2R 0RL, England

First published in the United States of America by Viking Penguin,
a member of Penguin Group (USA) Inc. 2012
Published in Penguin Books 2012

10   9   8   7   6   5   4   3   2   1

Copyright © John M. Barry, 2012
All rights reserved

THE LIBRARY OF CONGRESS HAS CATALOGED THE HARDCOVER EDITION AS FOLLOWS:

Barry, John M., ———.
    Roger Williams and the creation of the American soul : church, state, and the birth of liberty / John M. Barry.
        p.   cm.
    Includes bibliographical references (p. 427) and index.
    ISBN 978-0-670-02305-9 (hc.)
    ISBN 978-0-14-312288-3 (pbk.)
    1. Williams, Roger, 1604?–1683.  I. Title.
    BX6495.W55B37 2012
    974.5'02092—dc23        2011032995

Printed in the United States of America
Designed by Carla Bolte
Maps by Jeffrey L. Ward

*To Anne and Rose and Jane and Brown*

*and Smoke and Dell and E,*

*and all the others behind the fountain*

# Contents

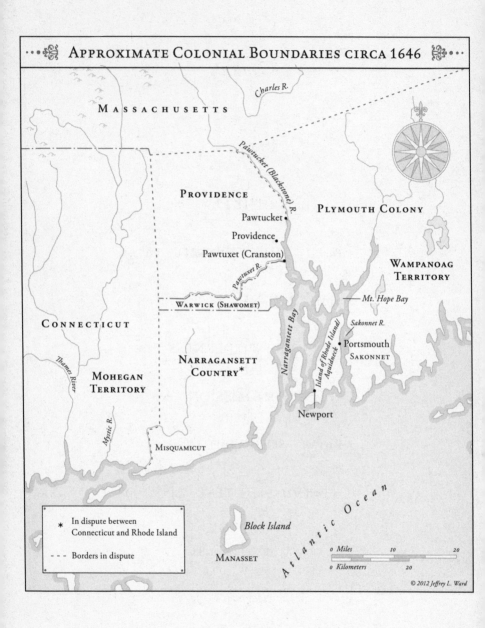

# Approximate Colonial Boundaries circa 1646

*Charles R.*

MASSACHUSETTS

PROVIDENCE

*Pawtucket (Blackstone) R.*

Pawtucket

Providence

Pawtuxet (Cranston)

*Pawtuxet R.*

WARWICK (SHAWOMET)

PLYMOUTH COLONY

WAMPANOAG TERRITORY

Mt. Hope Bay

*Sakonnet R.*

Portsmouth

SAKONNET

CONNECTICUT

*Thames River*

MOHEGAN TERRITORY

*Mystic R.*

NARRAGANSETT COUNTRY*

*Narragansett Bay*

*Island of Rhode Island/ Aquidneck*

Newport

MISQUAMICUT

* In dispute between Connecticut and Rhode Island

- - - Borders in dispute

*Block Island*

MANASSET

*Atlantic Ocean*

0 Miles 10 20

0 Kilometers 20

© 2012 Jeffrey L. Ward

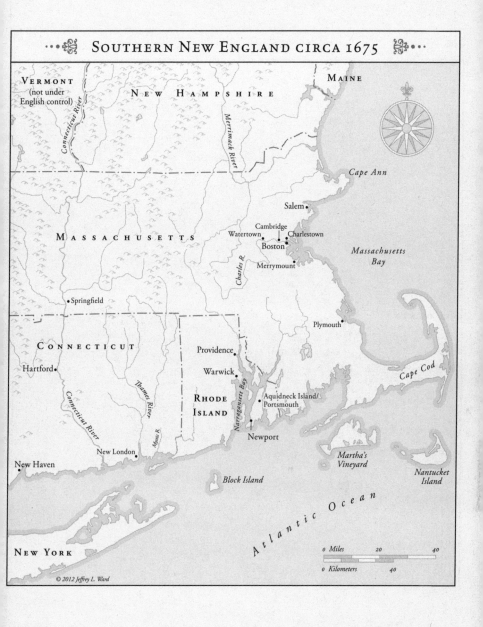

SOUTHERN NEW ENGLAND CIRCA 1675

VERMONT
(not under
English control)

NEW HAMPSHIRE

MAINE

*Connecticut River*

*Merrimack River*

Cape Ann

Salem

MASSACHUSETTS

Watertown
Cambridge
Charlestown
Boston

*Charles R.*

Merrymount

Massachusetts
Bay

Springfield

Plymouth

CONNECTICUT

Providence

Hartford

Warwick

*Thames River*

RHODE
ISLAND

Cape Cod

*Connecticut River*

Aquidneck Island/
Portsmouth

*Narragansett Bay*

*Mystic R.*

Newport

New London

Martha's
Vineyard

Nantucket
Island

New Haven

Block Island

*Atlantic Ocean*

NEW YORK

0 Miles        20        40

0 Kilometers        40

© 2012 Jeffrey L. Ward

# ❦ PROLOGUE ❦

Even the most bitter accusers of Roger Williams recognized in him that combination of charm, confidence, and intensity which a later age would call charisma. They did not regard such traits as assets, however, for those traits only made him more popular and thus increased the danger of the errors he preached in this, the Massachusetts Bay colony. With such a one as he, they could not compromise.

For Williams's part, neither his benevolent intelligence nor his Christian charity made him willing to compromise either. The error, he believed, was not his, and when convinced he was right he backed away from no one. His mentor Sir Edward Coke, once chief justice of England and arguably the greatest jurist in English history, had taught him that; when King James had declared himself ruler by divine right and above the law, Coke had contradicted him to his face. For that, the king had rewarded him with rooms in the Tower of London.

That precedent made the conflict between Williams and his accusers inevitable and thickened it with history, a history that stretched back long before Coke's defiance. And if the conflict began far distant in both space and time from Massachusetts, crossing both an ocean and centuries, it first came to a head there, in the cold New England winter of 1636. Its repercussions would be immense.

The Massachusetts authorities and Williams would have it out over their great dispute, but they would not settle it, nor is it settled now. For their dispute defined for the first time two fault lines that have run continuously through four hundred years of American history, fault lines which remain central to defining the essential nature of the United States of America today.

The first was the more obvious: the proper relation between what man has made of God—the church—and the state. The second was the more subtle:

the proper relation between a free individual and the state—the shape of liberty, the form American individualism would take. What Williams had largely already learned in England would lead him to prophesy the former; what happened to him that winter and after would lead him to articulate the latter.

No conflict was anticipated when Williams first arrived in Boston in January 1631 aboard the *Lyon*, a vessel which carried far more than him and a few other passengers. Its captain, William Peirce, had sailed in dead winter, the worst and rarest time to cross the North Atlantic, to keep a promise.

Less than a year earlier a fleet had carried nearly one thousand men and women to Massachusetts. They were not adventurers. They were like-minded Puritans who considered themselves loyal to the Church of England but disgusted with what they regarded as its corrupt practices, yet the crown and that church were putting intense pressure on them to conform to those practices. To escape that pressure, traveling as whole families and often with their neighbors, they had removed themselves from England and, with determination and purpose, had planted themselves in the wild that was America. As they embarked from England, Governor John Winthrop had reminded them of that purpose, stating that they would plant a "citty upon a hill" dedicated to God, obeying God's laws, and flourishing in God's image.

But they did not flourish and God did not bless them. Indeed, within a few months roughly a quarter of the entire population had died or was dying, starvation threatened the rest, many were fleeing back to England, and nearly all wondered if they had done right.

Anticipating that winter would utterly exhaust their resources, Winthrop had months earlier charged Peirce with resupplying the plantation. Peirce's return brought more than food, supplies, or even hope; he brought deliverance and, seemingly, a sign that the settlers had done right in leaving England, a sign that God had used the hard times merely to test the settlers' resolve. As the *Lyon* unloaded, Winthrop therefore declared a colony-wide day of thanksgiving and prayer.

He also hailed the arrival of young Williams, whom he called "a godly minister." Williams, who had already developed a reputation for scholarship and piety in England, had brought his family to this wild for the same purpose as the Winthrop group. And Williams had left England even after word of woes in Massachusetts had for the moment dried up interest in emigration, although in truth he had had little choice—English church authorities would likely have soon imprisoned him.

The Boston church confirmed Winthrop's opinion of Williams by immediately offering him a post. It was the greatest such post in English America and it held all the promise of the continent.

Yet Williams declined it, and he did so indelicately, spurning the church as insufficiently committed to the proper worship of God. This astonishing charge had made for tense relations between him and the colony's leaders ever since.

Now, five years later, the English settlement in Massachusetts had stabilized and begun to thrive. The planters no longer clung close by the rock and foam of the shore but had moved inland, rooting themselves, clearing thick forest and plowing fields. New immigrants, nearly all of them sharing in the same vision as the old, continued to arrive with each ship. Meanwhile, the government and clergy had set the colony firmly upon the path Winthrop had laid out.

Williams challenged both the government and the clergy. Had he been isolated, the authorities might have ignored him, might have left him to his own devices. But, after something of an odyssey, he had been called to minister to the Salem church, where passionate followers supported him. His teachings resonated outside Salem as well. Nearly all other clergy in Massachusetts and most lay leaders believed he threatened the very vision that Winthrop had described. He threatened, they believed, the success of that city upon a hill. He threatened, they believed, God's vision.

Williams did not dispute with them on any point of theology. They shared the same faith, all worshipping the God of Calvin, all seeing God in every facet of life, and all seeing man's purpose as advancing the kingdom of God. But Winthrop and his colleagues in power in the Massachusetts Bay colony had enormous disagreements with Williams over how to infuse human society with God's vision.

The Bay's leaders, both lay and clergy, firmly believed that the state must enforce all of God's laws, and that to do so the state had to prevent error in religion. This conviction they held fast to, for their souls and all the souls within the Massachusetts plantation depended upon it.

Williams recognized that putting the state to that service required humans to interpret God's law. His views were not yet fully formed—how Massachusetts dealt with him would itself influence their formulation—but he believed that humans, being imperfect, would inevitably err in applying God's law. Hence, he concluded that a society built upon the principles that Massachusetts espoused could at best lead only to hypocrisy, for he believed that forced worship "stinks in God's nostrils." At worst, it would lead to a foul corruption not of the state, which was already corrupt, but of the church, as it befouled itself with the state's errors. His understandings were edging him toward a belief he would later call "Soul Libertie."

The authorities in the Bay believed that Williams had become dangerous, that his views could infect the entire colony and cause its descent into sin. To prevent that, the General Court of the Massachusetts Bay colony decided on October 6, 1635, to banish him, ordering him to depart from its jurisdiction within six weeks. If he returned, the court had full discretion to impose upon him a range of punishments, from imprisonment to flogging, branding, the cutting off of his ears, the cutting out of his tongue, and execution.

The authorities had already extended one mercy. Williams was ill and winter was falling upon New England, so they suspended enforcement of the banishment order until spring. In return, Williams was to remain silent.

He did remain silent publicly, making no statements and preaching no sermons in the church he had once served. His most passionate supporters, however, had continued to come to his home. There, only in his own home, among his close comrades and supporters, he had spoken freely.

Word of this had reached Boston. In January 1636, without further admonition or warning, the authorities sent pursuivants—rough men, soldiers who had bloodied their swords in the brutal wars of Europe—to arrest him and place him on board a ship about to return to England.

Such an act went well beyond the banishment order. Williams could find several havens in America, beginning a few miles farther north in what later became New Hampshire. New Amsterdam would have provided haven as well, and he was already fluent in Dutch. (He would later teach his friend John Milton that language.) Or he could have gone to Virginia, or to the Summer Islands—Bermuda. In all these places, he would be safe.

In England, he could not be safe. The best he could expect in England was a jail cell. Nor would it be the comfortable rooms in the Tower where his mentor Coke had languished; Williams did not have the protection of rank. He might well face worse than simple prison. These were perilous and bloody times.

Winthrop, then deputy governor, knew of the plan to return Williams to England, and he knew also Williams's likely fate there. He both liked Williams personally and considered him a good and still godly man who had simply fallen into error. Secretly he sent Williams a warning that men were coming to arrest him and place him on board a ship. Williams acted upon the warning immediately. His wife and child would remain in Salem; the Bay had issued no sanctions against them. They would be safe until he could find refuge and send for them.

For himself, dressing against the winter, stuffing his clothes with the dried corn paste which Indians lived on for weeks at a time, with no time for sentimental goodbyes to friends, he fled his home, a burgher's cottage built to last and which would stand for two hundred and fifty more years, until it was torn down to make way for progress. Williams would never see it again.

In a moment he passed without the bounds of the village. The sea was close about him, but indications are he fled by land, swallowed by forest within a few steps. He would have found a kind of welcome in the forest; no other Englishman knew the Indian trails as did he, and no other Englishman was as fluent in Indian tongues as he. But if he found a welcome in the forest, he would find no comfort in it.

He fled in a blizzard. The snow fell softly but also thickly, until it rose above his knees. Each step became arduous, exhausting, and decades later he wrote of the weariness that overcame him then. He was not without company, however: packs of wolves haunted the forest. And the savage Indians haunted the forest too.

Yet it was the Indians who gave him shelter through all that winter. Until the end of his days the memory was ever in his consciousness that savages had saved his life, that his civilized fellow English, his onetime close colleagues, had banished him.

Roger Williams was no loner, no misanthrope, no recluse. He longed for nothing so much as community and fellowship, and especially church fellowship. They would all elude him. Yet he had the strength to live without that which he so longed for. He had the strength to follow the logic of his thought to its conclusion despite enormous personal cost.

That logic and thought seemed largely shaped by two men, each of them prometheans. The first was Edward Coke (pronounced "Cook"), who from the bench defied the crown, declaring, "For an Englishman's house is as his castle, *et domus sua cuique tutissimum refugium* [and each man's home his safest refuge]."[1] Coke's work and life exposed Williams to a deep understanding of state power, of individual rights, and of the law, not simply as practiced in the courtroom but as it defined the infrastructure of a society. The second was Sir Francis Bacon, who taught an entirely new way of thinking, a new way of inquiring, a new view of evaluating logic. That these two men so influenced him carried a certain irony, for Coke and Bacon despised each other and each spent much of his life trying to destroy the other.

Coke's influence was direct, Bacon's more subtle, but Williams built upon the grounding both provided him, adding his own insights and his own conclusions, leaving a legacy of his own. It would be he, not Thomas Jefferson, who first called for a "wall of separation" to describe the relationship of church and state which both he and Jefferson demanded. It would be he who created the first government in the world that built such a wall. And it would be he who first defined the word "liberty" in modern terms, and saw the relationship between a free individual and the state in a modern way.

It is always dangerous, often foolish, and sometimes dishonest to read into the past a modern meaning, or to extract from the past a lesson outside its context. But Roger Williams was in many ways so extraordinary as to create his own context, and, in this instance, the context he created almost four centuries ago does have direct relevance today. He was not the first person to call for religious freedom, but he was certainly the first to link that call to individual liberty in a political sense and to create a government and a society informed by those beliefs.

The settlers of the Massachusetts Bay colony did not expect this from him. They had considered him one of their own. Their plantation marked a coming together of congruous individuals and families into a whole and corporate body, a commonwealth. They intended their commonwealth to represent the fruition of their beliefs, and they were and saw themselves as a continuation of them.

Williams marked a departure, a departure so pronounced that in the words of John Quincy Adams—words not meant as a compliment—he was "altogether revolutionary."[2]

Part I

# THE LAW

# ❧ CHAPTER I ❧

This is not a biography. It is a story about the emergence of ideas. But those ideas did not come from books or theory. They came from living through extraordinary times, and they came from resisting two ambitious kings who compelled obedience—a resistance that led to revolution.

This is therefore a story about power. Those who know of Roger Williams generally think of him only in terms of the relationship of church and state, and certainly he is a central figure in the history of that debate. But he also came to have a deep understanding of political power, of the collision between England's "ancient rights and liberties" and a government justifying its acts by "reason of state," i.e., the national interest and national security, and by the theory of the divine right of kings, a concept which King James injected into English jurisprudence. Williams, although not a lawyer, also came to have a deep understanding of the fundamental precepts of English law. This book explores these questions by describing the evolution of these ideas in him and his translation of them into concrete form. Like most ideas, they evolved out of the interplay between his thought and his personal experience.

The personal experience included, during his teenage years when his views were forming, exposure not only to Sir Edward Coke and Sir Francis Bacon but to King James and his son King Charles, to their Privy Councils and courts, and to the leaders of Parliament. While trying to bring his ideas into fruition as an adult, he routinely dealt with and developed close friendships with such men as John Milton and Oliver Cromwell. One cannot know what precisely he took from such experiences. One cannot know the heart and mind of Williams or any other person. But one can stand where he stood, see what he saw, know much of what he heard and read, and thus come to some understanding of his perspective. This much is clear: his personal history was well grounded in English religious, legal, and constitutional history, just as was the larger history of the English Puritan exodus to America, complete with their vision of themselves as a new Chosen People. Religion and politics were ever mixed. As the historian Alan Simpson noted, "It is in the midst of the struggles between king and Parliament that the English [Puritan] discovers his mission. The confused strivings became fused with a providential purpose: a way is being opened for the establishment of Zion."[1]

This English history laid the foundations of American history; in particular, it built the infrastructure of American culture.

Roger Williams was born probably in 1603, at a time when England saw itself as surrounded by enemies without and riven by enemies within. International rivalries threatened to—and did—erupt into war, but even greater turbulence was being generated at home as the nation endured the death throes of feudalism and the birth pains of capitalism. Normally one could find peace from the attendant turmoil in the economy and society in religion. Instead, religion itself stirred that turmoil, for the history of the Reformation in England was dizzying.

The English Reformation began roughly one hundred and fifty years before Luther, when John Wycliffe translated the Bible into English and foreshadowed Luther in his criticisms of the Catholic Church. Wycliffe, later called "the Morning Star of the Reformation," died in 1384; forty-four years later and a decade after declaring him heretic, the Catholic Church ordered his body disinterred and burned and his ashes thrown into a river. England did not take another major step toward Protestantism for nearly two centuries, when Henry VIII, whom the pope had called "Defender of the Faith," wanted a male heir but failed to get papal approval to annul his marriage in order to wed again. So he decreed himself head of the Church of England and independent of the pope's authority. Parliament soon confirmed him in this and made a national hero of the long-dead Wycliffe.

But this English church superimposed a theology based on such Calvinist principles as predestination on a largely Catholic structure. From its beginning, then, English Protestantism contained within itself tensions identical to those which would ignite the righteous slaughters of religious war on the European continent.

When Henry's daughter Mary became queen, she returned the nation to Catholicism and married Philip, a future king of Spain. The marriage appalled all of England, for Spain was England's great and feared rival. Philip spent only fourteen months in England before returning home—he never set foot in England again. Meanwhile, in a reign of only five years, Mary burned three hundred Protestants at the stake, including Thomas Cranmer, who had been archbishop of Canterbury. In doing so, she also burned a horror of Catholicism into the psyche of English Protestants, a horror kept alive by John Foxe's *Book of Martyrs,* a multivolume history that recounted in graphic detail the stories of each of those killed by Mary.

Across the Channel, far worse slaughters were occurring. The single deepest river of red that flowed into that sea of blood occurred in 1572, when on St. Bartholomew's Day French Catholics suddenly fell upon their Protestant brethren and slaughtered them. Catholic histories generally put the number of victims at fifteen thousand; Protestant histories claim as many as one hundred thousand were murdered.

By then Mary had died a natural death. Her half sister Elizabeth succeeded her and turned England Protestant again. She also supported Protestants on the continent, including rebellious Dutch Protestants who sought independence from Spain. Thus in the space of twenty-five years England went from Catholic to Protestant to Catholic to Protestant, and from having a Spanish prince married to its queen to supporting the enemies of Spain.

For Elizabeth, Parliament passed a second Act of Supremacy—the first was for Henry VIII—which declared the monarch "Supreme Governor" of the Church of England. (Henry had been "Supreme Head" and could order the church himself; as a woman Elizabeth could not head the church and had to rule through its bishops.) This gave the crown power over the domain of God; it also made any challenge to church authority a direct affront to the crown.

To assure loyalty to both the crown and the church, Parliament required all officeholders, all members of Parliament, all priests, and even all university students to swear the Oath of Supremacy, stating, "I do utterly testify and declare in my conscience" to affirm the monarch as "the only supreme Governor of the Realm . . . as well as in all Spiritual or Ecclesiastical things or causes as Temporal, &c. &c. &c. So help me God." With the Act of Uniformity, Parliament also required all subjects to attend weekly worship at their parish church. "Recusancy"—failure to attend worship or even refusal to participate in the full liturgy—became a crime and a subversive act.

Most English subjects accepted the chaos of this churning worship and policy without complaint or, seemingly, even confusion, going about their lives, enjoying their pleasures, doing their duty, swearing required oaths, and worshipping passably if not passively. But if England seemed calm, it was not calm. Enough conspirators and assassins moved through the shadows to teach Shakespeare intrigue.

First Pope Gregory XIII excommunicated Elizabeth, absolved all her subjects from their duty to obey her, and decreed that killing a heretic—such as she—was no sin. Not long after, English Catholics set in motion several attempts to assassinate her. Her Catholic cousin Mary Queen of Scots was implicated in one conspiracy, tried for treason, and executed.

Then in 1588, Philip II, Elizabeth's brother-in-law, sent his seemingly invincible Spanish Armada against England, with the aim of making England Catholic once again. This Goliath fell to the English David. Ever after, English Protestants saw the victory as a sign that God had blessed them with a special providence. (In reality, Spain's heavy, sluggish galleons fell to a more numerous, faster, and more maneuverable force.)

Threatened by such very real foreign and domestic menaces, Elizabeth built a secret service; it in turn built nests of spies and offered rewards to anyone who offered "an information" about threats. The law and the spy system were aimed at Catholic enemies. During Elizabeth's reign several hundred Catholics were executed; many more died in prison. She did not kill purely because of religion as Mary had. Catholics were not executed simply for practicing Catholicism. English Catholics continued to worship secretly, and several powerful Catholic families continued to thrive even at court. Acts, not thoughts, concerned her. She said she would "open no window into men's souls."[2]

But Elizabeth also said, "There cannot be two religions in one State." Prime targets of her spy system were Jesuit priests who circulated and conducted Mass in a Catholic underground. One was John Gerard. The queen's attorney general was Sir Edward Coke and one of her favorites was Sir Francis Bacon. Both interrogated Gerard in the Tower of London. The questioning ranged from philosophical discussions to physical torture. Through it all Gerard denied plotting against the crown, confessing only that he had "endeavor[ed] to seduce people from the faith approved by English law, over to the Pope's allegiance."

Coke protested, "How could a man try to convert England and yet keep out of politics?"[3]

With the monarch simultaneously serving as head of the Church of England, one could not.

But if Catholics were the prime security concern, Elizabeth was also troubled by Calvinist critics of her Church of England who denounced its Catholic-like hierarchy and practices and its Book of Common Prayer, which they rejected as rote worship. Instead they sought a purer worship based solely on Scripture. These men and women became known as "Puritans," a term of derision and used as early as 1564. Nearly all these Puritans continued to belong to the body of the Anglican Church, which under Elizabeth tolerated considerable nonconformity.

In 1603 Elizabeth died. James Stuart, already king of Scotland for two decades, became king of England as well. Though he had been separated from his parents as a boy and raised a Protestant, his mother Mary Queen of Scots was Catholic, his father—who had been murdered—was Catholic, and his wife was Catholic. He soon formed an uneasy union between England and Scotland. Indeed, from the beginning, King James made his new subjects uneasy.

Over the next decades, even as the crown and hierarchy edged closer and closer to Catholic form and theology, even as this departure from Calvinist fundamentals created more and angrier dissent, the state's—and therefore the church's—tolerance of dissent declined. In the meantime, James viewed and exercised power in ways that not only marginalized those Protestants most devoted to Scripture but shook English law—threatening even the rights of Englishmen set forth in Magna Carta.

His acts in both religion and politics set off a series of increasingly powerful vibrations that would eventually shatter England. Those vibrations would first shake loose from England thousands of Puritans, Roger Williams among them, sending them to America with a purpose and vision that would ultimately inform the temper of the United States.

The first rumblings of trouble came soon after James's ascension. Though he was new to England, his years as king of Scotland and his personality had made him confident in his own authority and decisive in using it. Far from reassuring subjects who worried that England might compromise with Catholic forces within and without the nation, and thus compromise its Calvinist theology, he exacerbated their concerns.

He promptly reached a peace accord with Spain and committed himself to end persecution of Catholics loyal to his rule. These policies were not unreasonable. As he would later demonstrate, he was determined to establish himself internationally as a man who could build bridges between Catholic and Protestant that might bring real peace. Domestically, fines against Catholic recusants who broke the law by not attending Anglican services dropped by 80 percent from the last year of Elizabeth's reign to the second year of his.[4]

Despite this easing pressure against Catholics, in the first two years of his reign, three Catholic plots against him were uncovered. The most serious came in 1605, when English Catholics with links to Spain placed eighteen hundred pounds of gunpowder in a cellar beneath Westminster Palace; they intended to explode it when the king convened Parliament, killing him and as many legislators as possible. The discovery of the "Gunpowder Plot" is still celebrated as Guy Fawkes Day.

Coke prosecuted the traitors, who received the standard sentence of being hung, drawn, and quartered. (Traitors of high rank were beheaded.) The sentence expressed both the utter horror of the society toward rebellion and the brutality of the time. Each man was dragged to the scaffold over a hurdle with his head forced "downward, and lying so near the ground"—which often meant dragging his head through the foulest of sewage—"as may be thought unfit to take benefit of the common Air; For which cause also he shall be Strangled, being hanged up by the neck between Heaven and Earth, as deemed unworthy of both, or either. . . . Then is he to be cut down alive, and to have his Privy parts cut off, and burnt before his face, as being unworthily begotten, and unfit to leave any generation after him." Still alive, "His bowels and inlayed parts taken out and burnt, who inwardly had conceived and harbored in his heart such horrible Treason. After, to have his head cut off, which had imagined the mischief. And lastly, his body to be quartered, and the quarters set up in some high and eminent place, to the view and detestation of men, and to become a prey to the Fouls of the Air."[5]

Yet even in the face of assassination attempts, James continued to ease pressure on Catholics. He simultaneously encouraged an increasingly Catholic-style liturgy in the Church of England. At the same time, the word "recusant" came to be applied to Protestants who did not participate in the entire church service. The Anglican Church already had fissures. James drove wedges into them.

Even before James, English Protestants had begun dividing into three group-ings, all of which then accepted the Calvinist concept of predestination.

Those who came to be called "High Church" embraced the Book of Com-mon Prayer and a more Catholic-like worship, as well as the beauty and gran-deur of the cathedrals. James himself clearly preferred them, elevated clergy who favored these views, and in them he found support.

A second group who wanted simpler worship considered the Catholic Church the "Whore of Babylon," bloody and infinitely corrupt, a mortal threat to their souls. This they believed with as much fervor as they believed anything. There were gradations within this group, from moderates who were willing to endure High Church practices to the less malleable minority of Puritans. In them James exacerbated a previously existing discontent. They wanted simple worship and church governance as in Scripture. Therefore they resisted parts of the Book of Common Prayer and thought such liturgical practices as wear-ing the surplice lacked scriptural authority; hence, it was antithetical to true Christian worship. They bemoaned as foul superstition the signs and symbols of Catholicism remaining on Anglican churches, including not only statues of saints and stained glass but crosses and roods. Extreme elements among the Puritans desired to extirpate all trace of Catholic worship and carried on a kind of guerrilla resistance, smashing stained glass windows, tearing down roods, destroying images of saints, and stripping churches of ornaments.

In many parishes with sympathetic ministers, there existed almost a separate church of these purists, these "elect of God," these "visible saints"—as Puritans referred to themselves—within the larger church; clergy who believed with them often conducted separate worship for them alone. Such clergy also often did not conform to all Anglican practices. Nonetheless, both clergy and laity considered themselves fully members of the Church of England.

Still more radical Protestants—the Separatists—decried the Church of En-gland as so derivative of Rome as to be an abomination, entirely corrupt and representing the Antichrist. They wasted no energy smashing stained glass or holding services only for themselves within a larger church. Instead, they avoided all contact with the Church of England; they worshipped in their own, entirely separate congregations. They were tiny in number but considered dangerous to the state, and Elizabeth hanged several of them. Even under Elizabeth, tolerance had limits.

James made his own position clear on these matters soon after his coronation. More than one thousand ministers who sought a purer and simpler church signed the "Millenary Petition." Many of the signers were moderate and did not then fit the definition of Puritan. After being presented with the petition, the king convened a conference with bishops and several of the most moderate petitioners at Hampton Court Palace. It was an odd setting to discuss simplicity: this magnificent "royal pleasure house" included among its hundreds of rooms eighty chambers decorated with tapestries and marble pillars.

The petitioners soon learned that the king had called the conference not to listen but to impose his will upon the church. Indeed, he intended to impose his will upon Scripture itself. The English translation of the Bible then in use, the Geneva Bible, often referred to a king as "tyrant" and included marginal notes that offended him. (One such note read, "When tyrants cannot prevail by craft they burst forth into open rage.") So the conference, at James's direction, decided to produce a new translation reflecting his views on the obedience subjects owed authority. Appearing in 1611, the King James Bible proved the most popular book ever published in English.

At the conference, the king personally dominated discussions, dazzling the bishops present. One reported his astonishment at finding "a king and priest in one person [who could] propose, discuss, and determine so many important matters so soundly as I never look to see or hear the like again."[6]

But he did not dazzle those who desired reform. On the conference's first day, the king kept them waiting in a hallway while he met with his bishops. On the second day, they were suffered to kneel before the king and try to make their case while being cross-examined, interrupted, and harassed. James told one that if a student gave such answers, "[T]he rod should [be] plyed upon the poor boyes buttocks";[7] to another: "A turd for this argument";[8] to a third: "No bishop, no king!"[9] Later the king boasted, "*I have peppered thaime soundlie.*"[10]

In the end, he embraced the suggestions of his most conservative bishops and rejected virtually everything the reformers had suggested.

James also responded to Puritan attacks on Sunday games—he liked play and brought golf to England—by declaring that "after the end of divine service our good people be not . . . discouraged from any lawful recreation, such as dancing, . . . archery . . . vaulting or any other such harmless recreation, nor from . . . the setting up of Maypoles." Bishops were ordered to make Puritans "conform themselves or to leave the county, . . . so to strike equally on both hands against the contemners of our authority and adversaries of our Church."[11]

James did offer one accommodation. He allowed moderates with "painful consciences" to quietly evade conforming to those elements of worship which the church itself ruled "adiaphora," i.e., things indifferent. Regarding wearing the surplice, for example, he said, "I am so far from being contentious in these things (which for my own part I ever esteemed as indifferent) as I do equally love and honour the learned and grave men of either of these opinions."[12]

Nonetheless, his refusal to make any substantive accommodation with reformers and—more importantly—his subsequent choices of bishops slowly bent the Church of England back toward Catholicism, which in non-conformists built a reservoir of ill will. He was not only widening but deepening the fissures within the church. Only force could hold it together. He was quite content to apply the force necessary to do so. Believing his own authority came directly from God, James warned Puritans to comply "[o]r else I will harrie them out of this land, or else do worse, only hang them, that's all."[13]

Religion was not the sole cause of England's uneasiness. Three additional threads of rancor—the personal, the economic, and the political—were being woven into a cloth of contention, making James a king not beloved of his people.

Even his personal life created undercurrents of discontent. Those who knew details about it, especially Puritans and likely including the young Williams, could not reconcile their knowledge of his life with his position as head of the Church of England.

He had both lusts and a kind of cruelty. When hunting, he would rip open a dead stag and steep his feet in its blood and entrails. He would get courtiers, including women, drunk and laugh as they vomited. He considered nothing out of bounds. The morning after his daughter's marriage, he entered her bed-room and demanded she and her husband give an explicit account of the pre-ceding night.[14] It was impossible to be at ease around him. "His eye was large, ever rolling after any stranger that came into his presence, in so much as many for shame have left the room," noted one observer. His legs were misshapen and noticeably weak, giving him an odd gait when walking, making him appear off balance, and he was "of middle stature, more corpulent through his clothes than his body, yet fat enough, his clothes ever being made large and easy, the doublets quilted for stiletto proof, his breeches in pleats and fully stuffed . . . his fingers ever . . . fiddling about his codpiece."[15]

There was one other thing. As a youth in Scotland, his relationship with an older man—whom he made a duke and who left his embalmed heart to him—had all but sparked a mutiny among Scottish nobles. This quieted when he married Anne, with whom he had eight children. It then became easy to look away while he indulged his appetites with at least one other woman and a string of young men—until he encountered a youth called "the handsomest-bodied man of England."[16] His wife warned the archbishop of Canterbury, "This young man will become more intolerable than any that were before him."[17]

George Villiers was his name. James called him "my sweet child and wife," and referred to himself as "your dear dad and husband."[18] By age twenty-four Villiers had "all the honours and all the offices of the three kingdoms"—England, Scotland, and Wales—"without a rival," and James ultimately made him Duke of Buckingham. One contemporary satirist wrote, "Apollo with his songs / debauched young Hyacinthus . . . / And it is well known that the king of England / fucks the Duke of Buckingham." Their relationship endured: years later Buckingham would remind James of "the time . . . where the bed's head could not be found between the master and the dog."[19]

Many rulers have indulged their lusts with no harm to their nation or themselves. But Buckingham wanted involvement in the affairs of state and James welcomed him to those affairs, following his advice on questions ranging from war and peace to taxes. Nearly all the advice proved bad. Over time, Buckingham's role drove a wedge between James and his subjects. The king's subjects did not pour their bile onto him, but they did not withhold it from Buckingham. Indeed, it seemed they deflected their angers over all grievances onto him. He became the most hated man in England.

There was much to be angry about. In addition to all else, there was money. The government of England had been underfinanced for at least a century. Henry VIII had solved his financial problems the easy way: by engorging himself with the wealth of the Catholic Church. His several successors sucked the marrow from these bones, but by the time James became king there was no churchly wealth remaining upon which to feed.

The need for more money would have created frictions between any king, no matter how politic and frugal, and his nation. James was neither politic nor frugal. Elizabeth's operating expenses and income were roughly matched at £300,000, although she also left a war debt of £400,000. James's income grew marginally but his expenses soon exceeded £500,000. His extravagances masked the structural imbalance between the state's legitimate expenses and its income, and it allowed critics to charge that James's spending alone accounted for financial shortages. The royal coffers could never be filled, they claimed, because "the bottoms be out."[20]

Twice James summoned a Parliament to get money, and twice dissolved it without a solution. Angrily he told the Privy Council "no house save the House of Hell" could have treated him as had the House of Commons.[21] Brooding over this limit on his power, he complained that "All Kings Christian . . . have power to lay impositions" without any such inconvenience as a Parliament. "I myself in Scotland before I came hither" had it. The kings of "Denmark, Sweden . . . , France, Spain, all have this power."[22]

Placing much of the blame for Parliament's resistance on its Puritan members, he began melding his dislike of Puritans and his view of royal power. In fact, he had thought deeply about the issue of power and political theory, deeply enough to have read such works as Xenophon's *Cyropaedia* and to have written two books, *Basilikon Doron* and *The Trew Law of Free Monarchies*. In them he articulated a theory which accounted for his insensitivity to his subjects' concerns, a theory which further intensified the vibrations shaking England. That theory was the divine right of kings.

The essential elements of this theory were centuries old, and it had many supporters on the continent. Jean Bodin, the French philosopher who invented the phrase "political science," had argued for it not long before. James very likely read Bodin, but even if he did not he certainly took to the theory.

He declared "that even by God himself [kings] are called gods,"[23] and in 1610 explained to Parliament that if they would "consider the attributes to God, you shall see how they agree in the person of a king. . . . They make and unmake their subjects, they have power of raising and casting down, of life and death, of judges over all their subjects of all causes, and yet accountable to none but God only. . . . And to the king is due both the affection of the soul and the service of the body of his subjects."[24]

James stated that if a king governed badly, that did not justify resistance to his authority. Subjects should instead endure a harsh king's rule "without resistance but by sobbes and teares to God." Since God worked in ways unfathomable to humanity, to rebel against a bad king was to rebel against God. Indeed, even if a king attacked God, a subject had no right to rebel. In 1615 Richard Mockett published *God & King* in support of this position, arguing that even when "Princes in their rage may endeavor to destroy . . . Christ's church," the subject's "only means" for redress was "repentance for our sins, which have brought this chastisement upon us; and humble prayer unto God, who guideth the hearts of princes."[25] James liked Mockett's book so much that he ordered every householder to teach it to children and servants.

But James's views on royal authority collided head-on with English history. The concept that "the king can do no wrong" did exist in English law, deriving from Henry de Bracton, the great English scholar of the 1200s, who had concluded that no lord could be sued in his own court (this concept survives today in the doctrine of sovereign immunity). Even Bracton, however, stated explicitly that the king was under the law.

In addition, the idea of sovereign immunity did not exist in a vacuum. Several distinct English constitutional traditions limited the power of the king, beginning with the ancient witenagemot, a council of wise men. Before the Norman Conquest, kings were so far from omnipotent that in one period thirteen of fifteen in Northumbria had been deposed. After the Norman Conquest, William the Conqueror interrupted the witenagemot and did bring new laws with him but also continued such institutions as the hundred court and shire court, confirmed laws in use, reissued the earlier Code of Canute, and "summoned through all the counties of England the noble, the wise, and the learned in their law."[26]

Magna Carta, forced upon King John in 1215, of course limited the royal power. Yet Magna Carta was largely a summary of previously recognized rights and contained little that was new: for example, it simply copied language from the earlier Charter of Liberties in stating, "No free man shall be taken, or imprisoned, or disseized, or outlawed, or exiled, or in any wise destroyed; nor will we go upon him, nor send upon him, but by the lawful judgment of his peers or by the law of the land. To none will we sell, to none will we deny or delay, right or justice."[27] Several subsequent versions of Magna Carta were developed, and in 1297 King Edward I finalized it and also, in summoning Parliament, declared,

"What touches all should be approved of all, and it is also clear that common dangers should be met by measures agreed upon in common."[28]

In addition, both before and after Magna Carta, English kings had sworn at their coronation "to keep the laws and righteous customs" of England.[29] And Parliament had deposed kings, if only rarely. To justify ousting King Richard II in 1399, Parliament first read his coronation oath, then cited thirty-three separate violations of it and protested that he had claimed that the laws were in his own mouth and breast.[30]

Finally, feudalism never fully overcame older English traditions; as a result, Roman law, or "civil law"—developed under Roman emperors and favoring an absolute monarch—had far less impact in England than on the continent. Instead, "custom," which included certain rights of such local governments as London, as well as statute and, most importantly, common law, all also constrained the monarch.

Common law began both to take firm shape and to shape the country in the 1200s when Henry III sent itinerant justices across the country, making law "common" and consistent throughout England. Before that, crimes had often been considered a matter between the victim and perpetrator, where even a murder could be expiated by paying "wergeld" to a family—as is still the case in some societies in the developing world. Now crime violated "the king's peace" and was against the nation. Murderers were executed.

As common law spread, English lawyers entirely abandoned Roman civil law, while such abstruse concepts as frankalmoigne and "courts of the forest" survived as part of the "antient Rights and Liberties" of English subjects. This made common law more arcane and labyrinthine than civil law, but its very arcana, along with custom, created a web which restrained power, making England more resistant to absolutism than states on the continent.[31] Lastly, common law was grounded in property rights; for example, transforming land once held in villeinage, i.e., only with the approval of a feudal lord, into secure ownership. The nation at large came to value both the stability and the protection against arbitrary power which common law provided.

All this comprised the English "inheritance" of rights. All elements of this English inheritance imposed concrete limits on the crown which inherently contradicted the theory of the divine right of kings. And all this James, like all English monarchs for centuries, had in his coronation oath sworn to confirm and sustain. Thus, James brought his new views on royal power, royal pre-rogative, to an England which had come to value the stability of common law and fear the danger of arbitrary power, and to an England already disturbed by high Anglican worship pushing toward Catholicism.

He had all the awesome magnificence of the monarchy on his side, in a time when few thought of questioning a king. He had courtiers and lawyers to second him and justify him. But as he pitted the majesty of the crown against the majesty of the law, he encountered Sir Edward Coke.

## ❧ CHAPTER 2 ❧

It is ironic that the pedestrian skill of shorthand would introduce two such singular individuals as Roger Williams and Sir Edward Coke to each other, yet it was shorthand—a new, or newly rediscovered, technology—that brought the boy to the attention of the man. Romans had used shorthand at least a millennium earlier but it had disappeared into Europe's dark ages. After reappearing in England in 1588, it quickly took hold; by the time Williams was born, London grammar schools routinely taught it to their better students.

It was a skill useful to lawyers, and no man in all English history was more the lawyer than Coke. He personified a profession considered both so influential and so dubious that in 1372 the House of Commons had tried to bar lawyers from Parliament; little had changed when, in Coke's lifetime, Shakespeare wrote, "First, kill all the lawyers."

Many younger lawyers took notes in shorthand themselves, and Coke, who learned the law before shorthand's rediscovery, surely recognized the usefulness of that skill. Serendipity introduced Coke to Williams—stories differ about where they met, but all say Coke noticed the boy, then about thirteen, taking shorthand. Yet something other than the skill alone must have accounted for his taking Williams on. Coke was over sixty years old when they met and not a man easy with the new, nor is there any indication that he ever had employed a boy to take shorthand or ever did again. Something about Williams himself, his intelligence, his earnestness, his intensity, must have struck him.

They ultimately became so close that Coke "was often pleased to call [Williams] . . . his Son."[1] Williams reciprocated the affection. In thousands of pages of his surviving writing, Williams mentioned his actual father only once, in dismissal. But two decades after Coke's death, Williams referred to his "much honored friend, that man of honor, and wisdom, and piety. . . . How many thousand times since I had the honorable and precious remembrance of his person, and the life, the writings, the speeches, and the example of that glorious light."[2]

Coke gave example indeed, and Williams would observe the climax of Coke's collisions with the king. Those collisions went far beyond the personal, for the law and the monarchy were colliding, and shock of the impacts would resonate throughout England for decades; more than a century later in America they would still be resonating. Still, the beginnings of those collisions lay in the personal, and in the personality of Coke.

As an attorney Coke had represented great and important clients, and in representing his clients he always championed them. And even as an attorney he set precedents: in 1585 he won an acquittal by arguing that his client should not be tried twice for the same crime, helping to establish an essential element of modern jurisprudence. Subsequently he filled an extraordinary string of offices—he did not simply hold a position, he filled it, expanded it—including Speaker of the House of Commons, solicitor general, attorney general for two monarchs, chief justice of the Court of Common Pleas, chief justice of the King's Bench, as well as member of the King's Privy Council and of the Court of the Star Chamber. His greatest and most important client, however, was not the enormously wealthy Howard family, nor Queen Elizabeth, nor King James. His greatest client was the very law itself—the common law of England.

As a scholar, his great ambition was to, in effect, take down common law, to precipitate it out of the cloud of centuries of argument and judgment into the hard crystal of precedent, to then crack that crystal open by analyzing it, and finally to lock the pieces into place by defining precedent and law more firmly than could any legislative act. Coke pored through legal records predating the Year Books, which recorded judicial decisions beginning in the mid-thirteenth century, pored through the Year Books, pored through the writings of thirteenth-century jurist Bracton, fifteenth-century jurist Thomas Littleton, and many others. Beginning in 1600, he published annual commentary on contemporary cases that became known as Coke's *Reports*. Fortified by his knowledge of precedent and statute, these writings immediately ordered chaos, imposing themselves upon the courts and the legal profession; even his most profound enemies relied upon them. Publication of his deeper and more analytical work, *Institutes,* would be prevented by the crown's suspicion of him; these volumes would not appear until after his death.

As a judge, he set numerous precedents asserting judicial authority, any one of which was enough to make him a major figure in the history of the law. In the Bonham case, for example, he established the concept of judicial review of legislative acts, declaring, "When an Acte of Parliament is against common right and reason, the common law will control it and adjudge such Act to be void."[3] One hundred and fifty years later the Massachusetts Assembly quoted Coke in ruling the Stamp Act "null and void," and in *Marbury v. Madison,* which established judicial review in the United States, Chief Justice John Marshall borrowed from Coke in his decision.

Yet any single act of his as scholar or judge seems almost trivial compared with the entirety of his contributions. His very life came to epitomize a struggle between authority and liberty. Coke stood clearly on one side of this divide. His analysis and decisions wove themselves deep into English jurisprudence and constitutional history and eventually into the Constitution of the United States.

Coke became directly involved in American adventures in 1606 when he helped write the charter of the Virginia Company, which set an important precedent by guaranteeing that British subjects in the colony and their children "shall have and enjoy all Liberties, Franchises, and immunities . . . as if they had been abiding and born, within this our Realm of England."[4]

His work, his life, and his example also embedded themselves within Williams, for Williams took all this in as he took notes, and he inscribed it not on paper but into his own fiber. Later he would take it with him to the New World, where he would translate the inscriptions into what amounted to a new language.

Yet nothing in Coke's early life as a lawyer suggested that he would become an iconic figure, certainly not one who would defy the crown itself. A thin and angular man with long spidery fingers, he began his rise like so many others, by attaching himself to a patron and dedicating himself to advancing his patron's interests. After his success as an attorney led Elizabeth to favor him with appointments, that patron became the crown. He served her as solicitor general, Speaker of the House of Commons, and, in 1593, attorney general. His great rivalry with Francis Bacon began then; they competed for the post and Coke won it.

He remained attorney general through the queen's reign and early in James's. In all these positions, Coke advanced his patron's interests, even at the expense of the common law. He advanced his own interests as well.

Indeed, he seemed obsessed with his own interest, pursuing his own advantage in every sphere of life with singular purpose. Born to rank and wealth, he aspired to—and achieved—vastly higher rank and vastly greater wealth.

In those pursuits he used his brilliant intellect and his extraordinary and disciplined persistence; with a hunter's patience, he could lie in wait for weeks, months, even years before striking. But his primary tool was brute force. At law, he won by raining furious, heavy, often roundhouse and sometimes wild rhetorical blows upon opponents, then burying them under ad hominem attack and mountains of common law precedent—including distorted precedent. As a courtier, he used any and all tools which might serve him. Perhaps nothing epitomized his pursuit of advantage more than this: he had the right in certain legal circumstances to seize the estate of a suicide, and after a wealthy tenant drowned accidentally he threatened to attempt such a seizure unless the heir gave him a "present." He signed his threat, "Your loving friend, Edw. Coke."[5]

He could be pompous, self-important, and dismissive. His own marriage was filled with such acrimony that one man remarked that his wife would "ruin herself to overthrow him."[6] A brother complained he spoke even to him "as if he had been born Attorney General,"[7] and in his own reports of legal decisions he compared himself to Moses, the "first reporter."[8] Still, if Coke was ambitious, even avaricious, if he was a self-promoting egotist, if he cared about few people around him, he also had one trait that could redeem all his faults. He had courage.

Courage, like most attributes, is neutral in itself and can be employed for good or ill, but Coke demonstrated courage in a fight that could not benefit himself. It could only benefit the one thing that mattered more to him than triumph. That cause was the law, and liberty as expressed through the law.

For this, he had enough courage to knowingly not only sacrifice his self-interest but to put his life at risk. This courage of his was not the kind born of or limited to bold impulse, to the suddenness of the moment; it was considered, a deliberate position taken upon reflection. Ironically, it began to show itself after James rewarded him with a promotion, elevating him in 1606 from attorney general to chief justice of the Court of Common Pleas, the most powerful judgeship in England.

More than Coke's personal history would change with the appointment. To commemorate it, he gave colleagues rings engraved with the motto *Lex est tutissima cassis* ("Law is the safest helmet"). Henceforth, elevating the law meant elevating himself, but if ego leavened his courage, that only made it stronger. The common law itself became his client. It became that client's interest which he defended, and it became that client's interest which he advanced. As with all his interests, he did so not passively but aggressively, not by building a fortress but by launching attacks. Until now the crown had been his patron; now his target was the power of the crown.

Coke began the struggle in the courts, then with others advanced it to Parliament. Although Coke was without question a High Church Anglican, Puritans followed for their own purposes.

England had then three court systems: ecclesiastical courts, "prerogative" courts, and common law courts. Since the monarch headed the church, ecclesiastical courts were ultimately controlled by the state; thus, both the "prerogative" courts—so called because they were created by royal prerogative and carried the crown's authority—expressed the crown's will.

The most important ecclesiastical venue was the Court of the High Commission, which had its genesis under Henry VIII. With clergy as judges, the High Commission initially tracked down Catholic recusants and others regarded as dangerous heretics, such as the Separatists executed under Elizabeth. James, however, shifted its focus from finding Catholics to disciplining Anglican clergy who did not conform, who objected, for example, to using parts of the Book of Common Prayer. Usually the High Commission enforced discipline by suspending clergy from their livings, but it also claimed jurisdiction over the lay public and it had the power to flog, mutilate, imprison, and execute offenders.

Prerogative courts had broad jurisdiction and broad discretion. Because they were not bound by legal technicalities and could decide matters based on what seemed just, they were referred to as "courts of equity," of fairness. The Court of the Star Chamber—whose members included the king (but who rarely attended), his Privy Council, England's archbishops, and the chief justices of the two leading common law courts, King's Bench and Common Pleas—functioned as both an original court and a court of appeal and oversaw other courts, including common law courts. It could order torture, a rare occurrence in England, authorized on a case-by-case basis, and it could meet in secret session without indictments, juries, or witnesses. Defendants had no lawyers before it. Nonetheless, the Star Chamber was at its best "the poor man's court, in which he might have right without paying money."[9] Later, at its worst, the Star Chamber became a tool of the crown, used to give a patina of legality to acts against political opponents. Prerogative courts could also enforce decisions in ways common law courts could not. In a breach of contract, for example, common law courts could only order monetary damages; prerogative courts could order that the contract be enforced.

No bright line sent one routine case to a prerogative court, perhaps the Court of Chancery, and another to common law, perhaps the Court of Common Pleas. This last court tended to handle civil suits between *meum et teum,* "mine and yours." But so could prerogative courts. Lawyers chose the court system where they had the best chance of success. In effect, prerogative and common law courts competed jealously with each other, especially since court fees paid judges' salaries.

The obvious differences between the courts lay in procedure. Common law procedures were often esoteric and exacting, partly because some procedures derived from the days when, for example, an accused could win acquittal by swearing innocence. Swearing innocence sounds easy but was not; the oaths were complex and long, and the slightest mistake, even a slight stutter or hesitation, could be interpreted as proving guilt.[10] Similarly, a highly technical procedural error could determine the outcome of a common law case.

But a more subtle and substantive difference also separated the court systems. Common law courts had their grounding in Magna Carta and in property rights, in land law, which placed constraints upon the crown. Prerogative courts represented the sovereign power of the crown with few constraints. As an example, in common law courts, defendants could not be forced to testify against themselves, but prerogative courts employed the same oath ex officio used to hunt down enemies of the state. Defendants who took the oath and lied faced the awesome threat of losing their immortal soul. Those who refused to swear or to answer could be imprisoned. If they answered evasively, they were cross-examined, pinned down, assaulted with hypothetical questions designed to extract a truth.

The Jesuit Edmund Campion had called such interrogations "the Bloody Question." One example: *If the pope should send an army to England, for whom would you fight, the pope or the queen?* As fellow Jesuit John Gerard later said, "Whatever I answered I would be sure to suffer for it, either in body or soul." Campion failed in his answers, and was executed for indirect involvement in a treasonous plot. Gerard survived only by escaping prison and England.

Given that Common Pleas had jurisdiction only over civil suits, Coke as its chief justice would seem to have had little opportunity to assert the preeminence of common law over royal prerogative. He soon found some. He did so first indirectly, by challenging the High Commission's assertion of jurisdiction over laymen and its forcing the oath ex officio upon them.

To Coke, it was one thing to force this oath upon Catholics suspected of plotting to kill the monarch; it was another matter entirely to force it upon loyal Protestants concerned that Anglican Church practices were moving too close to Catholic practices. He seemed to have some sympathy for Puritans, if only because his favorite sister married one; the movement certainly interested him, for his library contained many Puritan tracts. He could do nothing to protect clergy, but he could protect laymen. So he began issuing "writs of prohibition" to block the High Commission from considering any cases that could be governed by common law. He also routinely issued writs of habeas corpus, ordering the release of laymen the commission had imprisoned.

Previously, habeas corpus had been used chiefly to enforce royal power—for example, to prevent lords controlling their own jails from arbitrarily imprisoning someone. A writ of habeas corpus demanded they conform to the king's law. Coke was now using habeas corpus to command an office of the king, a usage not yet fully established. And Coke went further still!: he asserted that since the High Commission had no jurisdiction over a layman, a layman would be within his rights to resist arrest by and even kill pursuivants—officers sent by the commission to arrest fugitives.

Then Coke directly challenged the king.

An Oxford don wrote a new legal dictionary in which he noted, "I have heard some to be of the opinion that the laws be above the King," but the king was "above the law by his absolute power. . . . And though at his coronation he take an oath not to alter the laws of the land, yet this oath notwithstanding, he may

alter or suspend any particular law that seemeth hurtful to the publick estate."[11] *
The king's lord chancellor, Sir Thomas Egerton—the lord chancellor was the
highest-ranking official in the government, surrogate of the king, and head of
chancery courts—agreed, "The monarch is the law. Rex est lex loquens, the
king is the law speaking."[12]

This was a breathtaking assertion. Parliament had justified deposing Richard
II partly because he had made a similar claim. Magna Carta explicitly stated
that the king was under the law, and English kings—including James—had
explicitly accepted this declaration in their coronation oath. One ramification
of Egerton's claim was that the king could judge any case before any court. In
Scotland James had declared it treasonous to deny this power; indeed, on his
coronation journey south he had personally heard charges against a criminal
and hanged him.[13]

Richard Bancroft, archbishop of Canterbury, sought to take advantage of
this assertion of royal power and asked James to personally decide a case. James,
pleased to establish a precedent in England, affirmed that he was "the supreme
judge; inferior judges [are] his shadows and ministers . . . and the King may,
if he please, sit and judge in Westminster Hall in any Court there, and call
theire Judgments in question. . . . The King being the author of the Lawe is
the interpreter of the Lawe."[14]

Eight days after making this statement, James summoned Coke before him.
It was not a private meeting. Bancroft was present as were several great lords,
and the king had summoned also all the judges of the common law courts of
Common Pleas and the King's Bench. Clearly James meant to bully Coke into
submission before all the judges. If James succeeded, he would establish this
new authority.

Bancroft began by stating that Scripture gave the king power to decide any
judicial proceeding. The king himself then interjected that the law "was
founded upon reason, and he and others had reason, as well as the judges."[15]

In reply Coke "greatly marvelled that the Arch-bishop durst inform the
King, that such absolute power and authority, as is aforesaid, belonged to the
king by the word of God." He continued, "True it was, that God had endowed
his Majesty with excellent Science, and great endowments of nature, but his
Majesty was not learned in the Lawes of his Realm of England . . . and

---

*The administration of George W. Bush made a similar claim.

judgment of Law . . . requires long study and experience, before that a man can attain to the cognizance of it; And that the Law was the Golden metwand and measure to try the Causes of the Subjects, and which protected his Majesty in safety and peace."

Coke was arguing the key point; he was arguing that the law was supreme. Irritated, James promised to "ever protect the common law."

Coke yielded nothing: "The common law protecteth the king."

James, angry now, snapped, "A traitorous speech! The King protecteth the law, and not the law the King! The King maketh Judges and Bishops. If Judges interpret the lawes themselves and suffer none else to interpret, then they may easily make of the laws shipmens hose"—i.e., sailors' socks, full of holes.

Coke did not retreat. Bracton had said a king could not be under any man— for then he would be subjected to those subject to him—but Coke reminded all that even "Bracton saith, *Quod Rex non debet esse sub homine, sed sub Deo et Lege*"—that the King should not be under man, but under God and the Laws.

For the king to be so contradicted was too much. He suddenly erupted. One man present reported, "His Majesty fell into that high indignation the like was never knowne in him, looking and speaking fiercely with bended fist, offering to strike him, &c."

Coke fell to his hands and knees. From there he beseeched "his Majestie to take compassion" on him and to pardon his zeal. Still James stood over him, ready to strike him, when Sir Robert Cecil, Coke's uncle by marriage and lord treasurer, suddenly knelt beside Coke and begged the king's indulgence. The king's moment of fury passed.

Yet Coke had yielded nothing. This meeting occurred on a Sunday. The next morning Coke issued a new prohibition against the High Commission to block charges against a layman. He went on to prohibit the oath ex officio: "No man ecclesiastical or temporal shall be examined upon secret thoughts of his heart. . . . The Ecclesiastical judge cannot examine any man upon his oath, upon the intention and thought in his heart. . . . *Cogitationis poenam nemo emeret*"—no man may be punished for his thoughts—"For it hath been said in the Proverb, 'Thought is free.' "[16]

Coke never articulated any coherent or overarching legal theory beyond stating his reliance on precedent and saying, "Reason is the life of the law; nay, the common law itself is . . . perfection of reason." Oliver Wendell Holmes disputed Coke on this, writing in *The Common Law,* "The life of the law has not been logic; it has been experience." However, understanding Coke's full meaning closes what seems a large gap between them. Coke also distinguished between "natural Reason and Judgment"—the ability to think through a problem—and "the artificiall Reason and Judgment of Law." By this he meant that custom, precedent, and procedure all influenced a legal judgment, and all involved knowledge and historical fact. Like a living thing, the law had evolved and adapted; its history influenced its response to a new circumstance as much as pure logic did, as when he paraphrased Chaucer in writing, "Let us now peruse our ancient authors, for out of the old fields must grow the new corn."

Coke also made few philosophical statements about liberty; for him, that English legal precedent protected it was enough. He saw liberty not only in political terms but in economic terms. To raise money, the crown had begun selling—among other things—monopoly rights; Coke consistently opposed monopolies. (The issue lies beyond the scope of this book, but monopolies became a major point of contention between the crown and Parliament.)

Given James's ahistorical advancement of the divine right theory, Coke's reliance on precedent, on history, was in its very conservatism pure rebellion. For he certainly understood that the law defined, underpinned, and sustained the infrastructure of society, the infrastructure of personal relationships. If he began with the concrete, with case law and not theory, he was creative enough to find—or distort—a precedent to justify any position he took. Thus he sounded conservative even at his most radical.

His reliance on precedent also represented the spirit of the times. England had become newly entranced with English history. History was popular. Even Shakespeare expressed, reinforced, and advanced this great and new interest in history. Common law was property law. Ownership of property had expanded enormously—absolutely enormously—as feudalism declined, as the modern era began. Property was inherited. As one scholar has noted, the tens of thousands who saw *Richard II* also saw Richard essentially disinherit Bolingbroke; they could easily see how that threat to his rights could amount to a threat to their own.[17]

The way England portrayed its history—as other nations do, transforming it almost into a mythology—both helped it separate itself from the rest of Europe and convince itself of its special and divine purpose. Oliver Cromwell proclaimed a sentiment not reserved to Puritans: "The dispensations of the Lord have been as if He had said, *England* thou art my first-born, my delight amongst the Nations. . . . [T]he Lord hath not dealt so with any of the people round about us."[18]

England's island status made it special. Its self-proclaimed leadership in church reform made it special. Common law, along with the accompanying rights and freedoms, made it special. Its conflicts with its king also made it special.

Those confrontations, forced by Coke, were just beginning. Another came when James heard the news that Henry IV, king of France, had been assassinated by a priest. He "turned whiter than his shirt." He issued a royal proclamation forbidding all recusants to come within ten miles of the palace and requiring every subject to take the Oath of Allegiance written after the Gunpowder Plot. Coke argued before the Privy Council that the king's proclamation had no force: "The Law of England is divided into three parts, Common Law, Statute Law, and Custom. But the King's proclamation is none of them . . . the King cannot change any part of Common Law, nor create any Offence by his proclamation, which was not an Offence before."[19] He was so convincing that the king's own council agreed and rebuffed the king.

Judges served at the crown's pleasure. Yet Coke was not so easy to remove. He had become a large figure, highly regarded, even a symbol, and his dismissal would cost the king credibility and access to Coke's connections and influence. The river of that influence ran both broad and deep. In addition, Coke had utility. Dismissal would cost the king Coke's nonjudicial services. For example, Coke had helped the crown set priorities on which debts to pay by distinguishing "eating debts, such as were taken up by interest, the second, crying debts, due to soldiers, mariners, tradesmen and such as live on labour, the third, pressing debts,"[20] which for political reasons had to be paid.

More than that, James seemed to like and respect Coke. Perhaps it was partly that James, considering himself an intellectual, enjoyed parrying with him. For James had no fear of surrounding himself with intelligent men. He had close to him another courtier eager to justify a great expansion of his power, a courtier who urged the king to put Parliament and the Puritans in their place. This courtier was more brilliant even than Coke. This courtier was Sir Francis Bacon.

## ❧ CHAPTER 3 ❧

It was a time of extraordinary men: in literature, William Shakespeare, John Donne, John Milton; in the sciences, William Harvey and Bacon himself; in law, Edward Coke; in political philosophy, Bacon's protégé Thomas Hobbes and, soon, John Locke. Other than Shakespeare, Bacon is often considered the most dazzling of them all.

Bacon's chief legacy lay in his contributions to scientific methodology, on the way people think rather than on what they think. With this legacy, he left a large mark on the world, and a large mark on Roger Williams as well. But even though Bacon performed many scientific experiments and inspired the founding of the Royal Academy, he did not view himself as a "natural philosopher," i.e., a scientist. He was far more ambitious than that. In 1592, he said, "I have taken all knowledge to be my province."[1]

He explored that province thoroughly, writing about religion, about science, about manners, about politics. His comments were penetrating and provocative, yet simultaneously deep enough to prove restful and require contemplation. One tribute to the depth of his understanding of human behavior is the theory that he wrote Shakespeare's plays. Ben Jonson said of him, "No man ever spoke more nearly, more prestly, more weightily, or suffered less emptiness, less idleness in what he uttered. . . . His hearers could not cough, or look aside from him, without loss. . . . The fear of every man that heard him was that he should make an end."[2]

But if knowledge was his province, his ambition and heritage placed him in an entirely different country. He was born to greater wealth and higher station than Coke, but his father died before fully providing for him. He did inherit a substantial sum, but he lived well beyond it and soon was in debt. Indeed, the way he spent, perhaps no living his father could have provided would have sufficed him.

And he came to know failure. Queen Elizabeth had been impressed with him when he was not yet a teenager; even then his conversation dripped intelligence, and he entered Cambridge at age twelve. Yet his effort to win a subsidy to allow him to pursue a life of scholarship failed. Most likely such a quiet life, with an income modest compared with that of great men, would have not satisfied his tastes anyway. Instead he pursued lives in two courts, one as courtier and the other at law. And everywhere he turned he seemed obstructed by Coke.

Their first conflict came when they both sought the post of attorney general. Coke got it. Soon after, largely because of Coke's opposition, Bacon failed to get the lesser post of solicitor general. Three years after that, while Coke was becoming one of the richest men in England, Bacon was arrested for debt.

As Bacon labored in a slow, arduous climb out of that darkness, Coke continued to obstruct him. They competed in court: Thomas Sutton, one of the wealthiest men in England, set up and left his fortune to the Charterhouse School to educate "poor" children, i.e., sons of the professional classes "whose parents may not have any estates of lands to leave unto them." Sutton's nephew contested the will. Bacon represented him. Coke represented the school. Coke won, depriving Bacon of a huge fee. But perhaps the greatest blow to Bacon came when he and Coke, after Coke's first wife died, competed for the hand of the enormously wealthy Elizabeth Hatton. Neither pursued her for love, but Coke did not need the money. Bacon did. Her wealth would have bought Bacon a great freeing—freeing him of the need for maneuver, of the need for obsequiousness, of the need to waste much of his life in the pursuit of gain. But again Coke won. Coke was fifty; his bride was twenty. That the marriage brought great unhappiness to both Coke and his wife could have given Bacon little satisfaction.

Without the marriage, while Coke ascended in audacious jumps, Bacon rose slowly, in small calculated steps. By his own admission and despite his enormous abilities, he did not seek advancement primarily through merit. Instead he played at court. Machiavelli was then a frequent subject of discussion and was often attacked for his immorality. Bacon admired him for "openly and unfeignedly . . . describ[ing] what men do, and not what they ought to do."[3] He emulated him both in his own essays and in practice, striving to become expert at dissimulation. In an essay he advised "the hiding and veiling of a man's self. . . . If you would work any man, you must either know his nature and fashions, and so lead him; or his ends, and so persuade him; or his weaknesses and disadvantages, and so awe him; or those that have interest in him, and so govern him."[4]

Bacon also had the curse of objectivity; his own interests did not blind him to the fullness of his reality. As he saw through others, he saw through himself and sometimes ruminated candidly about his own ambitions, talents, flaws, and means of ascent. Surviving portraits of Bacon show a man who appears wary, as if his gaze is not so much unfocused as darting about, simultaneously looking for an opportunity to exploit or a threat to avoid. In some of these portraits, portraits meant to flatter, he seems weary as well; in still others, he shows the cold detachment of the distant observer, a detachment so complete as to approach cruelty.

If he was wary, others were wary of him. Watching him, his own brother quoted Roger Ascham on courtiers: "To laugh, to lie, to flatter, to face; / Four ways in court to win men's grace." A contemporary described him: "His countenance had indented with age before he was old; his presence grave and comely; of a high-flying and lively wit, striving in some things to be admired rather than understood. He had a delicate, lively hazel eye; Dr. Harvey"— William Harvey, who both traced how blood circulates through the body, confounding beliefs of the time, and showed how embryos developed—"tolde me it was like the eye of a viper."[5]

One courtier observed, "He that will live at Court must make his dependency upon some great person, in whose ship he must embark his life and fortune. . . . He that settles his service upon one of them shall fall into disfavour of another, for a Court is an army ever at war, striving by stratagems to circumvent and kick up another's heels."[6]

Thus Bacon spoke of his need to "insinuate" himself with the powerful, explaining that "mean men in their rising must adhere."[7] The man to whom Bacon initially chose to adhere was Robert Devereux, the Earl of Essex. Bacon called his services to Essex "in a sort my vocation. . . . I did nothing but devise and ruminate with myself to the best of my understanding, propositions and memorials of anything that might concern his Lordship's honour, fortune, or service."[8]

Essex helped him collect several court positions that brought stipends; those stipends, along with his marriage to the daughter of a wealthy London alderman, improved his financial situation. But both his adherence to Essex and his marriage cost him something as well. To say he had an unhappy marriage rather understates it. He and his wife despised each other. He was homosexual and disinherited his widow in his will; she returned the favor by marrying her steward ten days after his death. In adhering to Essex, Bacon also chose unwisely. Essex dared a rebellion against Elizabeth.

Coke prosecuted Essex for treason, and he was beheaded. Bacon, again isolated, again confounded by Coke, wrote a vicious denunciation of Essex in an attempt to regain favor. After Elizabeth's death, to gain favor with James, whom Essex had long supported, he repudiated his denunciation.

Then, finally, Bacon succeeded in finding a stable patron and a steady rise, attaching himself to the king's favorite of favorites, the Duke of Buckingham, to whom he wrote, "I can be but yours, and desire to better myself, that I may be of more worth to such an owner."[9]

Finally also his abilities began to surface. Knowing James's ends, Bacon assured him that he might found a new and great age and advocated the expansion of the crown's power. He argued that the moral standards which apply to individuals do not apply to governments, and approved of war if it strengthened the state. (Bacon's last secretary would be Thomas Hobbes, philosopher of the authoritarian state.) In making these arguments he also confirmed in James, if only indirectly, the diminution of the ancient rights and privileges of England.

And always Bacon watched for his own opportunity. In 1613, when the chief justice of the Court of the King's Bench died, he found an opportunity.

The court vacancy gave him the chance to both revenge himself on Coke and elevate himself. Bacon advised James to "remove the Lord Coke from the place he now holdeth to be Chief Justice of England"—the grand if informal title of the vacant judgeship. Notwithstanding the title, the move would hurt Coke because King's Bench had narrower jurisdiction than Common Pleas; this struck at both his power and, since nearly every office in government was supported by fees, his income. Bacon further suggested that the current attorney general replace Coke on Common Pleas and that Bacon himself become attorney general. These moves, he argued, would "recover that strength due to the King's prerogative which it hath had in times past."[10] Bacon also suggested that James leave "dangling" before Coke the possibility of being named to the Privy Council, predicting that Coke would "thereupon turn obsequious."

James took Bacon's advice, except that he made Coke a privy councilor immediately. When Coke, with enormous reluctance, moved from Common

Pleas to the King's Bench two hundred and fifty feet away in the same Westminster Hall, he left weeping.

Bacon at last became attorney general, twenty years after first seeking the position. The appointment was received with some disfavor at court. One diarist wrote, "There is a strong apprehension that little good is to be expected from this change, and that Bacon may prove a dangerous instrument."[11]

At first, it seemed the moves would advance the crown's interests. The crown's need for funding had never abated and James did two things to alleviate it, both of which stirred intense opposition. Astoundingly, through the Spanish ambassador the Count of Gondomar, who had insinuated himself into James's confidence and who was said to personify Machiavelli's advice, James asked for Spain's financial help. That James could be so impolitic as to turn to the Catholic country his subjects so hated and feared marked both the level of his insensitivity to them and his need. Next he demanded "benevolences"—nominally gifts—from his subjects in lieu of taxes. James did not invent this idea. In the late 1400s Edward IV had demanded benevolences, but after his death Parliament had prohibited them.

On benevolences, this time Coke supported James. He privately called them an abuse while publicly stating that they were voluntary and therefore legal. He also gave generously himself. But if James believed that Coke had been tamed, he was soon disabused of that illusion.

A plaintiff who had lost a case in a common law court appealed to the Court of Chancery, the prerogative court presided over by the lord chancellor of England. Other than the king himself, the chancellor was the highest-ranking official in government. The chancellor was Egerton, who had earlier said, *The monarch is the law. Rex est lex loquens, the king is the law speaking.* The chancery court reversed the common law court and imprisoned a man named Glanvil.

Coke intended to show that the monarch was not the law speaking. Stating that once a common law court had ruled, the plaintiff could no longer appeal to Chancery, he issued a writ of habeas corpus to release Glanvil. To justify his position, he cited statutes passed in 1353 and 1402 that had been designed to block appeals from English courts to Rome (even while Catholic, England had seen its church in nationalistic terms).

Then Coke went further. He sought an indictment against Egerton. This was an extraordinary attack not only on Egerton but on the king.

James was outraged but in this case responded deliberately. He appointed a commission of legal scholars to consider the issues Coke had raised and render an opinion upon them. If this response seemed measured, it was well calculated. To chair the commission, he named Bacon.

Almost simultaneously, the *Commendams* case arose. It too involved a direct challenge to royal power, although in this case the crown was the aggressor. The details of the case are unimportant. What was important was that, likely as a rebuke to Coke, James declared his intent to, in effect, decide this case himself. James had earlier claimed the power to judge any case. Speaking for the king, Bacon forbade any common law court from hearing the case until the king made his wishes known. But a court did hear the case. Coke sent James a letter, signed by all common law judges, explaining, "Most dread and most gracious Sovereign . . . our oath is in these expresse wordes: That in case anie letters come unto us contrary to lawe, that wee doe nothinge by such letters, but . . . goe forthe to doe the law, notwithstaunding the same letters."[12]

A furious James replied to Coke, "We are therefore to admonish you, that since the prerogative of our crown hath been more boldly dealt withal in Westminster-Hall during the time of our reign than it ever was in the reign of divers princes immediately preceding us, that we will no longer endure that popular and unlawful liberty. . . . Out of our absolute power and authority royal we do command you, that you forbear to meddle any further in this plea till . . . out of our own mouth you may hear our pleasure in this business."[13]

James soon summoned Coke and the eleven other senior common law judges to Whitehall. They were arraigned like defendants before a table, facing the king, Bacon, and most of the Privy Council.[14] This was to be a public refutation of Coke's position, a humiliation of him and a humiliation of the common law. James began cross-examining all the judges. As he spoke his anger intensified. Holding Coke's letter, calling it "undecent and unfit for subjects to disobey the King's commandment," in a sudden burst of fury he ripped it to pieces.

Before the king's rage, the judges all fell to their knees, begging forgiveness. It was the second time Coke had asked forgiveness of James from his knees. But he was not cowed and, still on his knees, defended himself.

James turned to Bacon for support in legal argument, and Bacon began to berate and lecture the judges. Coke refused to remain on his knees for Bacon. Bristling, he started to rise and snapped, "The King's counsel learned are to plead before the Judges, and not dispute with them!"

Then James intervened and Coke fell silent, saying, "I will not dispute with your Majesty."

The judges now listened as Bacon and others of the king's allies railed against their position. Finally they were asked whether, should the king again tell them to halt a legal proceeding until his views could be heard, they would obey. Eleven of the twelve judges said they would.

Coke said only that he would do what "should be fit for a Judge to do."

Two weeks later, James convened a Star Chamber session, the first time a sovereign had attended since Henry VIII. In this grand and opulent setting in Westminster Palace—gilded stars on a deep blue ceiling gave the suite of rooms their name—he called Coke's ruling against Chancery "odious speech," then, buttressed by Bacon's legal research, he issued a formal decree that the prerogative court "our Chancery" would take precedence over common law. And he declared, "Kings are properly Judges, and judgment properly belongs to them from God: for Kings sit in the throne of God, and thence all judgment is derived. It is atheism and blasphemy to dispute what God can do; so it is presumption and high contempt in a subject to dispute what a King can do. . . . The absolute prerogative of the Crown is no subject for the tongue of a lawyer, nor is it lawful to be disputed."[15]

James then gave Coke a "vacation" to "review his . . . many extravagant and exorbitant opinions. . . . If, in reviewing and reading thereof, he find anything fit to be altered and amended, the correction is left to his discretion."[16]

James was referring to Coke's *Reports*. They were relied upon by every lawyer in every court in England. Even Bacon told James, "To give every man his due, had it not been for Sir Edward Coke's *Reports* (which though they may have errors . . . yet they contain infinitely good decisions and rulings over of cases) the law by this time had been almost like a ship without ballast."[17]

It took Coke five months to conduct his review. When he finished he met with Bacon, Egerton, and several other of the king's lawyers. Then he apologized for his errors and handed them a list of them: in thousands of pages he had found five minor mistakes of fact or translation.

James had not been seeking an excuse to dismiss him. He had been seeking an excuse to keep him. Coke refused to give him one. Bacon insisted that Coke's defiance amounted to "a scorn . . . to his Majesty," and urged James to remove Coke for "contempt and slander of his [Majesty's] government . . . a perpetual turbulent carriage, first towards the liberties of his church and the state ecclesiastical; then towards his prerogative royal and the branches thereof."[18]

James did not act. Bacon sent him seventeen specific instances in which Coke had curtailed royal power. James still hesitated. The only explanation for his reluctance to dismiss Coke is that he did not want to. But on November 16, 1616, Bacon wrote the king, "May it please your excellent Majesty, I send your Majesty a form of discharge for my Lord Coke from his place of Chief Justice of your Bench."

Finally, James signed it, informing Coke that "we at once remove and exonerate you from" the office. Bacon had seemingly triumphed. His archrival Coke was no longer a judge. A few months later Egerton died and James made Bacon lord chancellor of England, Lord Keeper of the Great Seal of England—the position his father once held—and the first Viscount St. Albans. In all the government, he was second only to the king in power.

As one of his first moves, Bacon had the High Commission build its own prison. The jailers of this prison had orders to refuse to obey common law writs of habeas corpus.[19]

But Coke was not vanquished.

## ❧ CHAPTER 4 ❧

It is not known precisely when the young Roger Williams began working for Coke, but he likely started about this time, as Coke resurrected his career—for Coke did not remain out of favor long. His return to favor would only be brief, and after it he would help set England on a slow march toward revolution, a revolution which commenced with a resolve to resist James's arrogation of power but gradually became infused with the passion of Puritans. Coke would lead the first part of that struggle; Williams watched from his side, each day learning more about power.

The revival of Coke's political fortunes was no accident. Rather, it demonstrated his ferocity and his determination to return to the game. He had an exceedingly beautiful fourteen-year-old daughter. Buckingham had an unmarried older brother who was so taken with Coke's daughter that he said he would take her "in her smock," i.e., he would marry her without any dowry. The prospective groom's advisers prevailed and Coke did provide a sizable one. But neither his wife nor his daughter, who lived apart from Coke, wanted the marriage; his wife forged a document that would have made it impossible. Coke proved the forgery. Bacon, knowing that any connection between Coke and Buckingham might threaten him, also tried to prevent it by granting Coke's wife legal custody over the daughter. Coke, accompanied by armed men, stormed his wife's home, and seized his daughter, forcibly carried her away, and had his wife arrested so she could do nothing further to interfere with the wedding.

Nonetheless, the groom was happy. The groom's happiness pleasured Buckingham. At the wedding itself, Coke gave his daughter to the king, who in turn gave her to the groom. After the wedding, only months after dismissing Coke from his judgeship, James restored him to a seat on the Privy Council.

(The groom's happiness did not last long. His bride so flaunted her "wanton"

ways that she and her lover were hauled before an ecclesiastical court. They
asserted the common law right against self-incrimination and refused to answer
questions; ecclesiastical courts did not recognize that right and excommunicated them.)

Williams, whenever his apprenticeship began, could not have escaped hearing talk at court about how Coke had regained favor. Indeed, twice the Privy
Council itself addressed legal issues involving Coke's marriage. Yet Williams
would also have seen that Coke had not compromised his purpose—to limit
the power of the crown. Only the battleground had changed. Coke could no
longer use the power of the courts to limit the sovereign, but the power of
Parliament remained at hand, whenever James called one. And he would have
to call one. The need for money would force his hand.

There, in Parliament and in the nation, the grievances Coke had articulated
would resonate, especially among those most suspicious of where the king was
taking his church. Meanwhile, Williams, standing in the back of the Star
Chamber and the Privy Council, his ears pricked and taking notes, was receiving an education.

Already Williams had seen much of life—and politics—growing up in London. London itself was a financial and commercial center, a great port, a center of intellectual ferment, a city whose theaters on the south bank of the
Thames drew twenty thousand people a week to plays. London was in fact
"drawing to it all the animal and vital spirits"[1] of the kingdom.

Williams's home in Smithfield was away from the center of activity, but the
name of his street, Cow's Lane, was the only relic of an earlier rural time. The
street itself was essentially a tunnel, cut off from the sun by multistory buildings whose second stories extended out over the lane.

Close by a huge livestock market operated, and half a mile from his home
one of the largest fairs in all England was held. Also close by was Newgate
prison. In 1612, a "vast Conflux of people" watched Bartholomew Legate, a
Separatist who completely rejected the Church of England, "burned to ashes"[2]
in London, while the bells of Williams's nearby parish church St. Sepulchre's
tolled in doleful celebration. Also in 1612 Edward Wightman, another Separatist, was burned at the stake in Litchfield. Williams's brother-in-law was also
named Edward Wightman, which would have brought that death directly into
Williams's home. Williams was then most likely eight or nine years old, clearly

old enough to have full awareness of both events. Legate and Wightman would be the last two people in England burned at the stake for heresy, although not the last to die for it.

Williams's near neighbors included Dutch expatriates—traders—and Williams learned their language, knowledge which later proved useful. The vicar of St. Sepulchre's was John Spenser, the king's chaplain and one of the scholars who produced the King James Bible. Numerous great men also worshipped there, including Captain John Smith. Smith had earned his captaincy fighting for the Dutch against Spain and for Austria against the Turks, then helped found and lead English colonies in Virginia and explored the region from Maine to Massachusetts, naming it "New England." His several books about his adventures made his name celebrated throughout London, and Williams could see him at worship every week.

In short, the great large world poured in upon Williams in Smithfield in ways that made the strange familiar. His own family was of modest middle-class means but not insular; it looked to this large world. He was named after an uncle who was high sheriff of Hertfordshire; another uncle was mayor of London in 1611. His father belonged to the Merchant Taylors Guild, a declining guild but one with a great and glorious history and whose fortunes were tied to international trade. One of Roger's brothers would become a merchant who routinely traveled to and traded with Arab countries; another would join Williams in New England.

His childhood seems to have been unhappy. In nine surviving volumes of his writings and letters, he mentioned his upbringing or his father only once, as he approached his thirtieth year, when he recalled being "persecuted in and out of my father's house these 20 years."[3]

Coke offered an immediate and breathtaking escape. Williams would have accompanied him to court, the Star Chamber, the Privy Council; an unnoticed amanuensis in the background, he nonetheless saw what Coke saw, listened as Coke listened. He did not simply read Coke's words; he heard Coke speak the words, he wrote down the words, he then translated those words from shorthand into a text Coke read and revised. Williams breathed Coke and lived Coke. His lessons were not something studied; they were lived. Williams was in the king's presence—and also present on occasion was the king's son who became King Charles—often enough to refer to it in a routine way. At least once he saw James receive a message from Coke "sore against his will."[4] Royalty did not impress him. He considered Charles "vicious, a swearer from his youth, and an oppressour and persecutour of good Men."[5]

The experience could not but affect him.

It is unclear why Coke took Williams on. There is no indication that he ever employed another boy to do the tasks Williams did, and his treatment of Williams seems out of character. But Coke was just passing sixty, a time when one begins to add up one's life. His own children had achieved little and wasted much, and as they entered middle age, he regularly had to extricate them from financial or legal difficulties. As Catherine Drinker Bowen wrote in her award-winning biography of Coke, "Coke's life was solitary. His wife lived apart; of eight children, only a daughter, Anne Sadleir, remained close." His children were "a disappointment irrevocable, irremediable."[6]

It was then that Coke encountered Williams, probably taking shorthand notes of a sermon. Williams was not only intense but *earnest*, earnestness reflected in his intelligence, enthusiasm, and vitality. Williams at age thirteen, fourteen, fifteen would have virtually trembled with all the possibilities of life, and perhaps Coke saw in the boy a new and final possibility. At any rate, whether from disappointment in his own children, or loneliness, or simple kindness, or Christian charity, or some exceptional potential Williams showed, Coke the aging lawyer came to take a deep interest in the future of this teenager—enough that Williams became that boy whom Coke sometimes called his son. Coke's affection for Williams was confirmed by his daughter, the one child who remained close to him. Anne Sadleir was no friend to Williams. Decades later, after the beheading not only of an archbishop but of a king, disgusted with Williams's Puritanism and involvement with revolutionaries, she called for hanging Williams himself. Yet in the same note in which she wished that he be hanged, she also conceded that her father "tooke such likeing to him" and considered him "so hopefull a youth."[7]

Williams clearly revered Coke, and loved him. According to an early-nineteenth-century historian who cited records no longer extant, Coke asked Williams's father to "let him have the care" of Roger, and the request was "readily granted."[8] It was then standard for most servants, and nearly all children in such positions, to lodge with their employer, who routinely supplied "meate, drink and apparrell & lodging." Employers also generally accepted parental responsibility for children in their service. Whether Williams lived with Coke or not, Coke did more than meet that responsibility.

His greatest gift was to bring Williams into his world, to give him his example, to educate him in all ways. Williams watched from intimate perspective as Coke and Bacon, one of the great jurists in history and one of the boldest thinkers of any age, maneuvered about each other with near-lethal intent. He observed both closely, observed as well the royal entourage, the ways of the courts both royal and legal, and international affairs.

For the world outside was about to burst into flames, and the sparks threatened to kindle England as well.

In 1618 James's son-in-law Frederick V, "elector" of the Palatine—a principality in central Germany whose leading city was Heidelberg—became the match when Calvinist Bohemia rebelled against its Catholic ruler and offered Frederick its crown. He accepted, and the conflagration ignited.

In the preceding century Christians had killed other Christians because they differed in how they worshipped Christ. A long, uneasy truce had settled over Europe, based on the doctrine of *cuius regio, eius religio,* i.e., in each principality, subjects would worship in whatever manner their ruler did. The truce had not prevented occasional eruptions of violence, and Protestants and Catholics had circled each other warily. Now they embraced with swords, muskets, and artillery.

A Catholic army quickly expelled Frederick from Bohemia. It also slaughtered Protestants and banned Protestant worship there. What came to be known as the Thirty Years War was under way, a war which one historian called "the most devastating the continent had ever known."[9]

Catholic forces next attacked Frederick's home province, the Palatinate. This directly involved England, since Frederick's marriage to James's daughter made the Palatinate the patrimony of a potential heir to the English throne. (Through this line of succession, the House of Hanover, whose reign ended with Queen Victoria's death, came to the throne in 1714.)

Bohemia's rebellion had appalled James and increased his suspicion of English Puritans. He rejected the idea that differences between subjects and king over religion could justify a revolt, "for what hath religion to do to decrown a king? Leave that opinion to the Devil and to the Jesuits, authors of it. . . .

Christ came into the world to teach subjects obedience to the king, and not rebellion."[10]

He also had advised Frederick to reject the offer of the crown of Bohemia. But now it seemed all England called upon him to help his son-in-law, so he reluctantly sent a token English force to do so.

Yet he also took steps that aroused England against him. Ironically, those steps came from his desire for peace. His personal motto was *beati pacifici,* "blessed are the peacemakers." Sincerely hoping to build bridges between Catholic and Protestant that might bring real peace and prevent English involvement in a larger war, he simultaneously attempted to mollify Spain. Fifteen years earlier Sir Walter Raleigh had been convicted of treason and sentenced to death. But Raleigh had not been executed. After more than a decade in the Tower of London, he had been released—although not pardoned—and he again started raiding Spanish possessions in the Americas. Upon Raleigh's return to England, Gondomar, the Spanish ambassador, demanded he be handed over to Spain for execution.

James formed a committee to advise him. Coke, who had originally prosecuted Raleigh and won the death sentence, spoke for the committee and urged James to give Raleigh a new trial before the Privy Council.[11] Instead James had Raleigh beheaded. This bowing of the knee to Spain, this murder of a symbol of English defiance of Spanish might, inflamed England. Raleigh's courage on the gallows exacerbated the inflammation. So did James's release of one hundred Catholic priests from prison.

Peace at this price was not popular. One critic wrote that James would rather "spend £100,000 on embassies to keep or procure Peace with Dishonour, than £10,000 on an army that would have forced Peace with Honour."[12]

Worse, James was pursuing a marriage of his son Charles to a Catholic—and not just any Catholic, but to Maria Anna, the "Infanta," princess of Spain and granddaughter of the king who had sent the Armada against England. No one in England had forgotten that. And no one in England had forgotten that Queen Mary had burned hundreds of Protestants at the stake. Many still alive remembered that horror; for those who had not, Foxe's *Book of Martyrs* reminded them; every Protestant church in England had a copy. (An abridged version was dedicated to Coke.) Nor had anyone in England forgotten the Gunpowder Plot—except, it seemed, James, the man targeted for assassination.

Devout English Protestants, and especially Puritans, felt threatened by

James's moves. They feared that under him their religion's hold on England would become tenuous. They feared that a turn toward Catholicism would corrupt England and bring God's disfavor. But they did not fear a return to the days of Mary, with Protestant martyrs burned at the stake. For this they would not allow to happen.

Even without the question of religion, the nation was in turmoil. The end of feudalism had pushed tens of thousands of English families off the land and sent them either wandering the countryside out of work or flooding London with poverty and discontent. The guilds had come under intense economic pressure as well, with enormous perturbation of markets, especially in textiles, which accounted for 90 percent of English exports.

James remained desperate for money. To raise revenue he sold anything he could sell. For a fee, James knighted more men in three months (one morning he knighted forty-six before breakfast) than Elizabeth had in forty-four years.[13] Peerages were sold—an earldom cost £10,000—and the House of Lords increased from 52 members to 126. Crown lands were sold. Government posts were sold; the purchaser profited by collecting fees over time. Even high posts were sold: Henry Montague, Coke's successor as chief justice of the King's Bench, bought the post of lord treasurer for £20,000. Even tax revenue was sold; the king sold the right to collect future taxes to a private "tax farmer" who paid cash.

Fees from the granting of monopolies became a revenue stream but they also became a great grievance in the country at large because they raised prices. The monopoly engendering the greatest grievance was the licensing of alehouses given to Sir Giles Mompesson, who had married into Buckingham's family and who split the licensing fees with James. This particular arrangement stripped licensing power and fees from justices of the peace, who were the bedrock of local English government; they soon lost their enthusiasm for James.

But the revenue from these sales yielded less and less, partly because James had little left to sell, partly because of supply and demand: the cost of the title of "baronet"—a title invented by James for the sole purpose of selling it—fell from £1,095 to £220.[14] James now had no recourse. His Privy Council, including both Coke and Bacon, urged him to call a new Parliament and trade an end to monopolies for new "subsidies," i.e., special taxes.

Late in 1620 James agreed, but he wanted to limit the subjects discussed to those issues, and he wanted to prevent critics from giving voice to complaints. He insisted that both "reason of state" and his royal prerogative justified and required public silence on foreign policy matters, be it the war in Europe or the possible marriage of Prince Charles to the Spanish princess. In his summons of Parliament, he called for defeat of "curious yet wrangling lawyers who may seek reputation by stirring needless questions."[15]

Precedent did suggest royal marriage was not a fit subject for discussion; in 1579, John Stubbes had published a pamphlet criticizing Elizabeth's possible marriage to a French Catholic; for this effrontery, he had his right hand chopped off. (With his left hand he took off his cap and shouted, "God save the queen!")

But Stubbes had not spoken in Parliament, and Parliament had a tradition, albeit a somewhat tenuous one, of free speech. As for the king's call for the defeat of his critics, although suffrage was limited to a fraction of the population, elections were free. The country would send whom it would.

In 1620, two additional and unrelated developments marked fundamental, even revolutionary change, although neither had immediate impact.

The first was a symptom of the age. In September, the *Mayflower* set sail from Southampton, carrying Separatists who had first fled to Holland a decade earlier, while the Church of England was preparing to burn Separatists at the stake. These pilgrims were by no means the first English to settle in America, but they were the first who left to create what in their own minds was a City of God.

The second helped create a new age. In November, Bacon published his extraordinary *Novum Organum, The New Organon or True Directions into the Interpretation of Nature,* in which he rejected Aristotle, logic, the Scholastics, and empiricism and called for something akin to the modern scientific method. Because Aristotle's interpretation of nature relied on reason as opposed to observation or experiment, Bacon said he "corrupted natural philosophy"— i.e., science—"by his logic," and "made his natural philosophy a mere bondservant to his logic, thereby rendering it contentious and nearly useless. . . . For he had come to his conclusion before; he did not consult experience, as he should have done, for the purpose of framing his decisions and axioms, but having first determined the question according to his will, he then resorts to experience, and bending her into conformity . . . leads her about like a captive in a procession. So that even on this count he is more guilty than his modern followers, the schoolmen, who have abandoned experience altogether." Although Bacon is today often called an empiricist—not a complimentary appellation among epistemologists—he also warned that "the Empirical school of philosophy gives birth to dogmas more deformed and monstrous than the Sophistical or rational school."[16] He argued instead for "[t]he evidence of the sense, helped and guarded by a certain process of correction." That process was experimentation; he noted that just as Proteus had to be bound fast before he would change shape, nature "exhibits herself more clearly under the trials and vexations of art than when left to herself."[17]

*Novum Organum* was a landmark work which established Bacon as inspiration and model and which would lead directly to the establishment of the Royal Academy. Williams likely did not read Bacon until he was older, but Bacon's ideas eventually seemed to lodge in his mind.

Bacon, no doubt showing off, sent Coke an elegantly printed, gold-encrusted copy of his great work. Coke could stomach nothing of Bacon, much less a philosophy which chose experimentation over precedent and denigrated logic; he wrote two comments in Latin on its flyleaf: "It deserveth not to be read in Schooles / But to be freighted in the ship of Fooles."[18] Under that, he added, "You propose to reconstruct the teaching of wise men of old. Reconstruct first our laws and justice."[19]

Coke intended to do just that.

On January 30, 1621, the new Parliament convened in Westminster Palace, which was a city of itself. Many people—Ben Jonson among them—lived and worked within it. Just outside were inns, shops, and alehouses, including three taverns named Hell, Heaven, and Purgatory. Events in and around the palace drew not only lawyers and scriveners for work but crowds of the "baser sort" thronging there for entertainment. "The citizens grow very tumultuous and flock by troops daily to the Parliament," said one member. "There is scarce passage between the two Houses, the Court of Requests is so thronged with them."[20]

The House of Commons met in a tiny chamber crammed with its more than four hundred members; only a decade earlier stepped wooden benches had been built so all could sit. The dark wood gave the chamber the feeling of the forest, hard but not impenetrable. The Speaker sat on a raised dais at one end. At the opposite end, inside the main door, a bar marked the point beyond which only members were allowed, and messages would come addressed to members at the "doors" of the House. Above the floor was a mezzanine reached by ladder from the floor, with a gallery above that.

Coke, as a privy councilor, was supposed to represent the king's interests. But the Commons chamber lay close by the King's Bench. He could hardly enter Commons without passing his old rooms there, a daily reminder of his former position and Bacon's role in his dismissal. Still, initially he did work with Bacon and others to help the king by finding precedent to allow Prince Charles to sit in the House of Lords; the king's supporters hoped Charles's personal presence would silence debate of his marriage plans.

But Parliament soon demonstrated its distrust of James by insisting that he spend any subsidies only on defending his daughter and son-in-law in Germany against Catholic armies. James bitterly confided—to of all people Gondomar, the Spanish ambassador and one of his few intimates—that this proved Puritans "loved [Frederick] more than they did" their king.[21]

In fact Puritans did not dominate this Parliament. James was largely conflating all Protestant critics with them. Religion played a major role in debate because the war in the Palatine was inspired by religion and because many feared that a marriage of Charles to the Spanish princess threatened the future of Protestantism in England. But it was not only Puritans distressed by James on these issues. Parliament's distrust of James was so great it put him on a tight leash. Keeping an army in the field would cost £900,000 a year, but it voted him only £150,000, meaning he would have to either keep this Parliament alive or call another.

Then Coke took Parliament further. Among Parliament's traditional rights was bringing "grievances" to the king's attention. Coke chaired the Committee on Grievances, an odd position for a privy councilor. And he lashed out at the king's claim that "reason of state," i.e., the national interest and particularly national security, could justify extraordinary action.

"Reason of state is often a trick to put us out of the right way," Coke said, "for when a man can give no reason for a thing, then he flieth to a higher strain and saith it is a *reason of state*."[22]

Coke had barely begun his attack on the crown. Parliament's formal name was the "High Court of Parliament," and Coke now insisted it was a court of record, able to fine, imprison, and impeach. Not in two centuries had

Parliament used its impeachment power. Parliament now asserted that power, asserted that the Commons functioned as "a grand jury for the whole commonwealth."[23] Coke, finding no precedent for the specific procedures he wanted, helped define new procedures, then varied them case by case, using whichever ones made conviction in the House of Lords, which tried those impeached, most likely.[24] Now Coke took aim, and he did not aim low.

Parliament brought down a bishop, and it brought down the president of the High Commission. It brought down Attorney General Henry Yelverton, and it brought down the monopolist Mompesson, who subsequently fled England to escape prison. (In vengeance Parliament jailed his attorney.)

James could have stopped it all by dissolving Parliament, but he still needed money. Then, not yet satiated by this feast of retribution, Coke hurled the full weight of all Parliament at his most important target: the lord chancellor of England, Keeper of the Seal of England, Baron Verulam, and Viscount St. Albans, Sir Francis Bacon.

In fact, Bacon was the most easy of prey, once Parliament found the stomach to devour him. Bribes had become so common in cases before the Court of Chancery, and Bacon had considered himself so invulnerable, that he had made no effort to hide his acceptance of them. Defenseless, he could only beg of the king, arguing, "Those who strike at your Chancellor, it is much to be feared will strike at your crown."[25]

But day after day Commons gleefully piled excruciating detail of guilt upon excruciating detail, each one another faggot for Bacon's pyre. The king thought of intervening, hesitated, and, in the face of these proofs, backed away. Bacon, after being impeached by Commons, crushed and humiliated, begged the Lords for mercy and offered his immediate "penitent submission" and resignation.

Coke wanted more than a simple resignation; he wanted Bacon utterly broken. Lords rejected Bacon's offer.

To avoid the humiliation of a trial, Bacon was forced to write, "The Confession and Submission of me, the Lord Chancellor . . . I do plainly and ingenuously confess that I am guilty of corruption; and do renounce all defence, and put myself upon the grace and mercy of your Lordships." To each charge he attested his guilt. In a subsequent communication he wrote, "I beseech your Lordships, be merciful to a broken reed."

He did not attend his sentencing. Nonetheless the ceremony proceeded in all formality and circumstance. Four-hundred-plus members of the House of Commons marched in procession down the hallway to the House of Lords, and their Speaker demanded judgment upon "a corrupt Lord Chancellor." Sir James Ley, chief justice of King's Bench, the seat Bacon had deprived Coke of, pronounced that judgment. Bacon was to be banned forever from any public office, nor could he come "within the verge of the Court." He was fined £40,000. And he was imprisoned in the Tower of London "at the King's pleasure."

It pleased the king that Bacon remain in the Tower for a single day, it pleased the king to remit Bacon's fine, and it pleased the king later to grant Bacon a full pardon. (Bacon died five years after his disgrace, from a pneumonia he caught while conducting a scientific experiment to examine how snow preserved food. In a summation of his life, he concluded that he had wasted himself "in things for which I was least fit, so as I may truly say, my soul hath been a stranger in the course of my pilgrimage.")[26]

Parliament did not please the king. It had taken from him his most able lieutenant and embarrassed his government. Yet it still had not given him the money he regarded as necessary. Therefore, rather than dissolve it, he adjourned it for several months. As another sign of displeasure, he briefly imprisoned his severest critics. He was applying pressure. Under pressure, people either collapse or stiffen.

In late November, James summoned Parliament back but forbade it from "licentious talking in matters of state."[27]

Parliament defied him. Only days after returning, on December 1, a Saturday, members sent the king a petition citing fourteen grievances—each one involving Catholics. It demanded enforcement of all anti-Catholic laws and—despite the king's prohibition of any discussion of Prince Charles's marriage or foreign policy—it "begged that our most noble prince may be timely and happily married to one of our own religion." And it directly called for war to protect the Protestant religion: "Let your Majesty take speedily and effectually your sword in your hand."[28] In return, Commons offered taxes but "for the relief of the Palatinate only."[29]

Gondomar saw the petition even before the king, to whom he sent an extraordinary note. It stated that if James did not "punish the insolence of this Commons" he "would have ceased to be a King here." Gondomar, who represented a nation far more absolute than England, also expressed regret that "I have no army here at present to punish these people myself."[30]

James needed no prodding from Spain to define his kingly powers. He chose now to enter the area not of policy but of constitutional law. He informed Commons he would "not deign" to read its petition, hear it, or answer it. He then commanded the Speaker of the House "to make known in our name unto the House, that none therein shall meddle henceforth with anything concerning our government or deep matters of state, and namely not to deal with our dearest son's match with the daughter of Spain, nor to touch the honour of that King or any other our friends and confederates." Such issues were "far above your reach and capacity," and discussions of them breached royal prerogative. He warned, "We think ourselves very free and able to punish any man's misdemeanours in parliament, . . . which we mean not to spare hereafter upon any man's insolent behavior there."[31]

The king had entered the area of constitutional law. It was Coke's area. Here, Coke, at sixty-nine years old a virtual living monument, led, with the Puritans strong beside him; together they were potent indeed.

The Speaker read the king's rebuke in all solemnity to the Commons. He read it a second time. He read it a third time. On each word in each reading he placed full dignity; each word fell like a lash. The members listened in unhappy and restless silence. After the third reading, they adjourned for the day. Members milled about discussing what to do next and met privately that night. Few were cowed.

When Commons reconvened, Coke informed his colleagues there was no precedent for the king's message. Commons defiantly passed a second, almost identical petition, again asking the king to act on "our former petition concerning religion" occasioned by "the danger of these times." Regarding the threat to punish "insolent behavior," Commons adopted Coke's language, reminding James of "the ancient liberty of Parliament for freedom of speech . . . a Liberty which, we assure ourselves, so wise and just a King will not infringe, the same being our ancient and undoubted rights and an inheritance from our ancestors, without which we cannot freely debate nor clearly discern of things in question before us."[32]

The conflicts between king and Parliament, especially Commons, were both escalating and hardening. The policy differences were great. The different views of the powers of a king were greater.

Not for three days did the king reply. He was not conciliatory. He said he was "needing no such lessons" from Parliament about its rights, denied that freedom of speech was "your antient and undoubted right and inheritance," saying it instead "derived from the grace and permission of our ancestors and us."[33] He had withdrawn that permission.

Coke declared, "The privileges of this House is the nurse and life of all our laws, the subject's best inheritance. . . . If my sovereign will not allow me my inheritance, I must fly to Magna Carta and entreat explanation of his Majesty. . . . When the King says he cannot allow our liberties of right, this strikes at the root. We serve here for thousands and ten thousands."[34]

Now Coke suggested a procedure that allowed them to assert parliamentary rights without giving the king a chance to confirm or reject them: "Let us make a Protestation, enter it into the *Journals* and present the *Journals* to the King— but not as requiring an answer."[35]

James would have to accept it. No procedure allowed him to do otherwise. Immediately Commons embraced the idea.

The king had been willing to endure this Parliament in order to gain a subsidy for an army, to be used not—he and Buckingham assured Gondomar— against any Catholic forces, but against Protestant Holland. The subsidy had not yet passed, but James's willingness to endure a Parliament had. As soon as he heard what Commons was about, without any further effort to get his money, James dissolved Parliament, saying he would not call another in his lifetime.

But Commons, rather than instantly obeying, stayed deep into the night to finish the work, to formally declare its and the nation's rights. The Protestation stated in part: "That the liberties, franchises, privileges and jurisdictions of Parliament are the ancient and undoubted birthright and inheritance of the subjects of England; and that the arduous and urgent affairs concerning the King, state and defence of the realm, and of the Church of England, and the maintenance and making of laws and redress of mischiefs and grievances which daily happen within this realm are proper subjects and matters of counsel and debate in Parliament; and that in the handling and proceeding of those businesses every member of the House of Parliament hath and of right ought to have freedom of speech."[36]

To this, James did respond. Returning to Whitehall, he demanded the Commons *Journal*. Angrily he ripped the page containing the Protestation out of it and ordered it "razed out of all memorials and utterly to be annihilated."

The Spanish ambassador reported home that the dissolution of Parliament was "the best thing that had happened in the interests of Spain and the Catholic religion since Luther began to preach heresy a hundred years ago. The Marquis of Buckingham has had a great part in this and deserves to be thanked."[37]

Then James summoned Coke to the Privy Council. There, silently, Coke endured the king's lacerating dismissal: "You have forgotten the duty of a servant, the duty of a Councilor of State and the duty of a subject." Coke would have no more intimacy, not even pretended intimacy, with the crown.

That was not all. The council then ordered "the Lieutennaunt of the Tower to receave into his custodie the person of Sir Edward Coke, knight, and to keepe him closse prisoner there until further order."[38]

Coke was not the only member of Parliament imprisoned. James soon released the others, but "his Majestie himself had . . . mencioned particularly" that Coke would be an "exception out of the Pardon."[39]

Bacon had remained in the Tower one day. Coke stayed for months. While he was there, the Privy Council launched a full investigation of him for treason. If he were found guilty, his estates, a very rich prize indeed, would be confiscated; they were inventoried in eager anticipation, with orders issued that no asset be removed, nor even a tree felled. In his rooms, in all his homes, the king's men pored over his correspondence, searched through his papers, seized books and read margin notes while inquisitors cross-examined him in the Tower.

He replied calmly, "[I]f the King desires my head, he knows whereby he may have it."[40]

The searches and cross-examination yielded nothing. Yet Coke remained in prison, week after week after week, living through a harsh winter, recording each day of his confinement and turning seventy there. Gradually the king granted him one privilege, then another; first, he could walk on the grounds; next, his daughter could visit. After more than six months, he was released under house arrest, then finally restored to full freedom.

He left the Tower unintimidated either by it or by the accusation of treason. Indeed, the threat had filled him with new energy. Back in his rooms at the

Inner Temple of the Inns of Court—the four Inns of Court were almost a physical incarnation of the law, providing a combination law school, residential hotel, and guild to the London bar—he ruminated on the future. Even now, in his seventieth year, he had not finished.

Nor had the king finished. He complained that "of late Writers and ungrounded Divines, do broach many times unprofitable, unsound seditions, and dangerous Doctrines to the Scandall of the Church, and disquiet of the State."[41] To silence criticism by Puritan clergy, he prohibited every "parson, vicar, curate, lecturer and minister in the realm" from "declar[ing] limit or bound" on the king; he prohibited Sunday afternoon sermons on anything except "some part of the Cathechisme," and any below the rank of bishop or dean from preaching on "deep points of Predestination, Election, or Reprobation."[42]

Later, the king's supporters were even more direct. When Coke and Puritans continued their attacks on the High Commission, the clergyman Richard Montagu, a rising favorite of the king's for his enmity to Puritans, wrote, "Before God, it will never be well until we have our Inquisition."[43]

In the midst of the turmoil of 1621, Coke and Williams parted. It was a happy parting. Coke had arranged for Williams to attend the Charterhouse School. Its history made it a proper place to train him. The grounds had once been a Carthusian monastery, and Henry II had founded that order's first English monastery as penance for the murder of Thomas Beckett. Henry VIII continued the bloody tradition: in 1535 four of its priests who had refused to conform to his new Church of England were executed. Sir Thomas More watched the arrests, and was himself executed two months later.[44]

According to school rules, Williams was too old to be admitted, but an exception was made as a favor to Coke. The school owed him its very existence, for he had defended it in court—against Bacon—in a dispute over the bequest which established it; he also served on its board, along with the archbishop of Canterbury, the bishop of London, the attorney general, and Robert Cecil, the lord high treasurer of England. For Williams's education[45] Coke paid £140—a huge sum, more than double the costs of Cambridge University. Williams repaid him by excelling at Charterhouse; upon his graduation the school's governors voted him an "Exhibition," a scholarship of £16 annually,[46] to Pembroke College of Cambridge University; this was enough for him to survive comfortably, particularly since he also won a prestigious scholarship from the university for his mastery of Hebrew, Greek, and Latin.

In 1623 Roger Williams entered Pembroke College. The English educational system encouraged the assemblage of existing knowledge, logic, and acceptance of authority and precedent. It did not encourage thought. For a young man of his experience it had to be stifling. Nor was he naïve about university life. He found university not a retreat from the world but the world intensified. The same year he entered Cambridge, William Knight, a graduate of Pembroke College, gave a sermon at Oxford suggesting that if a civil ruler unlawfully threatened a subject's life or chastity, the subject could lawfully resist. The High Commission imprisoned him and two scholars who defended him. The conditions of Knight's imprisonment led directly to his death. Both Oxford and Cambridge then burned all books by Pareus, a German scholar on whose work Knight had based his sermon. Subsequently, Cambridge formally declared "the kingly power . . . subject to none save God, all resistance to same was pronounced infamous."[47]

Not surprisingly, Williams later observed, "We count the Universities the Fountaines [of knowledge] . . . but have not those Fountaines ever sent what streams the Times have liked? and ever changed their taste and colour to the Princes eye and Palate?"[48]

Coke and Bacon had already provided his real education. That had come watching the two circle each other warily and with sinister intent, watching business being done in the Privy Council and the Star Chamber, watching Coke confront the king and go to the Tower of London for it.

Williams was studying books now. But he had not studied Coke in a book; he had heard Coke deliver his words, seen him perform them with all dramatic inflection, transcribed them with detail enough to win not a teacher's approval but Coke's own. Those words and not just Coke's delivery of them but Coke's infusion of them with his own life had taught him reverence for man's law, an abhorrence of absolutism, the flexibility of reason, and of course courage. Williams would later recall "the many thousand times" he thought of "the writings, the speeches, and the example of that glorious light."

Yet he had never given blind loyalty; as he had demonstrated when defying his father as a young boy, his fidelity was to his own reasoning. For not only Coke's ideas but Bacon's left a deep imprint on him. If he dismissed Bacon's life as a courtier, dismissed the advice Bacon gave to the king, dismissed Bacon's person, he yet learned from him. He learned from Bacon's writings. If in politics Bacon believed in and relied upon the authority of the king, in science he rejected authority, rejected reliance on logic alone, in favor of experiment and observation. In essence, Bacon taught the difference between reasoning and thinking, between using one's mind to advocate and using it to understand, between assembling evidence with an end in mind and allowing evidence to discover a direction.

(There is irony in that Bacon was far more accomplished in politics than in science, yet his personal history and views on royal power are forgotten while his impact on scientific inquiry has been memorialized. There is equal irony in that Hobbes, his last secretary, did substantial scientific work, greater than Bacon's, which has been forgotten, while his political works are still studied today. Some of Hobbes's writings were clearly responding to Coke. Hobbes called reading history a "frequent cause" for "rebellion in particular against Monarchy," and complained that law was based on "this false measure of justice, [which lawyers] barbarously call . . . a precedent."[49] However, history seemed to influence him: his observation about life without state authority being nasty, brutish, and short may well have been drawn not from theory but historical fact, from the days of the wergeld, when even murder was seen as between victim and perpetrator, before the king's peace settled over the land.)

From both these men—and from all the world about them—Williams derived his own path, his own view of the state, of law, of politics, and of the role of religion in the state. In his own way he would exceed even Bacon in his willingness to confront and accept the implications of evidence. He would envision a new and different place; then he would create it.

First he had some final lessons to absorb. Bacon was dead. Coke, however, would teach that last lesson, and he would teach it to a new king as well.

# ☙ CHAPTER 5 ❧

James died in 1625 at age fifty-nine. His decline had been slow and his death no surprise. While his body lay in state, John Donne, whom James had much liked, stood beside the bier preaching dolor. The country, however, greeted James's death with diffidence and turned to his twenty-four-year-old son King Charles I with more anxiety than hope.

James had fancied himself an intellectual and peacemaker. Charles spent his youth exploring the arts. Rubens called him "of all princes living, the most appreciative of good painting."[1] Sir Simonds D'Ewes described him as "full of delicacy and handsome features; yea, his hands and face seemed to me, especially, effeminate and curious."[2] But he approached his responsibilities with gravity, was no weakling, and although he was a maneuverer and liar, no one would ever accuse him of cowardice.

At first a reconciliation between monarch and Parliament seemed possible. Charles had served in Parliament, had his own relationship with its leaders, and said he "was never wearie of hearing Cooke, he mingled mirth with busines to so good purpose." In turn, Coke, at seventy-three still vital intellectually and physically and with no inclination to retire from public life, pronounced Charles "an excellent instrument . . . [who] obtained for us . . . many good laws."[3] Parliament met soon after Charles's coronation; in it, Coke still chaired the Committee on Grievances but said there could be no grievances against so new a king.

But Charles soon gave them some. Sharing with his father the belief in the divine right of kings and an insensitivity to the concerns of his subjects, he continued his father's expansion of royal power and impulsion of the Church of England toward Catholic practices. These paths intertwined; in fact, they moved toward convergence.

Historian Alan Simpson noted that Puritans lived a life of "holy violence under compression."⁴ As Charles advanced his agenda, as he intruded upon the political rights of English subjects and simultaneously weighed more heavily upon people uncomfortable with the direction of the English church, he increased the stress on this holy compression. Like a dam under pressure, the structure of the society began to leak. The first seepage was seen in Separatists fleeing England for Holland; next came thousands of Puritans who would leave England for America. Then, as Parliament confronted king, the dam would burst.

Earlier, while James still lived, there had been a single moment of national euphoria over Charles. It occurred when the plan to marry him to a Spanish princess collapsed. At Cambridge bells rang for three days, with bonfires each night, and the entire university assembled for an all-day thanksgiving with sermons and orations. It was the same throughout the nation: in London even the High Church Anglican William Laud, who would become Charles's favorite prelate, called that city's celebration, "The greatest expression of joy by all sorts of people that I ever saw."⁵

But that euphoria had itself collapsed when Charles married the younger sister of King Louis XIII of France. Henrietta-Maria was of course Catholic, and she brought a dowry of £250,000. Charles assured his subjects that his marriage would not affect policy toward Catholics. He lied. He had secretly agreed to relax enforcement of anti-Catholic laws. In return for this relaxation, France pledged cooperation in restoring the Palatinate to Frederick and Protestant rule, and Charles and Buckingham—the new king's closest adviser (as he had been James's)—wanted to wage war more aggressively than James had. After the marriage, however, France not only reneged on its pledge of help: it even refused to allow English troops to pass through its territory. That forced most of an English army to winter in the densely packed confines of a ship designed only to carry them across the Channel; in the choking, fetid close quarters, with fumes of human waste and vomit heavy enough to suffocate a man belowdecks, an epidemic raged, killing more than half the entire force. The survivors returned home without having even engaged the enemy. It was only the first of many foreign disasters, and all of them were blamed on Buckingham, whom Charles had made lord high admiral, commander of the navy.

Each military defeat, each diplomatic blunder, each failure to advance the Protestant religion abroad only deepened the sea of discontent made rough and whitecapped by the increasingly harsh discipline imposed by the High Commission. Worse, the Anglican Church seemed to many Protestants increasingly and dangerously sympathetic to Catholic theology. Meanwhile, the new queen's large household—where English Catholics attended Mass—soon became in Protestant eyes a nest of at best corruption, at worst treason.

The chief issue was predestination. Catholics had long complained that Calvin's theory of predestination meant that "Christ died to save only a few, and not for all of us." In Holland in the early 1600s, the Protestant Jacob Arminius addressed this by amending orthodox Calvinism; he proposed that God did not irrevocably predestine the "elect" for salvation, and that man found salvation through faith.

Those believing in predestination, including but by no means limited to Puritans, found this interpretation appalling. For one thing, it elevated humans beyond their capacity. God had offered Adam paradise in return for obedience. Adam had failed and damned mankind. Then God had by His grace offered salvation to Abraham and the seed of Abraham in return for faith. Humans again failed. Humans could only fail. Finally God, ever merciful, had sent his son Christ and again offered the covenant of redemption, this time through His grace, and only through His grace. Only God did not fail. God could not fail.

The idea that God only saved a few "visible saints," only the "elect," both terrified and reassured. It terrified because one could not know with absolute certainty that one was saved. Puritans constantly searched their own souls for evidence of having been saved, constantly doubted themselves. But it also reassured people that once God had chosen a person, salvation was irrevocable. As Puritan minister Ezekiel Rogers told one desperate woman, "When the Lord hath once given you a promise it shall always be true as ever it was."[6]

Arminians were saying that God could withdraw salvation, a terrible and terrifying prospect to all who believed in predestination. Arminianism also suggested that, by giving humans a role in their salvation, humans approached God as equals in attaining salvation. This was abominable heresy.

Nonetheless, Charles advanced to bishoprics High Church Anglicans who, though they denied being Arminians, were clearly sympathetic to Arminian views. They also made worship more Catholic in style, for example, by constructing rails in churches, separating clergy and congregation. Finally, Charles—even more than his father—increasingly saw Puritans as enemies of both his church and his government. Therefore the disciplinary machinery of the church focused more than ever upon Puritans who did not fully conform; indeed, it now demanded conformity to practices of which James had said, "[F]or my own part I ever esteemed as indifferent."[7]

Devout English Protestants, facing defeat by Catholics abroad and drift toward Catholicism at home, grew increasingly uneasy, especially given their awareness that on the continent monarchs had been arrogating power to themselves for decades. In Spain, the Cortes Generales were in steep decline; in France, the Estates General had last met in 1614 and would not meet again until the French Revolution; in the smaller states and principalities of Germany and Italy, princes routinely governed in arbitrary fashion. Therefore, despite the patina of goodwill in the Parliament which met upon Charles's ascension, Sir Robert Phelips warned his colleagues, "We are the last monarchy in Christendom that retain our original rights and constitutions. Let us not perish now!"[8]

Charles had built distrust, and this distrust had consequences. For two centuries, Parliament had given every king a lifetime grant of "tonnage and poundage"—customs duties to pay the ordinary expenses of government. Charles's first Parliament limited its grant of these duties to one year.

Without these funds, Charles went to new extremes to get money, engendering even more discontent. First he tried to raise money as his father had through a "benevolence," voluntary gifts to the crown. It yielded little. The Privy Council then called for a "Forced Loan." Hundreds refused to pay. He imprisoned seventy of the most prominent "Refusers." And, worse, he imprisoned them with no charge out of fear that the courts would declare the Forced Loan illegal. When common law courts issued writs of habeas corpus, his jailers refused to honor them. This imprisonment of knights, local leaders, and members of Parliament rocked the gentry, a class normally supportive of established authority.

This was not the only crown infringement on English rights. Without enough funds for its army and navy, the king's officers imposed martial law in some locales and billeted soldiers and sailors in private homes, with only the promise of future payment for board.

England had long prided itself on its liberty, on Magna Carta, on the freedom epitomized in Coke's comment, *Every Englishman's home is as his castle.* Collecting taxes without authority, imposing martial law during peacetime, imprisoning without charges . . . Charles was creating a constitutional crisis. He was radicalizing his critics.

Then Buckingham demanded £500,000 for a new military expedition. The crown had already borrowed from everyone who would lend and had long since run out of credit. In early 1628, Charles tried to borrow money from the city of London—again, despite owing it £349,000. The city refused. Charles sold the last large holding of crown lands to the city in exchange for the erasure of old debts and £120,000 in cash.

But he had nothing else to sell, and no one else from whom to borrow. The country, already roiling over the Forced Loan, would not pay another. With no options left, in early 1628 he freed all Refusers. Then, with the greatest reluctance, he called another Parliament.

The new Parliament had an extraordinary cast, men rich in intellect and principle and prepared for confrontation. Every Refuser—including twenty-seven who had been imprisoned—who ran for Parliament won election, while crown supporters fared poorly. Coke, age seventy-six, also served; it would be his last Parliament, and his most memorable one.

The king claimed to seek a reconciliation. Yet he was hardly conciliatory. He planned to bring one thousand German mercenaries to England, putting critics, who feared this force would become a Praetorian Guard, on alert and on guard. (The plan never came to fruition.) Then, in his opening address to Parliament, he warned that if it failed to give him "what the state at this time needs, I must, in discharge of my conscience, use those other means which God hath put into my hands. . . . Take not this as a threatening, for I scorn to threaten any but my equals."[9]

No member considered himself the king's equal, yet they bristled. Phelips responded, "It is well known, the people of this state are under no subjection, than what they did voluntarily consent unto, by the original contract between king and people; and as there are many prerogatives and privileges conferred on the king, so there are left to the Subject many necessary liberties and Privileges, as appears by the common laws and acts of Parliament."[10]

To many members, nothing less than English freedom seemed at stake. Sir Benjamin Rudyerd warned plainly, "This is the crisis of Parliaments; we shall know by this if Parliaments live or die."[11]

Soon after Commons convened, Coke echoed him and quoted a centuries-old law stating, "Loans against the will of the subject are against reason and the franchises of the land." Then he spoke of freedom, and of Magna Carta, "confirmed by thirty good kings and thirty good Parliaments."[12]

Commons formed a single committee—Coke was a member—to consider both grievances and supplying funds to the king. This committee promptly challenged the king's authority. It resolved that the king could not imprison any freeman either without cause or solely upon his order, that a writ of habeas corpus had to be honored, and that no taxes, loans, or benevolences could be demanded without Parliament's approval. The House approved this resolution and sent Coke and three others to present arguments for it to the House of Lords. There Coke spoke last, and asked for the Lords' endorsement of it.

While they awaited word from Lords, Commons turned to the issue of supply. It voted its intent to provide enough money to supply the expenses of government and wage war on the continent. The news delighted Charles, who said, "Now I see with this I shall have the affection of my people. I love parliaments. I shall rejoice to meet with my people often."[13]

But Charles failed to note that Commons had not actually given final approval of funding. Instead, even Sir Thomas Wentworth—by no measure a radical—had declared, "[L]et us be sure the subjects' liberties go hand in hand together" with money for the king. "Let us . . . not report it to the House until we have a bill for our liberties."[14] All Commons agreed that "grievances and supply go hand in hand."[15]

And Lords did not yield to Commons. Lords proposed revising the resolution Commons had passed to authorize the king to imprison someone without charge for "matter of state" until "a convenient time." Lords also added the statement that nothing in the resolution intruded upon "his Majesty's royal prerogative, intrinsical to his sovereignty and entrusted him withal from God."[16]

At issue was the fundamental nature of law, of the power of government, and of liberty. Was the king above the law, or bound by it?

Coke and James had clashed earlier over that precise issue. It had not then been decided. Now Coke was fighting it again. And this time he intended to force the king to accept his interpretation. But first he had to win Lords to his side.

In Commons, he contemptuously rejected the Lords' proposal. To allow imprisonment for a "matter of state" until "a convenient time" would, he declared, make "Magna Carta and the other statutes . . . fruitless. . . . Reason of state lames Magna Carta."[17]

He then identified the crux of the debate, the Lords' claim that royal prerogative was intrinsic in sovereignty and divine in origin. And he attacked it, pointing out that the Lords' interpretation "meant that intrinsical prerogative is not bounded by any law. . . . [It] is entrusted him by God and then it is due *jure divino,* and then no law can take it away. . . . We cannot yield to this. . . . Kings contended for it before Magna Carta and could never prevail."

He had little trouble convincing Commons. But for weeks debate continued with the House of Lords. Coke, his mind spry even if his body ached, took the lead in representing Commons there. Sometimes sarcastic, sometimes humorous, but always insistent and logical, he argued for common law and referred to English rights, the rights which gave liberty, as an inheritance. That rights were not a metaphysical idea but an inheritance, a kind of property, mattered. As Coke described them, they were something concrete, something owned; they were like land or a piece of jewelry; they belonged to the heir. Property was the essence of common law. William Stubbs, a leading English constitutional scholar, explained that personal freedom and political rights were "so much bound up with the relations created by the possession of land, as to be actually subservient to it. . . . The freeman is fully free because he possesses land, he does not possess land because he is free."[18] Law regarding real property was thus public law, constitutional law; how an individual held his property determined rights and responsibilities. So it was not surprising for Coke to ask, "Shall I be made a tenant-at-will for my liberties, having property in my own house but not liberty in my person? There is no such tenure in all Littleton! . . . It is a maxim, The common law hath admeasured the King's prerogative, that in no case can it prejudice the inheritance of the subjects." It would be absurd, he argued, to require due process of law before taking a man's property, yet not require due process before seizing his person. "The greatest inheritance that a man hath is the liberty of his person, for all others are accessory to it. . . . It is against law that men can be committed and no cause shown. . . . [I]t is not I, Edward Coke, that speaks it but the records that speak it. . . . The king could not imprison by word of mouth."[19]

"If this be law," Phelips echoed, "what do we talk of our liberties?"[20]
*Was the king above the law, or bound by it?*

Charles tried to prevent any legislative action by going in person to the House of Lords and giving his "royal word" to hold Magna Carta and associated statutes "to be all in force," then twice demanded to know whether Parliament would "rest upon his royal word and promise." But he also warned that there should be "no encroachings upon that sovereignty or prerogative which god hath put into his hands for our good."[21]

Parliament would not rely on his word, especially with that limitation. Coke suggested that Parliament require the king to acknowledge English liberties in a legislative way. He proposed sending a "Petition of Right" to the king to define the rights of his subjects and Parliament and the limits on the royal prerogative. Though called a "petition," it was not to be a request granted by the king's grace; it would be a resolution voted by Parliament and assented to by the king. King and Parliament together, representing a unified nation, would give it the strongest possible legal force and make it binding upon the crown.

Commons adopted Coke's suggestion, and he was central in drafting the petition. It incorporated the earlier resolutions prohibiting forced loans, benevolences, or "any tax, tallage, aid, or other like charge not set by common consent, in parliament." It prohibited billeting soldiers in homes and the exercise of martial law in peace. It required honoring writs of habeas corpus. And it reaffirmed Magna Carta and associated statutes, reaffirmed the principle older than Magna Carta that "no freeman may be taken or imprisoned or be disseized of his freehold or liberties . . . or in any manner destroyed, but by the lawful judgment of his peers, or by the law of the land . . . [and] that no man, of what estate or condition that he be, should be put out of his land or tenements, nor taken, nor imprisoned, nor disinherited nor put to death without being brought to answer by due process of law . . . no offender of what kind so ever is exempted from the proceedings to be used."[22]

Due process was critical. The honoring of writs was critical. Prohibiting arbitrary imprisonment by anyone, including the king himself, was critical. The petition closed by requiring all crown officers—including the king's judges—to follow the law as defined by the petition: "That in the things aforesaid all your Officers and Ministers shall serve you according to the Lawes and Statutes of this Realme."[23]

The petition passed the House of Commons unanimously. Coke was chosen to present it to the House of Lords. There he read the petition out loud and was answered by "profound silence."

After long debate, Lords agreed to the petition, asking Commons to add only one statement. But that one statement emasculated all the rest. It stipulated that the petition did "leave entire that sovereign Power, wherewith your majesty is trusted."

Commons reacted with fury and contempt. Coke uttered one of his most famous sentences: "*Magna Carta* is such a fellow as he will have no sovereign." He continued, "If we grant this, by implication we grant a sovereign above all these laws. . . . We must not admit of it, and to qualify it is impossible. Let us hold our privileges according to the law."[24]

As member after member echoed Coke's points, anger resonated in Commons, then spread to London. Buckingham spoke of billeting hundreds of soldiers in the city. The lord mayor of London swore the city would resist them "in blood."[25]

Faced with uproar in Commons and possible uproar in the streets, Lords yielded. Without alteration, it unanimously passed the Petition of Right.

The Petition of Right had now passed both Commons and Lords without a single dissenting vote. But for it to have force, the king had to agree to it. For days, Charles pondered his response with "so many wise men." On June 2, 1628, he came to Parliament to give his reply, sitting upon the throne in the House of Lords. He began graciously: "I am come hither to show you that, as well as in formal things as essential, I desire to give you as much content as in me lies."

But he did not agree to the petition. Instead, he gave an evasive reply, then ordered Parliament to pass supply "and entertain no new business."

Instead, Commons met in a surly mood, shouting down defenses of the crown by a privy councilor, launching bitter attacks on policy. The House of Lords met in comparable distemper. It is not clear who suggested passing a "Remonstrance" attacking not Charles personally—such a move would be unthinkable—but his ministers, especially his most hated minister Buckingham. One was suggested in both chambers, and Commons began debate.

Charles intended to stop it. He ordered Commons to "proceed to business"—pass the supply—and "entertain no new matters." He also specifically ordered it to refrain from anything "which may lay scandal or aspersion on the state-government, or ministers thereof."[26]

But John Eliot rose in Commons and seemed about to mention Buckingham's name. Suddenly, the Speaker of the House interrupted and silenced him. In tears, the Speaker stated that the king had commanded him to silence "any that should go about to lay an aspersion on ministers of state."[27]

They were not revolutionaries in this Parliament. All within Parliament did honor this king as God's anointed. Even Eliot, who had gone to the Tower for advocating Buckingham's impeachment in 1626 (and would die in the Tower later for giving new offense to Charles), said, "It is our King we serve. We wholly rely on his goodness, and on none else."[28]

Yet the king had spurned the Petition of Right and now was trying to suppress the privileges of Parliament—indeed, its most important privilege. The king to whom all had sworn loyalty was forbidding them to speak within Parliament itself. Charles Rex was doing this.

To violate the king's explicit instruction seemed impossible. Silence fell upon the House, upon the whole great chamber. The silence reverberated with meaning. John Pym, one of Parliament's most influential members, rose, began to speak, then broke into weeping and sat down. Coke rose, began to speak, then broke into weeping; even he sat down, silenced by the gravity of the king's command. Another member proposed they do no business whatsoever but protest by sitting in silence. Finally Nathaniel Rich rose. They could not remain silent, he said. They had a duty to speak. He insisted they speak. "We must speak now or forever hold our peace!"[29]

Pym, still weeping, now seconded him. The weight of the moment was upon the House, the weight of knowing that the king would dismiss Parliament and might not call another. Phelips too felt the need to speak even while declaring, "I fear it is the last time that I shall ever speak in this House."[30]

Then Coke took the floor: "Our liberties are now impeached. . . . Let us take this to heart." He called for a reading of the Protestation of 1621, that protest which James had physically torn from the Commons journal. He recounted from history instances when members of Parliament had spoken in defiance of an order from the crown. Though they went to the Tower for it—as all knew he had gone to the Tower—could they do less? "Now, when there is such a downfall of the state shall we hold our tongues? How shall we answer our duties to God and men? . . . Why may we not name those that are the cause of all our evils? . . . Nothing grows to abuse but that this House hath power to treat of it. What shall we now do? Let us palliate no longer. . . . The Duke of Buckingham is the cause of all our miseries, and till the King be informed thereof we shall never go out with honor, nor sit with honor here. That man is the grievance of grievances."[31]

Coke had pronounced Buckingham's name. It was the first explicit violation of the king's order. And suddenly nothing was held back. In great shouts of support, members shouted Buckingham's name, blamed him for all that was wrong, blamed him for war and for failures in war. Vitriol poured out of their mouths, pure vitriol.

Religion entered the debate. First one member then another attacked Buckingham, accusing him of treason for helping "papists"; another charged that his religious leanings meant "no less than the subversion of the whole state."[32]

There was a growing anger in the chamber, indeed a kind of mad fury. The Speaker had left the chamber to inform Charles of events and now returned with the king's order to suspend debate for the day. Members obeyed, but the next day they returned and returned to the attack. As the House grew increasingly raucous, others sought a way out. There was a way out: for the king to agree to the Petition of Right.

Members of both Commons and Lords begged the king to do so. Even Buckingham urged it. Finally, Charles came again in person to the House of Lords. With hundreds of members of Commons standing at the bar, the Petition of Right was read. A note was passed to the clerk, with the king's reply: *Soit droit fait, comme il est désiré*. Let right be done, as is desired.

He had agreed to the Petition of Right. In agreeing, the king was recognizing—for this moment—the concept that the law was sovereign. The law was over the king.

"We reach here," judged Winston Churchill, "the main foundation of English freedom, the charter of every self-respecting man at any time in any land."[33]

# ❧ CHAPTER 6 ❧

I n defeat, Charles moved toward confrontation. Because he still had need of money from Parliament and seemed finally to have some chance of getting it, he prorogued rather than dissolved Parliament. It was to return in six months. But in those months he virtually dared it to restrain him. He ordered that the printed edition of the Petition of Right including his agreement to it be "made waste paper," replacing it with a version containing his evasive first response. He claimed the right to collect tonnage and poundage with no further parliamentary action. And he declared that Parliament did "neither mean [to] nor can hurt my prerogative."[1]

Then Buckingham was assassinated. The murderer leaped from a crowd, stabbed him, and did not flee, shouting that he acted out of patriotism, that the Remonstrance Commons had passed justified his act. Virtually all England seemed to agree. Soldiers lined the streets to protect the funeral procession from the crowd, a crowd whose noise sounded "more like joy than commiseration." As a precaution against desecration, the coffin in the procession was empty; Buckingham's body traveled to its grave in secret.[2] Charles tried to have the assassin tortured, but his judges would not allow it. Crowds flocked to his jail to pray for him until he was hanged at Tyburn.

The assassination had no effect on policy. If anything it hardened Charles. Buckingham had been his confidant, his friend, almost his peer. The murder only isolated the king further and drove him closer to his Catholic wife; this marriage, once difficult, had become a union of love. And now Charles moved ever more aggressively in regard to the Church of England, both using it to expand royal authority and shifting the emphasis of its theology.

Critics had earlier charged that the church was drifting toward Catholicism; now they feared that drift was become a riptide. It was no longer only Puritans who worried that this was so. And the issues of authority, conformity, and freedom in both political and religious spheres were converging.

Earlier Roger Manwaring, a minister, had preached that kings were Gods and that the king's command to pay the Forced Loan meant that subjects "could not refuse the payment without peril of damnation."³ This view had offended the archbishop of Canterbury, who forbade the printing of the sermon. Charles, supreme governor of the church, had it printed and distributed widely, then effectively suspended the archbishop from his duties. Parliament impeached Manwaring. Charles pardoned him and made him royal chaplain, and pardoned other clergy inimical to Parliament as well, including one who had preached that even if a king's command was "against the laws of God, or of nature, or impossible" subjects had to obey "without resistance or railing."⁴

Even more disturbing to the king's critics was Richard Montagu, the man who had called for an English Inquisition. In a book, Montagu denigrated Calvin and reduced specific doctrinal points of difference between the Church of England and Catholicism from forty-seven to eight.⁵ He also spoke of God's grant of absolute power to the king, and attacked Parliament so viciously that Parliament charged him with criminal sedition. Coke, no Puritan, called Montagu's book "as dangeroys a book as I ever saw."⁶

Charles responded first by blocking the charges against Montagu. Then he made him a bishop and a member of the Privy Council. But the most important man Charles advanced was William Laud.

Laud was a short man, prickly about his height, and described as "low of stature, little in bulk, cheerful in countenance (wherein gravity and quickness were all compounded), of a sharp and piercing eye, clear judgment." Even church colleagues had attacked him for "popish" views, for saying that Rome was a true church. He had also served as a spy, reporting "the names of many Churchmen, marked with the letters O [for Orthodox] and P [for Puritan]" to Buckingham for Charles.⁷ Orthodox were to be advanced, Puritans silenced. Laud became such a favorite that Charles had him officiate at his coronation, then in July 1628, a few weeks after the confrontation between king and Parliament over the Petition of Right, Charles named him bishop of London and member of the Privy Council.

Though the nominal leader of the church remained the archbishop of Canterbury, Laud ruled in fact. (Five years later, Laud did become archbishop of Canterbury.) He became a powerful voice on the Privy Council and in the Star

Chamber, ever supporting the king's authority, and he controlled the High Commission. Through it he began purging the Church of England of dissent. Indeed, he termed his policy "Thorough" and he intended it to be thorough.

Charles's politics had already pushed moderates into opposition. What he was doing now concerned the nation's soul. His actions made the conjunction of religion and the Petition of Right not only reasonable but inevitable. The king himself called Puritans "enemies of monarchs."[8] Samuel Brooke, master of Trinity College, Cambridge, and a High Church man, called "Puritanism the roote of all rebellions and disobedient intractableness in parliaments, &c., and all schisme and sauciness in the countrey, nay in the Church itself."[9] Montagu openly speculated about a reconciliation with Rome and flatly declared, "A Puritan is worse than a Papist."[10]

The king was forcing those disquieted by the direction of the Anglican Church into extreme opposition. Said Phelips, "To be an honest man is now to be a Puritan."[11]

Parliament returned in January 1629. Coke, pleading the infirmity of his seventy-seven years, did not attend. But many now were ready to confront the king. Roger Williams would himself soon enter the scene, if still in a secondary way. It would be his final lesson as an observer, and he would watch the conjoining of the issues of church and state.

Williams was a young man now, a Puritan, passionate in belief, and a cleric. He had graduated from Cambridge in 1627 and had begun work toward an advanced degree but abandoned those studies, likely because Laud instituted a new requirement that all those getting a degree had to swear that the entire Church of England service conformed to Scripture. This Williams could not do.

By then the High Commission had made it impossible for a new Puritan cleric to find a church post. But wealthy estate-holders had family chaplains, and Puritans among the wealthy used these chaplaincies as havens for Puritan clergy. In a few months, Laud would close this loophole by requiring new family chaplains to be approved by a bishop, but just before this loophole closed, Williams became family chaplain to Sir William Masham in County Essex.

No definite evidence connects Coke to Williams's hiring, but Masham and Coke were both members of the Inner Temple, and Masham, his father-in-law Sir Francis Barrington, and his brother-in-law all served with and supported Coke in Parliament. Masham and Barrington had also gone to prison over the

Forced Loan, and Barrington's wife Lady Joan Barrington had shared his prison rooms rather than be separated from him. Barrington had become ill in prison and died shortly after his release, further embittering the family toward the crown.

Essex was more thickly peopled with Puritans than any other county in England, and in Essex the Barrington-Masham family was arguably second only to Robert Rich, Earl of Warwick. Though now a widow, Lady Joan routinely received visitors active in politics, and many important conversations took place in her home. Her nephews and frequent visitors included Oliver Cromwell and Edward Whalley, two men later central to the killing of a king, while two of her sons, Sir Thomas and Sir Robert Barrington, and her son-in-law Masham served in this Parliament. Williams's new post thus put him at the center of Puritan political and religious activity. And all the family took to Williams, liking him—Masham called him "a good man and a good friend"[12]—and more importantly trusting him.

When Parliament reconvened, Masham and his two brothers-in-law returned to London. They brought Williams with them, believing he would prove useful. Not only did they trust him, but his connection to Coke meant both that many parliamentary leaders knew him and that he understood the issues and the process. He quickly took over a key if minor role. Letters would include blunt talk about "cyvill government" and "divers abuses to be reformed," and they worried that their letters "should come to other hands." Of one possible messenger, Sir Robert Barrington said, "I am very fearful to send any letters by him."[13]

They did not fear using Williams. He became their messenger and carried not only their letters but his own reports—for he was present at many of the events over the next few weeks—back and forth between London and Essex, and very likely to and from those involved in the events in London. He had much news to carry.

Parliament returned in a combative mood. John Selden, one of the leaders of Commons, immediately launched into an attack on the crown for violating the Petition of Right, particularly by collecting tonnage and poundage without Parliament's approval and for seizing goods of merchants who refused to pay it. But in the less than six months during which Laud had served as bishop of

London, his aggressiveness had shifted Parliament's focus from its rights to religion.

Indeed, Walter Erler stated that he had initially wanted to "postpone the business of religion" to concentrate on rights but now realized that was impossible "without settling religion. . . . For I dare boldly say never was there a more clear connection between the matter of religion and the matter of state."[14] A majority shared his views. One member after another recounted outrages in the church. Phelips warned, "Now fall these things, at a time when our religion is almost extirpate in Christendom."[15] Protestants were retreating before Catholic armies everywhere in Europe; in England too they were in retreat. Phelips went so far as to suggest that the conflict over rights had only been a ruse "thrown in by [Arminians] that have drawn a cloud over our sun, our religion, to divert or interrupt us in the prosecution of them."[16]

Francis Rous worried, "How the see of Rome doth eat into our religion, and . . . the laws and statutes of this realm . . . for an Arminian is the spawn of a Papist."[17] Oliver Cromwell gave his first speech in Parliament, accusing a schoolmaster of "flat Popery at Paul's Cross."[18] "For the first time," observed historian Conrad Russell, "the Commons as a whole regarded the growth of Arminianism as a conspiracy to alter the doctrine of the Church of England."[19]

Commons considered defining by law the doctrine of the Church of England. Parliament had passed the law making the crown supreme over the church; logically, then, Parliament had the power to control the church with other laws as well. Members insisted that no theological doctrine or worship decided by a religious convocation was valid without the "assent of the state," and by that they meant themselves.

On February 24, 1629, a Commons committee warned of a dangerous design "aiming at the subversion of all the protestant churches of Christendom," for which evidence abounded at home and abroad. Protestants in Germany and France were "in great part already ruined." Ireland was "almost wholly overspread with Popery." And under Charles and his father, even in England, their own England, "we observe extraordinary growth of Popery." In a direct charge to the king, it concluded, "If our religion be suppressed and destroyed abroad, disturbed in Scotland, lost in Ireland, undermined and almost outdared in England, it is manifest that our danger is very great and imminent."[20]

Not in centuries had such distrust and antipathy existed between Parliament and the crown. Assessing all this, Robert Barrington gave Williams a letter to carry home. "We have brought the business of religion . . . and against both popery and arminianisme . . . into the house and with one consent ordered that it should be the maine business and first in agitation. I pray God direct us in this soe waighty business, the success whereof is and will be the foundation of our happiness or missery."[21] Barrington added, "You shall heare more of this business, it is a very fowle one.[22]

Something fundamental was occurring here. Sir Benjamin Rudyerd warned, "If the king draw one way, and the parliament another, we must all sink."[23]

That was now happening. Facing this chaos, even such activists as John Pym and Dudley Digges tried to pull back. For they feared that in trying to gain all they would lose all. But Parliament did not pull back. It moved forward.

For a moment the king tried to calm the circumstances, and saw to the adjourning of Parliament for a week. He hoped yet for a legal grant of tonnage and poundage, which he explained almost in apology he was collecting only out of "necessity." He hoped yet for compromise.

There was sentiment toward compromise. Even the Barringtons—who had gone to prison rather than pay the Forced Loan—hoped for cooling. Thomas Barrington agreed that "Princes should in policye have somm time and way left to evade when point of honor is in competition." He also thought it "better to take reasonable satisfaction" than to insist on harsher measures which would "lett fall the end of our desyres."[24]

Yet there was no movement toward compromise. Instead, a growing and dismaying sense of inevitability, a fear that Parliament would be dissolved, hung over the city. Barrington found among "all men that wish well to church or commonwealth mourning for this threatening evell."[25]

As that threat seemed increasingly certain, John Eliot was determined to "go not out like sheep scattered, but to testify to the world that we have a care of their safety and religion."[26] He and his allies had a plan. They wrote a resolution, a resolution of fear and fury, and they intended to demand a vote on it. The next morning, as the doors of Commons opened, the physically strongest and most ferocious of his supporters took seats in the front of the chamber by the Speaker's chair, where the king's allies normally sat. Other supporters took places in the rear, by the doors. When Speaker John Finch gaveled the session to order, Eliot began to read his resolution.

The Speaker refused to put the question to a vote. Instead, he began to rise—and his rising would end the session. Suddenly young brawny men rushed the chair and pushed him back down, back into his seat, forced him down. Others sealed the doors in back. When the Speaker protested that he was acting upon the king's order, expecting those holding him to desist, Denzil Holles shouted, "Zounds, you shall sit as long as the House pleases!"[27]

There was chaos now, chaos in the House "no man allmost knowing what to doe; the distraction was so sodaine, and so greate."[28] Word went to the king to call out the guard. Fights erupted as some members tried to free the Speaker. At the back of the hall, a messenger from the king pounded on the locked great door, a noise that reverberated through the House. Eliot threw his resolution into the fire to destroy evidence.

The floor erupted in bedlam and commotion, all yells and pushing and fists. Dudley Digges was Coke's old ally, no friend to the king, yet he moved to adjourn. He was ignored. The pounding on the great door intensified.

Finally Eliot and his allies gained a semblance of control of the floor. Holles at the top of his lungs shouted words as violent as the day, attacks on evil "counsels" to the king, on Arminian and papist traitors. Then Holles bellowed out three resolutions:

"Any merchante or person whatsoever [who] shall voluntarily yield or pay the said subsidies"—anyone who cooperated with king—"[was] a betrayer of the liberties of England and an enemy to the same."[29]

"Aye!" shouted the Commons.

The king's messenger and the king's soldiers hammered on the door, the sound echoing through the chamber.

"Whosoever shall bring in innovation of religion, or by favour or countenance seek to extend or introduce popery or Arminianism or other opinion disagreeing with from the true and orthodox Church, shall be reputed a capital enemy to the kingdom and commonwealth."

*A capital enemy, a traitor subject to death.*

Holles put the question. "Aye!" shouted the Commons.

Holles shouted out the next resolution, that any who "counsel or advise the taking or levying of the subsidies of Tonnage and Poundage, not being granted by Parliament . . . [was] a capital enemy."

*A capital enemy, a traitor subject to death.*

"Aye!" shouted the Commons.

Now, finally, Commons adjourned, and members poured out of the House chamber in a flood of flight. Almost as promptly several parliamentary leaders were arrested. (John Eliot would die in the Tower three years later. His son asked permission to bury his body at home. An unforgiving Charles replied, "Let Sir John Eliot be buried in the church of that parish in which he died.")[30]

All the travail of this Parliament, all its compressed fury, Williams witnessed. He saw much. Said Robert Barrington, "Mr. Williams who walkes the city will be able to say more than I can."[31]

This last assignment as observer had furthered his education, and his intimacy with power. Much of his sensibility he had of course already derived from Coke, but now, older, more mature, without Coke, he was coming to his own understanding. He was proceeding toward this understanding as a devout Christian, neither a lawyer nor revolutionary. Yet he would articulate legal principles and a definition of freedom more original and more far-reaching than his mentor's, and he would become a revolutionary.

Watching Parliament's dissolution could have brought him no pleasure, nor could he find pleasure in carrying back to Essex one more letter from Sir Thomas: "I love not to be a messenger of evell tideings, yet my desyres are so greate to inform you with the occureunts of the times. . . . This daye in Parliament . . . no man allmost knowing what to doe; the distraction was so sodaine, and so greate. . . . He whose hart bleedes not, at the threates of these times, is soe stupid; I pray God send us better grounds of comfort, and with all to be armed for the worst that can befall us. . . . What the particulars were, you have an eye witness to report."[32]

With that witness Roger Williams ended his apprenticeship.

Part II

# THE COVENANT

## ❧ CHAPTER 7 ❧

The king held all real power. Parliament's one bridle on him was refusing extraordinary funds for war. Charles had dissolved Parliament without getting enough war funds, forcing him to make peace with France and Spain. In that peace England, having suffered only defeats, won nothing beyond the end of war, and the end of war brought no peace within England.

For in all other areas Charles did as he would. He did as he would to the extent that he violated Parliament's express prohibitions, including collecting tonnage and poundage. He did as he would to the extent that this period without parliaments—eleven years passed before circumstances compelled him to call another—became known as the era of Personal Rule.

With it a new tone came to England, and a new sense of disquiet. Among Puritans, especially, that disquiet was becoming desperation. Eventually, that desperation sent thousands of Puritans fleeing to America, where their vision would define—and still defines—the national consciousness of the United States. And as Charles relentlessly increased his pressure on both English liberties and Puritans, the desperation spread well beyond Puritans and erupted first in the beheading of an archbishop, then civil war, and finally the beheading of a king.

The slow march toward that unhappy end had now begun. Immediately after dismissing Parliament, Charles issued new "Royal Instructions." In them he ordered that "hereafter none do presume to print or publish any matter of news, relations, histories, or other things in prose or in verse that have reference to matters and affairs of state, without the view, approbation and licence" of the government.[1]

Soon he began using the Star Chamber in ways that made it symbolize the abuse of power, and made the phrase "Star Chamber proceeding" into an epithet hurled for the next four centuries at legal proceedings marked by extreme judicial abuses and predetermined outcomes. Regarding Anglican doctrine, he commanded that "all further curious search be laid aside and these disputes shut up."[2] To strangle any comment by the ministry, he also ordered that all afternoon sermons be converted to catechizing by question and answer only. In addition, his lord high treasurer, his chancellor of the Exchequer, and his secretary of state were secret Catholics, a fact much suspected and deeply resented.

All about them, then, Puritans could see the church changing, and all the changes were away from simplicity, away from, in their view, Scripture. Even the physical church was changing. Laud moved the communion table out of the nave to the east end of each church, which forced changes in the siting of family pews and gave great offense, railed it off, which separated priest and congregation and gave greater offense still, and renamed it the altar, which smacked of Catholicism. These tangible changes exemplified the enormous theological gap between Charles and Laud on one side, Puritans on the other, for those changes shifted the emphasis in worship away from each worshipper's relationship with God toward the sacraments and priestly power. And while Puritans complained of crosses and demanded simplicity, Laud relished the great cathedrals, relished stained glass, relished crucifixes, and relished formal ceremony, all of which he called the "beauty of holiness."

To Puritans, this so-called beauty represented corruption. They never forgot that, because of the queen, Catholic Mass was openly celebrated in royal palaces, and they regarded making the sign of the cross as superstition, while stained glass and the surplice signified a violation of Scripture, an unholy priesthood, even a seducing Satan. John Milton expressed those feelings when he complained that Charles "bemoanes the pulling down of crosses and other superstituous Monuments, as the effect of a popular and deceitful Reformation. How little this savours of a Protestant."[3]

Meanwhile, the High Commission tolerated no criticism. If its pursuit of nonconformists did not equal the Spanish Inquisition in brutality, if the English church burned no one at the stake after 1612, it still executed at least some "heretics" and it still used violence to discipline critics. Alexander Leighton attacked bishops as "unChristian and satanic." The High Commission had him arrested and kept in Newgate prison in an open cell, exposed to rain, frigid temperatures, and snow for fifteen weeks. He survived but was too sick to attend his own sentencing—to a £10,000 fine and life in prison. Life sentences in English prisons were often remarkably short terms. London was unhealthy enough. Prisons were outright pest-holes, breeding grounds for infectious disease which feasted on those with immune systems damaged by lack of heat, poor diet, and great stress. And before Leighton's life term began, he was to enjoy another, briefer sentence: he was tied to a stake to receive thirty-six stripes with a heavy cord upon his naked back, then placed in the pillory for two hours, then branded in the face with "SS" for "Sower of Sedition." Then his nose was split and his ears cut off. This was no clean dissection; the executioner sawed off his ears in a slow, bloody mess. Only then did he go to prison.

Reportedly, when this sentence was pronounced, Laud pulled off his cap and gave God thanks for it.[4]

Leighton had openly attacked the hierarchy. But most Puritans, especially most Puritan clergy, did not attack the hierarchy; they hid from it. As Laud changed the inside of the churches, however, so he sought to change what was in the hearts and minds of Puritans. If Elizabeth had refused to make windows into men's souls, Laud had no such reticence.

At every turn Puritans felt, and were, under assault. At every turn, spies returned "informations" about their preaching and their worship, such as a typical report about Cambridge University's Puritan-leaning Emmanuel College: "At surplice prayers they sing nothing but certain riming Psalms of their own appointment, instead of Ye hymns between ye Lessons. And at Lessons they read not after ye order appointed in ye Calendar but after another continued course of their own."[5]

And at every turn, Laud closed off one avenue after another for Puritan relief, seeking to force full conformity, or force nonconformists into the open. He ordered the English ambassador in Paris to stop attending Huguenot services because they were too Calvinist in theology.[6] He sealed off the loophole, just after Williams escaped through it, which allowed family chaplains to evade surveillance. He required all clergy lecturers—Puritans were commonly lecturers, for they believed that the process of coming to God began with listening to the Word—to wear a surplice and hood, and to read from the Book of Common Prayer before lecture. He insisted that ministers kneel at communion, make the sign of the cross at baptism, and conform in all other ways.

Under his direction, under his policy of "Thorough," the High Commission ceased investigating Catholics and searched out all Protestant dissent. It shrugged off the limits Coke had once imposed upon it and began exercising power far more expansively than ever, began searching out even "conformable Puritans"—those who obeyed such rules as wearing the surplice but who nonetheless favored simpler worship. The oath ex officio allowed it to discover such outward conformists and inward dissenters. It sought out this dissent with the intent of crushing it.

Laud considered this purge of the church necessary for the survival of the state. He reasoned that "as the spirit of God is one . . . he that divides against the unity of the church practises against the unity of the spirit."[7] Without such unity, he believed, the church would disintegrate, and without the church, the state would disintegrate: "It is impossible in any Christian commonwealth that the church should melt, and the State stand firm. For there can be no firmness without law; and no laws can be binding, if there be no conscience to obey them; penalty alone could never, never do it. And no school can teach conscience, but the church of Christ."[8] He argued that a state that sinned would collapse either slowly and "inwardly" because sin meant a "drop away from all foundation in virtue, in steadiness in justice," or explosively, as Sodom and Gomorrah had, because of "God's punishment for these sins."[9]

Few in England, whatever their religious conviction, disputed that. With near unanimity Puritans certainly agreed: typically, Francis Rous said, "As religion is decayed, so the honour and strength of this nation decayed."[10]

But agreement by Laudians and Puritans on the need for conformity and unity only intensified the passionate and increasing enmity between them. Puritans were obviously in no position to impose their views on the entire Church of England; they were struggling to survive within that church.

Indeed, in a church within the church was the only way Puritans did survive: in those parishes with sympathetic ministers, they often comprised a small almost secret congregation who worshipped separately, "betwixt ourselves, to the stirring up of ourselves to greater godliness."[11]

Stamping out such worship was one of Laud's goals. He pressed forward. Even James had been "indifferent" to many of the practices to which the High Commission now demanded conformity. Charles and Laud were not indifferent to them.

Neither were Puritans indifferent.

Under siege, Puritans believed they had retreated as far as they could. Yet Laud pushed further.

Meanwhile, other turmoil troubled England.

Great change is never easy. In England one kind of world, the world of feudalism, was coming to an end, while another, the modern age, was birthing. For most great lords and peers of the realm, this change was good; they no longer had to support private armies and, since cannon had made castles obsolete, their wealth now went into great country houses and estates and magnificent homes in London. For nearly everyone else, change meant a terrifying instability, a seasickness at the center of their lives.

Hard times compounded the instability. Prices were tripling while real wages were falling. Superior Dutch technology all but destroyed England's textile industry, by far its most profitable foreign trade. The Privy Council worried the industry had "so much decayed . . . that many poor people are ready to mutiny for want of work."[12]

In May 1629, weavers in several towns in County Essex, the most Puritan county in the nation, rioted. Hard times, not religion, caused the riot. In one parish, two-thirds of the entire population lived in poverty—poverty as defined by the barest minimum of standards of the time.[13] One man wrote that "the almhouses are filled with old labourers. Many there are who get their living with bearing burdens; but more are fain to burden the land with their own bodies. Multitudes get their living by prating [trickery], and so do numbers more, by begging. Neither come these straits upon men always through intemperancy, ill husbandry, indiscretion, &c., as some think: but even the most wise sober and discreet man go often to the wall; when they have done their best."[14]

Under James, the Midlands had erupted in armed rebellion over the enclosure of lands. More violence erupted under Charles, after he sold off the last of the royal forests to raise money and the new owners drove people off those lands and enclosed them. Even Laud called himself "a great hater of depopulations in any kind, as being one of the greatest mischiefs in the kingdom."[15]

The hard times sent a river of desperate poor flooding through society, and the flood left behind a deposit of fear. Perhaps the fear was justified. One shire had twice as many felony indictments in the 1620s as it had had forty years earlier, and triple the number it would have forty years later.[16]

The flood poured into all cities, especially London, whose population exploded from roughly 200,000 at the beginning of James's reign to almost 400,000 by the end of Charles's. It did not enjoy happy growth. Hordes of beggars sometimes made the streets all but impassable. In 1608 James protested new buildings in the city because they "doth draw together such an overflow of people, specially of the meaner sort, as can hardly either be fed and sustained, or preserved in health, or governed, which doth not only threaten, but hath already bred and brought forth at divers times dearth of victuals, infection of plague, and manifold disorders."[17]

He was right. Even when plague did not haunt the streets, London saw far more funerals than baptisms. As in all large cities, many more died in London than were born there, a circumstance which would continue until modern public health practices in the late nineteenth century. Population growth came only from the constant influx of people leaving the country for the city.

Nor was trouble limited to London. Vagrants everywhere were branded with a "V," and a third offense for vagrancy could lead to a death sentence. As the economy sank, tradesman turned against tradesman. Wrote one, "A man can hardly anywhere set up a trade, but he shall pull down two of his neighbors. . . . Each man is fain to pluck his means, as it were, out of his neighbour's throat."[18]

Puritans expected society to be ordered and rational, and in a society every person had a place valued equally by God. With the church hierarchy and the crown turned enemy, with prices ever rising, with business short, with those dispossessed of land moving about the country like pieces of litter blown by the wind, with London reeking of sin and superstition, society no longer seemed ordered and rational. It was unsurprising that many Puritans were coming to believe what one Puritan pamphlet said: "We are those upon whom the end of the world has fallen."[19]

Puritans believed in Scripture and in history, and saw the latter as fulfillment of the former. The end of the world was foretold in Revelation, and some saw the roiling as a sign of that history. And if England's troubles were actually the first signs of Armageddon, then reform of the church would move history forward, toward Christ's reign. Retreat would give ground backward, to the Antichrist. Under these circumstances, for Puritans now any further bending of the knee, any further yielding to Charles and Laud, was impossible. To do so risked all. It risked breaking their covenant with God.

For decades, English Protestants in general and Puritans in particular had had no doubt that God had chosen England as His own land and themselves as God's new Chosen People. Three-quarters of a century earlier, John Foxe in his *Book of Martyrs* had portrayed England as replacing ancient Israel as God's chosen, had said the English had a special covenant with God. Later, Bishop of London John Aylmer said bluntly, "God is English."[20] Now, Milton wrote, "God is decreeing to begin some new and great period in his Church, even to the reforming of Reformation itself: what does he then but reveal himself to his servants, and as his manner is, first to his Englishmen."[21]

God proved His love for England by delivering England. Thomas Hooker, a leading Puritan minister, explained, "Above all other deliverances that in '88 [the Spanish Armada] was a great deliverance, but we specially record . . . the gunpowder plot . . . [when] the choicest of the nobles and the council, when King, Queen, and nobles were there assembled for the glory of God in one instant should have been miserably blown up and torn in pieces. . . . It is the Lord that delivers England."[22]

But God, Puritans were convinced, had expectations of England in exchange for blessing it, for God worked through covenants. God expected England to abjure sin. Hooker preached—and no Puritan would have disagreed—"Mark the agreement between us and the Lord. He propounds the law and saith, Dt 28, Lev. 26, that if we will keep the law he will bless us abundantly in all things. . . . It is a sweet thing that the Lord hath bound himself by oath to us, to keep covenant with us. . . . The Lord's people take a corporal oath and a curse upon themselves if they do not keep covenant with the Lord."[23]

In Puritan eyes, under Charles and Laud England was now breaching that covenant. In Geneva Calvin had banned playing with cards, dice, or ninepins. In England Puritans saw about them not only such games but drunkenness, whoring, bear-baiting, and bull-baiting, while James's *Book of Sports* had explicitly called for dancing and Maypoles. The problem was not only the sin and corruption of life in the cities. It was the behavior of the crown and the Church of England: the crown's refusal to seek out and punish Catholics, the open celebration of Mass in royal palaces, the Church of England's drift toward Catholicism. So Puritans feared that God might abandon England. As early as 1622, after the confrontation over the Protestation between Parliament and the king, mainstream Puritan thought had become deeply pessimistic. Typically, John Winthrop, a layman, bemoaned to his brother-in-law "the present evill times, and the feare of worse. . . . The Lo[rd] looke mercifully upon this sinfull lande, and turne us to him by some repentance, otherwise we may feare it hath seene the best dayes."[24]

Yet England had only sunk deeper into sin since then, appalling God. Sins were, as Hooker said, "the ground of Sodom and Gomorrah. To humble and to reform our sins is the best means to maintain the safety of a kingdom or nation."[25]

When plague struck England in 1625, Puritans believed it signified an explicit warning from God to return to His ways. Yet England had not come back to God. In the next few years, while God inflicted blood and defeat upon Protestants on the continent, He delivered England again, for England had escaped this war. Hooker noted, "[O]ur wives are not husbandless, our children are not fatherless."[26] Still England had not come back to God.

The Reverend Hugh Peter worried over all these blessings in a sermon: "Shall we after all thy mercys be damned? God forbid. How hath God wept over England. Come Lord knock once more & enter; give us holy consideration to thinke . . . & finding hell our end, let us abhore ourselves. . . . Bow & buckle our hearts at last."[27]

Yet English hearts did not bow and buckle. The sins of daily life were not abjured. The crown and the Church of England grew more corrupt each day.

Most dangerous were attacks on Puritan ministers, Hooker said: those ministers "are the defenders of states, churches, and commonwealths . . . [who] by their fervent prayers and supplications stop the wrath and indignation of the Lord, and so keep back judgment from us, as Moses stood in the gap, Num. 16:48. . . . The enemie to God's faithful ministers are the greatest adversaries that the Church or State hath; for they spoil the munition of the land. . . . So if thou hast set thyself to oppose and secretly undermine any that is a true faithful minister of Jesus Christ, know, thou art a traitor to thy King and country, because thou persecutest him who labors in his place to keep back wrath from seizing upon the land."[28]

To Puritans, "a true faithful minister" could only be one of their own, not one of Laud's. And Laud was persecuting these true and godly ministers, these very men whose presence protected the nation. He was driving them from their livings, sending some into prison or into hiding. He was endangering England. For if the English believed their country's chosen place in God's heart was secure, they were sadly mistaken. Warned Hooker, citing Judges 10:13, "When the sin of a nation comes to full ripeness and perfecion, then the truth is, the Lord will save and deliver them no more."[29]

God had made Israel His Chosen People yet the Jews had broken their covenant. God had left them. God could make any people—any people—His

Chosen. Hooker begged his listeners to rally to the covenant, to renounce sin, to pray, to beseech God, lest God "rather go into Turkey and say unto them, 'Thou art my people, and I will be your God.' "[30]

John Wilson preached in 1628, "What hath God found in England? . . . He looks for obedience but beholds rebellion, contempt. He looks that we should be brought to a right frame by all our blessings, his pains, his judgments. . . . But we grow worse and dishonor him. God is going; his glory is departing, England hath seen her best days, and now evil days are befalling us: God is packing up his Gospel, because no body will buy his wares, nor come to his price."[31]

Wilson's phrasing reflected a Puritan refrain. Echoed Hooker, "God is packing up of his gospel, because none will buy his wares nor come to his price. . . . Oh therefore my brethren, lay hold on God, and let him not go out of your coasts. . . . Let not thy God depart. O England, lay siege about him by humble and hearty closing with him. . . . Suffer him not to go far, suffer him not to say 'Farewell,' or rather, 'Fare ill, England.' "[32]

# ❧ CHAPTER 8 ❧

Persecuted and hunted, enduring the harshest of economic times, believing that God might abandon England, but not yet ready to rebel against their lawful monarch, many Puritans began considering escape. Some followed earlier Separatists and fled to the continent, especially to Dutch provinces where the Calvinist Dutch Reformed Church was the state church. But few found satisfaction there, for it was neither English nor the holy community they had envisioned. Many among them became increasingly determined to create a community that was both. Only one place afforded them any realistic opportunity to do so: America.

America had beckoned to Europeans for a century and a half. The very name "New World" resonated with infinite possibility and provoked immense curiosity. Yet Europe was also fully familiar with America. Even the concept of the "noble savage"—although the actual phrase came later—had already entered European consciousness in 1580 in Montaigne's well-known essay "Of Cannibals." Though Catholic, Montaigne was appalled and shaken by the St. Bartholomew's Day massacres, and his essay implied that Indians* had higher moral standards than Europeans. He had also observed American Indians puzzled by men serving the child-king Charles IX at the French court.

By 1600 Europeans had mapped America's shores, dug gold from America's belly, fished America's seas, penetrated deep into America's river valleys, dressed in America's furs, smoked America's tobacco, and planted "plantations" on America's coasts. (The word "colony" did not come into general use until the next century; in the seventeenth century a colony was a "plantation" and colonists were generally called "planters.") By 1600, the Spanish, the French, the

---

*This book will retain the 1600s usage of the word "Indian" for those now called Native Americans.

Dutch, the Italians, the Portuguese, and the English had all explored the Americas and established themselves there in greater or lesser degree.

For England, it was lesser. The first English exploration came early: in 1497, Henry VII authorized John Cabot—a Genoese sailor, not an Englishman—to "conquer, occupy and possess . . . [and acquire] dominion, title and jurisdiction" over lands occupied by "heathens and infidels." Cabot rediscovered Newfoundland—Vikings had discovered it, named it Vinland, settled it, then abandoned it—and even kidnapped three natives whom he brought back to London. And nearly everything said in English about the New World promoted it, beginning with Sir Thomas More's *Utopia* in 1516, a novel in which the hero traveled three times to America. Promotion continued with the 1555 translation of an influential Spanish book recounting "what commoditie" America could supply "to the hole christian world,"[1] and the 1577 translation of the French guide *Joyefull Newes out of a Newe founde World*. That same year an English sea captain brought home an Eskimo who paddled a kayak on the Avon River.[2]

Nonetheless, England did nothing to follow up on Cabot's voyages. Absorbed by its internal travails as it became Protestant, then Catholic, then Protestant again, it sat dormant while other European states actively pursued—and found—wealth in the New World.

As early as 1494, Spain and Portugal agreed to a line, later adjusted, dividing their interests in South America. By the middle of the 1500s Spain dominated the southern hemisphere and had penetrated deep into North America. In 1543 Spaniards even witnessed a great Mississippi River flood—the flood created an inland sea stretching one hundred miles across—and in 1565 established a permanent settlement at St. Augustine, Florida.

Nor was France dormant. In 1524, France sent Giovanni Verrazzano to inspect the Atlantic coast from the Carolinas north to Nova Scotia. Several French settlements followed, and though they did not thrive, the French did explore eastern Canada and the Mississippi valley, establishing trading ventures and, like Spain and Portugal, converting Indians to a Catholic Christianity. In the 1560s French Protestants—driven, much like English Puritans, by persecution to create a godly refuge—settled in South Carolina. But God did not prosper them. The planting collapsed, with survivors forced into cannibalism. A second planting of Huguenots near present Jacksonville, Florida, became an American victim of European religious wars when a Spanish commander in

1565, appalled by this "evil sect" of Calvinists, "made war with fire and blood" upon it. He slaughtered three hundred and fifty male captives, sparing only women, children, a few men who convinced the Spanish they were Catholic, and four "carpenters and caulkers of whom I had great need."[3]

Only after Spain, largely because of the infusion of wealth from America, became the most powerful nation in Europe did England finally recognize the need to compete in America. Elizabeth sent privateers to steal Spanish gold, and in 1578 authorized Sir Humphrey Gilbert to seize "remote heathen and barbarous lands."[4] Soon after, she granted Gilbert's half brother Sir Walter Raleigh a patent to plant settlements in America. Despite failures— a first plantation on Roanoke Island in North Carolina was withdrawn and a second disappeared without a trace—the infinite possibilities of the New World began to inspire the English imagination. This was not coincidental. Raleigh paid Richard Hakluyt to write of those possibilities. Hakluyt and his nephew and namesake were true believers and their writings had enormous impact. *Principall Navigations, Voiages and Discoveries of the English Nation*, published in 1587, expanded the English mind with its accounts of all the wide world, of Africa, of Russian steppes, of trade in the Near and Far East—and of America. The Hakluyts unceasingly urged establishing many plantations and bemoaned the failure "to reduce this savagae nation to some civilitie."[5]

Their arguments found increasing resonance, spurred by increasing curiosity, increasing ambitions, increasing greed, and increasing envy. By the early 1600s, France had built an extraordinarily lucrative and extensive North American fur trade, a cash crop of the north. Fishing was almost as lucrative, and five hundred English ships a year were visiting the great fishing banks off Newfoundland.

Many of them sailed south down the Atlantic coast and brought back news of a land of opportunity, a fecund land. In 1602 an Englishman spent a few weeks on what is now Martha's Vineyard, reporting, "We stood a while like men ravished at the beauty and delicacy of this sweet soil" whose farmland "in comparison whereof the most fertile part of England is but barren."[6] In 1605 George Weymouth went up the Kennebec River in Maine and recounted "profits we saw the country yield."[7] (Weymouth also kidnapped several Indians and carried them back to England. One was a man named Squanto, who made it back to America only to be captured by another Englishman and sold with twenty other Indians into slavery in Spain; from there he returned to America once again, eventually proving of great help to the later Plymouth plantation.)

Finally, in 1606 James chartered two Virginia Companies, one each for the northern and southern reaches of the Atlantic coast. Both had well-connected investors, and Coke helped write their charters, guaranteeing to British settlers and their children all the rights of English subjects. This guarantee carried enormous import for settlers. So did Coke's ruling in a subsequent court decision that the crown had control over colonies.

The following year both companies attempted to plant colonies in their grants. The northern company, organized by Sir Fernando Gorges, sent one hundred and twenty men to Maine's Kennebec River. One of the coldest winters on record greeted them. Nearly all survived, but in the spring they abandoned the site, built a ship, and returned to England in it. Gorges, however, never gave up his interest in building an empire in the area that would become known as New England.

The southern company planted a colony at Jamestown, Virginia. Taking root proved hard. In 1608 John Smith sent back a candid account of its difficulties, but boosterism first entered America's bloodstream when it was published with an introduction stating that "the worst being already past," new investors "may at ease labour for their profit, in the most sweete, coole, and temperate shade."[8] In 1610, a minister reassured parishioners that the sea voyage was "so faire, so safe, so secure, so easie, as though God himself had built a bridge for men to passe from England to Virginea."[9]

In truth, the voyage was terrifying to those unfamiliar with the sea, and the Jamestown colony itself was a death trap. Men came to make their fortunes and found their graves instead. Initially all planters were men, usually unskilled and brutal men, often the "basest" men, including prisoners shipped from Newgate, yet even they could not survive.[10] Nearly two-thirds of the first settlers died within a year of arrival. A dozen years later, things had not improved: between 1619 and 1621, 4,270 immigrants arrived, but in 1622 the colony's total population was 1,240. Some immigrants had left, but most had died. Then came "the Great Massacre." Whites had treated Indians with brutality, and in March 1622 an Indian uprising killed one-third of the colonists. As a result, the king revoked the company charter and Virginia became a crown colony.

Mortality rates did not improve. In the last half of 1622, one thousand new colonists arrived, but soon "there are perished above 500" of them.[11]

Thus the more northerly coast was considered more receptive, despite its hard winters. Smith sailed along it and called the whole northern region New England. He also recommended it to those who "have great spirits and small meanes."[12] Of Massachusetts, he said, "Of all the four corners of the world I have yet seen uninhabited, could I have but means to transport a colony, I would rather [there] live than anywhere else."[13]

The name New England stuck, and so did the idea it embodied: England new again! Simultaneously, America received spectacular publicity when John Rolfe, a Jamestown colonist, returned to England with several Indians, including his wife, Pocahontas, who had reputedly saved Smith's life and who was presented to King James. Thus did America enter the English imagination. Even the mounting death toll in Jamestown did not deter those seeking profits or a place for themselves. It already seemed the future. Book after book said so, proselytizing for America with such titles as:

*Englands Way to Win Wealth, and to employ Ships and Marriners . . .*

*A True Discourse of the Present Estate of Virginia, and the successes of the affaires there till the 18 of June, 1614*

*A Discourse and Discovery of Nevv-Found-Land, With many reasons to proue how worthy and beneficiall a Plantation may there be made . . .*

*New England Trials. Declaring the Successe of 80 ships employed thither within these eight years . . .*

Even John Donne called England the "Suburbs of the old world" and sought a post in Virginia.[14]

There was always opportunity for those bold enough to seize it by the throat, and hardy enough to survive. A London play of the time portrayed Virginia in a way future Americans saw their Wild West: "where any man may be an alderman, never a Scavener . . . and never a slave . . . a land where there is no more Law then conscience, and not too much of either."[15]

So far Europeans, especially the Spanish and French, had approached the Americas like miners; they extracted gold from America either directly by digging into the land or indirectly by following rivers into the heart of North America and taking furs. And at first the English crown and other English imaginers of wealth were as money-driven as any. John Smith contemptuously reported that in Virginia "there was no talke, no hope, no worke, but dig gold, wash gold, refine gold, load gold."[16]

But others in England saw deeper. They saw the land itself as the prize. They saw the future in it. Puritans saw this most clearly—for they were seeking to build not a new world nor even a new England, but a New Jerusalem.

There was something else. The Spanish, French, and Portuguese had all justified their American incursions—despite their accompanying brutality, slaughter, and slavery—by saying they brought natives to Christ. The English too spoke of bringing natives to Christ. As the Thirty Years War soaked the European continent in blood, as the French and Spanish spread Catholicism in the Americas, the English felt the need to convert Indians not only to spread the Word of the Lord but to build a bulwark against the further spread of Catholicism. More than that, many Puritans believed that if the battle with the Antichrist was commencing, they had to convert the Indians. The Resurrection could not come until all the world heard the Gospel.

For the English who settled much of New England were coming to see more than the salvation of the Indians in their arrival. Those English who would plant there saw their own salvation in it.

In 1620, a newly created Council for New England took over the authority and privileges of the northern Virginia Company. The council included many of the old company's backers, and Gorges still led it, still pursued his dream of an empire in America. James granted the council all the land between the 40th and 48th parallels (roughly between Delaware Bay and the St. Lawrence River), and allowed it to subdivide and charter colonies within this grant.

But the first permanent New England settlement was unauthorized. A group of Separatists—known today as the Pilgrims—had earlier fled England for Holland. Initially they had flourished there. In fact, they became so established that the Dutch state paid salaries to their clergy. Life became routine—too routine. But these Separatists were men and women who believed life should test them at every turn: they feared fat contentment, feared the too-easy life, feared their children losing their English heritage and becoming too like the Dutch. Indeed, they considered an easy life an "affliction." William Bradford wrote, "Yea, some preferred & chose ye prisons in England rather then this libertie on Holland, with these afflictions."[17]

So they abandoned their refuge in Holland and passed through England to take ship on the *Mayflower* for America. They had planned to settle on Long Island but landed instead at the site of an abandoned Indian village on the Massachusetts coast. Disease had left it empty and desolate. A "three years Plague"—probably smallpox brought by Europeans—had begun in 1617 and "swept away most of the inhabitants all along the Sea Coast, and in some places utterly consumed man, woman and childe, so that there is no person left to lay claim to the soyle."[18] The epidemic killed 90 percent of the Indians in much of coastal New England. Here a community of nearly one thousand Indians had lived, but now "bones and skulls . . . made such a spectacle," wrote one man, "it seemed to me a new found Golgatha."[19]

The English did not fear this plague. They believed God had used it to clear the land for them. They called it Plymouth Plantation. Ninety-nine passengers disembarked from the ship. In less than a year only fifty were still alive. But from that point the plantation grew, if only slowly. Three years later the population was one hundred and eighty, with dwellings scattered for half a mile beneath a fort built atop a hill.

Not all were Separatists; their group included both some irreligious adventurers and some who were devout Church of England adherents. The Pilgrims referred to these individuals as "particulars" or "strangers." They came as individuals, all men, seeking fortune; the Pilgrims came with families and livestock and a desire to build a home. The two did not mix well. Bradford, the governor, dismissed them contemptuously as adventurers who were "about building great houses . . . as if they would be great men and rich all of a sudden."[20]

Many of these adventurers left Plymouth, scattering themselves northward up the New England coast. The plantation, weak as it was, also banished some few, including Church of England minister John Lyford for using the Book of Common Prayer in worship.

Simultaneously, Sir Fernando Gorges renewed his efforts to colonize New England, sprinkling Englishmen along the coast from Massachusetts to Maine. A few of these men, none of them Puritans, liked what they found, dug in, and survived. Then came the first enterprise organized by Puritans.

Unlike the few, isolated Separatists in Plymouth, a plantation with little promise or ambition and no support in England, this Puritan enterprise carried within it the seeds of and ambition for a new world. With it, the religious conflict in England crossed the ocean.

The seed for the enterprise was born in flame. In 1613 fire had roared through the English town of Dorchester, nearly destroying it. Puritans there believed God had sent "fire from heaven" to punish the town for its sinfulness. Led by Reverend John White, a man of "great gravity and presence, [who] had always influence on the Puritanical party, near to and remote from him,"[21] they decided to purge sin from the town. They would make of it a beacon, a model for all England to emulate. They would make it a New Jerusalem.

They wanted not only to stamp out sin—and judging by the number of out-of-wedlock births, behavior did change—but to create a true common-wealth with charity and help for the poor. The good citizens raised taxes and built a municipal brewery, dedicating its profits to the poor. Dorchester thrived, built new almshouses, funded education, even gave money to neighboring towns in distress: "All able poor were set on work, and . . . maintained by the profit of the public brewhouse; thus knowledge causeing piety, piety breeding industry, and industry procuring plenty unto it."[22]

Many of the people who had rebuilt the town, White chief among them, wanted to expand this model and link godliness and profit. In 1624, the company sent a group of settlers to Cape Ann on the northern tip of Massachusetts Bay. This area was already used seasonally by fishermen, and the company planned to profit by creating a permanent settlement to service the hundreds of English ships that fished nearby waters. The investors hoped that this enterprise would ultimately create a flourishing Puritan colony which would convert Indians and establish the true Protestant religion, as Puritans defined it, in America. The company sent an expedition equipped to erect large buildings, make saltworks, and start an almost industrial-scale enterprise. But the enterprise yielded neither godliness nor profit. Its leader "proved a very drunken beast, did nothing (in a maner) but drink, & gusle, & consume away ye time & his victails; and most of his company followed his example . . . so as ye loss was great."[23]

Then fire, as if sent by God, struck anew, destroying the great saltworks. An even greater disaster threatened in a confrontation with Plymouth colonists over fishing rights, exacerbated by religious antagonisms. Puritans, despite their conflicts with the English hierarchy, considered themselves fully congregants of the Church of England. Now, on this wild Atlantic shore, amid the tall green sea grass waving in the dunes, with all of a whole new boundless world to share, English men, Protestants, offered death to other English men, also Protestants.

By then Roger Conant, whose brother was one of the Dorchester Company's founders, had joined this settlement. He was a salter—an expert at preserving fish—and had left Plymouth with his wife and child for this even lonelier spot. He intervened and made peace. His intervention made him de facto leader of the colony, and he declared the location ill-suited for their purpose. In 1626, after two years of failures, he led an exodus of about thirty people, mostly men but a few wives and children and cattle, to the base of the cape to a site called Naumkeag, forty miles by sea north of Plymouth.

This location had a harbor well sheltered, with plenty of freshwater from springs and ponds and made easily defensible by steep hills rising from the sea called "Castle Rock" and "Darby fort." The location also had extraordinary natural beauty; waves breaking on one stretch of sand made such unusual sounds that it was called "singing beach," and a chasm in a rock formation was so narrow that waves rushing in drove spray fifty feet high. Conant loved it and wrote a letter to English friends in which he expressed hope that New England might prove a religious refuge for Puritans.

The English backers did not love it. Relocating the settlement had been the final straw. Preferring to write off their investment of £1,000 rather than send good money after it, they sent a ship for all in Naumkeag, paid all wages due, informed the colonists they were abandoning further support of the venture, and offered to return to England any who desired it.

But the ship also carried a personal reply from White to Conant's letter. White, speaking for himself and not the company, begged him to remain and promised to procure a charter and further financial and logistical support.

On the edge of the lonely continent the settlers debated the future. Their sponsors had abandoned them. Plymouth, the only permanent English colony within hundreds of miles, overflowed with hostility toward them. Their tiny settlement was yet insubstantial, a sand castle on the beach, with the great Atlantic bleak and gray beyond it.

What was there to stay for? Many chose to return to England. Lyford, who after banishment from Plymouth had joined the enterprise and served as its minister, announced his plans to go to Virginia and pleaded powerfully for the rest to accompany him. Most wanted to.

Conant did not. In three years he had, first, crossed the ocean with his family to America, then tried to make a home three times in three settlements, only to uproot his family again and again. He now planted himself firmly and reminded all of White's promises. Those who stayed, he insisted, "should soon have more company"—new planters, a charter, and supplies. The debate went back and forth. Finally he declared that he and his family would stay at Naumkeag, alone if they had to, "to wait the providence of God."

His stand firmed others. They too would stay planted, here. Years later Conant wrote how Naumkeag "was in great hassard of being deserted. I was a means, through grace assisting me, to stop the flight of those few that then were heere with me, and that by my vtter deniall, to goe away with them, who would have gone either for England or mostly for Virginia, but thereupon stayed to the hassard of our liues."[24]

In Virginia one hazarded one's life as well, just by being there. Lyford was dead within a year.

A year later the settlers in Naumkeag were still waiting for the promised charter. More desperate than ever, they sent one of their own back across the ocean to advance their cause.

As winter began gripping New England, the messenger was rowed in a longboat through the harbor's sifting water to the next ship that dropped anchor. The ship hoisted sail and headed out to the open sea, leaving them fragile and alone on the cold sand.

The Reverend White intended to keep his promises to Conant. Soon after the confrontation between Charles and Parliament over the Petition of Right, he saw to it that Puritans in this newly dividing and radicalizing England finally sent a reply, a reply which made a dramatic statement and reflected a different approach to colonization.

The old approach had focused on immediate financial gain, but none had materialized. Therefore those interested only in profit abandoned the venture. The Dorchester Company disintegrated, like a handful of sand sifted through one's fingers. But White, several other original company investors, and new investors formed a new company initially called the New England Company, then the Massachusetts Bay Company. In 1628, while Parliament and king wrestled over the Petition of Right, this company received a patent from Robert Rich, the Earl of Warwick, a Puritan leader and friend and neighbor of the Masham and Barrington families, who had replaced Gorges as head of the Council for New England. Members of the new company wanted profits, yes, but they did not expect gold mines or a new trading route to India. They were patient and would look to families to produce goods and markets. Most also had Puritan sympathies; they valued the New World largely because they foresaw creating a Puritan haven there.

They sent fifty planters, nearly all of them Puritans, to Naumkeag. These settlers were the first of what would become a flood, and they, like those who followed them, came as families—only a dozen of the fifty were grown men—along with livestock and supplies. This mix of people could hardly have differed more from the carousing single young men who adventured to Virginia.

The company board, determined to appoint only "such as are sound both in profession and confession, men fearing God and hating bribes," also sent John Endicott to take charge as governor. It considered him "a fit instrument to begin this wildernesse-work, of courage bold undaunted, yet sociable, and of a chearfull spirit, loving and austere, applying himselfe to either as occasion served."[25]

Others had a lesser opinion of him. One detractor mocked him as "the great swelling fellow of Littleworth."[26]

In fact he did his duty, had considerable competencies, and was honest, but he was not quite so sociable and loving as they imagined. Little is known about his early years, but he seems to have soldiered in some of the most brutal religious battles in Europe. He had a high opinion of himself and a combative personality, along with bluster, ferocity, and pride. His seal reflected him: a death's head—a skull with one horizontal bone. He was a man absolutely true to his convictions but also easily convinced, which made him variable, unpredictable, and therefore doubly dangerous.

Upon his arrival he quickly outraged not only Conant but all the "Old Planters" by immediately declaring his authority over the settlement, including over their land, dictating rules and, according to an opponent, ordering that "he that should refuse to subscribe [to his authority], must pack."[27] After angry protests, the company in London and he backed off, guaranteed Old Planters all "lands which they have formerly manured," plus "a further proportion" to be worked out, and a role in government.[28] The new arrivals and Old Planters reconciled over this agreement, and so did Endicott and Conant personally. To commemorate it, and perhaps also to remind themselves of the need for it, they renamed Naumkeag "Salem," Hebrew for "peace."

Plymouth remained apart, an independent colony with, by then, its own charter. The first settlement of the Massachusetts Bay Company was now established.

On March 4, 1629, while Old Planters and new reconciled, back in England the Massachusetts Bay Company received a royal charter, confirming the earlier charter from the Council for New England, to the region between the Plymouth colony and present New Hampshire. (Fernando Gorges already claimed some of this territory; he later challenged this charter in court.) Shortly after Parliament dissolved in disarray, the Bay Company affirmed in the most concrete way both its commitment to the colony and its different approach to colonizing by sending five ships carrying three hundred and fifty more settlers, many of them intact families and nearly all Puritans, to plant themselves in Salem. These were "not the weak, unfit and prodigal" but "good Governors, able Ministers, Physicians, Soldiers, Schoolmasters, Mariners, and Mechanics of all sorts. . . . The frame of the body is thus formed and furnished with vital parts, and knit together with firm bands and sinews."[29]

To accompany the new planters, the company hired three Puritan ministers to engage in "preaching, catechizing . . . teaching, or causing to be taught, the Company's servants and their children, as also the savages and their children."[30] The situation in England made the posts even more attractive than the generous salary and three servants that went with it. One offer seems to have gone to Roger Williams, who declined.[31] Still, the company was quite pleased with the ministers it did hire: Francis Higginson and Samuel Skelton, who were under extreme pressure from Laud. (A third minister was hired, went to Salem, but returned to England.) And as a sign that the company was making of Massachusetts a true new world, a godly place, it appointed Higginson and Skelton—fugitives from the law and Laud in England—to the eight-person governing council which advised Endicott.

Higginson had once been a conformist, but Thomas Hooker had convinced him that High Church practices had no scriptural authority. He had ceased countenancing these practices and became pastor to a group of Puritans who met privately. For this, a spy returned an information against him. Expecting arrest and imprisonment, he preached a farewell sermon using Luke 21:20–21: "And when ye shall see Jerusalem compassed with armies, then know that the desolation thereof is nigh. Then let them which are in Judea to flee to the mountains; and let them which are in the midst of it to depart out."[32]

He then did depart, with his wife and eight children.

The voyage itself opened a new world to him, its smells and sights ones of wonder and amazement. Higginson wrote to England, "We saw a mountain of ice, shining white as snow, like to a great rock or cliff on the shore. . . . Now we saw an abundance of mackerel, a great store of great whales huffing up water as they go. Some of them came near our ship. Their greatness did astonish us. . . . There backs appeared like a little island. . . . We saw many schools of mackerel, infinite multitudes on every side our ship."[33]

Then, as they neared their destination, he reported, "The sea was abundantly stored with rockweed and yellow flowers like gillyflowers. The nearer we came to the shore the more flowers in abundance, sometimes scattered abroad, sometimes joined in sheets nine or ten yards long, which we supposed to be brought from the low meadows by the tide. Now with what fine woods and green trees by land and these yellow flowers painting the sea, made us all desirous to see our new paradise of New England, whence we saw such fore-running figures signals of fertility afar off."[34]

The colonists had more than just fertility and opportunity in mind. As they approached America, they felt the whole world before them and history unrolling with it. They intended not merely to survive, but to make that history, to fulfill what they regarded as their role in it.

On June 22, 1629, they landed at Salem. The deep harbor allowed the ship to anchor close ashore, and the creak and groan and sweat of unloading cargo onto small boats began, with the greatest difficulties moving cattle. Salem was then still a tiny and primitive village of about ten houses "and a faire House newly built for the Governor."[35] One hundred or so of the passengers stayed there, and most others settled between the Mystic and Charles Rivers in the area soon called Charlestown, where they pushed aside two English settlers—Thomas Walford and his wife—already there. In both places, the immigrants made "what haste we can to build Houses so that within a short time we shall have a faire Towne."[36]

They intended not only to plant in this new world. They intended to fulfill the purpose of the planting, to define the ethos of this world, to infuse it with the Puritan political and religious convictions under assault in England. They were Christian soldiers and they had begun to march.

# ❧ CHAPTER 9 ❧

While those new arrivals familiarized themselves with the new world, back in England in late July 1629 the leaders of the Massachusetts Bay Company held two meetings almost simultaneously, one hundred miles apart. Both had immense impact on the future of the plantation.

In London, the company's "General Court"—in effect a stockholders' meeting—convened. At this meeting Matthew Craddock, the true "governor" of the company—Endicott only represented it in New England—proposed "to transferr the government of the plantacion to those that shall inhabite there, and not to continue the same in subordination to the Company here, as now it is."[1] Craddock argued that this would "induc[e] and encourag[e] persons of worth and quality [to] transplant themselves and their families thither."[2]

Craddock's proposal was in fact an enormous step. Giving control to those in Massachusetts would have the practical benefit of preventing the misunderstandings and poor governance that had plagued the Virginia Company, whose leaders in America reported to London and were often confounded by decisions made there. In effect, it transformed an investment company into a true colony which could pursue its own interest. Craddock also intended to transfer the charter itself, the physical document itself, which would also afford considerable protection to the plantation from the crown and the hierarchy of the Church of England. This was so because altering the charter was vastly easier to do legally with the actual document to hand. Sending the sole original to America put its recall out of easy reach, and also made it far more difficult for any English enemy to amend in any way the rights it conferred. The Atlantic Ocean thus added a real buffer to the legal one, helping guarantee that the Bay Company could build a safe retreat, a godly enterprise, a New Jerusalem. No final action on this proposal was taken that day, but it had broad support and was subsequently approved.

The second meeting critical to the future of Massachusetts was held one hundred miles north of London, at the Sempringham castle of the Earl of Lincoln, a Puritan who had offered livings and sanctuary to several Puritan ministers, including Samuel Skelton. There, members and associates of the company—men who would certainly have known what Craddock was proposing in London—convened to plan the actual settling, financing, and governing of the colony, and the conversion of Indians.

Three ministers who were not members of the company attended. In fact, they rode together for the last few miles to the meeting. Their conversation was pregnant with future conflict.

Two of them, Hooker and John Cotton, were established, prominent Puritan clergy who knew each other well. Their lives had intersected at numerous points, and both had long since attracted Laud's attention.

Of Hooker, the informer Samuel Collins—who said he would be "utterly ruined" if his reports were not kept secret—wrote Laud, "I have lived in Essex to see many new ministers and lecturers, but this man surpasses them all for learning and . . . gains more and far greater followers than all before him." Hooker also attracted and inspired many younger ministers. Collins reported that these ministers "spend their time in conference with him . . . and preach . . . what he hath brewed."[3]

Hooker told them that when they preached, "Let there be fire in it."[4] There was certainly fire in him. But what made him unusual was not his fire. It was his particular ability to reassure his listeners about their salvation, to assuage the terrifying doubt which Puritans lived with. No Puritan could ever be absolutely certain of his or her own salvation, and that uncertainty generated enormous tension, even fear, a fear that never fully loosened its grip. He had personally endured such fear, privately writing of how he did "suffer thy terors, O Lord,"[5] and declaring he could "compare with any man living for fears."[6] But his great sympathy for those in terror of damnation, his belief that a broken heart must precede God's grace, his assurance that a life of sin and corruption did not mean one could not receive grace meant that, as one admirer said, he "had no superiour, and scarce any equal, for the skill of treating a troubled soul."[7]

At the time of the Sempringham meeting, Hooker knew the High Commission was eyeing him. He had so far managed to avoid direct confrontation with it, at least partly because he did use parts of the Book of Common Prayer. His popularity also gave him some protection; Collins had warned Laud that taking harsh action against him would "prove very dangerous," like holding a wolf by the ears. So for now Laud let him continue to preach while monitoring him closely.

Cotton, like Hooker an immensely popular and educated scholar, was less concerned than Hooker about his immediate safety. Minister of St. Botolphe's in Boston, Lincolnshire, he had so far evaded discipline by being even more politic than Hooker. He had reason for being politic: as a small boy he lived only a few yards from where the heads and quartered bodies of three executed Catholic priests had been stuck on pikes until they rotted.

So Cotton conciliated. After Puritans far more extreme than he smashed stained glass windows, defaced statuary, and destroyed crosses at his church, the High Commission investigated his involvement. The investigator exonerated him, reporting that Cotton had said "they might as well refuse the kings coyne because crosses were on it, as forbidd the crosses, and therefore the examinant is p'suaded that Mr. Cotton never did conyv at the cutting of thos crosses."[8]

Later, when Cotton was queried about his refusal to kneel in church, he wrote a pained letter to his bishop, saying study and prayer had shown him "the weakness of some of these grounds against kneeling which before I esteemed too strongly. . . . Besides I shall never forget what your Lordship gravely and wisely once said to me—'The ceremonies I doubted of were nowhere expressly forbidden in Scripture: the arguments brought against them were by consequence deduced from Scripture; deduction of consequences was a work of judgment; other men's judgment (so many, so learned, so godly) . . . did as infallibly deduce just consequences to allow these things as mine own to doubt them.' "[9]

Such expressed willingness to reconsider his own course had preserved him so far. Simple evasion also helped; an assistant presided over parts of the liturgy he objected to. Another Puritan minister noted, "Of all men in the world I envy Mr. Cotton, of Boston, most; for he doth nothing in way of conformity, and yet hath his liberty, and I do everything that way, and cannot enjoy mine."[10]

At the same time, "the flexible Mr. Cotton," as historian Edmund Morgan called him, knew he could not remain untouched indefinitely. He had too much visibility. He had always had visibility. As a twenty-five-year-old rising academic star at Cambridge he was regarded "as another *Xenophon,* or *Musa Attica*."[11]

And for all his surface flexibility, he had conviction. He also had the typical history of torment over the question of whether he was himself saved. At Cambridge, the preaching of Richard Sibbes had given him courage; Sibbes taught that sorrow and humility were good but discouragement was "evil." Hearing this, knowing his own fears, Cotton had changed his own preaching style; he abandoned massaged and clever rhetoric to aim instead at the heart. At a sermon before a huge Cambridge audience, he unveiled his new style. The response of these academics, come to be wowed by intellectual gamesmanship, was negative, but soon after the lecture a distinguished Aristotelian came to Cotton and asked how he could save himself. This convinced Cotton of his course.

Cotton had emphasized the heart and God's grace ever since. Yet he also said, "*Zeale must be according to knowledge;* knowledge is no knowledge without zeale, and zeale is but a wild-fire without knowledge."[12]

His unique mix of scholarship and zeal conveyed hope more than did other ministers, and his ability to create in his listeners a greater sense of intimacy with God made him hugely popular. His sermons drew large crowds— sometimes several thousand—from outside parishes even though worshippers were supposed to attend services at their own parish church. Given his popularity, Cotton knew he was under scrutiny. If his flexibility had won him more freedom than his Puritan fellows had so far, Laud was determined in his thoroughness to make the church inflexible.

The third minister attending the conference was Roger Williams, whose chaplaincy with Masham put him at the epicenter of Puritan activity not only in the region but in all England. He lacked the credentials of Hooker and Cotton but he was young yet, a full generation younger than Hooker and Cotton. Considered a man of great promise, he was suffused with an eager enthusiasm, a confidence in his own judgment, and a certain impatience with his elders. The Massachusetts Bay Company had already offered him a post in New England. He had rejected it, saying he would stay in England "so long as any . . . libertie affoorded."[13] His living as a private chaplain insulated him somewhat from the High Commission's inquisition, but his presence at the meeting also testified to his interest in America and his understanding that liberty might not be afforded him much longer. So he had been invited to join those of greater accomplishment.

While their horses trod the road toward Sempringham, Williams demonstrated his self-confidence and impatience. Or perhaps it was simply arrogance. The three ministers discussed theology and its political implications, especially the Book of Common Prayer. Hooker and Cotton did use it. Williams challenged them for doing so. Noting that he made no compromises on the issue, he cited Scripture to explain why he "durst not joyn with them in their use of Common prayer."

Cotton rejected his arguments, saying they "seemed sandie" but not elaborating. Cotton's answer condescended; it was the kind of answer a teacher gave a pupil. He justified his own use of the book by explaining that he selected only the best prayers.[14]

Williams was unimpressed. Both Cotton and Hooker were formidable men, but Williams had known greater men and had heard the king himself rage and swear in fury. His response to the king had been disgust, not trembling. Their debate went unresolved, but already Williams was taking a more radical position even than these ministers under scrutiny from Laud. And already he was demonstrating another trait: the willingness to confront authority.

At the Sempringham meeting itself, all were of the same mind. All those present agreed that creating an entire commonwealth of the godly was the primary goal of the settlement. The discussion focused on identifying what was necessary to secure success and planning how to acquire it. They would start by collecting an entire community of the godly, a new Chosen People "of good ranke, zeale, meanes, and quality."[15] They would carry no troublers of Israel, no hangers-on, no adventurers indulging foolish personal ambitions. They determined to assemble a fleet to transport this community in an entirety, complete of itself: in the next decade 40 percent of those emigrating from London to Massachusetts would be women, triple the percentage going to Virginia even now, two decades after Virginia was established; one-third of those going to Massachusetts would be children younger than fourteen, compared to less than 4 percent going to Virginia.[16] These men at Sempringham planned carefully the particular skills those families would carry with them, skills needed to make the colony self-reliant. Planning was no theoretical exercise for them; many of them knew that they and their own families would sail with the great fleet. Their own lives depended upon their foresight.

In Salem, meanwhile, Endicott was busy organizing a colony whose population had abruptly quadrupled. He intended to rid it of all those he regarded as troublesome, and he promptly returned to England five teenaged boys who were, as a later historian put it, "discovered to follow practices, which were physically and morally injurious to themselves and others."[17] This was likely masturbation; the boys were fortunate that expulsion was their punishment.

Simultaneously, with little thought as to the implications, he set important precedents in Massachusetts by taking two other actions. First, he declared that government would be based upon laws which in all causes would follow the rule of God's word. One Englishman who had settled in the area before Endicott's arrival complained that Endicott refused to include the caveat that "nothing be done contrary or repugnante to the Lawes of the Kingdome of England."[18] His complaint was ignored.

Endicott next took an equally aggressive step. Unlike Plymouth settlers, the Massachusetts Bay Company members insisted that they ever remained loyal members of the Church of England. Higginson had explicitly reiterated that from the prow of his ship as it departed England, proclaiming, "We will not say, as the Separatists were wont to say at their leaving England, 'Farewell, Babylon! farewell, Rome!'; but we will say, 'Farewell, dear England! farewell, the Church of God in England! . . .' We do not go to New England as separatists from the Church of England, though we cannot but separate from the corruptions in it; but we go to practise the positive part of church reformation and propagate the gospel in America."[19]

But three thousand miles of ocean separated Salem from Laud. The ocean freed Higginson. In a direct assault on the king's and the hierarchy's power, he and Skelton now agreed that the authority to call a minister belonged only to a group "of beleevers . . . joyned together in covenante."[20]

This declaration also reflected Puritan power in the New World. In England, when groups of Puritans often gathered within the larger parish church, these "visible saints" often signed a written covenant pledging themselves to live a godly life and to support each other. Here in Salem that inner church was to become the whole church membership. Here in Salem thirty visible saints signed the church covenant, and the church organized itself around these thirty. Two hundred were present at the organization of the church, but only those signing the covenant were fully church members.[21]

This new church chose Skelton as pastor and Higginson as "teacher," essentially as its theologian. (This seems somewhat odd, given that Skelton was more the scholar, had given the Bay Company a list of books to provide the plantation, and had brought a sizable personal library which eventually became the basis of Harvard's course of study.)

Equally subversive, the congregation conveyed authority to the ministers by a laying on of hands. In a singular ceremony, the ministers bowed their heads while the elders placed their hands upon them and spoke of the power of the Word of God, while all witnessing the act were flushed with godliness. Later, when such ceremonies became an issue in England, those associated with the Massachusetts Bay Company insisted that the ceremony was optional and even unnecessary. But no one could pretend that church services in Massachusetts from this moment forward did not routinely depart from standard Anglican worship. Massachusetts ministers did not wear the surplice, did not kneel, did not make the sign of the cross, did not use Common Prayer.

Most of the several hundred who did not sign the covenant approved. Especially the new arrivals approved; they had come to America in the hope of such godly practices. Many and perhaps most of them entirely shared the theology of the saints, aspired to be saints, but did not sign because they yet doubted their own qualifications as saints. The full community would worship with the others, but only church members could partake of the communion or in church government.

But two brothers did not approve. Samuel and John Browne were hardly troublemakers. Company leaders in London had informed Endicott that they were "men we do much respect."[22] The company had ordered Endicott to place one on the governing council, and the other had earned his own place on the council. Nor did the brothers now confront the Salem church. They simply "gathered a company together, in a place distinct from the public assembly, and there, sundry times, the Book of Common Prayer was read unto such as resorted thither."[23]

Endicott determined that this worship constituted a threat to the order of the community. He determined to bring the weight of government down not upon those who violated the king's decrees on religion, but upon two good subjects who in their piety and loyalty conformed to them. But they did not conform to the ways of Salem. He also brought down upon them the full weight of the community, a weight fashioned into a weapon, used now for the first time in the Massachusetts Bay colony. It would not be the last.

Endicott called the Brownes to account at a public meeting which grew increasingly contentious. The Brownes, though isolated, did not retreat. As they were attacked, they lashed out, accusing Skelton and Higginson of making the church Separatist, attacking the government, charging that Endicott was acting illegally. Endicott now had cause to declare "their speeches and practices tending to mutiny and faction,"[24] and decided to expel them. When they wrote letters of complaint to England, he confiscated the letters. Since he was sending them back to England, seizing the letters accomplished nothing except to enrage the brothers further.

Upon their return to London, furious, they complained in person to the Bay Company, whose leaders concluded that Endicott had jeopardized the entire enterprise, an enterprise carrying risk enough without attracting Laud's attention to it—without in effect taunting him. Salem in general and Endicott in particular had also demonstrated an impulsiveness and independence that had to curbed. The Bay Company board ordered Endicott to avoid anything which "may have ill construction with the State here, and make us obnoxious to any adversary,"[25] and "to bee very sparing in introduceing any lawes or comands wch may render yorselfe or vs distatefull to the state heere," for toward the state "wee must and will haue an obsequious eye."[26] Ten members of the company signed the letter admonishing Endicott. One of them was John Winthrop.

John Winthrop had attended the Sempringham meeting and had decided to emigrate himself, but he had reached that decision with considerable reluctance. Earlier, when his son John Winthrop Jr. had considered joining the Endicott party, he had opposed emigration, writing, "I am loth you should thinke of settlinge there."[27] But much had happened since then and, driven by both personal and public causes, he saw himself as having no choice. The personal came first.

At the time, Winthrop was not a large figure in England. At forty-one years of age, an age when men had well started upon if not fulfilled all that they would achieve in life, he was not a man of great accomplishment, not a man who consorted with or maneuvered around great lords or the royal court, not a man who had risen far of his own. Nor had he been singed by some unachieved ambition or hope that made him restless and unsettled. Rather, he lived a life of diligence and duty. He was calm and calming to those around him; a measured man, a man of intelligence, perception, and weight, he saw the breadth and depth of other men and of things, he saw consequences. He gave ballast to a room. But if he was a man seemingly at rest, that appearance hid an enormous but perfectly balanced tension between his great passions and his determined control of himself.

His passion rarely showed itself yet nonetheless informed his life. That passion was his religiosity, and he felt it in a way as intensely and personally as any intimacy between man and woman. In his journal *Experiencia*, he wrote of "the most sweet love of my heavenly husband, Christ Jesus" and of "thy marriage chamber." Almost with eroticism, he reported that Christ had "married me to himself, so as I am become truly one with him . . . methought my soul had as familiar and sensible society with him, as my wife could have with the kindest husband; I desired no other happiness but to be embraced of him; I held nothing so dear that I was not willing to parte with for him. . . . I was so ravished with his love towards me, far exceeding the affection of the kindest husband that being awaked it had made so deep impression in my heart, as I was forced to unmeasurable weeping for a great while. . . . O my Lord, my love, how wholly delectable thou art! let him kiss me with the kisses of his mouth, for his love is sweeter than wine: how lovely is thy countenance! how pleasant are thy embraces! my heart leaps within me for joy when I hear the voice of thee my Lord, my love. . . . Oh how was I ravished with his love!"[28]

That same passion, filtered through his character and circumstances, would ultimately transform him into a man of consequence. He would become, as even one of his severest critics later conceded, "a man of men."[29]

That came later. So far he had a respectable legal practice but nothing more. A graduate of Cambridge and member of the Inns of Court, his greatest accomplishment was earning appointment as a justice of the peace for Essex because of merit. Justices of the peace had wide-ranging authority, and Winthrop exercised his with decisiveness but also with graciousness, a judicial temperament, moderation, political sensitivity, and an inclination toward—but no absolute commitment to—mercy. Perhaps he even showed wisdom. He had a center, and this center was weighty enough to steady others.

He turned away from this centeredness to pursue pure self-interest once, when his son John Jr. informed him that an attorney at the Court of Wards "is yesterday dead, so as now that place is void." This was a cesspool of a court which controlled the estates of many wards, children too young to make their own decisions. The court did not protect these children; instead, its three court attorneys received large fees for in effect selling the rights to exploit their estates. Wards often came of age to find their estates pillaged. Both his son and his brother-in-law Emmanuel Downing, who already held a position as an attorney at this court, urged him to "come up with all speed" to London to seek the post before a "King's or Duke's letter may be a means to make it disposed another way."[30]

Winthrop seized this main chance, received the appointment, and subsequently sent a "present" to the man who had appointed him. For his time at the court he found rooms in the Inner Temple where he would have routinely crossed paths with Coke. According to a recent biographer, Winthrop stopped short of taking full advantage of opportunities that could have made him wealthy. Those who took fuller advantage, including his brother-in-law, might have considered him foolish for his restraint.[31]

Now, however, he wanted to be shut of this corrupt court. He wanted to be shut of all England. Now, against the advice of many friends, he began taking steps that made it nearly impossible to reverse his decision on emigrating. One was to purge himself of the venality at the Court of Wards. After resigning his position, he wrote his wife that he was "still more confirmed in that Course which I propounded to thee. . . . The Good Lord direct and bless us in it."[32] Two weeks later he added, "[W]here we shall spend the rest of our short time I know not. The Lord, I trust, will direct us in mercy. My comfort is that thou art willing to be my companion in what place or condition soever in weal or woe."[33]

The onset of the king's Personal Rule, the intensifying pressure on Puritans, and the deteriorating English economy also drove his decision to emigrate. In a letter to his wife he expressed a common sentiment among Puritans, that "the Lorde hathe admonished, threatened, corrected, and astonished us, yet we grow worse and worse, so . . . he must needs give waye to his furye at last." On the continent their fellow Protestants had been "smitten . . . before our eyes, and [God] hath made them to drinke of the bitter cuppe of tribulation even unto death; we sawe this, and humbled not ourselves, to turne from our evil wayes, but have provoked him more then all the nations round about us:

therefore he is turning the cuppe towards us also, and because we are the last, our portion must be, to drinke the verye dreggs which remaine: my deare wife, I am veryly perswaded, God will bringe some heavye Affliction upon this lande, and that speedylye."[34]

The decision to leave gave him neither joy nor release, but his quiet and fated acceptance of its necessity did not make him any less committed to it. He was desperate, and desperate men cling to a solution all the more when it seems the only solution. Soon he became a compelling voice for emigration. Within a few weeks after the Sempringham meeting he wrote a draft "General Observations for the Plantation of New England,"[35] which made the case for doing so.

He was hardly the first to argue for emigration. One pamphlet written a few years earlier seemed to speak directly to Winthrop in saying, "I know many who sit here still, with their talent in a napkin, having notable endowments, both of body and mind; and might do great good if they were in some places; which here do none."[36] Another argued, "It be the people that makes the Land *English,* not the Land the People. . . . Take and reckon that for your Country where you may best live and thrive" and not remain in "that countrie which . . . is indeed, weary of you. She accounts you a burthen to her, an encombrance to her."[37] Another told the "truly Pious" that New England offered "the oportunity to put in practise the workes of piety."[38]

His own "General Observations" offered nothing new. But it was designed explicitly for a Puritan audience, and, like a legal brief, it laid arguments out concisely, examined them thoroughly, presented objections, and rebutted them. And it circulated widely among that audience.

It spoke of the hard economic times: "This land grows weary of her Inhabitants, so as man which is the most precious of all Creatures, is here more vile and base, then the earth they tread upon: so as children, neighbors, and friends (especially if they be poor) are rated the greatest burdens, which if things be right, would be the chiefest earthly blessings." By contrast, America offered opportunity: "The whole earth is the Lord's garden, and He hath given it to mankind with a general commission (Gen. 1:28) to increase and multiply and replenish the earth and subdue it."

Most of its arguments, however, related to religion. One was, "It will be a service of great consequence to the church of god to carry ye gospel of Christ to those parts of the world, and to raise up a bulwark against ye kingdom of

Antichrists which the Jesuits labor to raise up in all parts of the world." Another reflected Puritan criticism of High Church practices, as in the complaint that "the fountains of learning and religion"—Oxford and Cambridge—"are so corrupted that most children are perverted, corrupted, and utterly overthrown by the multitude of evil examples and licentious government of these seminaries."

And it warned anew that Protestantism was under such assault that it was both a Christian responsibility to support emigration and a possible means to save oneself. "All other Churches of Europe being brought to desolation," it stated, "and our sins for which the Lord already begins to frown upon us and to cut us short, do threaten evil times to be coming down upon us, and who knows, but that God hath prepared this place for a refuge for many whom he means to save out of the general calamity."[39]

To the Puritans, at stake was not simply a personal decision whether to emigrate. At stake was, at least in the eyes of many who did emigrate, even the fate of the world.

A minority but a growing number of English Protestants saw themselves as at the beginning of the Last Days, at the opening skirmishes of Armageddon. They saw themselves as participants in this battle. Indeed, they saw themselves as key. For before Christ's reign could begin, the Gospel had to be carried throughout the world. Carrying it to the Indians not only offered salvation to the Indians but brought the world closer to the end times. Emigration not only meant escape from the wrath of God in England. It meant they were soldiers on the side of Christ, against the Antichrist. There could be no higher calling.

And, all that had happened between the king and Parliament, all the assaults which Laud and the High Commission had launched, made many Puritans worry that their world was trembling. It was as if great blows had struck a tuning fork and the trembling was threatening to shake England apart.

On August 26, 1629, in Cambridge, a dozen leaders of the godly faction of the Bay Company, John Winthrop among them, signed an agreement pledging to emigrate and binding themselves to each other: "Now for the better encourragement of ourselves and others that shall joyne with vs in this action, and to the end that euery man may without scruple dispose of his estate and afayres as may best fit his preparacion for this voyage . . . [we] doth hereby freely and sincerely promise and bynd himselfe in the word of a Christian and in the presence of God, . . . we will be ready in our persons and with such of our seuverall familyes as are to go with vs and such provisions as we are conveniently to furnish ourselves withal, to embarke for the said plantacion by the first of March next."[40]

One could not retreat from such a pledge.

Two days later the company's General Court formally voted "by the erection of hands" to confirm the earlier recommendation "that the government and patent should be settled in New England." The significance of this transfer of authority was lost on no one. Next came the selection of a governor; ever since the fiasco with the Brownes, the company had lacked confidence in Endicott.

The position interested Winthrop, Sir Richard Saltonstall, Isaac Johnson— likely the wealthiest of the emigrants; his wife was married to an earl, and Winthrop's flagship the *Arabella* was named after her—and Jon Humfry. Winthrop was both the poorest of the group and the lowest-ranking in the social hierarchy. But he had been active enough in the company by then that he had been judged. On October 20, 1629, the General Court "having received extraordinary great recommendations of Mr Jhn Winthrop, both for his integrity and sufficiency as one being very well fitted and accomplished for the place of Governor. . . . The said Mr Winthrop was, by erection of hands, chosen to be Governor for the ensuing year, to begin this present day."[41]

Events would show that the company had chosen well.

Winthrop had committed everything within himself and everything he had control over outside himself to the venture. All four candidates for governor would eventually go to Massachusetts; Johnson died there soon after arriving, while Saltonstall and Humfry eventually returned to England. For Winthrop, there was no going back.

He had already decided this. At the same time he wrote "General Observations for the Plantation of New England" he also drafted "Particular Considerations in the Case of J:W:." In it he searched his own heart about the decision to emigrate. His notes suggest the kind of governor he would make.

Some of his thinking reflected self-awareness and humility, along with an admission of defeat that few men would make, especially to themselves. He wrote, "My meanes heere are so shortned as I shall not be able to continue in this place and imployment where I now am: and a souldier may with honor quitt his ground rather then be forced from it." He added in a margin note,

"When a man is to wade throughe a deepe water, there is required tallnesse, as well as Courage, and if he findes it past his depth, and God open a gapp another waye, he may take it."[42]

But he also wrote lines that reflected not only self-confidence and a sense of duty and dedication but absolute conviction that, despite any failures he had experienced, he could lead this venture into America. And he had absolute conviction that in doing so he was doing the work of God. He noted the "inwarde . . . inclination of mine owne heart to the worke. . . . In my youth I did seariously consecrate my life to the service of the Churche (intendinge the ministry) but was diverted from that course . . . but it hathe ofte troubled me since, so as I thinke I am the rather bounde to take the opportunitye for spendinge the remainder of my tyme, to the best service of the Churche which I may." He recognized that "if I should let passe this opportunitye, that talent which god hath bestowed on me for publike service, were like to be buried." He also noted that "in all probabilitye, the wellfare of the plantation depends upon my assistance, for the maine pillers of it being gentlemen of high qualitye, and eminent partes, . . . are determined to sitt still, if I deserte them."[43]

In the next few weeks and months, he disentangled himself from his life in England, divesting himself of property and encumbrances and, given that he was to build a home in Massachusetts proper for a governor, arranging the transport of favored furniture, wall hangings, and the like. He also fitted himself to and took on the responsibilities of the role of governor. He began by telling those who had invested in the Bay Company primarily to make money that "the eyes of all the godly are upon you" and urging them to "deny your own profit" for the gain of "the Gospel which you profess."[44] The fact that investors never did much pressure those in Massachusetts to return a profit demonstrates both the Puritan zeal of the investors and their excitement about the plantation.

Then he turned his focus on the concrete: fitting out a fleet of ships and guiding an exodus of close to one thousand people. It was an immense task, suffocating in detail. For the trip itself, the experience of having sent several hundred emigrants to Salem gave some understanding of logistical needs. In November 1629—for a voyage that would commence the following March—Winthrop ordered 14,700 brown biscuits, 5,300 white biscuits, thirty hogsheads of beef, six hogsheads of pork, and two hundred tongues.[45]

But that was only for the voyage. Planning for the colony itself vastly exceeded that in complexity. The plantation needed much more than supplies. It needed to become self-sufficient quickly, meaning it required not only farmers but carpenters, brickmakers, fishermen, salters, shipwrights, seamstresses; it needed kettles and pans, ladles and ploughs and hoes; it needed seeds for apple trees, seeds for quinces, seeds for currants, for cherries, for hemp and flax; it needed cattle, dogs, pigs, horses, even rabbits and tame turkeys. It needed not only nails but people skilled in the making of tools to make nails. It needed the means to grow or make all that was known to English kitchens and manufacture, and all the tools to transform a wilderness into something as close to English society as possible. Everything English society had, New England needed. If it could not be made in New England, sufficient supply had to be provided; if it could be made in New England, sufficient skill had to be transported to make it.

Many of those embarking on this voyage were men of some wealth, and these men traveled not only with their own families but with servants and servants' families, whose passage they paid. Either the company or a sponsor paid the passage for skilled laborers. Winthrop himself brought at least four entire families as part of his own household and personally recruited many others, for example successfully recruiting a man of "godlinesses and abilityes" in surgery whose present place did not "afforde you such sufficient and Comfortable imployment as your giftes doe require."[46] He preferred finding a skilled godly person—a Puritan—but he was practical enough to recognize that the skill itself mattered more, as long as the man who had it was not lacking in character. As governor, he also had the authority to reject passengers he deemed unsuitable.

Others associated with the company—including those in Massachusetts—recruited as well. Winthrop could talk only of his hopes for America. From Salem, Francis Higginson wrote of life there. He sent a letter that became known as *New Englands Plantation* and which circulated widely beginning in October or November 1629. "The fertility of the soil is to be admired," he wrote. "About three miles from us a Man may stand on a hill and see diverse thousands of acres of ground as good as need to be, and not a Tree in the same." Hence, not a tree had to be cleared from these fields, fields so fertile that, extraordinarily, even "little children here by setting of Corn may earn more than their own maintenance. . . . Great pity is to see so much good ground for Corn and Grass as any is under the Heavens, to lie altogether unoccupied when so many honest Men and their Families in old England through the populousness thereof, do make a very hard shift to live one by the other."[47]

Finally, the men involved with the Massachusetts Bay Company had no illusions about the world they lived in. They knew war, war on the continent, war in Ireland, and war on the seas. They knew that pirates took English captives and sold them into slavery, and they knew that civilized men, including Englishmen, put their enemies' heads on pikes.

Therefore they determined to transport—along with cattle, horses, cows, goats, and pigs—the great English mastiffs, dogs of war. As one man who would himself emigrate advised, "The People of Christ . . . [must] behave themselves in War-like Discipline," prepare "with all diligence [to] provide against the Malignant adversaries of the truth . . . [and] store yourselves with all sorts of weapons for war, furbish up your swords, Rapiers, and all other piercing weapons. . . . Spare not to lay out your coyne for Powder, Bullets, Match, Armes of all sorts, and all kinde of Instrument for War . . . in that Wildernesse, whither you are going."[48] And so they also provided artillery "for a Fort, with Muskets, Pikes, Corslets, Drums and Colours, with all provisions necessary for the good of man."[49] They sent enough that one Salem resident reported, "We have great Ordnance, wherewith wee doubt not . . . to keep out a potent Aduersary."[50]

Combat veterans were recruited, and England's finest military experts were consulted. After talks with England's master gunner and the commander of London artillery, Winthrop sent his brilliant son John Jr.—he would become a founding member of the Royal Society—to sketch the design of a harbor fortification and to recruit the skilled labor to build it. The son also drew the plans of, as he informed his father, "Corne milles sawe miles &c.; . . . if there be made any use of it, I desire New England should reape the benefit."[51]

They were, they believed, ready.

### ✸ CHAPTER 10 ✸

Winthrop and his colleagues had pledged before God to embark by the first of March 1630. They failed to do so, but very soon after, a fleet of eleven ships creaked at anchor at Southampton, rising and falling with the tide, while men lowered hogsheads of supplies to carry the emigrants through the voyage and the first months of settlement.

A few weeks later, one thousand emigrants accompanied by friends and family come to say goodbye crowded into the small, quiet port unaccustomed to so much human freight. Most of the emigrants expected never to return, never to see their homes again, never to see England again. They were to give up everything, each and every thing to which memory attached, each field into which their sweat had soaked, each tree along the lane, each barn, each cobblestone, each tavern, each gravesite for a child or spouse or parent, each friend, each brother, each sister, each aunt, each cousin. For most, departure was wrenching. Winthrop wrote to one friend, "[M]y soule is knitt to you, as the soule of Jonathan to Dauid: were I now with you, I should bedewe that sweet bosome with the tears of affection: O what a pinch will it be to me, to part with such a freinde!"[1] He would travel alone; his wife was pregnant and would follow later. She was his third wife—the first two died—but he loved her completely, addressing her in letters "mine own, mine only, my best beloved," "my love, my joy, my faithful one." In parting they had agreed that each Monday and Friday between five and six o'clock each would think of the other, believing in their love that this would connect them across the Atlantic.

A sense of defeat haunted some of those leaving, while concern that they were deserting England in its time of need must have haunted others. Their stomachs churned with anxiety as well, anxiety over the voyage itself, for most had never been on a ship at all, much less had they ventured upon a voyage such as this—and anxiety over what they would find in America.

Yet anxiety was allayed by faith. Puritans felt God everywhere present; each moment and each object resonated with that presence. Those departing felt God with them, felt God's intimate, direct touch, giving them not only hope but conviction, a conviction shimmering within them like a holy thing. They found reassurance also in that they were not traveling as individuals, that they belonged to this community of pilgrims, that not only families but clusters of families and neighbors were transplanting themselves in groups. Several hundred came from County Essex, Winthrop's county, and many came from within a few miles of Winthrop.

In the middle of March, on the eve of departure, John Cotton preached them a sermon, "God's Promise to His Plantation." Cotton was not then himself embarking, but he had come with many of his parishioners from Lincolnshire—another center for the godly—who were leaving. His sermon had a purpose: to clear his listeners' minds of doubt, to confirm in them their belief that God required that they proceed.

Cotton's audience that day likely far exceeded one thousand; he was a celebrity, his sermons events. Emigrants heard him, those come to say farewell heard him, townspeople heard him. He did provide some secular rationale, stating that because "Tradesmen cannot live one by another, but eate up one another, in this case it is lawfull to remove." He also denied that those departing were impractical people who "dreame of perfection in this world."[2]

But the main point of his sermon rested upon 2 Samuel 7:10: "Moreover I will appoint a place for my people Israel, and I will plant them, that they may dwell in a place of their owne, and move no more."

He justified the emigrants in their departure, justified them that in abandoning all that they had known, every tangible thing in their lives and every tangible thing tying them to England, that they were fulfilling God's purpose, and that God would take care of them. They had lawful reason to desert England, he told them, lawful reason to occupy vacant land, lawful reason "to plant a Colony, that is, a company that agree together to remove out of their owne Country, and settle a City or Common-wealth elsewhere."

He urged them to "feede [the Indians] with your spiritualls," advised, "Goe forth, every man that goeth, with a publicke spirit, looking not on your owne things onely, but also on the things of others," reminded them, "God is said to plant a people more especially, when they become *Trees of righteousnesses*."

And he told them God "promiseth them firme and durable possession . . .

they shall have peacable and quiet resting there, The sonnes of wickednesse shall afflict them no more . . . hee would make them a good people, a choice generation."

They would be a new Chosen People, God's people. There could be no greater privilege. But he concluded with a warning: "If you rebell against God, the same God that planted you will also roote you out againe. . . . When the Israelites liked not the soile, grew weary of the Ordinances, and forsooke the worship of God. . . . As they waxed wearie of God, so hee waxed wearie of them, and cast them out of his sight."

There was also another sermon preached to the voyagers, one preached by John Winthrop. Such was the measure of conviction conveyed first by Cotton, then by Winthrop, that it seems not a single person out of a thousand at the last moment withdrew from the voyage.

Winthrop titled his sermon "A Modell of Christian Charitie." Ironically, given all the importance attached to it, historians do not know where he delivered it. They once thought he preached it at sea only to those on his own ship, but they now consider it more likely that he gave it to all the colonists before departure. The fleet sailed only a few days after Cotton spoke, so Winthrop may well have delivered it at this same gathering. At any rate, copies of it soon began to circulate. And his message resonated. Over the next few years numerous Puritan ministers echoed his vision and his words in defining the purpose of the plantation.

His message has resonated ever since. There was a subtle but vital difference that made his purpose both much more ambitious than Cotton's and much more profound. Where Cotton primarily reassured listeners that they were doing the right thing, Winthrop focused more on what that right thing was. As a result, he went beyond Cotton. He went far beyond. He spoke intending to define, in a reasoned and undramatic way, the task that the colonists were embarking upon. In that ambition he succeeded.

Winthrop articulated what many of his audience not only believed but felt in their *bowels*—a word then in common use to denote a thing both intimate and integral to one's being. And what he said has also etched itself into the being of what became the United States of America; it has filled its soul, defined its purpose, poured itself into its concrete. Nearly four centuries after Winthrop spoke, one historian concluded that his words have been "[e]nshrined as a kind of Ur-text of American literature."[3] In 1999 on the eve of the new millennium, the *New York Times* asked the prominent Harvard theologian Peter Gomes to identify the greatest sermon of the preceding one thousand years; he selected Winthrop's.[4] It has inspired and continues to inspire, largely because of a single choice of phrasing, a choice which came directly from the Bible, from the sermon on the mount in Matthew.

Yet it represents only a single side of the American ethos and mythos. What it omitted, Roger Williams would supply. Williams would never say anything quite so eloquent, and his vision—though routinely given lip service by a majority—even today is rejected by a large segment of the American community. But it is the breadth and depth of their combined views and the tension between them which has driven the spirit of America.

To a modern reader, much of Winthrop's sermon is remarkable. To Winthrop's contemporaries, it was neither remarkable nor original. But their very familiarity with his two main themes helps explain why it resonated so deeply.

He first spoke of Christian charity, of Christian love. He saw society as truly holding its wealth in common, hence as being a commonwealth; it had economic inequality in it, it had inequality of rank, but there was no inequality in value. This was entirely consistent with contemporary views of the body politic.

William Perkins, a particularly influential Puritan theologian, had articulated this view twenty years earlier: "A vocation or calling, is a certain kinde of life, ordained and imposed on man by God, for the common good. . . . [A] king is to spend his tyme in the governing of his subjects, and that is his calling; and a subject is to live in obedience to the Magistrate, and that is his calling. . . . The author of every calling is God himselfe; and therefore Paul saith; *As God hath called every man, let him walke.* . . . The final cause or ende of every calling . . . [is] *For the common good.* In mans body there be sundrie parts and members, and every one hath his severall use and office, which it performeth not for it selfe, but for the good of the whole bodie; as the office of the eye, is to see, of the eare to heare, and the foote to goe. Now all societies of men, are bodies, . . . the common-wealth also."[5]

Winthrop opened his sermon echoing Perkins, saying that God "hath soe disposed of the condition of mankind, as in all times some must be rich, some poore, some high and eminent in power and dignitie; others mean and in submission. . . . [Yet] it appears plainly that noe man is made more honorable or more wealthy, &c., out of any particular and singular respect to himselfe but for the glory of his creator and the common good of the creature, man."[6] Like Perkins, he compared different parts of the body, each fitting together, to different roles people played in society, explaining that "every man might have need of other." He considered such dependence a good thing, since "from hence they might all be knitt more nearly together in the Bonds of brotherly affection."

He spoke of "two rules whereby we are to walk one towards another: JUSTICE and MERCY. . . . [M]an as he was enabled so withal is commanded to love his neighbor as himselfe. Upon this ground stands all the precepts of the moral law, which concerns our dealings with men. . . . [E]very man afford his help to another in every want or distresse. . . . The lawe of the Gospell propounds likewise a difference of seasons and occasions. There is a time when a christian must sell all and give to the poor as they did in the apostles' times. There is a time allsoe when christians (though they give not all yet) must give beyond their ability . . . whereby our Christian brother may be relieved in this distress . . . rather than tempt God."

And he said, "Love is the bond [that] . . . makes the worke perfect . . . ourselves knitt together by this bond of loue, and, live in the exercise of it, if wee would have comforte of our being in Christ."

Winthrop used the word "love" neither metaphorically nor philosophically. He meant it in an intimate, passionate, and tangible way. To Puritans, Christ was the husband and his church the bride. Winthrop envisioned a similar intimate and personal union with Christ. He applied this concept of love when he said they would "seeke out a place of cohabitation and Consorteshipp under a due forme of Government both ciuill and ecclesiasticall," and referred to the "bond of marriage between him [God] and us, wherein hee hath taken us to be his, after a most strickt and peculair manner."

"Love" mattered also because of Winthrop's pragmatism. He recognized that feelings, not reason, drove men: "The way to drawe men to workes of mercy, is not by force of Argument from the goodness or necessity of the worke; for though this course may enforce a rational mind to some present Act of mercy . . . yet it cannot worke such a habit in a soule." Consistent behavior could only come from "frameing these affections of love in the hearte which will as natively bring forthe the other, as any cause doth produce effect."

The second theme of Winthrop's sermon carried a more somber, even ominous message. He spoke of the covenant between the emigrants and God and their need to obey "holy ordinances." He warned that "truthe in profession onely" meant failure, and that God would not "beare with such faileings at our hands as he dothe from those among whome wee have lived."

They had become the Chosen of the Lord, they were now like Israel, and "he tells the people of Israell, *you onely have I knowne of all the families of the Earthe, therefore will I punishe you for your Transgressions. . . .* When God gives a speciall commission he lookes to have it strictly observed in every article. . . . Thus stands the cause betweene God and us. We are entered into Covenant with Him for this worke. . . . [God] will expect a strict performance of the articles contained in it; but if wee shall neglect the observation of these articles . . . and, dissembling with our God, shall fall to embrace this present world and prosecute our carnall intentions, seeking great things for ourselves and our posterity, the Lord will surely breake out in wrathe against us; be revenged of such a people and make us knowe the price of the breache of such a covenant. . . ."

"Wee must delight in eache other," he said, "make other's conditions our oune; rejoice together, mourne together, labour and suffer together, allwayes haueving before our eyes our commission and community in the worke, as members of the same body. Soe shall wee keepe the unitie of the spirit in the bond of peace. The Lord will be our God, and delight to dwell among us, as his oune people, and will command a blessing upon us in all our wayes. . . . Wee shall finde that the God of Israell is among us, when ten of us shall be able to resist a thousand of our enemies; when hee shall make us a prayse and glory that men shall say of succeeding plantations, 'the Lord make it like that of New England.'"

Then Winthrop spoke the words which transformed his sermon into something quoted by modern presidents, something that has informed America's view of itself and even much of the world's view of America.

"For wee must consider that wee shall be as a citty upon a hill. The eies of all people are uppon us. Soe that if wee shall deale falsely with our God in this worke wee haue undertaken, and soe cause him to withdrawe his present help from us, wee shall be made a story and a by-word through the world. Wee shall open the mouthes of enemies to speake evill of the wayes of God, and all professors for God's sake. Wee shall shame the faces of many of God's worthy servants, and cause theire prayers to be turned into curses upon us till wee be consumed out of the good land whither wee are a goeing.

"I shall shutt upp this discourse with that exhortation of Moses, that faith-full servant of the Lord, in his last farewell to Israell, Deut. 30. Beloued, there is now sett before us life and good, Death and evill, in that wee are commanded this day to loue the Lord our God, and to loue one another, to walke in his wayes and to keepe his Commandements and his Ordinance and his lawes, and the articles of our Covenant with him, that wee may liue and be multi-plied, and that the Lord our God may blesse us in the land whither wee goe to possesse it. But if our heartes shall turne away, soe that wee will not obey, but shall be seduced, and worshipp and serue other Gods, our pleasure and proffitts, and serue them; it is propounded unto us this day, wee shall surely perishe out of the good land whither wee passe over this vast sea to possesse it.

"Therefore lett us choose life, that wee, and our seede may liue, by obeyeing His voyce and cleaveing to Him, for Hee is our life and our prosperity."

On March 20, 1630, the *Arabella,* which carried Winthrop, and the *Ambrose, Hopewell,* and *Talbot* weighed anchor off Southampton and crossed to the Isle of Wight. They waited at Cowes for wind to leave. When they did finally catch the wind—not until March 29—it blew hard, hard enough that Winthrop's son Henry, who had gone ashore "to fetch an oxe & 10," could not return to the ship even with it at anchor. He would have to follow. Already they had lost any chance that the entire fleet of eleven ships could assemble and travel together. Yet they did not get far, and dropped anchor again farther west on the Isle of Wight at Yarmouth.

There, on April 7, Winthrop made his first formal political statement as governor, sending ashore *The Humble Request of His Maiestes Loyall Subjects, the Governour and the Company late gone to New England,* probably with former company governor Matthew Craddock, who came on board with several oth-ers to bid farewell and godspeed. This document became known as simply the *Humble Request.* In it Winthrop and other signatories pledged to "their Brethren in and of the Church of ENGLAND: For the obtaining of their Prayers, and removal of their Suspicions" that they were not Separatists, that they were entirely loyal both to England and to the Church of England, and that "such hope and part as wee have obtained in the common salvation, we have received in her bosome, and suckt it from her breasts."[7]

On April 8, 1630, the four ships hoisted anchor once again, heading out into "the English Sea," the Channel. Still in the Channel, the captain worried that eight sails in the distance were pirates. He mustered twenty-five of Winthrop's landmen who could handle muskets, assigned them posts on deck, loaded the cannon for war—the *Arabella* carried twenty-eight—and experimented firing "a ball of wild fire fastned to an arrowe, out of a Crosse bow which burnt in the water a good tyme," wrote Winthrop. "It was much to see how cheerfull and Comfortable all the Companye appeared, not a woman or childe that shewed feare. . . . [O]ur trust was in the Lord of hoastes."[8]

Ready, the captain turned his small fleet into the approaching sails. They soon relaxed; the ships were English, bound for Canada and Newfoundland.

On April 10, Winthrop spied out the Lizard, the extreme tip of Cornwall. Finally they reached the open vast Atlantic. He would never see England again.

No voyage across the Atlantic was easy. Overcrowding made it harder. Quarters teemed with people and livestock. Even Winthrop, who had a cabin, his own bedding, and servants, slept in one bed with two of his sons. Life for most was far more densely packed; the area belowdecks soon grew noxious enough that the captain complained that "our lande men were very nastye and slouenly, & that the gunne decke where they lodged, was so beastly & noysome with their victualls, and beastlynesse, as would muche endanger the healthe of the shippe."[9]

Yet they adjusted. Routine settled over them as it later settled over Williams and all those who later left England for America. The ship became their world. They caught fish and kept them alive and fresh in a tub on deck. They tracked their distance and location. They worshipped each day, and each day heard a sermon. And many days they saw men disciplined—one man was locked into bolts, while another, for cheating a child over biscuits, had "his handes to be tyed vp to a barre & hanged a basket with stones about his necke & so he stood for 2 howres."[10] Storms initially terrified all, added intensity to worship, and drove these four ships far enough apart that one arrived twenty days after the first. Yet by six weeks into the voyage even violent weather became routine, the passengers "so acquainted with stormes, as they were not sick nor troubled, thoughe we were much tossed 48: howers together . . . continually in a high growne sea."[11] Three weeks later they were closing on America: to avoid the shoals—the water in some spots only a few meters deep—of the great fishing ground George's Bank between Maine and Cape Cod, "we sonded in the morninge & againe at noone, & had no gronde. [W]e sonded againe about 2: after noone, & had gronde about . . . 80. fath: a fine grey sande. . . . In the great Cabbin *thankesgivinge*."

On June 6, the fifty-ninth day at sea, "we sawe the shore." They sailed down the coast of Maine. By now they were passing places noted on maps, "a ridge of 3 hilles . . . it lyes near Aquamenticus . . . a small hill to the Southward of the Turks heades."[12] Passing within sight of Cape Ann, they saw a ship at anchor and a dozen shallops. They caught mackerel and met another shallop with Englishmen in it, fishermen. They could see the land, smell the land, all but taste and step upon the land. Then, on the twelfth of June, 1630, they anchored at Salem and shot off two cannon in celebration. But they found nothing to celebrate in the chilling facts ashore.

Plymouth had suffered many deaths in its first year before stabilizing, but Bay Company leaders thought they had learned enough from that terrible experience not to repeat it. They were wrong.

Less than a year earlier they had sent three hundred and fifty colonists across the Atlantic. Winthrop found "above eighty of them being dead . . . and many of those alive weak and sick."[13] Those in Winthrop's fleet had expected relief upon arrival. Salem had expected the fleet to give them relief. More than one hundred indentured servants were waiting for supplies that the company had a contractual obligation to provide; the fleet carried no such supplies, and the breach of contract freed those servants. But freedom without food gave little satisfaction. For there was little food. "All the corn and bread amongst them all [was] hardly sufficient to feed them a fortnight,"[14] reported Thomas Dudley, soon the plantation's deputy governor and a frequent rival of Winthrop, adding that Salem itself "pleased us not."[15] About ten houses lined a dirt street, heading up a hill from the water; the handful of other buildings were little more than huts and hovels.

Not even Salem's church offered respite. Skelton and Higginson allowed only passengers who belonged to a church whose congregation had signed a covenant to participate in the Lord's Supper. Winthrop himself was excluded. They refused to baptize a child born at sea of parents from a noncovenanted congregation.[16]

This directly contradicted the promise made in the *Humble Request*.

Winthrop made no known protest, but word of the exclusion made its way to England. There many, including John Cotton, subsequently upbraided the Salem ministers for their actions.

Amidst this somber and dismal welcome, Winthrop and other company leaders dined ashore with Endicott, Skelton, Higginson, and probably Conant and a few others. They informed Endicott that he was now replaced as governor. Then they began searching for appropriate sites to plant the nearly one thousand men, women, and children in their fleet. Salem clearly could absorb few.

They searched with urgency. Already they had missed the planting season and they had to build homes. Sharp New England nights would begin to arrive in a few months, and close upon them would follow winter.

And if the desperate straits of the first Bay Company expedition gave the new arrivals any sense of superiority, they were soon disabused of their smugness. Death visited the newest arrivals early, and it came often. Winthrop's own son Henry, twenty-two years old, drowned only a few days after arriving, when he tried to swim a river to retrieve a canoe; likely tidal currents were too strong for him. ("My son Henry, my son Henry, ah my poor childe,"[17] Winthrop wrote his wife.) But such deaths could happen anywhere. Special to America seemed the "fevers and scurvy" which were taking "diverse amongst them, not sparing the righteous."

As early as mid-September, "much mortalitie" had occurred. Isaac Johnson and his wife Lady Arabella—for whom the flagship of Winthrop's fleet had been named—died. The surgeon Winthrop had personally recruited died. Sickness was so widespread and so debilitating that the plantation lacked the manpower to move cannon into place to command the harbor. This made them vulnerable militarily; worried that Catholic powers might attack, Winthrop and others decided to abandon their plan to concentrate the population in one area. Instead the colonists dispersed.

Work had already begun at one site. Earlier Endicott, upon orders from London, had begun construction of a large governor's mansion and several other buildings at Charlestown, about twenty miles south and slightly east of Salem, on the south bank of the Mystic River. Perhaps one hundred and fifty English men, women, and children already lived there. Now more joined them. Settlers also occupied Roxbury, Dorchester, and Watertown.

In a race against winter in each town, wells were dug, a street laid out, a few houses were built rapidly by those who traveled with servants. But most of those in each town, still too weak to build homes, "pitched some tents of Cloath" or "built them small Huts" in which they waited helplessly for winter.

Charlestown quickly—but temporarily—became the largest town. People there soon covenanted to form a church. John Wilson was chosen as pastor and installed with "imposition of handes." Winthrop, far more politic than Endicott had been on this issue, carefully stipulated that this imposition of hands "was onely as a signe of Election & confirmation, not of any intent that mr. wilson should renounce his ministrye he received in Englande."[18] Thus Winthrop's church continued to affirm the Church of England as a true church. Within a few days nearly one hundred people signed the church covenant and were admitted to membership. Soon, however, church membership would become far harder to attain.

But in Charlestown the increased population could not subsist with the single freshwater spring—unreachable at high tide—so far found. Across the river on the Shawmut peninsula was a free-flowing spring. William Blackstone, a devout man but no Puritan, already lived on the peninsula, but he could hardly claim all of it. In September Winthrop and many others moved there— Winthrop had his mansion taken apart and rebuilt there as well—and renamed it Boston, partly to honor John Cotton of Boston in England, partly because some of the emigrants came from old Boston. The Charlestown church removed with them, becoming the Boston church. The move came late in the year—very late for those who had to start building shelter. But by the end of October, with winter fast coming on, Boston had about one hundred and fifty inhabitants.

Those who remained in Charlestown nursed anger, even a sense of betrayal, for having been abandoned. That worsened as illness hit Charlestown especially hard: there "almost in every Family Lamentation, Mourning, and woe was heard, and no fresh food to be had to cherish them."[19] Bickering and hostility spread.

Charlestown was hardly alone in suffering. By the end of 1630, barely six months after arrival, approximately two hundred had died. Among them were twelve of those close enough to Winthrop that he regarded them as part of his own household—those who worked for him directly and indirectly and their families.

Two hundred more returned to England. Many went back on the *Lyon*, a ship whose master, William Peirce, Winthrop trusted utterly; fully aware of the difficulties the colony faced, Winthrop gave Peirce orders for emergency supplies and counted upon his return.

By then, on its way across the ocean was a letter to Winthrop from his brother-in-law Emmanuel Downing, warning him to "bestow not much cost in building where you are, but do advise that you do speedily send about the discovery of some fitter place to the south, where you may enjoy . . . milder winters and fruitfuller harvests."[20] A second letter followed that "the Iudgment of most men here [is] that your Colonye would this winter be dissolved, partly by death through want of Food, housing, and rayment, and the rest to retorne or flee for refuge to other plantations."[21]

Then came winter. They had never known winters like this, far more biting than any they had suffered in England, biting enough that they had no measure of it, with snowdrifts deep enough to lose a man in and with wolves howling thick in the wood. "The weather held tolerable until the 24th of December, but the cold came on then with violence," noted one report. "Such a Christmas eve they had never seen before. From that time to the 16th of February their chief care was to keep themselves warm, and as comfortable, in other respects as their scant provisions would permit. The poorer sorts in tents and miserable hovels, and many died of the scurvy and other distempers. So short provisions, they lived on clams, musseles, ground nuts and acorns instead of bread."[22]

Winthrop was himself bewildered at "this strange land, where we have met many troubles and adversities."[23] But he was hardly willing to quit. He wrote his wife that God had only "stripped us of our vain confidence in this arm of flesh, that he may have us rely wholly upon himself." God was testing them. He, and the bulk of those who had come with him, were undeterred, determined to do far more than succeed: they were determined to demonstrate their faith and their conviction.

"ISRAEL," as the godly in Massachusetts often now called themselves, had—regardless of hardship—found their home, their place of peace, their Rehoboth. Winter only hardened the survivors' conviction; it was not diminished. They intended still to erect more than just new buildings and towns; they intended still to erect Jerusalem itself, anew. There would be no retreat.

Winthrop could do nothing about disease. But he could and did proceed to advance the purpose of the plantation. He focused on establishing order and orderly procedures of government. The charter called for a governor, deputy governor, and up to eighteen "assistants," also known as "magistrates," and the governor chaired monthly meetings of the Court of Assistants. These assistants or magistrates combined the power of a legislator—making laws at regular meetings—with that of an English justice of the peace; they could issue warrants, empanel juries, conduct trials, and sentence offenders to whippings, stock and bilboes, disfigurements. But two assistants died and seven returned to England, leaving only eight to serve for now on the Court of Assistants. Endicott was the only assistant in Salem.

In October 1630 Winthrop held the first meeting of the General Court. This had been essentially a stockholders' meeting in England, but here only the men already assistants qualified to participate in it. Recognizing the need for a government with a broader base, Winthrop invited the public to attend. He then announced that, with the concurrence of the assistants, he would expand membership of the General Court, effective at the next meeting, to include all "freemen." The assistants also agreed that in the future the freemen would elect assistants. This did not mean that Winthrop believed in democracy. He quite definitely did not, and he routinely denounced "democraticall" government. The authority to rule, he believed, came from God. Even elected rulers embodied God's authority and received their authority from God.

But if the assistants agreed to expand the General Court, they reserved to themselves alone the power to make laws, choose the governor and deputy governor from among themselves, carry out the executive responsibilities of government, and appoint officers to enforce laws. Winthrop did not reveal that the charter gave the full General Court the power to make laws, so reserving this power to the assistants violated the charter. His doing so would later create enormous hostility.

At the next General Court in May 1631, 116 men, nearly all the men in the plantation who were not servants, elected the magistrates. These beneficiaries of the expanded suffrage now promptly limited it. They decided that to ensure "honest and good" voters, "for time to come noe man shalbe admitted to the freedome of this body polliticke but such as are members of some of the churches within the lymitts of the state."[24]

In the future, then, only church members could vote. And church membership soon became difficult to attain. Winthrop and his fellow magistrates also attended to establishing another kind of order as well. They attended to Thomas Morton.

The territory granted to the Massachusetts Bay Company was not empty of English when Winthrop arrived. A handful of individuals were scattered about the coast, men and in a few cases families who had remained after prior attempts to establish settlements. In addition to Blackstone in Boston, prior arrivals included Thomas Morton and Samuel Maverick. Maverick had built a large and fortified home complete with artillery on Noddle's Island in Boston harbor, close by the mainland. (Logan Airport now occupies the site.) One Puritan called Maverick "a man of very loving and curteous behaviour, very readye to entertain strangers, yet an enemy to Reformation, being strong for the Lordly Prelaticall power."[25] Nonetheless, Maverick had graciously hosted Winthrop when they were first exploring sites for settlement.

Both Maverick and Blackstone went their own ways and left the Puritans to their own devices, and no outright hostility developed between them and the Puritans. Nonetheless, the Puritans eventually pushed both of them out. Blackstone soon removed himself, declaring that he had left England to escape the Lord Bishops and was leaving Massachusetts to escape the Lord Brethren. It would be several years before Maverick went back to England, though he would return and have suitable revenge.

Morton, however, was a different case. A full-spirited Elizabethan and son of a gentleman soldier, Morton had a bit of Falstaff in him, hardened by a streak of defiance. He learned the law at the Inns of Court and played lawyer before seeking adventure and fortune, arriving in Massachusetts in 1624 as one of a group of about thirty men, most of them indentured servants. The group's leader soon departed for Virginia. But Morton became a fur trader and stayed.

He had offended Plymouth first, a few years earlier, by encouraging the servants in his own settlement to free themselves of their indenture. Plymouth's leaders feared this would mean they could "keep no servants . . . [because] all the scume of the countrie . . . would flock to him."[26] He offended them even more in his manner of living. He flaunted being, in his own words, "a carnal man," sleeping with Indian women and calling his small settlement "Merry Mount." In this, he mocked them, and he mocked them as well by erecting a huge Maypole, "a goodly pine tree of 80 foote longe," and dancing with his Indian women about this great, tall, stiff rod. Finally, he traded guns to Indians to increase fur production.

Plymouth deemed his way of living "licentiousness" and "a school of atheisme."[27] They claimed to "stand more in fear of their lives and goods from this wicked and deboste crue, then from the Salvages themselves."[28] They were also offended because he cost them money. His Maypole served as "a faire sea marke" to attract coastal traders, and he routinely bested Plymouth traders in competition for furs, Plymouth's only export. Although he lived outside Plymouth's territory—where it had no jurisdiction—the colony arrested him and sent him back to England.

In England the law had set him free. He had promptly returned and resurrected Merrymount. Endicott had then moved against him, and he had moved with force, without any legal justification—even a Puritan account concedes the charges were "trumped up."[29] King James had expressly approved of Maypoles. Endicott had torn Morton's down anyway, then imprisoned him to await this General Court.

The Bay colony had the power to deal with Morton as it chose. It chose rough treatment. The court ordered him "sett into the bilbowes" and extirpated all sign of his existence by burning Merrymount "downe to the ground in the sight of the Indians."[30] It also sent Morton "prisoner into England" a second time. And he was sent penniless, his goods having been seized to pay for his transportation, his debts, "& to give satisfaccon to the Indians for a cannoe he unjustly took away from them."[31]

Back in England the law freed him again. And Morton would seek later vengeance on Massachusetts.

The punishment of Morton was symptomatic of a Calvinist order Winthrop and the other magistrates imposed. They quickly built a jail. They forbade dice and card playing. They forbade smoking in public. They fined a man who drank too much and ordered him to wear on his back a sign with "'drunkard' . . . written in great letters."[32]

But what most offended the magistrates was any affront to their authority. They took special umbrage at those who sent criticism to England or threatened to challenge the plantation's authority in an English court. Typically, Henry Lynn was "whipped & banyshed, for writeing Lettres into England, full of slander against our government, & orders of our churches."[33]

Banishment was an extreme measure; anyone who returned after banishment risked severe punishment, including hanging, at the discretion of the court.

Nor was Lynn alone in receiving harsh treatment. Of particular note was the case of Philip Ratcliffe. Massachusetts authorities described him as a servant who uttered, according to Winthrop, "most foul, scandalous invectives against our church and government." A source unsympathetic to Puritans, however, said he was not a servant but an agent of Matthew Craddock, the former governor of the Bay Company and still its leader in London, and that he uttered those invectives only after a debtor broke a promise to repay him and instead warned him to pray for his soul. The magistrates did nothing to the debtor. But Ratcliffe "was censured to be whipped, lose his ears, & be banisshed the plantation, which was presently executed."[34]

Massachusetts was asserting itself truly, marking out the boundaries of the city Puritans envisioned. They would have it, at any cost. Winthrop wrote his wife, "It is enough that we shall haue heauen, though we should passe through hell to it. We heere enjoye God and Jesus Christ, is not this enough?"[35]

## ✤ CHAPTER 11 ✤

God's people in Massachusetts had found their home. Roger Williams was
now seeking one.

He did not lack for ambition, and his life with Coke had exposed him to
position and wealth. If attaining these things was not his chief goal, he did not
despise them, and he continued to enjoy them as chaplain to his friend
Masham, and as invited intimate of Masham's in-laws the Barrington family.

Williams was certainly a winning young man. His enthusiastic and warm
nature, insightful intelligence, boldness and youth combined to give him a
certain charm—the charm of great promise. Also charming was the fact that,
despite all that he had observed at Coke's side, despite the reek of corruption
and hunger of ambition which he had observed, still he saw the best in and
expected the best from others. These traits could win him friends and advancement. Less charming and even troublesome could be his honesty, the fact that
he did not calculate the effect of his words, and his willingness to follow a
thought logically to its end no matter the dangers it exposed him to. In short,
he remained innocent, in some ways naïve. Indeed, his innocence approached
arrogance. Innocence and arrogance are of course close cousins; each presumes
upon others, and only a thin line divides them. The innocent expose themselves
to the world, expecting no harm to come to them; the arrogant expect the
world to make way for them. Whether it was innocence or arrogance, or ambition, or simply that he was in love, Williams soon made a request which ended
in humiliation, a humiliation which seemed to mark him permanently.

Masham's mother-in-law Lady Joan Barrington was a serious woman who
at seventy years of age was more strong-willed and imperious than ever. Possibly the wealthiest woman in the county and very likely the most political,
she counted among her close friends the earls of Lincoln, Bedford, and Warwick, all of them prominent Puritans. Warwick, a man singularly involved with

colonial affairs, wrote her that in judging a clergyman he would "sooner your recommendation than all the bishops in this kingdome."[1]

Her opinion and those of the bishops were likely to be very different. She and Masham supported in one way or another at least seventeen clergymen under pressure from Laud, providing them livings, giving stipends, and allowing some to reside indefinitely as guests. Numerous ministers dedicated books to her, and many leading Puritan theologians visited her.

She and all her family had never ceased their involvement in politics, and her home continued to be frequented by the leaders—including her nephew Oliver Cromwell—of what would become a revolution. This would have made the post of chaplain at her son-in-law's nearby estate a heady place for any young minister, even one who had seen great events from Coke's side.

In this time of tumult Williams had also seen great events at the side of her sons and son-in-law; with them he had been trusted, a colleague, not a servant. It was his time now, time for full adulthood, time to become a principal.

In April 1629, following the dissolution of Parliament, he wrote Lady Barrington an overreaching letter, a letter which would leave him scarred. In it he informed her of his desire to marry her niece Jane Whalley, adding, "I acknowledge myselfe altogeather unworthy and unmeete for such a proposition."

She agreed that he was unworthy for such a proposition. Her opposition meant that the match became instantly impossible.

Williams was not only rebuffed but humiliated. He had considered himself equal to her son and son-in-law. Her rebuff meant that he had no such rank. He responded by informing her that he and Jane "hope to live together in the heavens, though the Lord have denied that Union on Earth." Then he struck back. Williams would likely have known that Lady Barrington had particular and frequent terrors and depression over the question of her salvation. He struck at her weak point. He further informed her that out of his deep concern for her soul he was required to remind her how close she was to her "everlasting home. . . . [Y]our candle is twinckling and glasse neere run. The Lord only knows how few minutes are left behind." He therefore was compelled to urge her to repent, for, "(Madame), the Lord hath a quarrel against you."[2]

Ministers often reminded even their patrons of the proximity of the infinite future, but not in the tone in which Williams wrote. She wanted no guidance from him. Her fury in response chilled him. Both her daughter Elizabeth and Masham were extremely close to Williams and urged her to forgive him. She did not. Not long after, Williams became seriously ill—he was expected to die—and Masham told his mother-in-law he was as a dying man pleading for her understanding. Only then did the breach heal even superficially.

Whether Williams's attempt to marry above his station reflected love or ambition, the rebuff left a mark. For the rest of his life he never again did anything that seemed aimed at preferment or self-advancement. For the rest of his life he seemed almost consciously to reject any such move, or indeed any move that might advance him in a worldly way. Although he would ever remain full aware of rank, it seemed almost as if he felt wordly advancement would compromise him, even shame him. Indeed, he would make few compromises of any kind again.

The first indication of his increased intransigence came two months later, when he argued with Hooker and Cotton over the use of the Book of Common Prayer on the way to the Sempringham conference. Meanwhile, both his and Jane Whalley's broken hearts mended well and quickly. Within weeks, Jane was married to William Hooke, another young minister but one who was the son of a gentleman. (A few years later they removed first to Taunton, Massachusetts, then became early settlers of New Haven; they subsequently returned to England and Hooke became chaplain to the family of Jane's cousin, Oliver Cromwell.) That Hooke was acceptable but he was not must have galled Williams.

Williams himself moved on as well. Mary Bernard, who had likely nursed him during his illness, lived in the Masham household as "maid," a position that more closely resembled companion than servant, to Lady Masham's daughter. Williams approached Masham, who felt responsible for properly situating Mary, about wedding her, and Masham wrote Lady Barrington for approval: "Fit matches in these partes are rare. We had best take the first that come (having your approval) fearing the longer she staies the harder itt will be to bestow her."[3] This time she approved, for the couple was marked out as decisively below the Masham family.

They married seven months after Williams wrote his letter to Lady Barrington. The bride seems to have been the daughter of the Reverend Richard Bernard, a prominent Puritan author of more than thirty books. His first was a translation of the Roman playwright Terence which went through at least six printings. (Terence wrote such lines as, "Where there is life, there is hope," and "I am a man. Nothing human is foreign to me.") Some historians believe

Bernard's *The Isle of Man*, published in 1627 and regularly reprinted over the next century, gave John Bunyan the idea for *Pilgrim's Progress*. Bernard was disciplined for such nonconformity as refusing to make the sign of the cross, but he was in essence a "conformable Puritan," compromising with his bishops to retain his position. Williams called him "upright in the mayne, but of very great weaknesses."[4]

No extant letters suggest Williams felt passion for his bride anything like that which he had expressed for Jane. But, in his late twenties, with his moment of passion passed and few eligible women available, Williams filled the only proper position for a man. He became the head of a household.

Duty can be a passion, but usually it is a joyless one. A duty performed out of love can, however, bring joy. If Williams did not show any particular love for his wife, at least not initially—they seemed to grow together over the years. And he loved God. He loved God with a boundless joy. To the extent that he believed performing his duty brought him closer to God, he would find joy in his duty. Now, with his wife, it was time to make his own mark wherever that might take him.

In the weeks and months before the departure of Winthrop's fleet, pressure from Laud on Puritans continued to intensify. Laud was determined to rid the English church of what he called "unworthy ministers which pester the church."[5]

Earlier Williams had committed himself to remain in England so long as any liberty afforded. His chaplaincy had offered a shield; the private world of the Masham estate of Otes hid from view his defiance of the orders to wear the surplice, to make the sign of the cross, to use Common Prayer, to limit his preaching, and in general to yield to authority.

But that shield was disintegrating. Laud knew well that many Puritans had found shelter as private chaplains, and he now had King Charles demand the names of all chaplains. Laud clearly intended to investigate them and purge nonconformists. He warned each diocese, "I pray you . . . not to fail" in producing the names, "for if you should . . . I must discharge myself upon you."[6]

Williams could not survive an investigation. Far more moderate clergy than he were being disciplined; he had an example even at Otes. A guest of Masham then was the Reverend Arthur Hildersham, a man so moderate and respectful of authority that King James had once allowed him an audience in which to present reformers' views. Yet Laud's High Commission sent him twice to prison and fined him thousands of pounds. Hildersham considered the present the darkest time. While at Otes he wrote, "Now is the tyme come wherein . . . all of my judgment"—i.e., all those who shared his beliefs—"are cast out as men utterly unprofitable and unfit to God."[7] A few weeks after writing those words, despite his great age and unthreatening behavior, Hildersham was again disciplined by Laud, suspended from the small living he had managed to attain, with the threat of still worse hanging over him.

As Hildersham was being disciplined anew, John Pym and Oliver St. John, two leaders of Parliament who had tried to limit royal power, were visiting Masham and the Barringtons. They brought the latest political news from London. The news was not good.

The king had well started upon his Personal Rule, and he was with vigor collecting the taxes which Parliament had decreed were illegal for him to collect. He also fully supported Laud's efforts to force conformity upon the church. To that end, Laud had just removed Nathan Beard, a Puritan minister supported by the Barringtons, from his post, with more severe discipline to come. A correspondent writing about this to Lady Barrington, concerned that spies were everywhere, noted, "I know not which way to send a letter saife."[8]

Late in 1630 Laud readied new orders requiring use of the Book of Common Prayer and personally interrogated several Puritan clergy, including Thomas Shepherd. Shepherd reported that Laud referred to Puritans as a "malignant faction" and charged that they tried to deceive him more than "ever was man by Jesuit. At the speaking of which words he looked as though blood would have gushed out of his face, and did shake as if he had been haunted of an ague fit . . . by reason of the extreme malice and secret venom. . . . He fell then to threaten me, and withal to bitter railing, calling me all to naught, saying, 'You prating coxcomb, do you think all the learning is in your brain?' "[9]

Laud soon turned his attention to John Rogers of Dedham. Rogers had a magic name; when Queen Mary had made England Catholic again, his namesake was the first Protestant minister burned at the stake for adhering to his faith. In addition, Rogers's relative Richard Rogers had helped define Puritan theology and wrote that "to be hated of the world, to be reviled, persecuted, slandered . . . is a sign that we are blessed."[10] Laud blessed John Rogers, starting with removing him from his ministry.

Thomas Hooker was a close friend of Rogers and, on a temporary basis, took his place in the Dedham pulpit. An earlier warning that to move against Hooker was to hold a wolf by the ears had kept Laud from disciplining him. But now Laud's control over all the clergy was tightening into a stranglehold, and Laud's underlings urged "the oppressing and rooting out . . . of such a one from amongst us."[11]

Hooker was promptly removed as minister. He opened a grammar school, intending to remain quiet and in shadow. But the High Commission was now searching the shadows, and it ordered him to appear. He put up a bond to guarantee his appearance. Then he preached a farewell sermon which compared the fate of ancient Israel to England's: "And who would have thought that Jerusalem would be made a heap of stones, and [Jews] a vagabond people? And yet we see God hath forsaken them. . . . The Lord is said to dis-church or dis-charge a people, Hos. 1:9. There God saith, '. . . ye are not my people, and therefore I will not be your God.'. . . As if God should now say to England, 'Plead, plead with England, all ye that are my ministers in the way of my truth, and say unto her, let her cast away her rebellions, lest I leave her as I found her in the day of captivity and bondage under the blindness of popery and super-stition.'[12]

"When men will not be bettered by God's corrections, he will break them in pieces,"[13] he warned. "The famine hath been threatened, the plague inflicted, and the sword is coming."[14]

Then, a step ahead of the pursuivants and fearing prison, Hooker absconded from his bond and fled for Holland.

Roger Williams knew any inquiry into his beliefs would doom him. Many who took far less extreme positions than he—Hooker among them—had already faced the High Commission. Some had only lost their livings, but others had gone to prison after enduring heinous physical mutilation.

An English prison in the 1600s was a place where not even the rats ate well. The dampness penetrated the soul, and the mind grew moldy. Few emerged from prison with their health intact; many died there. Prison even for the likes of Sir Francis Barrington—who had been given relatively roomy accommodations and his own food—was severe enough that he did not long survive his release. For Williams life in prison might have been especially harsh; not only was he unknown, young, and defiant, but his association with Coke would have marked him as an enemy not only of the hierarchy but of the king as well.

In late November Williams seems to have received a warning that Laud and the High Commission were about to turn their attentions to him. Hooker had fled to Holland. So had many others. Williams already knew Dutch; he had learned it as a boy from the Dutch enclave nearby. Possibly he mastered that language to please his father—the knowledge might have been useful to his trade—or possibly it reflected simple intellectual curiosity about people different from himself and a facility with languages.

But Holland was threatened by the advance of Catholic armies, and Williams might have already understood what Hooker was learning, what those who voyaged on the *Mayflower* had learned: that Holland was no home for an Englishman. William Bradford, by now governor of Plymouth, had written before leaving for America that some of his colleagues had preferred prisons in England to liberty in Holland.

Thus Holland held no attraction for Williams. But America did. Whether he had read Winthrop's sermon or not, he knew the plans, indeed the determined and convicted intent, to make of Massachusetts a city upon a hill. Free of Europe's afflictions, it was to be Rehoboth, a place of respite and peace and God's glory.

With his wife, part of his library, and little else, he made his way to the port of Bristol. He fled without happiness. Decades later he wrote that "when Bp Laud pursued me out of this Land," leaving England still "was bitter as Death to me." It was also "bitter as Death to me when I rode Windsor way to take ship at Bristow, and saw Stoke-Howse"—Edward Coke's home a few miles north of the town—"where that blessed man was."[15]

Coke had done everything for him, opening to him all the world, had been father to him. He loved Coke, and he believed Coke loved him. Yet Williams knew Coke's sense of duty, knew that he was a fugitive in flight from lawful authority, knew that Coke was wedded to the High Church, knew that the High Commission did have authority over him since he was a minister. Decades later Williams wrote, sorrow still stinging his words, "I durst not acquaint him with my Conscience and my Flight."[16]

And so Williams passed by Coke's home without attempting to say goodbye. Of America's afflictions, of the deaths in the Massachusetts Bay colony, he certainly knew: even with the delay of weeks to cross the ocean, word of the colony's travail had already spread throughout the Puritan community in England. The very ship and captain with whom he sought passage to America had been sent by a desperate Winthrop to bring back emergency supplies. It also carried Winthrop's wife and young child, and Winthrop's son John Winthrop Jr. was handling final arrangements of the voyage.

Winthrop's son and Williams were the same age and had much in common, including their deep interest in Bacon's scientific method. While in Bristol waiting for the ship to sail, the two became fast friends. They would see each other again, in America. Williams also had the whole voyage to become close to his new friend's mother, Winthrop's wife, which helped secure his relationship with Governor Winthrop as well.

On December 1, 1630, Roger Williams and his wife, Mary, boarded the *Lyon* to face the North Atlantic in dead winter, bound for the New World.

Part III

# THE NEW WORLD

## ✠ CHAPTER 12 ✠

The North Atlantic storms most violently in winter, so few ship captains and fewer travelers chose to spend those months upon it. The storms then were themselves more dangerous, and ice made sailors' lives treacherous. But Peirce, master of the *Lyon*, had no choice; he knew the desperation of the Bay colony and he had promised Winthrop to return with supplies. Williams too had no choice but to cross in winter what he later called "the terrible Atlanticke ocean."

The sea did not disappoint. Williams and the handful of other passengers— not the hundreds who packed the ships in Winthrop's fleet—endured a "verye tempestuily"[1] voyage to America. Human and animal smells made life below rank, with little respite, but to go above decks risked one's life. Mountains of waves broke over the ship, tossing and shaking it. Great winds coming out of the northeast buffeted it, ice coated the deck itself, icicles hung from the rigging—ice could hang so heavy on the rigging that it could capsize a ship— and the wind drove needles of frozen spray into exposed skin. A man on a similar voyage described day after day of "a sore and terrible storm, for wind blew mightily, . . . the sea roared and the waves tossed us horribly . . . with no little terror . . . to our mariners." If the mariners feared, those who had never been at sea before trembled with horror as from their quarters they heard sailors "running here and there, loud crying one to another. . . . The waves poured themselves over the ship. . . . There came a fearful gust of wind."[2]

Yet on the *Lyon*, God was merciful: only a single death occurred, when waves washed a youth overboard in one of the storms. Those on deck, helpless to lower a boat, watched him straining to stay afloat, rising and falling on huge swells for a quarter of an hour before the sea swallowed him. Finally, on February 5, 1631, the ship anchored safe amid great and dangerous ice floes in Boston harbor.

The voyage was a fitting portent for Williams; his time in Massachusetts would prove tempestuous, icy, and dangerous. Ultimately, he would find himself cast adrift in winter and swallowed by wilderness.

Initially, however, he enjoyed the warmest of receptions. John Winthrop's first mention in his journal of the ship's arrival noted, as if giving thanks, that this "godly minister" had come. Winthrop mentioned Williams even before recording either the arrival of his own wife and infant child or the tons of relief supplies the ship brought, supplies which would keep the Bay colony—or simply "the Bay," as the planters there now called it—alive.

For the situation in the plantation was desperate. Public stores of food had run out, and some colonists were living like the Indians without having learned their skills, trying to dig clams out of tidal flats and find nuts and acorns on the ground "with much difficulty in winter time."[3]

Winthrop had lived up to his sermon by giving away his personal stores of food, handing the last of it out the same day—but before—the ship was sighted. Even so, it was not enough. He reported, "The poorer sorte of people (who laye longe in tentes &c.:) were much afflicted with the Sckirvye, & manye dyed."[4]

Deaths from scurvy were one thing, at least, that the *Lyon*'s arrival could stop. Sailors already knew citrus juice cured scurvy, so Peirce carried a large store of lemon juice. He distributed it. (Another century passed before James Lind, in a classic scientific experiment, proved citrus juice was a cure and preventive, although fifty more years passed before the British admiralty accepted the proof.)

For this and for the relief from the threat of outright starvation which the other supplies provided, Governor Winthrop and the other magistrates called for a day of prayer and thanksgiving. The celebration, while deeply felt, was nonetheless muted. Winter, and hardships, continued. Those who had built homes lit great fires for warmth, but in several buildings these fires proved too great—the flames escaped the hearth and burned down the home. Wolves howled outside settlements each night and feasted on cattle; the government offered a bounty for their heads.

By the time winter ended, roughly 40 percent of those who had accompanied Winthrop had either died or returned to England. In a letter written March 28, deputy governor Thomas Dudley warned friends in England that "we yet enjoy little to be envied but endure much to be pitied. . . . [I]f any come hither that can live well at home, he commits an error, of which he will soon repent him."[5]

Such opinions had already been carried back to England by other letters and by the colonists who had fled Massachusetts. In 1630, over one thousand emigrants left England for New England, all of them hopeful. In 1631, fewer than one hundred did, all of them desperate. For only those desperate to escape England would take the risk. The rest of England's Puritans were waiting to see if Massachusetts could survive.

Yet the Bay *was* surviving. Energy poured into clearing fields, cutting roads, and constructing buildings in 1630 began to pay off. In 1631, unlike the year before, crops were planted early enough to produce a harvest; other industries— fishing, fur trading, lumber, and shipbuilding (the straight tall trees of the New England forest made magnificent masts)—were taking seed as well and offering fine prospect. America did that spring seem filled with promise. The very sky itself was full. Indeed, of all the sights of New England, the most remarkable indicator of America's seemingly infinite vastness and bounty was in the sky: great flocks of birds—birds in the "millions and millions," birds whose flights have "neither beginning nor ending"[6]—flew over "all the towns in our plantations so many . . . , that they obscured the light."[7] (These were almost certainly passenger pigeons which, though now extinct, once quite literally did fill the sky; they were so plentiful that, rather than shoot them, the English strung nets between trees to catch them as if they were fish.) Such an infinity of life could not be found anywhere in Europe, not even in myth; here it was real.

And, most importantly, the colonists had made no compromises in their pursuit of what they perceived as God's purpose.

This was the world which Williams entered, a world of hardship but hardship limned with promise. No inns had yet been built, so leading citizens of Boston or Charlestown entertained him and his wife. He was a most desirable guest. After all, two years earlier the Bay Company had tried to entice him to New England with the offer of a ministry, and even William Hubbard, one of his later and most severe critics, conceded his reputation had preceded him and he was "of good account in England, for a godly and zealous preacher."[8] In addition, he carried news of England. Once the Massachusetts plantation began thriving ships arrived and departed often, sometimes several a week, but the *Lyon* was the first ship in months and the colony was nearly as hungry for news as it was for supplies. That and Williams's intimate knowledge of the situation in both the Puritan and the pro-Parliament communities made his reception much like that of another minister who arrived a year later and found himself "so importuned" with offers of lodging "that it was a trouble to know what friend to gratify."[9]

Still, Williams was neither willing nor able to remain a guest indefinitely, and, arriving with only his wife, his academic training, and a library of cherished books, he had no money, no resources, no post, and no practical skill. (He was hardly the only one who brought a library; Winthrop's numbered one thousand volumes.)

Luck, however, seemed to smile on him. John Wilson was minister at the Boston church, but he was returning to England to fetch his family. Although he promised to come back, he would be absent many months at least. The leaders of the Boston church decided, unanimously, to offer Williams the position of "teacher" in their church, essentially its theologian. The church could make room for both Williams and Wilson, who upon his return—if he returned—could pastor the congregation.

For Williams, a man no older than twenty-eight and possibly younger, this was an extraordinary opportunity. Indeed, it was an opportunity of a lifetime. It meant far more than simply ministering to a congregation. He was being invited to occupy one of the most important positions in English America, a position which would give him influence over and make him a partner in defining and creating an entire society, an entirely new order in this new world.

Yet Williams did not leap at the offer. Instead, he met with church leaders to discuss their precise church practices. He did not like what they told him. He had hidden himself at Cambridge, he had hidden as the Mashams' chaplain, and he had fled to America. Now, three thousand miles and an ocean distant from Laud, he would not hide himself any longer.

He declined their offer, explaining, "I durst not officiate to an unseparated people."[10]

His response offended as much as astounded. The most powerful men in the plantation had unanimously invited him to join them, to become one of them. He had not only rejected their offer and them, had not only rebuffed them; he had found error in them and in their ways.

They would not forget his answer, and it colored his relations with most of those in authority in Massachusetts for the rest of his life.

Winthrop himself responded by writing a tract titled *Reasons to proue a necessitye of reformation from the Corruptions of Antechrist which hath defiled Christian Churches, and yet without absolute separation from them, as if they were no Churches of Christ.*[11] In it, he agreed with Williams that the Church of England had become defiled. But he did not agree with Williams's conclusion. Separation smacked too much of rebellion.

Soon Williams went even further in his critique. He suggested something radical enough to make the foundation of this new society quiver and shake.

Obedience to God was the very foundation of Winthrop's city on a hill. That obedience meant conforming to God's laws, and those laws began with the Ten Commandments. The government intended to enforce these commandments.

Williams attacked this intent. He stated that magistrates had no authority to enforce "the First Table." By this he meant the first four of the Ten Commandments (as numbered by Calvinists and the Church of England; other denominations number the commandments differently). The First Table regulated human duty to God: to have no God before Him, to make no graven images, to not take the Lord's name in vain, and to keep the sabbath holy.

All in Massachusetts, Williams included, considered duties to God infinitely more important than duties to man. Still, Williams was asserting that these most important duties lay outside the sphere of government. The state, he said, had no authority to inject itself in any way into an individual's relationship with God. It must enforce only the commandments in the "Second Table": those which govern human relations, such as the injunctions forbidding murder, theft, lying, adultery, and covetousness.

This was far more than an attack on the jurisdiction of the government of Massachusetts. It had equal implications for England. English magistrates enforced laws derived from the First Table. English magistrates fined those who failed to attend church, disciplined blasphemers, sent heretics to prison, cut off their ears, bored their tongues, and sometimes imposed the ultimate sanction. Governments in virtually all of Europe did the same.

Williams's position did not come from any sympathy for Separatists. Most

Separatists believed the government should enforce the First Table and blamed government's failure to do so for corruption in the church. Henry Barrowe, an early Separatist leader—until the High Commission had him executed in 1593—wrote, "Yet now if I be asked who ought to abolish this idolatry . . . and to depose these antichristian priests: to that I answer, the prince, or state. . . . Only the magistrate may pull down the public monuments of idolatry."[12]

Williams's surviving writings do not make clear how he arrived at his position. It may have derived at least partly from Coke's efforts to restrict the High Commission and protect individuals from the state. It may have derived from similar views expressed twenty years earlier by the first English Baptists. They had worshipped secretly near Williams's home—and many had been sent to Newgate prison, a few hundred yards away from his home, where at least one of them, Thomas Helwys, died. Another of these prisoners wrote a treatise arguing for religious toleration; it was smuggled out of prison and sent to King James. Later Williams quoted this treatise; he may have already known of it.

But it was in the self-interest of Baptists to advocate this position; were the state to adopt it, it would protect them from persecution. Advocating it was not in Williams's self-interest; in Massachusetts, since such a position ran so contrary to the views held by Winthrop and others in power, advocating it made him vulnerable and exposed him to attack.

Whatever the source of Williams's views, this very first criticism of the Bay authorities expressed the essence of his later thought. That thought would eventually develop into a systematic and comprehensive formulation of religious and political freedom, of the appropriate exercise of power by the state and by the church, and of an individual's rights and the limits on those rights.

This first criticism would cost him for the rest of his life. And it began to cost him immediately.

Boston and Salem sat less than twenty miles apart, but the distance between them seemed much greater. Travel between them often required a voyage by boat; overland travel was arduous and even, depending on the weather, dangerous. In addition, Boston was the wealthiest community in the plantation and Salem, despite being the oldest community, was probably the poorest. Winthrop's replacement of Endicott as governor symbolized the diminution of Salem and the shift of economic and political power to Boston. Indeed, Salem seemed somewhat of a backwater even in Massachusetts. Few travelers with the Winthrop fleet settled there, preferring to carve out a home from utter and raw wilderness than to build there. In sum, the rest of the colony seemed to share in Dudley's sardonic dismissal that Salem "pleased us not."

Not surprisingly then, Salem nursed a lingering resentment toward and desire for independence from Boston. Its church members also felt that they more closely approached worship according to Scripture than did other churches in the Bay. They believed that this brought them closest to Christ, and they yearned for this intimacy as passionately as any human yearned for anything. They had demonstrated their strict adherence to their worship in preventing even those arriving on the Winthrop fleet from participating in the Lord's Supper unless they already belonged to a covenanted church. And Endicott had a connection to Coke; details of that connection have not survived, but they were enough that Endicott had been present when Coke finalized the arrangements for the marriage of his daughter to Buckingham's brother—the marriage which returned Coke to the Privy Council.[13] Lastly, the recent death of the Reverend Francis Higginson had opened a position there.

All this made the town perfect for Williams. Immediately after rejecting the Boston offer, he went to Salem, and Salem embraced him. His natural charm, the sweetness of his spirit, his biblical scholarship, the logic with which he offered exegesis and explanation and the intensity of his conviction won him admirers. He was quickly at home.

On April 1, John Wilson sailed for England on the *Lyon,* which had remained in American waters carrying cargo up and down the New England coast. His departure left the Boston church without a minister; to fill the gap, Winthrop and Dudley would "prophesy," i.e., give lay sermons, a common practice in Puritan churches, although normally prophesying only augmented worship led by clergy.

On about that date, the Salem church offered Williams the vacant post of teacher to its church. He accepted with alacrity, giving Salem both a prideful moment and further offense to the Boston church.

Those in Boston had other ideas. On April 12, a Court of Assistants—the governor and his fellow magistrates—convened in Boston. Many of these magistrates, including of course Winthrop and Dudley, belonged to the Boston church. Endicott, the only magistrate from Salem, did not attend. In his absence the court debated what to do about Williams, then wrote Endicott that they "marveled" that the Salem church "would chuse [Williams], without advising with" them. They suggested to Endicott that Salem "forbeare to proceede until they had conferred about it."[14]

The court was not formally prohibiting the Salem church from engaging Williams as teacher. It was simply warning them against it. It was not ordering Endicott to do anything. It was only "desiringe" that he intervene.

The court also informed Endicott that he himself was about to go on trial. He had gotten into a dispute with a man named Thomas Dexter over money, and the two had run into each other on a Salem street. Endicott explained to a correspondent, "If you had seen the manner of his carriadge, with such daring of me with his armes on kemboe &c. It would have provoked a very patient man."[15] Endicott was not a patient man, much less a very patient one. So he had beaten Dexter to the ground with his fists, although he now conceded, "I was too rash in strikeing him, understanding since that it is not lawful for a justice of the peace to strike."[16]

The court could view his assault as a very serious crime, or as a minor altercation. Punishment could range from jail, to stripping him of his position as a magistrate, to an insignificant fine. Endicott was thus in the power of the court. He was also the most powerful man in Salem, and he had great influence over the church there.

Endicott paid a small fine for the assault, and, for the moment, the Salem church withdrew its offer to Williams.

Sometime between late May and the middle of August 1631, Roger Williams and his wife Mary departed the Bay for what was then the entirely separate colony of Plymouth Plantation.

# ❧ CHAPTER 13 ❧

Plymouth had a ready supply of sweet freshwater, accessible food—clams in broad and sweeping mud flats, fish in the harbor and streams—and a great hill rising from the harbor that commanded the area and was easily defensible. Those advantages had lured the *Mayflower*'s passengers into settling there. But those advantages were a trap.

The harbor was neither deep enough nor roomy enough to support commerce, no great rivers could carry a trader into the interior, and the site lay a considerable distance from sources of fur. In addition, although the soil could and did produce crops, it was generally poor even by New England standards. This trap meant that Plymouth could and did survive and even grow, becoming solidly established in the decade since its founding. But it could not thrive.

Williams cared less about thriving, however, than living. In his late twenties, he had spent his life so far under patrons: first Coke, then schoolmasters, then Masham. Soon after his arrival in Plymouth, his first child, a daughter, was born. It was time to make a home. It was time to make his own way. Now, rather than attempt to support himself as a minister, he made a home by digging in, rooting himself; he became a farmer, digging in the soil, husbanding cattle, raising squash and Indian corn. He was finally fully independent, free of any responsibilities to anyone except himself, his wife, and his God. His energy went into fulfilling those responsibilities and into weaving himself into the fabric of all that went on about him in Plymouth.

He was welcomed. He was a social and sociable creature. Two governors, Edward Winslow and William Bradford, praised and befriended him. Bradford called him "a man godly and zealous, having many precious parts."[1] Winslow described him as "a man lovely in his carriage," spoke of "the love I beare to him and his,"[2] and even called him "the sweetest soul I ever knew."[3]

He became active in the church. Every Sunday and sometimes during the week he would prophesy, and on Sundays he and pastor Ralph Smith would propound questions and then explore them in conversive debate. The church never offered him a formal or paid position—possibly because Plymouth authorities did not want to offend their Massachusetts counterparts—but he became an unpaid assistant pastor. Even years later, after he had fallen far from favor, Bradford recalled that "his teaching was well approved, for the benefite of which I still blese God, and am thankfull to him, even for his sharpest admonitions and reproufs, so farr as they agreed with truth."[4]

One sign of how well things were going for him was his continued relationship with Winthrop. A little over a year after Williams arrived in Plymouth, Winthrop and Wilson, who had recently returned from England, visited there, traveling partly by boat and partly on foot; while there, they attended one Sunday service which included prophesying by Williams. Winthrop made note of it in his journal, but there is no indication of any concern about Williams's remarks. Although only one letter between them from this period survives, it is thick with evidence of a broad and deep connection between them: it has an intimate tone and refers to business dealings—Winthrop and Williams sometimes represented each other in business—politics and policy in the Bay, and church developments in both Boston and Plymouth. Williams was clearly the inferior in the relationship, clearly sought to please Winthrop, yet he did not hold back his opinions. Massachusetts had recently been roiled by the question of whether a person could be both a church officer and a magistrate and decided one could not. Williams approved: "You lately sent Musick to our Eares, when we heard, you perswaded (and that effectually and successfully) our beloved Mr. Nowell to Surrender up one sword."[5]

In that same letter, Williams also referred to one aspect of his activities which would have repercussions more far-reaching than he could have imagined. He wrote, "I am no Elder in any church . . . , nor ever shall be if the Lord please to graunt my desires, that I may intend what I long after, the natives Soules."[6]

Winthrop had already very consciously spoken words which would launch one tradition in American thought, a tradition of Christian people charged not only with redeeming themselves but with inspiring the world. Williams's involvement with Indians would, like his earlier position on enforcing the First Table of the Ten Commandments, contribute to the beginnings of an entirely different tradition of American thought, a tradition of individualism, law, rights, and freedoms.

————

Converting Indians had always been one of the main—arguably *the* main—justifications for every effort to plant in America. Even the Virginia Company had claimed that "the *Principal* and *Maine Endes* . . . were *first* to preach and baptize [Indians] into *Christian Religion*,"[7] later stating that "all Europe are looking upon our endevors to spread the Gospell among the Heathen people of Virginia."[8]

But in twenty-five years Virginia had done little to evangelize Indians. The Massachusetts Bay provided the same justification for settlement, but with greater conviction. Conversion of the Indians mattered particularly to Puritans for the perceived good of the Indians, to prevent the Catholic Church from gaining millions more adherents—both the Spanish and French sent priests to the Americas whose task was to convert Indians en masse—and because they believed that spreading the Gospel was a necessary prerequisite to Christ's return. Many Puritans also believed the Indians were the Lost Tribes of Israel. Yet after three years of Bay Company involvement in New England, despite the Puritans' absorption in the Lord, nothing had been done to convert a single Indian.

Williams took it upon himself to act. Independent of any church or outside charge, he began traveling among several tribes and even entertaining them in his own home. Partly to enable him to evangelize, partly out of natural curiosity, he also had a "Constant Zealous desire to dive into the Natives language, . . . to gain their Toung."[9]

He believed that one could not become a Christian without a full understanding of what Christianity meant, and he refrained from any efforts to convert Indians until his fluency in their language was adequate to explain Christ's message. In the meantime, he developed relationships with many Indians, relationships which led to friendships and trade. His trading soon carried him throughout southern New England, up into Cape Cod, south into Narragansett Bay.

He brought Indians English axes, knives, mirrors, spades, clothes. They gave him furs and "wampum"—strings of shells, collected on beaches and strung together, that served as money among Indian tribes and which was also becoming accepted in Plymouth and Massachusetts. The lack of any European specie, of English or French or Spanish coin, limited colonial commerce; using wampum increased the money supply and spurred growth.

And while Williams traded, while he struggled to communicate and learn

Indians' language, both necessity and curiosity drove him to observe the Indians closely, note their habits, predilections, mores, culture. His journeys through the woods thus led him into an intellectual journey as well, a journey which brought him to an unsought and undesired destination. He had already in effect questioned the entire system of church and government in Massachusetts. Now his intellectual journey carried him irrevocably toward an equally provocative position. Logic, experience, and his understanding of common law—a legal tradition so dependent upon property rights—forced him to this place.

His position would estrange him from many of his fellow planters, but he did not shy away from it.

The concept of the "noble savage" had entered the European consciousness fifty years earlier,[10] but Williams did not romanticize Indians. Far from it. He was not a naif, could drive a hard bargain himself, spoke with disgust of staying in their "filthy smoak holes," and occasionally when angry called Indians "wolves with men's minds."

But he also stated, "Nature knows no difference between Europe and Americans in blood, birth, bodies, &c. God having of one blood made all mankind."[11]

This opinion was hardly unique. It was of course the Christian view that all souls were equal before God. But it was one thing to voice such an opinion, it was another to believe it and to act upon its truth.

To so act was unusual even in the seventeenth century, when belief in rough equality between peoples was more common than later. Distinctions then were based less on race than on religion and military power, both of which were conditional and subject to change. Even slavery did not have the connotations, especially racial connotations, it later took on. Every English subject on every ocean voyage risked capture by pirates who sold into slavery captives who were not ransomed. John Smith, the most prominent English explorer of North America, had been enslaved; his story was well known and his autobiography, which included details about his capture, slavery, and escape, was hugely popular.

In addition, English writers reminded readers that Britons themselves had once lived much as the Indians did. Thomas Harriott's *Brief and True Report* included images "of the Pictes which in the olde tyme dyd habite one parte of the great Bretainne . . . to showe how that the Inhabitants of the great Bretainne have bin in times past as sauvage as those of Virginia."[12] William Camden in his massive sixteenth-century history *Britannia* similarly said that Britons had been savages until their conversion to Christianity, after which they became a great people; he implicitly equated Indians with the English, writing that an Indian woman "painted about the eyes and balls of the cheek with a blue colour like the ancient Britons."[13] So it is not surprising that an Englishman marrying Pocahontas and bringing her to London created not scandal but celebrity.

Williams too compared Britons to Indians; speaking also of painting faces and bodies, he said, "[W]ee may remember it of some of our Fore-fathers in this Nation."[14]

But if such a comparison was common, his comprehension of the essential equality of peoples was uncommon. Similarities were not theoretical to him. They were to him tangible, measurable facts, and they derived from observations, the observations of an anthropologist. He noted, "The sociableness of the nature of man appears in the wildest of them, who love society; Families, cohabitation, and consociation of houses and towns together." "The wildest of the sons of Men have found a necessity, (for preservation of themselves, their Families and Properties) to cast themselves into some mold or form of Government." "They apprehending a vast difference of Knowledge betweene the *English* and themselves, are very observant of *English* lives. . . . [T]hey are greatly affected with a secret hope concerning *themselves*."[15]

It was knowledge or the lack thereof that made Indians different, not race. And he recognized Indian knowledge, observing that Indians farmed the forest itself. They did so by controlling fire, mastering it, and transforming it into a tool. They themselves told him of its importance, and even speculated that the need for fuel had brought the English invasion of their land: "This question they oft put to me: Why come the *English*men hither? and measuring others by themselves; they say, It is because you want *firing*, for they, after having burnt up the *wood* in one place . . . [t]hey are faine to follow the *wood;* and so to remove to a fresh place for the *wood*s sake."[16]

He made other, much more important observations regarding fire also—more important because they had legal and political ramifications. He did not turn aside from these ramifications. In the spring and in November, after cutting large trees for firewood, Indians lit controlled burns. The burns had little impact on nut-bearing trees or blueberry heaths, but they cleared fields for planting and cleared dead underbrush from forests. This clearing of underbrush eliminated competition for nutrition in the soil and for sunlight and opened the way for thick, straight, and impossibly tall pines to climb high, upwards of one hundred feet high. Oak, maple, cherry, and other trees also abounded. At the same time it encouraged the growth of live flora, which increased the deer population, and eliminated dry twigs, which helped Indians stalk prey.[17]

"The Natives," Williams observed, "hunted all the Countrey over, and for the expedition of their hunting voyages they burnt up all the underwoods in the Countrey, once or twice a year, and therefore as Noble men in England possessed great Parkes, and the King, great Forrests in England onely for their game, and no man might lawfully invade their Propriety: So might the Natives challenge the like Propriety in the Countrey here."[18]

The legal justification the English depended upon to claim land in America was that it lay unoccupied and unused. But Williams's observations and his grounding in common law, which he well knew linked the law itself to property, pushed him toward an inevitable conclusion: the Indians used the land and therefore they owned the land. In fact he stated, "The *Natives* are very exact and punctuall in the bounds of their Lands, belonging to this or that Prince or People. . . . And I have knowne them to make bargaine and sale amongst themselves for a small piece or quantity of Ground."[19]

Williams was not alone in noting this. Even Winslow, the Plymouth governor, conceded, "Everey Sachim knoweth how farre the bounds and limits of his own country extendeth; and that is his own proper inheritance. . . . In this circuit whoever hunteth, if they kill any venison, bring him his fee. . . . The great Sachims or Kings, know their own bounds of limits of land, as well as the rest."[20]

But if that was true, no English king had legal right to grant ownership over any part of America, for not even a king could grant what he did not own. In turn, no planter could claim ownership of any land unless he had purchased it from the rightful owners, the Indians.

Apparently Williams took his concerns privately to Plymouth authorities, and they asked him to write a treatise explaining them. He did so.

The act of writing makes a thought concrete, forces one to give shape and structure to inchoate ideas. And he had been trained in argument at Cambridge; students prepared "disputations" meant to make a point, not simply to offer analysis. His entire experience with Coke had taught him to do the same. His views may have been tentative before, but as he put words to paper he seems to have been tentative no longer. This treatise has not survived, but, judging from events, rather than back away from his conclusions he went further.

The consideration of royal charters and grants brought him to a second issue. James had claimed to be the first Christian king to discover these lands. That statement was patently false. Williams also objected to the description by both James and Charles of Europe as "Christendom," since all of Catholic Europe—and for that matter much of Protestant Europe—was outside what Puritans regarded as Christ's true church.

Williams was unwilling to dismiss these royal assertions as harmless grandiosity or hyperbole. He not only rejected the validity of any royal land grants but declared that King Charles had told "a solemne public lye."

Even in the Separatist community of Plymouth, these were extraordinary, explosive assertions.

His position on the legal title to land did not challenge the ownership of all land in Plymouth and elsewhere in English America; in many instances planters had reached accommodations with Indians which would have satisfied his legal objections. It was still unsettling enough. Calling the king a liar, however, was frightening, if only because of the political implications.

At least two versions of what happened in Plymouth, written long after the fact by Williams's enemies, portray him as aggressively advancing his views on the question of Indian ownership of the land, but well-documented events in the Massachusetts Bay colony suggest that on this issue his behavior was muted. He seems to have discussed the problem privately and only with those in authority.

Controversy is rarely welcome in any community; nowhere was controversy less welcome than in Puritan New England. Puritans wanted no disturbance of the social fabric. He disturbed it. Many members of the community continued to support him, but Bradford now called him "very unsettled in judgmente" and accused him of "fall[ing] into some strang opinions, and from opinion to practise; which caused some controversie betweene the church and him, and in the end some discontente on his parte."[21]

Sometime during his second year at Plymouth, he asked for dismissal from the Plymouth church—after covenanting with the church, he could not simply leave. "Though some were unwilling to, yet through the prudent counsel of Mr. Brewster (the ruling elder there) . . . the Church at Plimoth consented to his dismission, and such as did adhere to him were also dismissed, and removed with him."²²

Sometime in the summer or early fall of 1633, a little more than two years after leaving Salem, Williams returned to it. A group of supporters went with him.

Bradford considered that best; he thought the Bay far more able to handle Williams and any trouble he might cause than Plymouth. And Plymouth sent "some caution to [Massachusetts magistrates] concerning him, and what care they ought to have of him."²³

That same year of 1633, England was opening itself in some ways to new and even exotic things: one example—bananas were sold there for the first time. But in the Church of England, Laud continued his efforts to seal shut any openings; he ratcheted up pressure another notch.

Early in 1633, while Williams roiled Plymouth, the Reverend John Cotton was summoned to appear not only before the High Commission but before Laud himself. He sought help from the Earl of Dorset, who, after trying unsuccessfully to intervene, warned him, "You must fly for your safety."²⁴

Already several nonconformists—not Separatists but Puritans who considered themselves loyal to the Church of England—had died in prison, and Cotton had none of the martyr in him. Explaining that flight was not flight— it was instead "a confession of our faith" because it meant that faith was "dearer unto us, than all the enjoyments from which we fly"²⁵—he disappeared into the Puritan underground. His second wife, Sarah, was pregnant and he was, though forty-eight years old, still childless. Nonetheless, he wrote her that she could not follow him not out of concern for her pregnancy but because "if you should now travel this way, I fear you will be watched"²⁶ and he would be discovered.

In disguise and using an assumed name, he went into hiding in Surrey and in London, staying sometimes at the homes of Henry Whitfield and John Davenport, who later founded respectively Guilford and New Haven, Connecticut. But he could not survive long in England. Four possible havens were open to him: Holland, Barbados, Bermuda, and Massachusetts. Thomas Hooker helped him choose between them.

Four years and a lifetime earlier, Hooker, Cotton, and Williams had ridden together on horseback to the Sempringham meeting, which had planned the path of the Massachusetts Bay Company. Not long after that ride and despite his willingness to compromise over the Book of Common Prayer, Hooker had fled to Holland, where he had remained since. But in a letter to Cotton he now called Holland "miserable" because the Dutch Calvinists had no "heart religion, they content themselves with very forms, though much blemished."[27]

Hooker himself planned to return secretly to England to find passage to Massachusetts. Cotton decided. He also would go to the new Boston.

While Cotton was preparing to leave, Hooker did return to England, but not secretly enough. Informers led pursuivants to the Reverend Samuel Stone's home in Towcester, where Hooker and Stone sat talking. A pounding on the door froze them, but "smoking of tobacco," Stone boldly threw the door open and demanded to know what they wanted. They declared that they had come to arrest Hooker. Stone told them with "a braving sort of confidence" that he had seen Hooker not an hour earlier at another house in town. The pursuivants hurried away. So did Hooker and Stone, who now also had to flee.[28]

The High Commission set a watch at every major port of embarkation for all three men, Hooker, Cotton, and Stone. But in July 1633, they evaded the watch at Downs, a small port in Kent; disguised probably as servants—servants were nonentities in England, often ignored by port clerks who inspected outbound ships for fugitives, and prominent Puritans routinely disguised themselves as servants—they were rowed out to the *Griffin,* a three-hundred-ton ship crowded with two hundred emigrants, their freight, and their livestock. Cotton's wife and stepdaughter joined him. From Downs, the ship skirted the coast of England to its southern tip, evaded more pursuivants at the Isle of Wight, then sailed west toward the Atlantic but still in English waters. The three men remained in disguise. Not until well out into the Atlantic did they reveal themselves, but once they did they made the voyage a most godly one. Cotton preached each morning, Hooker each afternoon, Stone each evening. Halfway across the ocean, Cotton's first child, a son, was born. He named the boy Seaborn.

On September 4, 1633, the ship reached Boston. It was not only a new Boston but a new Cotton. The church promptly offered to him the post of teacher (Wilson remained pastor) which Williams had earlier rejected. Cotton accepted, and he made of his acceptance a formal and deliberate articulation of his true position. Only now, an ocean removed from Laud, did he dare do so. First he indicated that the congregation—not the bishop or the king—controlled its own church, next he joined the church, then he went through the formal process of having the congregation choose him. The church made his ordination a major event, a fast day, a celebration with laying on of hands and ministers of other churches present.

Meanwhile Hooker and Stone settled themselves at Newtown (it later changed its name to Cambridge; Hooker's home stood in the present Harvard Yard). With much less fanfare but consistent with the same theory of church governance, the Newtown church chose them as pastor and teacher.

Of all the Puritan ministers England had produced, with Cotton and Hooker the Bay was now home to two of the most respected. Cotton soon became so convinced of the rectitude of his decision to flee that he denigrated those who remained in England, writing a minister there that he had chosen "rather to remove hither than to stay there that we might enjoy the liberty not of some ordinances of God but of all, all in purity." Those in England, by contrast, were willing "to sit down somewhere else under the shadow of some ordinances when by two months travail [they] might come to the liberty of all."[29]

Now, here in Massachusetts, Cotton saw himself as neither beginning over nor continuing his old life. He saw his life as coming to fruition. He saw himself as leading the way to, as foretold in Revelation, that final, last judgment. En route to that glorious end, he would come to judge Williams.

# ❧ CHAPTER 14 ❧

By 1633, the Massachusetts Bay colony was no longer scratching for survival at the surface of the land. It had become well planted, rooting itself in many ways. Those who had crossed with Winthrop had grown crops and raised cattle, begun industries and entered commerce, cleared fields and built fences. They had built barns and homes, too, solid-framed homes, well finished and furnished. Even Salem's circumstances had improved. In short, the plantation had settled; its early troubles had dropped away like sediment settling out of a standing glass of water—still present but no longer a problem.

With that settling, with new arrivals not having to face the desperate times of their predecessors, immigration exploded. For not only had conditions in Massachusetts improved but conditions in England had deteriorated. On August 5, 1633, the long out-of-favor archbishop of Canterbury, George Abbot, died. Charles elevated Laud to that see, making him supreme in the church but for the king alone.

Puritans started fleeing England by the thousands. Of all emigrants—not just Puritans—leaving London for the Americas in 1635, less than 25 percent went to New England. But of those who left London and came originally from such English counties as Essex where Puritans were strongest, 95 percent went to New England.[1] (Many Puritans also went to Bermuda and Barbados.)

Massachusetts in fact began to boom because of those immigrants—in the 1630s the "Great Migration" poured twenty thousand into the plantation—because of the money they carried, because they bought land and necessaries. Ships visited Boston routinely; commerce became so profitable that some masters specialized in voyages there, making several round trips a year. Every ship carried a cargo that made Massachusetts more like England. Roughly one-third of immigrants were servants. A letter to John Winthrop the Younger describes this growing normalcy: "You shall also reciue in this shipp 3 wolfe doggs and a bitch with an Irish boy to tend them. . . . [H]e be bound to your father for fiue yeares; . . . very willingly he hath bin at [a Protestant] church 4 or 5 times; he . . . doth not loue to heare the Romish rel[igion] spoken against, but I hope with gods grace he will become a good convert. . . . The fellowe can reed and write reasonable well which is somwhat rare for one of his condition; and makes me hope the more of him."[2]

The wealthy imported apple and pear trees, roses and other flowers from England. Endicott became known for his apple and pear orchards; he referred to his three-hundred-acre farm—acres granted to him gratis by the colony, as it granted thousands of acres to other leaders of the plantation—simply as "Orchard." He was the original Johnny Appleseed; apple trees soon spread throughout New England.

If salt marsh remained a dominant feature of the Boston landscape and the sea still sometimes swept across the narrow neck connecting the town to the mainland, if its main street was yet a rutted dirt path, both the town and the plantation were thriving. All things seemed right in the plantation. So they seemed, for a while.

Roger Williams had no difficulty making a full life upon his return to the Bay colony. His house reflected his position; it was spacious, the home of a burgher, of a family man, of a man of some accomplishment and stature. He already had a following, both those who had come with him from Plymouth and those who had wanted him to be teacher in the Salem church. That church particularly welcomed him back, and in effect now gave him—unofficially—that same post it had earlier offered and which had not been filled.

Therefore in November 1633 Samuel Skelton, the pastor, brought him along to a regular meeting of all the Bay's clergy; the meetings were held "once a fortnight," with ministers rotating as hosts, and at them "some question of moment was debated."[3] But this evening Skelton and Williams objected to the very fact that such meetings occurred. Sensitive to precedent and jealous of freedom, they feared they "might growe in tyme to a Presbiterye or Superintendancye, to the preiudice of the Churches Libertyes."[4]

Winthrop insisted in reply that "thise feare was without Cause, for [those present] were all cleere in that pointe that no Churche or person can have power over another Churche."⁵

Winthrop was conveniently ignoring what Skelton and Williams could not forget: Bay magistrates had already imposed their will on the Salem church when they opposed its hiring Williams. The fact that magistrates and not clergy had intervened only made that intervention more serious; as in England, the state had exercised power over the church.

Given that Skelton had been attending the regular meetings without complaint until Williams arrived, given the warning from the Plymouth authorities about him, Winthrop was now concerned about Williams. He asked him for and received the treatise which Plymouth had requested he prepare.

Winthrop, Cotton, and several other assistants and ministers read it. They were not pleased. On December 27, 1633, the governor convened a meeting of the assistants in Boston—Endicott again did not attend—to discuss it. The question of Indian ownership of land was secondary. According to Winthrop, the assistants were "muche offended . . . that he Chargeth Kinge Iames to have tould a solemne publicke lye," and that he "did personally apply to our present Kinge Charles"⁶ passages in Revelation which implied "our Kinge" sided with the Antichrist and "committed Fornication with the whore,"⁷ i.e., the Catholic Church in the person of the queen.

Winthrop and the assistants "advised with some of the most iudicious ministers who muche condemned mr willms error," then ordered Williams to appear at the next full General Court. The charges "which will cheifly be layd to hi[m]" were his insults to the king and his "concluding vs all heere to lye vnder a sinne of vniust vsurpation vpon others possessions."⁸

His summons was not for a trial, for the verdict had already been reached, but "to be Censured"⁹ and further punishment decided.

Yet the best solution seemed to be to bring Williams into the fold, especially since he had developed a following. Endicott, Cotton, Wilson, Hooker, and others talked to him about his treatise, and Winthrop conveyed his own "divers Argumentes to confute the said errors."¹⁰ All of these men were intelligent, forceful, and, with the possible exception of Endicott, excellent and trained debaters. They each had private conversations with Williams, disputing his points and warning how dangerous his treatise was to him personally, to

Massachusetts, to all Puritans. The pressure on him was intense, mounting, and coming from everywhere. They lovingly wanted Williams to yield, to recant, to understand his error. They wanted him to conform.

This time he proved uncharacteristically malleable. He was apologetic and penitent, and "returned a verye modest & discreat answeare . . . [to] the Councell, verye submissively: professinge his intent to have onely to have written for the private satisfaction of the Governor &c. of Plymouth: without any purpose to have stirred any further in it, if the Governor heere had not required a Copye of him."[11] To prove his willingness to yield, Williams "offer[ed] his book or any part of it to be burnt &c."

Offering his own work to be burned was an unmistakable act of submission, if not quite a recantation. The magistrates now wanted to hear from Cotton and Wilson. Given Williams's willingness to submit, the ministers had no difficulty concluding that "further Consideringe of the aforesaid offencive passages in his booke . . . might well admitt of doubtfull interpretation they fonde the matters not to be so evill as at first they seemed."[12]

Williams had not publicly divulged his position. He had simply given the governor and assistants, upon their request, a private treatise written at the request of Plymouth authorities. All proceedings had been confidential. No harm had been done. Williams appeared in private before Winthrop and the assistants "& penitently gave satisfaction of . . . his loialty, so it was left &c. nothinge doone in it."

Williams had conformed, and in conforming had escaped—for now.

The question of Massachusetts and conformity has drawn the attention of many historians, who have gone through fashions of interpretation. Current fashion argues that earlier historians overstated required conformity in Massachusetts, and one can without question find individuals who deviated from the norm yet escaped discipline. This book does not argue that the state or the church brought a hammer down upon absolutely everyone who did not conform in all ways. But this author does believe that the earlier emphasis on conformity is a more accurate representation of the way things were. Conformity was central to Winthrop's city upon a hill. More than in any other English-speaking society, the idea and the ideals of this society were well defined. Massachusetts was purpose-driven and its purpose was to advance God's interests upon earth. The definition of that interest was nearly universal within Massachusetts. It was clear to everyone in the society. That individuals within that society fell short of the idea and the ideal did not mean that the society encouraged their falling short, or encouraged individualism. It meant only that humans sinned.

Winthrop had articulated the society's ideals clearly and explicitly in his sermon "A Modell of Christian Charitie." Conformity was to be to the perceived will of God. One of the Bay's leading ministers said the plantation would "endeavour after a Theocracy as near as might be to what which was the glory of Israel."[13]

Technically, the Bay was not a theocracy. Consistent with the admonition to render unto Caesar the things that were Caesar's, and to God those which were God's, the plantation prohibited a minister or church officer from simultaneously holding a government office. (For this reason some historians have argued that Puritan Massachusetts actually advanced the concept of separation of church and state.) But if not a theocracy, Massachusetts was theocentric. The week was filled with church services, including two on Sunday, each of which lasted roughly three hours. Services required concentration and effort, from all concerned; they became so consuming that the government actually had to ban them on some days, partly to relieve pressure on the ministers to prepare sermons, partly because the services interfered with work.

Far more important than the time spent in worship was the fact that the Puritan view of Scripture, of God's purpose for them, lay at the epicenter of the plantation and informed every activity within it. Those who controlled both church and state never forgot their goal: to build the New Jerusalem. And those who controlled both church and state also worked in perfect unison to build that perfect society, defined by them as a society which perfectly obeyed God. Before any consequential decision, the governor and magistrates actively sought the opinion of the leading ministers; they sought out Cotton, sought out Wilson, sought out Hooker, Nathaniel Ward, Richard Mather, and others. Those in control of the society were also in perfect unison in seeing themselves, seeing their new society, as playing a vital role in the progress toward what they regarded as God's ends. That made Massachusetts more even than a theocentric society; every decision and every act was seen from, justified by, or rationalized to accord with an eschatological perspective. Hubbard, a contemporary and the official historian of the plantation, said of Cotton, "Whatever he delivered in the pulpit was soon put into an Order of Court, if of a civil, or set up as a practice in the church, if of an ecclesiastical concernment."[14] Those who controlled the society also believed in authority—beginning with the Word itself—and stability. In their ideal society, each individual had a certain calling fixed and determined by God and all callings fitted together to make society function. Everything was to be fixed and stable. There was to be discipline without discord. The General Court even passed laws to stabilize profits and wages, though the government preferred compliance to come "in a voluntary way, by the counsel and persuasion of the elders, and example of some who led the way, they were brought to more moderation than they could be by compulsion."[15]

Disagreements were to be worked out in love and friendship, with the most bitter disputants swearing their love for each other and coming together as in a family. In 1636 Boston went so far as to prohibit a resident from filing a lawsuit until after the church heard the dispute.[16]

The family was like the commonwealth and the commonwealth was to resemble the family. As one leading Puritan explained, "A familie is a little Church, and a little commonwealth, at least a lively representation thereof, whereby triall may be made of such as are fit for any place of authoritie, or of subjection in Church or commonwealth. . . . [I]t is a schoole wherein the first principles and grounds of government and subjection are learned: whereby men are fitted to greater matters in Church or commonwealth."[17]

This "little commonwealth" was so important that Massachusetts required all persons to live under "family government."[18] Unmarried men and women could not live alone; they had to find a family, board there, and subject themselves to family discipline. That discipline promoted order.

John Robinson was a Separatist who had defied the authority of the Church of England, yet he too decried rebellion, preaching, "And surely there is in all children . . . a stubbornness, and stoutness of mind arising from natural pride, which must, in the first place, be broken and beaten down; that so the foundation of their education being laid in humility and tractableness, other virtues may, in their time, be built thereon. . . . For the beating, and keeping down of this stubbornness parents must provide carefully . . . that the children's wills and wilfulness be restrained and repressed. . . . Children should not know, if it could be kept from them, that they have a will in their own."[19]

The will was based on pride, and pride interfered with the community. The will, based on pride, created discord. The will itself, the pride that it represented, was to Puritans "fruit of natural corruption and root of actual rebellion against God and man."[20]

Massachusetts tolerated private dissent, but it insisted upon, it demanded, it compelled public uniformity, public conformity. The compulsion came from the discipline of the law and even more from the pressure of the community.

But the very demands of godliness also created an inherent tension. Each individual was required to obey the law of God and man, and man based his law on God's. And each individual was to seek God, and to seek God in the most personal way; each individual was expected not only to read the Bible and to ponder upon it—but also to act based on one's interpretation. Yet to pursue one's individual will, if that will was in error, meant rebellion against God and man. When was it willful, rebellious, and sinful to follow one's conviction? When was it God's will that one do so?

In Massachusetts, the answers to these questions were defined by what the governor, the other magistrates, and the leading clergy perceived as God's law. The plantation's leaders wanted not so much to expel dissenters, contemners, and the ungodly, nor even so much to force conformity upon them. The plantation desired most to shepherd dissenters back into the flock. They wanted not to compel but to convict them of their error—using "convict" in the seventeenth-century sense as a synonym for "convince" or "demonstrate," to make them people of conviction—to have them of their own volition renounce their old path and embark upon a new, and then to enfold and embrace them.

The method they employed came from the Bible: admonition. They employed it gently at first, then with increasing pressure, based on Matthew 18:15–17: "Moreover if thy brother shall trespass against thee, go and tell him his fault between thee and him alone; if he shall hear thee, thou hast gained a brother. And if he shall neglect to hear thee, tell it unto the church."

Then, Hooker advised, "You must use all means to reclaim them. You must reprove them sharply, counsel them compassionately, and strive with them mightily, that so you may bring them home to know [Luke 19:42] 'the things belonging to their peace' here and everlasting happiness hereafter."[21]

In Massachusetts all of life involved God, and so the church did not limit its admonitions to theology. Robert Keayne was a wealthy merchant who over-charged his customers. His church admonished him, and the admonishment haunted him the rest of his life. Drunkards were admonished and shamed by being forced to wear the letter "D" for an extended period of time. All this was done with love, to correct error. If an individual continued in error and rebellion, church pressure increased. And if admonition failed, the churches had no recourse. They excommunicated members.

Citing 2 Thessalonians 3:14, *And if any man obey not our word . . . note that man and have no company with him, that he may be ashamed,* Hooker continued, "Observe it: it is very reasonable a man should do so; for he that will not receive good by the society of the members of Christ, it is fit he should be cast out from having any communion with the members of Christ."[22]

Excommunication was an extreme and dramatic act. John Wilson declared to one poisoner of the congregation, "In the name of our Lord Jesus Christ and in the name of the Church . . . I do exclude you not only from the fellowship of the church in all public ordinances of the same, but also from private fellowship and communion with any servants of God in the church. . . . *I doe cast you out. . . . I doe deliver you up to Sathan. . . .* I doe account yow [*sic*] from this time forth to be Hethen and a Publican. . . . *I command yow* in the name of Christ Jesus and of his Church *as a Leper to wthdraw* [*sic*] *your selfe.*"[23]

All church members—including members of other churches—were not only to refrain from joining with "excommunicate persons" in any "religious communion" but also to withdraw from "any civil familiar connexion, as sitting at table"[24] with them. No other church member—not a cousin, not even a husband or child—could eat with them, greet them on the street. This public shunning, this isolation, was an enormous burden, especially in a society in which most members regarded themselves less as individuals than as part of a community, as part of the common weal.

The causes of excommunication need not reflect great evil. Pride was a great sin, indicating failure to yield. One man was excommunicated for marrying a woman his church considered "vaine, light, and proud, . . . and much given to scoffing."[25] (One can imagine this woman's view of the church.) Another man was excommunicated for idleness and being "somewhat proud."[26]

Excommunication was by no means always permanent. The excommunicate had control. All he or she had to do was to capitulate, to yield, to recognize the error and abandon it to be welcomed back—lovingly welcomed back, without recrimination and with full forgiveness—into both the church and the society. Indeed, repair and reconciliation were expected. The church like the government sought rehabilitation, not revenge. The ability to end one's own suffering intensified the pressure to yield, made it build and build.

The pressure to conform, even when not directly applied, caused some to leave voluntarily. One who left had preceded the Puritans in the area. William Blackstone had warmly welcomed Winthrop to what became Boston. He was a temperate and serious man, but he soon had enough of New Jerusalem and removed himself into wilderness, outside the bounds and bonds of Massachusetts or Plymouth, to what is now the Blackstone River in present Rhode Island.

The government took greatest offense at what it regarded as "contempt of authoritie"—in effect any public criticism or resistance. It responded by demanding submission. It required this even when no crime had been committed. After the Court of Assistants levied a tax to pay for fortifications, the pastor and ruling elder of the Watertown church warned their congregation that paying the taxes could bring "themselues & posteryty into bondage."[27] The court issued warrants for all who protested. After discussion, the protesters admitted error. This was not enough. The magistrates required them to retract their opposition in writing, and read their retraction to the Watertown church.

When an offender submitted to the government willingly and full in spirit, punishment was lessened and sometimes waived. When there was no submission, the state ordered whippings, mutilation, and imprisonment. It also had a power comparable to excommunication. When all else failed, when all efforts to bring a wayward spirit home were rebuffed out of pride and willfulness, when all hope for that lost soul vanished, the state could banish.

Any banished person who returned to Massachusetts was subject to punishment, up to and including death, at the discretion of the magistrates. Massachusetts banished people unhesitatingly: in 1630 and 1631, the colony banished fourteen people—nearly 2 percent of its entire population.

They were contaminants, refuse, offal. And the state cast them out.

# ❧ CHAPTER 15 ❧

In England, Massachusetts was attracting unfavorable attention.
Massachusetts clergy did not use the Book of Common Prayer, did not wear the surplice, did not allow crosses—considered Romish—in any building, especially in a meeting house. Persons wishing to follow the order of worship of the Church of England not only were unable to do so but could remain in the plantation only if they did not publicly protest.

But there was protest aplenty in England. It came from those banished or punished by Massachusetts who sought revenge, and it came from Anglicans who visited and returned home. Puritan friends in England warned those in Massachusetts they were being called "Hereticks . . . and that your preachers in their publique prayers, pray for the gouernor before they praye for our kinge and state . . . that you neuer vse the Lords prayer, that your ministers marrie none"—Puritan marriage ceremonies were civil, not religious—"that you count all men in England, yea all out of your church, in the state of damnacion."[1] Another writer cautioned that "your frends heer . . . haue much to do to answer the vniust complaints made to the Kinge and counsell of your gouernment there."[2]

Even Sir Simonds D'Ewes, a strong Puritan supporter of the plantation, warned Winthrop that Massachusetts was going too far. Winthrop replied, "For your counsell of Conforminge ourselves to the Ch of E, though I doubt not that it proceeds out of your care for our wellfare: yet I dare not thanke you for it; because it is not conformable to Gods will revealed in his worde; what you may doe in E where things are otherwise established, I will not dispute, but our case heere is otherwise: beinge come to clearer Light and more Libertye . . . we may freely enjoye it."[3]

But others, even some friends, believed the light was not so much clear to them, as blinding.

In England, meanwhile, new and intertwined threats had emerged. Determined to extirpate, to rip out "branch and root" all religious nonconformity, Laud widened and thickened his web of spies. Homes of Puritans in England were raided and letters were seized; other letters were intercepted, copied, and delivered and recipients spied upon. People feared putting anything in writing. One correspondent of Winthrop the Younger reported that people "write to their utter Ruine (if they take not heed) for let them be assured, theire letters will come to light that write against our state ciuill or ecclesiasticall, and the Starchamber hath punishments for such lybellers, and a longe arme to reach them."[4] Another said, "As concerninge anythinge in our nation, you may haue relation by worde of mouth . . . badd times, and great fear of worse."[5] And another: "how it fareth . . . is safer to be related by those that come to you then to be committed to paper."[6]

Even those who had proven their loyalty to the king found themselves out of favor if they crossed Laud. Sir Robert Heath had championed the royal prerogative in disputes with Parliament and Coke over the Petition of Right. Charles had rewarded him by making him chief justice of Common Pleas. But he was a Calvinist, unhappy over Laud's direction of the Church of England, and Laud convinced Charles to dismiss him.

Then Laud began defining offenses against the church as treason, which brought defendants into the Star Chamber—where defendants could neither have an attorney nor refuse to answer even self-incriminating questions. When Williams had assisted Coke there, few cases had involved politics; the court had pursued equity. Now Charles and Laud exploited its lack of common law procedural safeguards to make of it a tool of power.

One victim was William Prynne. He had written a lengthy attack on the morality of stage plays and had called female actors "notorious whores." After his work was published, the queen acted in a play. He could not have known earlier that she would do so, but he was arrested. In February 1634, he was brought before the Star Chamber and sentenced to a £5,000 fine, expulsion from the Inns of Court, deprivation of his Oxford degree, the loss of part of his ears and time in the pillory, and life imprisonment. Now, in the Tower, he was continuing to write attacks on Laud—reportedly he wrote some on the walls of his cell—and his attacks were being smuggled out.[7] For this, he would later suffer more torture and a second sentence of life imprisonment. (He ultimately had full revenge prosecuting Laud for treason.)

Thousands of Puritans were now fleeing England, fleeing Laud's efforts, as they perceived it, "to bring into the Church, downe right poperie."[8]

Yet their flight did not satisfy Laud. He complained of "an universal running to New England, and God knows whither, but this it is, when men think nothing is their advantage, but to run from government."[9] Laud intended to pursue those who had run, and Sir Fernando Gorges gave him a ready vehicle in which to do it. Gorges had long sought a New England empire and had created the Council for New England but, distracted by England's wars against France and Spain, had given up his chairmanship of the council to the Earl of Warwick, who had granted the charter to the Bay Company. England was no longer at war and Gorges was no longer distracted. He wanted his chance at empire back, and demanded the return of the patent given to the Bay.

He took his case to the Privy Council, which ruled in the colonists' favor. But Gorges did not give up. He brought to the Privy Council's attention Philip Ratcliffe—the man who had uttered an oath about Puritans after a debtor refused to repay him, and who lost his ears and was flogged for it—and several others expelled from the Bay. Thomas Morton, whom Massachusetts had expelled after looting his fortune and destroying his giant Maypole, presented his own case and other legal arguments against the colony to the council. In response, the council created a Commission for Regulating Plantations. And it named as chair William Laud.

Laud soon convinced the Privy Council to order Craddock, the leader of the Massachusetts Bay Company in England, to return the company's charter. This was the first step to rescinding the company's rights to govern Massachusetts, just as James had dissolved the Virginia Company in 1624 and made Virginia a royal colony. Craddock explained he could not return the charter, for it was in Boston. This delayed action against the colony, but it hardly ended the threat.

Laud also attempted to starve the Bay of further Puritan immigrants— and of the money they carried—beginning in February 1634, when he had the Privy Council forbid twelve ships from sailing for Boston. Subsequently he ordered all those embarking for New England to swear an oath of loyalty to the crown and reaffirm the crown's supremacy over the church; then he added the requirement that all emigrants show affidavits from two justices of the peace and a minister asserting their loyalty to the king and to the Church of England. And all shipboard services had to use the Book of Common Prayer.

Initial enforcement of his orders was strict. The Reverend Richard Mather traveled in disguise and under an alias and reported that "searchers" came on board his ship "and viewed a list of all our names, ministered the oath of allegiance to all at full age, viewed our certifacates from the ministers in the parishes from whence wee came . . . and gave us tickets."[10] But under pressure from merchants upset over the disruption of trade, port authorities grew lax.

Nonetheless, the attempt to prevent more Puritans from going to Massachusetts was as clear a threat to the colony as the order recalling the charter. Laud's pressure on all those who did not conform would eventually lead to a bloody civil war and his beheading, but for now he rested easy. It was Laud's enemies who feared.

There was one other rumored action. As the colony continued to make excuses for not returning the charter, rumors spread that a military expedition might come to seize it and rule the plantation.

Massachusetts leaders expected all within the plantation to yield to them, to conform to their ways, but they were not about to yield to any outside power, not even English power. In April 1634, the Court of Assistants prepared to build a "sea fort," a floating gun battery to be anchored in Boston harbor. The assistants justified this publicly as a defense against French forces in Canada and the Dutch in New Amsterdam (now New York). But Laud was the proximate cause. That was proved by the assistants' decision to also impose a loyalty oath.

It was assumed that all freemen, being church members, were loyal, but all adults who were not freemen had to swear to "submit to the authority of the governor, and all the other magistrates there, and their successors, and to all such laws, orders, sentences and decrees as now or are hereafter lawfully made."[11] Two refusals to take the oath meant banishment. A month later, the full General Court echoed that step by requiring new freemen to swear faithfulness and submission to the government of Massachusetts and to "yield assistance and support thereunto."[12]

Absent from these loyalty oaths was any mention of loyalty to the king of England. The omission escaped the notice of no one.

Simultaneously, the freemen were tightening their own control over the plantation, even including over Winthrop. Three years earlier suffrage had been restricted to male church members who were not servants. A majority of men may have then been church members, but during those three years, three years during which the population grew enormously, church membership became increasingly exclusive. Initially, one had had to do little more than sign the church covenant to become a member. That soon changed: to join a church now, potential members had to prove themselves "visible saints," had to prove that they were among the precious few elect whom their Calvinist God would save. This forced potential members through a stringent and arduous process that included standing before the entire congregation and presenting evidence that God had made the seeker a saint, had made the seeker one of His "stones" upon which He would build the New Jerusalem. This was no pro forma ritual. It was an intimidating, difficult, rigorous, and by no means always successful test. In most churches the congregation had to vote unanimously to accept the new member. Those who either did not seek or were rejected from membership could worship in a church—in fact, the law required them to do so. But they could not belong to a church.

As a result, only a minority of the population, and a decreasing minority, were church members and qualified as freemen with voting privileges. One historian has found that only 21.2 percent of London emigrants to New England in 1635 were known to have *ever* been admitted to church membership.[13] Whether this number can be extrapolated to the entire population is unclear, but clearly most men could not vote. Since church members tended to be more successful than average, voters also became increasingly wealthy—left-leaning historians have referred to Massachusetts as an oligarchy—increasingly puritanical literally and figuratively, and increasingly inflexible.

There was another change, too. In 1631, when Winthrop had made all freemen members of the General Court, freemen were given the power to elect the magistrates. But those magistrates had reserved to themselves, acting as the Court of Assistants, the power to legislate and to choose the governor and deputy governor from among themselves. Subsequently, freemen had demanded that the entire General Court, not the assistants, elect the governor and deputy governor. This proposal had incensed some assistants, particularly

Thomas Dudley, the deputy governor. He and Winthrop had often clashed, and even had one confrontation when Dudley "rose with great fury and passion, and [Winthrop] grew very hot also, so they both fell into bitterness."[14] The two had, lovingly, mended their relationship, or so they said. And Winthrop had convinced the assistants to cede the power of choosing the governor rather than fight with the body of freemen.

But in May 1634, the freemen expressed extreme discontent with their governor, and they acted upon their discontent.

The trouble began with Watertown, where resentment against Winthrop lingered; twice the Watertown church had taken positions at variance from the Court of Assistants and twice the church had been forced into a very public "retraction and a submission."[15] Also, Winthrop and other leaders of the plantation had voted themselves and such close associates as John Wilson thousands of acres, justifying it as compensation for the time they devoted to government or advising it.[16] This had caused more resentment.

Now all the freemen, led by those from Watertown, demanded to see the charter itself. Winthrop had no recourse but to agree. The freemen promptly discovered that the charter gave the whole General Court, not the assistants, the power to make law. The assistants had knowingly been exercising that power in violation of the charter. Winthrop defended the magistrates with arcane reasoning, but the General Court now insisted it exercise the legislative power granted by the charter. The freemen's one concession was, in recognition of how unwieldy writing law would be in a General Court open to all freemen, to have each town begin sending "committees" of two or three delegates to the General Court.

On election day a river of anger ran high against Winthrop. Cotton preached a sermon of support which reflected an ultimate endorsement of authority, declaring, "A magistrate ought not to be turned into the condition of a private man without just cause . . . no more than the magistrates may turn a private man out of his freehold &c., without publick trial, &c."

Cotton's words did no good. Dudley was elected governor. Winthrop received barely enough votes to remain an assistant. Nor did the votes reflect liberality. Far from it. Electing Dudley was a move toward inflexibility. He was known as a hard man. In England he had loaned corn at 33 percent interest for a single harvest season; in New England he had attacked Winthrop's leniency, attacked him for showing too much mercy, attacked him for having too much of his Christian charity, attacked him even for delaying the enforcement of a banishment order. Winthrop had done so because expelling the man in winter might have led to his death.

No freeman expected Dudley to show charity, and his election indicated that a majority of them did not want him to.

Roger Williams was withdrawn from this controversy, but these developments troubled him. Chiefly the loyalty oath troubled him, but not because it failed to require loyalty to the king. The oath troubled him because it intertwined church and state. For the moment, he did not much voice his objections to it. For the moment, he did not engage. Salem and his life among the Indians were his refuges.

To him, Salem had become the bright spot in all of the Americas. And if the rest of the Bay looked somewhat askance at Salem, Salem looked back with steady eyes. The Old Planters had arrived before the Massachusetts Bay Company took charge of the colony and they remained somewhat aloof even in Salem; the rest of the plantation they saw as latecomers. Endicott and those others who first settled under the Bay's auspices also had a sense of priority. Endicott had governed when Boston did not even exist, nor did Newtown, nor Watertown, nor Roxbury. After Winthrop came, Salem and its church had continued to pursue their own course, had nominally bowed to the rest of the plantation while continuing to show flashes of independence from it. The streak of resistance to, independence from, and resentment toward the Boston government ran through both the town and Williams personally. Salem and he were well matched, and he had influence and standing there, however the rest of Massachusetts saw him.

And there Williams planted and harvested crops and deepened his involvement with Indians. He now considered himself fluent enough to say, "I could debate with them in a great measure in their own language." His fluency was noticed. One report to England noted that he "in a special good intent in doing good to their soules, hath spent much time in attaining to their language, wherein he is so good a proficient that he can speak to their understanding and he to theirs, much loving and respecting him for his love and counsel. It is hoped that he may be an instrument of good amongst them."[17]

He desired to expose them to Christ, but it was not only that. Intellectual curiosity, an anthropologist's curiosity, drove him forward as well. He wanted to learn all about them, to understand how they grew corn, how they raised their children, how they hunted, how they traveled, how they fished, how they governed themselves, how they worshipped. To do this, he chose in his words "to lodge with them in their filthy Smoakie holes," which required of him discipline and "a Painfull, Patient spirit."[18] It helped that the Indians knew him as "a public speaker both at Plymouth and Salem, and therefore they perceived him to be an English 'sachem,'" a chief.

He also traveled throughout southern New England. New Englanders had so few horses that most people, including even Winthrop, moved through the country by sea where possible or on foot when necessary. The most common vessel was the shallop, a boat of fourteen to twenty feet that could be sailed or rowed and required several men to handle it. Also in use were pinnaces, a larger vessel capable of an extended ocean voyage. Williams, lacking the resources to own either, got about by canoe, sometimes likely with a sail rigged; if too small to carry much cargo, it could access the shallowest marshes and streams.

Canoeing even in protected bays meant confronting sometimes breaking surf and routinely strong currents, heavy swells, whitecaps, and wind; occasional exposure to open ocean increased the danger exponentially. Handling a canoe required skill; Williams became adept and would use a canoe for the next fifty years. That required physical labor, hard labor, muscle-numbing labor, skin-blistering labor. Even when the canoe was rigged with sail and the wind was sufficient, sail was useless for surf, in marshes, in streams. And when wind was not sufficient or a sail was not rigged, covering not simply a mile or two miles but tens of miles in a day meant digging a paddle into the water stroke after stroke after stroke after stroke. Doing this day after day after day after day hardened the hands, built the forearms, the triceps, the shoulders, the back, the legs. To do that in summer, the air thick with humidity, exposed to sun hours at a time, and in winter, the air so cold that breathing sent sharp tiny stabs into the lungs, the spray from the sea freezing to hair, required great physical hardiness. This would have given Williams a hard, powerful body. Such labor would have also given him a sensibility of his own physicality unusual compared with those ministers—including all other Massachusetts clergy—supported financially by their congregations. Those who labor as Williams did, when they also have intellect and education, often develop both great confidence in themselves and some disdain for those who do no physical labor. Years later Williams would show such disdain, writing, "I know what it is to Study, to Preach, to be an Elder, to be applauded, and yet what it is to tug at the Oar, to dig with the Spade, and Plow, to labour and travel day and night amongst English, amongst Barbarians."[19]

Events now brought him, and his evolving beliefs, back into the arena.

# ❧ CHAPTER 16 ❧

The summer of 1634 was the hottest the New England English had yet experienced.[1] Politics made it hotter. In July, the magistrates dropped the plan for the floating gun battery in favor of fortifying Castle Island in the harbor and placing several batteries of artillery there, which provided much stronger defense.

Then one of Salem's Old Planters, a man sympathetic to the Church of England, received a letter from Thomas Morton. Morton, apparently considering him a friend and ally, gleefully related that he was near success in revenging himself upon Puritans for his banishment, the destruction of Merrymount, and the loss of his fortune. He was preparing to argue the case to rescind Massachusetts's charter before the King's Bench, and there was to be force behind his argument. Not only was the charter about to be recalled but a governor-general representing the crown—and Laud—was to be sent over to take control of the colony. On August 4, the man gave the letter to Winthrop.

Morton's report—and the earlier rumors—proved true. The Privy Council had authorized Gorges to travel to Massachusetts to seize the charter and take charge of New England. The next General Court overwhelmingly decided they would neither give up their charter nor yield power to Gorges or any other governor appointed by the crown. Instead, they prepared for war.

The plantation in fact bristled with weapons, from artillery to pikes and muskets, and maintained large stores of powder. Colony organizers had also recruited soldiers with combat experience on the continent and in Ireland, and each town had "trained bands," militias which regularly performed military drills. Attendance at drill was compulsory for men, and they had to supply their own weapons. Given potential threats from the Spanish and Dutch in the south, the French in the north, and the Indians all about them, this made sense. But the plantation had always worried as well about the threat it preferred not to discuss.

Now that last threat, from England itself, had become real. The General Court ordered trained bands to drill frequently, and those drills took on seriousness and urgency. It also decided to fortify several additional locations which commanded the harbor and to place a beacon on a high point overlooking it—Beacon Hill—to alert the colony to suspicious ships.

On more routine matters, the court reached easy agreement in condemning "costly Apparrell & immodest fasions."[2] But two other issues made this meeting both lengthy and contentious. The first was a request by Thomas Hooker and a group of freemen for permission to remove to near present-day Hartford, Connecticut, which was then wilderness. The request per se did not cause the most dissension, but it created the second controversy—over a struggle for control.

The very fact that Hooker sought permission to leave demonstrated that Massachusetts was a "common wealth" in reality as well as in name. It meant that there was an order to things, that even those wanting to leave perceived their responsibilities to the whole, and that authority was to be respected.

In the soggy thickness of the days, the deputies argued the case, their sweat soaking through the full garments they wore. One reason to move was not spoken of publicly: the rivalry between Cotton and Hooker. What was spoken of was "want of land"; the Hooker group needed more land for cattle and farming; they felt already cramped. They also insisted that the English, although they had no legal authority to occupy this wilderness, needed to claim the region for themselves. It was rich country, fat with beaver and with the fertile ground of a great river valley. Failure to establish an English presence would cede it by default to the Dutch, who had built a fort and trading post in the area.

Winthrop opposed their leaving, arguing, "[W]e were nowe weake, & in danger to be assayled," and that the Hooker contingent was "knitt to vs in one bodye, and bonde by Oathe to seek the wellfare of this Common wealth."[3]

Then came the vote. Governor Thomas Dudley, two assistants, and three-fifths of the deputies representing the towns voted to grant Hooker permission. But Winthrop and three other assistants did not. The governor and assistants had voted four to three against giving permission. This raised a new issue. The issue was power.

Earlier, when the General Court had taken from the assistants the power to legislate, Winthrop had claimed that the charter still gave the assistants a "negative voice," i.e., a veto over legislation, and that a majority of *both* the town representatives who now made up the General Court and the assistants had to agree for legislation to pass. His was an abstruse argument with little to support it, for the patent explicitly gave the General Court legislative power. But the question of Hooker's removal to Connecticut now became a test case for Winthrop's theory.

All present understood what the negative voice meant. It meant the de facto creation of an upper body of the legislature. The assistants in their role as magistrates—the words "assistant" and "magistrate" were used interchangeably—already exercised all the executive power of the government and much of the judicial power, and the Court of Assistants met monthly to transact government business between meetings of the full General Court. Allowing them to overturn actions of the General Court was too much. Israel Stoughton, a leader of those opposed to the veto, expressed astonishment that "though all the country and three of seven of the magistrates do like and desire" something, a bare majority of assistants could prevent it. "I know none that have read the patent (except the magistrates) that esteem it their due."[4]

The governor and assistants had split over the question of Hooker's moving. But on this question of power, they unanimously supported Winthrop. As Winthrop reported, there "grewe a great difference between the Governor & Assistantes . . . & the deputyes" who refused to "yeild the Assistantes a negatiue voice."[5]

Winthrop's account barely hints at the ferocity of the division. Red-faced men shouted angry words at one another, and, uncharacteristically, Winthrop himself was among the angriest. The assistants and deputies could agree only to adjourn for two weeks, hold a day of humiliation throughout the colony, and "seeke the Lord" for guidance.

When the court reconvened, nothing and no one had changed. Rather than further inflame the plantation by defying the magistrates, Hooker and those who had planned to go with him remained. (Eventually, with permission, they did leave, settling about fifty miles up the Connecticut River from the coast.)

By persistence, even ruthlessness, and by Hooker's setting a precedent of in effect honoring the negative voice, Winthrop established the assistants' claim to veto power, effectively creating a legislature with two houses.

Soon after, Winthrop denounced Stoughton as a "troubler of Israel," "a worm," and "an underminer of the state."[6] Then he had Stoughton, an elected deputy to the General Court, stripped of office, and a legal brief Stoughton wrote on the issue was burned.

Meanwhile, the day of humiliation led to an even deeper unsettling of the plantation.

On August 2, shortly before the conflict in the General Court erupted, Samuel Skelton died. He had formed the first church in the Bay colony, but if he was beloved in Salem his thorniness had provoked the rest of the colony, beginning the day Winthrop arrived in America, hungry for worship after months at sea, when Skelton had refused to allow him and others to participate in the Lord's Supper.

Roger Williams, already unofficially teacher of the church, added the also unofficial responsibilities of pastor. Considering himself "charged by my office with the feeding of that flock," he began preaching three sermons a week. The fact that he was not formally consecrated in either position allowed him, the church, and the magistrates to avoid conflict. But when the General Court sought reconciliation by adjourning for a day of public humiliation, a day of searching private souls and public acts for anything that offended the Lord, Williams felt it his duty, his obligation, to speak out.

He later explained, "[W]hen in apprehension of some public evils the whole country profest to humble it self and seek God, . . . I discovered eleven public sins for which I believed and do, it pleased God to inflict and further threaten public calamities. Most of which eleven, if not all, that church then seemed to assent unto."[7] The "public sins" committed by the colony's government and by the king were not ones he newly discovered. But he had held silent about them until now. He could no longer, now that his "thoughts so deeply afflicted [my] Soule and conscience."[8]

He repeated his objections to government enforcement of the first four of the Ten Commandments which governed the individual's behavior toward God. Three years earlier, because of his position on this question, the magistrates had shouldered him out of the colony. He also voiced new objections to both government-compelled church attendance and the loyalty oaths; they too, he believed, improperly mixed church and state. (His reasoning was not that of most modern supporters of separation; rather, he sought to protect the church, believing the profanity of the state could only contaminate the church's purity.)

Finally, he made public what had been his private complaints, denouncing "the sinne of the Pattents, wherein Christian Kings (so calld) are invested with Right by virtue of their Christianitie, to take and give away the Lands and Countries of other men."[9]

He was not entirely isolated in the Bay colony ministry. In Roxbury, John Eliot also used sermons to attack public sins, some of the "faylinges as he conceived" of the Bay government. The government decided that Eliot "should be dealt with by mr Cotton mr Hooker & mr Welde to be brought to see his error, & to heale it by some public explanation."[10] The next Lord's day, Eliot issued a public apology.

Williams had greater conviction. Earlier he had offered his writings to be burned. He would make no such offer now, and he would make no apology. Pushed inexorably by his logic, Williams argued that the Massachusetts charter was irrevocably besmirched; they had to return it to England and get a new one. He even called for a letter of reprimand to be sent directly to Charles I, king of England.

Winthrop and his colleagues believed—and would not forget—that he "had broken his promise to us, in teaching publickly against the kings patent, and our great sin in claiming right thereby to this countrie, &c."[11]

Williams was, the magistrates felt, showing contempt for their authority. They were correct.

In obedience to the General Court, each town's trained band had begun drilling hard. The bands seethed with the ferocity of continental war: breastplates, helmets with knife-like edges, pikes, swords, and muskets. Each band comprised a brutal killing force. Earlier, the Plymouth colony's Miles Standish had demonstrated the lethality of a few determined, well-armed Europeans in combat; he had cut through a group of Indians like a scythe cutting corn.

Endicott commanded the Salem band. As it drilled for war against their own king, a war they would fight on God's side against that king, he looked up at the king's banner under which his men and all trained bands drilled. Fixed on the banner was a cross, the red cross of St. George, a symbol suggested to an earlier English king by the pope.

Puritans believed that any cross violated the Second Commandment, to make no graven images of God; they considered it superstition and idol worship. For this reason Puritan extremists had smashed stained glass windows and destroyed crucifixes in English cathedrals. Here in New England, churches were simple buildings, rectangles or squares, without a nave, without ornamentation, with only a podium for the minister to speak from, certainly without a cross as adornment. Winthrop had gone so far as to object to the name of a place called "Hue's Cross" where people forded a stream, renaming it "Hue's Folly."

To train under such a symbol as the cross of St. George, a cross linked to a pope, was anathema. At best, it betrayed all that Puritans stood for; at worst, it represented a grievous offense to God. In a sudden burst of fury, or zealotry, or inspiration, Endicott slashed at the flag with his sword, slicing the cross out of it.

Endicott's action fired the plantation. Richard Brown, a Watertown elder who had once argued that even the Catholic Church was a true church (and had been roundly chastised for it), formally complained in November to the Court of Assistants. Others worried that Endicott had jeopardized their safety, that England would see his act as rebellion enough to justify an armed invasion.

Yet a majority of the colony seemed to consider the presence of the cross in the flag so abhorrent as to justify Endicott's act. Even so measured a man as Winthrop leaned toward this view.

On November 27, 1634, a Court of Assistants met at the home of Dudley, Winthrop's successor as governor, to consider Endicott's action. At that same court a complaint was also lodged against Williams for his sermons attacking the charter and the king.

The court immediately decided to send a letter signed by all the magistrates to authorities in England, stating that they considered Endicott's act "very unlawful" and that they planned "to punish the offenders." But they took no action against him, nor against Williams.

Williams the assistants seemed to put on hold. Regarding Endicott, they invited the opinions of several ministers in attendance. The ministers contradicted each other—Cotton supported the destruction of the cross, Hooker opposed it—so the magistrates convened a meeting in Boston attended by every minister in the plantation. Still the clergy failed to reach consensus.

If the magistrates hesitated about Endicott and Williams, they did not hesitate about the threat from England. A few weeks later the Court of Assistants made explicit what had been implicit in their decision to fortify the harbor and prepare for war. They declared, "If a general governor be sent out of England . . . not to accept him, but defend our lawful possessions."[12]

Rather than allow a royal governor to interfere with the way of life they were building, they would rebel against their own king. If they perceived themselves as weak in comparison to the vast power of all England, there is no sign of it. They believed God favored them.

Three months later, on March 4, 1635, Endicott was summoned to a full General Court. Still no decision was reached on punishment, but on the issue he won. The court created a "Commission for militarye Affaires . . . which had power of life and limbe"[13] and which "appoint[ed] colors for every company . . . and left out the cross in all of them."

This General Court then replaced the old loyalty oath with a new one, requiring "every man of or above the age of sixteen" to take an "Oath of Fidelity" to Massachusetts authorities alone—again excluding any mention of loyalty to the king. And the court did "intreate of the elders and brethren of every church within this jurisidiction, that they will consult & advise of one uniforme order of discipline in the churches, agreeable to the Scriptures, and then to consider how farr the Magistrates are bound to interpose for the preservation of that uniformity & peace of the churches."[14]

Dudley also pushed for action against Williams. Cotton asked for delay, offering "with the consent of my fellow elders and brethren a serious request to the magistrates that they would be pleased to forbear all civill prosecution against him, till we ourselves (with our churches) had dealt with him in a church way. . . . [M]y selfe, and brethren hoped, his violent course did rather spring from scruple of conscience, (though carried with inordinate zeal) then from a seditious Principle."

The ministers planned to admonish him for his errors and bring him to the correct view. Dudley told them they "were deceived in him, if we thought he woud condescend to learne of any of us. And what will you doe . . . when you have run your course, and found all your labour lost?"

Cotton replied, "[W]e hoped better things . . . and endeavour for the deed."[15]

Williams did meet with several ministers on numerous occasions. He may well have even welcomed the meetings, given his confidence in the correctness of his opinions. Perhaps he even thought he could convert them. He could not. But they pressed upon him, and they pressed hard and frequently. And he bent.

On the questions of landownership, the validity of the charter, and his attacks on Charles, they repeated all the legal and scriptural arguments Winthrop himself had laid out to rebut Williams three years before. The chief argument was that plague had emptied the country of Indians, proving that the Lord intended them to have the land. Williams had already dismissed that argument, finding his own much stronger.

Nonetheless and for the second time on these issues, he yielded. But he did so not because of substantive arguments which convinced him of his error; he did so for political reasons, recognizing that further advocacy of his position risked causing chaos in the colony and provoking harm to it in England. Later he wrote that "Councells from Flesh and Blood supprest" his views and "Worldly policie at last prevailed."[16]

Williams stopped speaking to these issues. But the General Court had created new issues in requiring all males to take the oath of fidelity and in seeking to establish a uniform order of church discipline. Williams objected to both these actions, and he would speak to them.

The question of church discipline was an old one; upon his return to Massachusetts he had protested the monthly gatherings of clergy precisely because of concern that they would grow into a disciplinary institution. Winthrop had dismissed this fear as "without Cause" and asserted that "no Churche or person" would ever have power over another church. Now the state was explicitly calling for just that.

Yet of more immediate concern to Williams was the loyalty oath. Cotton justified it, arguing that "upon intelligence of some Episcopal and malignant practices against the country"—i.e., upon learning of the threat of a governor-general who would impose Laud's Church of England upon New England—the magistrates and General Court decided "to take trial of the fidelity of the people, not by imposing upon them, but by offering to them, an oath of fidelity." Those who refused it, he said, suffered only in that magistrates "might not betrust them with place of public charge and command."[17]

Cotton's analysis was, to put it gently, disingenuous. Anyone twice offered the oath, and who refused twice to take it, was subject to banishment. To put it less gently, Cotton was lying.

Williams objected to the oath on two grounds. His views would develop beyond—much beyond—what he stated at this time, but even now his protests went to the core of the relationship between church and state. He objected, first, because the state was requiring an oath of all its subjects, including the most corrupt. Forcing "unregenerate" persons to swear before God forced them to take the Lord's name in vain. This profaned God. This created sin. This violated one of God's fundamental commandments. And since the requirement was imposed by a vote of the General Court, it involved all persons in that sin.

But he had a more subtle and deeper problem. He argued that "an oath was part of God's worship,"[18] that "Christ's prerogative [was] to have his office established by oath."[19] Swearing an oath was a serious and spiritual act; it represented striving after God, seeking God, submission to God. An oath linked God and the swearer. Yet this oath—an oath before God to perform a worldly act—instead linked the state and its subjects. Requiring men and women to swear fealty to the state—to *swear* this, to pledge before God and to God for an earthly purpose—equated an earthly and necessarily corrupt kingdom with God's holy kingdom.

This too took the Lord's name in vain. It trivialized God. Worse, by equating human society, the world in all its corruption, with God's kingdom, it reeked of human pride. This too was sin. This too was anathema to him.

Williams began to protest in Salem. Cotton reported that he "vehemently withstood" the magistrates and that he "drew not a few good people toward his conclusions"[20] not only in Salem but throughout the plantation.

Almost immediately, the governor and assistants met and "sent for mr williams."[21]

No record of this meeting exists, but references to it make clear that the magistrates called upon numerous ministers, almost certainly including Cotton, Hooker, Richard Mather, and John Eliot, to confront Williams and rebut him. All were Cambridge graduates, trained in disputation. Their debate would have been abstruse, intense, and sharp, with words for swords. Williams would have answered one while another, then another, was thrust at him. Winthrop reported nothing of the debate itself, only that Williams "was heard before all the ministers and verye cleerly confuted."[22]

Williams very clearly did not consider himself confuted. Nor did most of the plantation. To the contrary, his position resonated throughout the colony. This resonance in fact grew strong enough "to force the Court to retrace its steps and desist."[23] It stopped administering the oath, a fact which, Cotton noted, caused "the authorities . . . serious embarrassment, the more, [for] his reputation for sanctity."[24]

Williams began to push upon his advantage, pressing anew his old complaints. He attacked forced tithes and giving tax money to ministers, insisting, "No one should be bound to maintain a worship against his own consent."[25] And as before, he preached that the state should concern itself only with the world: it should discipline only acts of persons against persons; it was profane for it to involve itself in the First Table. On these issues too he began to find resonance. He found such resonance in Salem that the church there was finally ready to make him, formally and officially, its teacher.

The magistrates as they had before joined with ministers and elders from several churches and "advised the Church at Salem, not to proceed to choose him to office in the Church."[26]

When these magistrates and ministers gave advice, they expected it to be taken. Despite the pressure, despite efforts to agitate the congregation against him, five weeks after the General Court ordered the imposition of the oath "the major part of the church made choice of" Williams as its teacher.[27]

The magistrates were defied again, and embarrassed again.

Next came further embarrassment. A committee selected by the General Court to investigate Endicott's defacing the flag issued its report. It proposed that the colony use an older flag which bore no cross and used the colors red and white to signify the houses of Lancaster and York, to which King Charles traced his English ancestry. As for Endicott, the report found that his greatest offense was not the act itself. Although that had given "occasion to the state of England to think ill of us,"[28] his greatest offense was exceeding his own authority "and not seeking advice of the court." By acting alone, he had implied that the other assistants would allow the cross; he was "laying a blemish also upon the rest of the Magistrates, as if they would suffer idolatry."[29]

The report perfectly expressed the sentiment in the plantation. The threat from England and Laud was real. Nonetheless, Endicott's destruction of the flag had such widespread support that the report had to defend the other assistants for not having acted themselves.

The committee also recommended, and a full General Court subsequently concurred, that Endicott was to be punished, but solely for exceeding his authority. His sentence: to be barred from office for one year. He would lose his position as assistant and magistrate. Even this seemed to stun Endicott.

The colony soon received bad news followed by the best news. Gorges was laying *quo warranto* papers before the King's Bench, demanding the Bay Company show cause why the colony's charter should not be revoked. Morton was one of those arguing the case. Emmanuel Downing, Winthrop's brother-in-law, and Richard Saltonstall succeeded in delaying the proceedings. But Gorges was building a "great shippe" expressly to carry himself and an armed force across the ocean to seize the charter.

Then, in June 1635, Massachusetts learned that Gorges's warship, upon its launching, broke apart. To nearly all in Massachusetts, this proved that God favored them. Such favor confirmed them in their course. Later, when the Privy Council under Laud's prodding again demanded the return of the charter, the magistrates seemed to capitulate, writing, "We dare not question your Lordships proceedings in requiring out patent to be returned. . . . [If] in anything we have offended his Majesty or your Lordship, we humbly prostrate ourselves at the footstool of supreme authority; we are sincerely ready to yield all obedience."[30] But they did not return the charter.

Meanwhile, the magistrates turned to Salem. Endicott's challenge to their authority had just been resolved, but the magistrates could hardly consider the resolution a victory. Even so, and embarrassing as the episode may have been to them, Endicott had not so much defied them; he had simply gone past them in the same direction.

Williams's challenge was greater, for he directly and explicitly opposed them. Half a century later Cotton Mather called Williams "the *first rebel* against the divine *church order* established in the wilderness."[31] Mather was correct. He might just as well have called him the first rebel in the wilderness.

Also in June, the Salem church formally installed Williams in the church office as teacher. In other such ceremonies in Massachusetts, leading clergy from other churches participated and celebrated. For Williams's ceremony,

Cotton was not present, nor Hooker, nor Mather, nor any other minister. In making Williams teacher, Salem had defied not only the magistrates but the elders of other churches.

In some ways, to the magistrates and other ministers at least, this defiance of Salem was worse than that of Williams. It was one thing for an individual to struggle against authority, and Williams's actions seemed still no more than well-intentioned error. True rebellion came when a community of people rose up, as Salem had. All Salem had defied the authorities.

The same General Court which finally settled upon the modest punishment of Endicott also received a request from Salem. The town wanted to expand, and acquire land in Marblehead Neck.

This gave the state opportunity not only to bring Williams to heel, but to finally impose its will on Salem. It would not let that opportunity slip past. The court did not act on Salem's request. Instead, the assistants delayed action "because they had chosen mr williams their Teacher." They would use the request to gain leverage over the town. To the next General Court, noted Winthrop, "mr Williams of salem was summoned & did appeare."[32]

# ❧ CHAPTER 17 ❧

The General Court convened in Boston July 8, 1635. It quickly brought Roger Williams "under Question before the magistrates & Churches for diverse dangerous opinions." Winthrop reported these dangerous opinions to be "1: that the magistrate ought not to punishe the breach of the first table, otherwise than in such Cases as did disturbe the Civill peace. 2: that he ought not to tender an oathe to an vnregenrate man. 3: that a man ought not to pray with such [unregenerates], though wife, Childe, &c. 4: that a man ought not to give thankes after the Sacrament, nor after meate, &c."[1]

The first two charges were the essential ones. The first cited Williams's objection to the state enforcing the first four commandments of the decalogue, which in his view placed it in the position of judging what humanity owed God. The second raised the question of the loyalty oath.

The third and fourth charges—the fourth involved the question of when precisely during a meal to say grace—even in the Massachusetts of that time would not normally have generated charges by even a single magistrate, much less would they have risen to the level of the full General Court. Their inclusion suggests the common prosecutorial tactic both then and now of burdening defendants with every conceivable offense. Their inclusion also makes particularly noticeable by their absence Williams's far more dangerous opinions: his attacks on King Charles and his claim that planters had no claim to land that was not purchased from the Indians. The absence of these charges meant that Williams had satisfied the authorities by abandoning his public profession of these positions.*

---

*No official record survives containing an account of the trial, and a discrepancy exists between Winthrop's account of the charges and other accounts which do include the land issue. I have relied on Winthrop's summary for two reasons. First, he wrote his account more or less contemporaneously. The earliest other surviving account was written almost a decade later, and other

The assistants seem to have barred Williams's supporters from the court while "desireing" all the ministers of the plantation "to be present." Such a request—an order really—was unusual, signifying the importance attached to the event. It seems all clergy did attend. Already they were cooperating with the magistrates against Williams; already all the churches in the Bay were preparing to jointly admonish both the Salem church for installing Williams as teacher and Williams himself. Admonishment was the first, threatening step toward more severe discipline.

Williams thus faced a pointedly hostile court. One after another, magistrates and clergy cited Scripture in attacks upon his statements and their ramifications. Criticism rained down upon him. He withstood it. If his supporters were barred from attending, if no attorney represented him and no witness spoke for him—no account mentions any—he knew that outside the court he was not isolated.

Defending himself, he started by saying that magistrates were "properly and adequately fitted by God to preserve the Civill state in civil peace and order, as he hath also appointed a spiritual government and governors in matters pertaining to his worship and the consciences of men."[2] None of his judges would have disagreed with that statement, even though it separated church and state. Their interpretation of what constituted "civil order," however, was radically different from his. His real defense rested upon the fact that none of the charges amounted to a "breach of the holy or civil peace, of which I have ever desired to be unfeignedly tender."[3]

This echoed Coke's jurisprudence, much of which could be expressed in his ruling, "*Cogitationis poenam nemo emeret,*" that no man may be punished for his thoughts, expanded to include the freedom to speak one's thoughts. Whether Williams considered, much less cited this is impossible to know, but he had spent years exposed to it, exposed to the idea of free speech.

"[M]uch debate . . . about these things" ensued, noted Winthrop. Whatever the debate, the position of all the assistants and clergy was foreordained.

---

accounts came long after that; some of these later accounts clearly contain inaccuracies—for example, incorrectly stating that Williams was charged with defacing the flag. I have also considered Williams's own observation that the land issue was brought up (see below) "[a]fter my publike triall and answers at the generall Court." So this issue was raised and discussed at this same session of the court, but not in the trial proper. The later accounts likely conflated the actual charges cited by Winthrop with the informal discussion in the same venue.

Winthrop stated that "[a]ll magistrates & ministers" judged Williams to be "erronious & verye dangerous," but the jury was the entire General Court. Winthrop made no claim of unanimity or even near-unanimity among deputies.

Any support Williams may have had among those deputies did not, however, weigh in his favor, nor did the fact that Salem stood with him. According to Cotton, the magistrates and clergy held that his support only made him "the more dangerous."[4]

The court of course found him guilty, but the verdict did not end the court's condemnation of him.

"After my publike triall and answers at the generall Court," Williams later wrote, one assistant rose and condemned him anew, repeating the charges already made and adding that Williams "holds forth . . . that we have not our land by patent from the King, but that the natives are the true owners of it, and that we ought to repent of receiving such a patent."[5]

On this one issue, Williams had yielded to "Worldly policie" considerations and had ceased discussing it. But he had not changed his mind. Now, under attack again, he gave back a "Rockie" edge, reiterating his position and his reasoning. There was no hint of recantation on this or any of the other issues.

The court had not pronounced sentence, and it asked the ministers for their advice. The ministers had tried with love to show Williams his errors, they had clearly confuted him, but he had nonetheless out of pride and obstinacy maintained those errors. They now "professedly declared . . . that he who should obstinately maintaine suche opinions . . . were to be removed, & that the other Churches ought to request the magistrate so to doe."[6]

It was up to the court to accept or reject the advice. It was up to the court whether to banish him. It deferred a decision for now.

Finally, the court turned its attention to the Salem church. In the wake of the court's judgment on Williams, little more needed to be said. It condemned the church's "Callinge him to office," judging it "a great Contempt of authoritye."[7]

Even so, as with Williams, it decreed no punishment for Salem. It delayed. It also again deferred acting on the town's request to annex land, continuing to use it as leverage.

For now, "fine tyme was given to [Williams] & the Church of Salem to consider of these thinges till the next general Court," Winthrop noted, "& then either to give satisfaction to the Court or els to expect the sentence."[8]

Neither Williams nor Salem was intimidated. Rather, the General Court had "incensed" Williams, Endicott, and much if not most of Salem. They believed the court and the colony's clergy had far overstepped their authority. The town stood by Williams, for now.

Cotton and others repeatedly met with him, trying to convince him to give satisfaction by recanting, by conforming. Cotton later wrote, "I spent a great part of the Summer in seeking by word and writing to satisfy his scruples."[9]

But Williams was in no mood for concessions. He had forced the magistrates to retreat once. He intended to force the magistrates to retreat again. He planned to build support outside Salem, to convince the members of other churches that, even if they believed he was in error, the magistrates had both behaved abominably and set a dangerous precedent. They had, he charged, chosen to "punish two or three hundred of our town for the conceived failings of the church; we see not how any cloud . . . can hide this evil from the eyes of all."[10]

Confident of his position, he and Samuel Sharpe, the Salem elder, now wrote a letter to each church in the Bay to which a magistrate belonged, urging the churches to "admonish their Magistrates"[11] for committing "a haynous sinne"[12] and "of their open transgression of the rule of justice."[13]

Sharpe and Williams expected their letters to be read publicly in each church. They were naïve. The letters were addressed to and belonged to the congregation and not the church officers, but it was church officers—men who had already condemned both Williams and the Salem church—who opened them. Not one read the letter to his congregation. Outraged anew, Williams and Sharpe demanded that the letters be read. But they had no power to enforce their demand.

Then, suddenly, for the second time in his life, Williams fell seriously ill at the height of a crisis. Whether this was coincidence or his illness was caused entirely by stress is impossible to know. But his symptoms were real enough; he could not even speak. Cotton gloated that this demonstrated God's disapproval of him, that God did "stop your mouth by a sudden disease and to threaten to take your breath from you."

At the same time, the magistrates and Cotton launched new attacks through their own churches, which now wrote directly to the Salem church, hoping its congregants "might hear us" and in turn force Williams to hear them. Elders, clergy, and laymen from around the colony also began to weigh heavily upon individual members of the church at Salem. In every contact, in every business dealing, those from Salem heard that they were in error, had to respond to questions. Did they seek to splinter the plantation? If Williams was right, why then had God silenced him? Why had God struck him down? Did they have such confidence in Williams as to choose his interpretation over such scholars as Cotton and Hooker? What good to Salem could come of this fight? Did not all in the plantation love one the other?

As the pressure intensified, Cotton noted, "The church finally began to hearken to us, and accordingly began to address themselves to healing of his spirit."[14]

Some Salem church members urged Williams to reconcile with the magistrates. Williams believed only "fear of persecution" caused them "to say and practise what to my knowledge with sighs and groans many of them mourned under."[15] Nonetheless, the move stung him.

On September 3, the General Court met again. Now the assistants turned ruthless; they would have their way. Salem's deputies arrived prepared for a full debate. The assistants had no intention of allowing such a debate, of allowing the "spreading of his Leaven to sundry."[16] They refused to allow Salem's representatives to take their seats.

Endicott angrily "protested against the proceedings of the Court." The assistants jailed him for contempt of authority.

Imprisonment was a humbling experience for him, utterly humbling, and it brought an enormous change in him. However aggressive, impulsive, and passionate he was, he was neither a rebel nor an original thinker; rather, he absorbed the views of people around him, reflected them, and in the passion of the moment and the authority of the moment he transformed them into action. He was one of those who do what others only think. Actions can in themselves create new realities, but he neither created new thought nor thought to create. If he was a man who followed one pathway with passion and vigor, he was also one who could be deflected onto a new path; he was a malleable man, a man who could be convinced. Now the pressure made him bend until "he gave place to the Truethe."[17] Only hours after being jailed he "acknowledged his fault, and was discharged."[18]

His acknowledgment of error was no act; it set him on a new path. He never again supported Williams. Far into the future, he would prove as vigorous an enemy as he had been an ally.

That same day the court made clear that it would discipline not only Williams but all who stood with him, ordering "Mr. Samuel Sharpe . . . to appear at the next particular Court, to answer for the letter that came from the church at Salem, as also to bring the names of those that will justify the same; or els to acknowledge his offence, under his own hand for his own particular."[19]

Finally, the court demanded "satisfaction" for the letter Williams and Sharpe had sent the churches of the commonwealth, in which they had "reproached and vilified the magistrates and deputies of the General Court." If a majority of "the freemen of Salem shall disclaim the Letters sent lately," the town could then "send deputyes to the General Court."[20] It could also annex the land the town wanted. The government of the colony was once again conflating the entire town of Salem with its two church leaders.

All the weight of the plantation's government now pressed upon Salem. All the weight of the churches of the plantation, of the clergy and elders, now pressed upon Salem. And all the weight of money pressed upon Salem as well. The men of business in Salem, and all those within it who sought to expand into Marblehead Neck, recognized the practical benefits of finding some compromise—and, lacking that, of yielding.

Under this weight, besieged by repeated entreaties and repeated assaults, repeated pleas and repeated threats, the church of Salem had already begun to bend. Now it began to crack.

Williams himself drove a wedge into the crack. His illness left him still unable to speak, so he wrote to his own church that he would no longer communicate with other churches in the Bay and demanded that the Salem church do the same. If not, he would cut off his own communication with it.

He was demanding absolute fealty. In doing so, he pushed too hard by far. The first Lord's day after the meeting of the General Court, Sharpe, who had with Williams called for admonishing the magistrates, read Williams's latest letter to the Salem church demanding that it separate itself from the other churches in the Bay. This demand "grieved . . . the whole church."[21]

The congregation by erection of hands chose to remain in communion with the rest of the Bay, and to accept the land.

Endicott had fallen away from Williams. Now the church and even Sharpe had. Williams awaited his next court appearance and sentencing alone.

Shortly before the next General Court convened, two "great shippes" dropped anchor in Boston harbor. While sailors used hoists to unload a cargo of cattle and goods, the ships creaking in swells, passengers lumbered down gangplanks. At least five were noteworthy, including John Wilson, the Boston minister whose post Williams had been offered so many years earlier, Thomas Shepard, another prominent minister, and Winthrop's son John Winthrop Jr. Both Wilson and Winthrop Jr. were returning from their second trip back to England; such back-and-forth travel was not unusual, and demonstrated the close interaction and communication between the plantation and there.

Winthrop the Younger had already made a mark in his own right, and two English peers, Lord Saye and Sele (one person) and Lord Brooke, had asked him to plant a settlement that became Saybrook, Connecticut. Charming, highly intelligent—even brilliant, accomplished enough as a naturalist that he became a founding member of the Royal Academy and counted as friends many of the leading scientists of the day—and extraordinarily capable, he was also a man who calculated and weighed things, a man charming and competent enough to win trust even while his unceasing attention to his own ends made him untrustworthy. He and Williams had met and become close in England, and they would remain on intimate terms for the rest of their lives. For Winthrop Jr. and his father this relationship would prove useful; for Williams it would prove damaging, although he would never know the son was using him.

Two more men arrived who would play large roles in both English and American history. The Reverend Hugh Peter had fled England for Rotterdam, until he found himself "persecuted by the Englishe Embassador, who would have brought his & other Churches to the Englishe discipline"[22]—Laud's reach had extended that far. So Peter now fled Rotterdam for New England. He was traveling under an alias—as were Wilson, Shepard, and several other Puritan clergy on the ships—to escape Laud's spies. Once in New England, he replaced Williams at Salem and compelled that congregation to conform to the view of the Massachusetts clergy. Later he would return to England and become a powerful voice on the parliamentary side during the English Civil War, powerful enough that he ended his life on the gallows, drawn and quartered for his role in killing a king.

Lastly, the ship brought Sir Henry Vane the Younger, only twenty-two years old, the highest-ranking nobleman yet to come to America. A devout Puritan, he was not driven out of England; his rank protected him from Laud. Still, he "forsooke the Honors & prefermentes of the [king's] Court, to enioye the Ordinances of Christ in their purity here,"[23] and to help in the building of New Jerusalem. He arrived amid much fanfare and his rank won him instant deference, so much that, despite his youth, only a few months later the freemen elected him governor. In some ways he was much like Williams: an enthusiast, a man of courage, of intense feeling, of sincerity. He and Williams immediately formed a friendship that would last the rest of their lives and prove of utmost importance. Vane too would return to England and become an important and powerful figure, arguably second only to Cromwell. He too would end his life on the gallows.

Williams had been ordered to appear at the October General Court in Newtown. It gathered in the town meeting house, a large, simple structure that served for both worship and public functions. Plain but not rustic, it was well finished with clapboard and sufficient windows to let in much light. If it had none of the ornamentation that Laud called the beauty of holiness, its very simplicity reminded all that no simple confession nor act of contrition could mollify God's fury, nor assure one of salvation. God's merciful grace moved with entire mystery, and the struggle with evil was personalized, particular, and intimate. If the structure lacked even the decoration or the spire typical of later New England churches, its simplicity still went beyond the merely functional to convey a certain grace.

There was, however, nothing graceful about what happened inside on this day. The court met in full formality and what grandeur the Puritans allowed, and the assistants had again called upon "all the ministers in the Baye . . . to be present."[24] They all did attend, including the newly arrived Shepard and Peter, who had brought fresh tales of Laud's persecution of Puritans. So it was with unintended irony that Governor John Haynes began the proceedings against Williams by citing Romans, 16:17, "Now I beseech you brethren, mark them which cause divisions and offenses contrary to the doctrine ye have learned; and avoid them."

No official record exists of the proceedings,[25] but according to Winthrop's journal entry, the court addressed the letters Williams had written "to the Churches Complayninge of the magistrates for iniustice, extreame oppression &c.: & the other to his owne churche, to persuade them to renounce Communion with all the Churches in the Baye, as full of Antichristian pollution."[26]

These were in effect new charges, subsuming the earlier ones. The court considered itself generous and patient. It gave Williams every opportunity to recant. Instead, he "iustified both these Lettres, & maintained all his opinions."

Again, the court demonstrated its patience. Again, it offered him "further Conference or disputation" with learned clergy, who could show him his error.

Williams declined.

The court offered to delay proceeding against him for one more month.

Williams once again declined. He would have this out, finally, here and now.

The court chose for its champion Thomas Hooker, who so long ago had ridden with Williams to the Sempringham conference. He carried himself with such majesty that it had been said he could put a king in his pocket.[27] Cotton's grandson Cotton Mather, best known for his role in the later Salem witchcraft trials, also credited Hooker with "a singular ability at giving answers to cases of conscience."[28]

The two men were capable of debating for hours. Each had been trained to debate at length, each could cite Scripture flawlessly, and each could interpret that Scripture. Williams could cite the principles of English law as well. All surviving accounts of this debate were written by Hooker's supporters, and all say Hooker triumphed, to the extent that he ultimately silenced Williams, that "Mr. Williams thought better to hold his peace, then to give an Answer."[29]

Williams likely would have disagreed with what his silence meant, but Winthrop summed up accurately: "Mr. Hooker . . . could not reduce him from any of his errors."[30]

Guilt or innocence had never been at issue. The only question was whether Williams would recant, apologize for offending the magistrates and the clergy, and conform.

He had not and would not.

Cotton wanted Williams gone. Nearly all clergy and elders did. But Cotton and Wilson seem to have been the most active, the most virulent, the most convincing in arguing against him. Over the preceding days and that night they spoke with magistrates and deputies. Later Cotton claimed the sentence was "neither done by my counsell nor consent." But he also admitted telling at least one magistrate "of mine own marvell at the weaknesses, and slendernesse of the grounds of his opinions, notions, and courses, and yet carried with such vehemency. . . . Truly, said I, I pity the man, and have already interceded for him . . . [but] have now no more to say in his behalf."³¹

Williams believed Cotton did much more than simply wash his hands of the matter, and stated that "his memory faild him. . . . [D]ivers worthy gentlemen . . . solemnly testified, and with teares, that they could not in their soules have been brought to have consented to the sentence, had not Mr. *Cotton* in private given them advice and counsell."³²

Winthrop reported that "all the ministers, save one, approv[ed] the sentence."

Condemnation from the clergy perhaps Williams expected. But he also came under attack from a new quarter, an unexpected quarter, and one which must have pained him. Winthrop continued, "[H]is own church had him under question also for the same cause; and . . . openly disclaimed his errors, and wrote an humble submission to the magistrates acknowledging fault in joining with Mr. Williams in that letter to the churches against them."³³

When the court convened in the morning, no further discussion occurred. The governor pronounced the sentence: "Whereas Mr Roger Williams, one of the elders of the church at Salem, hath broached & dyvulged dyverse newe and dangerous opinions, against the auchtoritie of magistrates, . . . and yet mainteneth the same without retraction, it is therefore ordered that the said Mr. Williams shall dep[ar]te out of this jurisidicoon within sixe weekes."³⁴

Williams's break with Massachusetts, and his break with the Salem church, was now complete.

The sentence stunned Williams. Indeed, for the rest of his life he seemed never quite able to accept it, never quite to believe it could have happened. He understood how a church might expel him, might excommunicate him. But he could not then grasp, could never grasp, how he could be banned from civil society. In his view, he had done nothing except exercise the rights held by all free Englishmen. Coke himself had extended the full protection of English law to the American colonies in a 1608 ruling.

There was no doubt about the gravity of the sentence. Banishment had certainly been imposed before, but the colony had not issued such a sentence in three years, and none of those expelled earlier had been such respected contributors to the community as Williams. Despite the Salem church's abandoning him, the town "was in an uproar, for he was esteemed an honest, disinterested man, and of popular talents in the pulpit."[35]

Defenders of Massachusetts then and later insisted the plantation banned Williams for civil reasons, not religious ones. Later defenders of the colony particularly emphasized his position on Indian ownership of the land to justify the expulsion. Yet Winthrop's listing of the formal charges omitted this important charge even while including such trivia as whether to give thanks before or after eating. Massachusetts's defenders also insisted that Williams could have believed anything he chose and remained in the plantation had he only refrained from publicly stating his beliefs.

But whatever Cotton and others argued later, at the time of the trial the magistrates understood that the only significant accusation was the first one which Winthrop stated: the relationship between the state and the church, as embodied in the state's enforcing those of the Ten Commandments which defined humans' responsibility to God, and Williams's right to express an opinion on that relationship. He had committed no act of rebellion, nor even of disloyalty. He had only expressed his beliefs.

That was the only real accusation. The others were dross. Although Williams was also charged with opposing the magistrates' use of the loyalty oath, he had convinced so many in the plantation of the correctness of his view that the magistrates had ceased imposing it. Banishing all who shared his view on the oath would have banished half the plantation.

Nor could they expel him for his position on land rights; he had acceded to their demand of silence on that. But on the question of the state imposing the views of the Puritan church, on this question, pushed by Cotton and others, it could and would act.

The sentence spoke to much more than Williams's personal circumstances. It defined the course of settlement in New England. More importantly, it opened a fissure in America, a fault line which would rive America all the way to the present. That fissure opened over the question of the role of government in religion and of the reverse, the role of religion in the government.

Puritans in Massachusetts did believe a division between church and state should exist. The question was where to draw the line. The General Court had earlier asked some clergy not only to develop "one uniforme order of discipline in the churches" but "to consider how farr the Magistrates" should go "for the preservation of that uniformity" in the churches. The result was the treatise *A Modell of Church and Civil Power.*

Its informing principle, and the essence of what Hooker had argued in his disputation with Williams, was that the state was the "nursing father" of the church. This view was hardly unique to New England Puritans. In England Laud believed the same, and so did those Puritans in disguise and under aliases who were hiding from his pursuivants.

Roger Williams did not believe the state should be nursing father to the church. He saw society differently. His views were as yet nascent, and they would develop over the course of his remaining life. He would voice them in America and in England, and they would inform one side of the great fault line in America.

That came later. For now he retired to Salem to prepare for his banishment.

While dealing with such quotidian particulars as selling his house to raise money, he considered where to go. The Plymouth colony seemed at first a possibility, but Plymouth authorities were unwilling to offend Massachusetts by sheltering a man it had banished. Settlements in present New Hampshire and Maine might have received him; they stood outside the Bay's jurisdiction and were less dependent on it than Plymouth. But the arc of Williams's own ideas increasingly turned toward something more radical: freedom.

Freedom. It was clearly on his mind. Less than a month after his sentencing his wife bore him a daughter. He named the child Freeborne.

Freedom. He had seen his mentor go to the Tower to protect English freedom. He had watched Parliament struggle with the king to reassert English freedom. But he could not find freedom in England. Indeed, during John Wilson's most recent trip to England, Winthrop had referred to him by a code name in letters for fear that Laud's spies would intercept one, learn of Wilson's presence, track him down, and imprison him. Williams was far more critical of the Church of England than Wilson had ever been. For him a return to England meant certain prison, likely after being whipped, having his ears cut off, and his tongue bored. Prison itself would probably be for life, which was likely to be fairly short. No, there was no freedom for him in England.

But one option seemed increasingly attractive. His trading with the Indians had opened possibilities for him in territory where no English lived, in territory where he could find freedom. He began to plan a settlement beyond the bounds of the Massachusetts Bay colony, a settlement untouched as well by the Church of England. The land to the north was spoken for. He looked to the south.

Then he once again fell ill. Whether it was a recurrence of whatever had struck him during the summer, whether it was still another manifestation of stress, is impossible to know. He himself seemed to believe he had simply worn himself to the point of collapse. By "labours on the Lords dayes, and thrice a week at Salem"—he was referring to his past preaching—and "by labours day and night in my Fields with my own hands, for the maintenance of my charge; by travells also by day and night to goe and return from their Court . . . it pleased God to bring me neare unto death."[36]

It was now early November 1635. Because of his illness and to avoid forcing him to leave in winter when travel and resettlement was both difficult and dangerous, the magistrates agreed to delay his banishment. He could remain until spring—so long as he did not publicly preach his dangerous doctrines. Since he no longer worshipped in the church, this was an easy condition to agree to.

But a few supporters began to gather in his home; some prayed there, with him. Williams believed he was doing nothing wrong in his home. Coke had called the home inviolate, had written that "the house of every one is to him as his Castle and Fortress as well for defence against injury and violence, as for his repose."[37]

Word of the private gatherings reached Boston. Cotton had warned against the "spreading of his leaven to sundry that resorted to him."[38] On January 11, 1636, Winthrop, then an assistant, reported that the governor and assistants "mett at Boston to consult about mr. Williams" and his "entertain[ing] companye in his howse & to preache to them." But the magistrates' real concern was that Williams "had drawn above twenty persons to his opinion, and they were intended to erect a plantation about the Narragansett Bay, from whence the infection would easily spread unto these churches, the people being, many of them, much taken with the apprehension of his godlines."[39]

The magistrates did not want a refuge from themselves established just beyond their boundary and control. They wanted no one "infected with his extravagances" to settle close by their borders.

To prevent it, at least some magistrates advocated executing Williams.[40] Most felt this was too extreme an action, and one that might cause uproar in the plantation. Instead, despite knowing his likely fate in England, they "agreed to send him into England by a ship then ready to depart."[41]

Whatever happened to him there, they would be able to claim they had done nothing to him themselves. They could wash their hands of him. Winthrop continued his report: "Whereupon a warrant was sent to him to come presently to Boston, to be shipped, &c. He returned answer that he could not come without hazard of his life, etc."[42]

Two physicians testified that he was too sick for a trip to Boston, much less across the ocean, and a committee of Salem residents pleaded before the Governor's Council, a recently created group to make decisions between meetings of the court, to grant a delay. Instead, the governor ordered "a pinnace . . . sent with commission to Capt. Underhill, &c., to apprehend him, and carry him aboard the ship."[43]

One week earlier this same Governor's Council had reprimanded Winthrop for "his too much leniency to disaffected souls." Nonetheless, now he did something he never admitted publicly. He sent warning to Williams that he was about to be arrested and sent to England.

John Underhill was a professional soldier, a man not to be trifled with, and he would soon show himself to be a killing machine. He took fourteen men with him. Then, in the dead heart of winter, a great blizzard came out of the northeast, with heavy gale. The pinnace hove to in Boston harbor, waiting out the storm. For four days Underhill waited. It was a great storm, leaving snowdrifts as deep as a man.

It was likely with a great but secret pleasure that Winthrop reported, "[W]hen he came to his house, they found he had been gone three days before, but whither they could not learn."[44]

Part IV

# THE WILDERNESS

# ❧ CHAPTER 18 ❧

Roger Williams's home, a solid burgher's house which would stand another two and a half centuries, sat not far from the center of Salem, but forest was still close upon it. While the storm held those intending to arrest him in Boston, Williams entered that forest and quickly disappeared into it. He never saw Salem again.

He entered the wilderness ill and alone.* To make one's way through deep snow one has to lift one's foot high, place it, then lift the other foot high; it is like perpetually climbing stairs. To do so for any distance is utterly exhausting; he had to do it for miles. Perhaps he either was faking his illness or it was a manifestation of his mind; it is difficult to imagine how a seriously ill person could have survived this trek. Or perhaps he felt the strength of the Lord fill him.

Winthrop described that winter as "a very bad season." The cold was intense, violent; it made all about him crisp and brittle, the moisture from his breath freezing to his face. The cold froze even Narragansett Bay, an extraordinary event, for it is a large ocean bay riven by currents and tidal flows. But the cold may also have saved his life: it made the snow a light powder. Exhausting as it was to move through, step after step after step for miles, it lacked the killing weight of heavy moisture-laden snow. The cold also froze rivers and streams which he would otherwise have had to ford.

The violence of the cold, the desperation of his flight, the depth of the snow, the exhaustion of making his way left a mark on him. Thirty-five years later he would refer to that "Winter snow wch I feele yet."[1] So also leaving its mark was

---

*Some accounts suggest that a young servant named Thomas Angell accompanied him, but this supposition first surfaced more than a century later and contemporary documents do not support it.

the disillusionment that came with losing a faith which had been fixed and immobile. It was not his faith in God that he lost. It was his faith in man.

For another kind of cold scarred him also. Men who had been his fellows, his colleagues, his friends had cast him out. For the rest of his life he could never comprehend their stolid coldness, how he could be "driven from my house & land & wife & children," how he could "be denied the common aire to breath in, and a civill cohabitation upon the same common earth and also without mercy and humane compassion be exposed to winter miseries in a howling Wildernes?"[2]

He most likely made for the Wampanoags, the closest tribe to the south beyond the boundaries of the Bay colony. He had long traded with the Wampanoag sachem Ousamequin; for years he had "spared no cost toward them and in Gifts to Ousamaquin Yea and all his."[3] That investment proved a wise one. But it was still thirty miles to Wampanoag territory; possibly on his way there other Indians sheltered him for some nights. Wherever he stayed, he survived only because Indians took him in. There was no comfort in this shelter. For fourteen weeks he did "not know what Bread or Bed did meane." Moving from place to place, enduring "distressed wandrings amongst the Barbarians," and "destitute of food, of clothes," during the worst of it "I may say as Jacob, Peniel, that is, I have seen the face of God."[4]

He never gave a full accounting of his experiences that winter, saying only that "the ravens fed me in the wilderness." The memory of these "Barbarians" caring for him after the English cast him out never left him.

The memories could not leave him: the ice of that winter and the ice of those he had regarded as friends and colleagues had left a burn upon his heart. The latter left the hottest scar, for during that winter Cotton wrote him several letters, at least one of which was carried by Indians to him. It was marvelously taunting, saying that if he "perished" among the "Barbarians, . . . your bloode had been on your owne head; it was your sinne to procure it, and your sorrow to suffer it."[5]

Decades later Williams vividly recalled receiving the letter, that its heated ferocity and frozen rigidity "stopt" him. The fact that Cotton sent it at all, sent it knowing the desperate straits he was in, sent it as if to exult in his troubles, stopped him. More even than his banishment, it isolated him, made him feel "cut off."

In the seventeenth century, that term—usually spelled "cut of"—meant not simply isolation; it meant violent death. It connoted an outcome absolute and final. It referred to one man killing another, usually in battle; when the fight was between Indians, "cut off" meant the victor had beheaded the loser. Williams frequently used the term in his letters and tracts; he used it so often, over so many years, so much more than other writers, that a reader cannot help but note it and cannot help but wonder at its significance to him. Each usage seems to reflect his unceasing, unremitting inability to comprehend why he had been cut off by Massachusetts, and his bitterness over it. His use of the term suggests the extent to which what happened to him became an obsession, even as he went on with his life. He was no loner, much less a misanthrope. He was a social creature, a man who made friends easily and often, a man who enjoyed the society of others.

Yet he was now cut off, cut off at any rate from the human society of Massachusetts, cast adrift emotionally, mentally, and physically, cast into the ocean of wilderness surrounding an island of civilization. Being adrift in a new world, he began exploring, probing, thinking. And he thought deeply.

Through the winter Williams remained alone. His family would not join him until he made a new home. In the spring he settled upon a site suitable, he believed, for that home. It was a forested spot but with adequate soil, freshwater, and close access to Narragansett Bay and the world beyond. If he did not speak of it as his own city upon a hill, he nonetheless intended for it to be a new kind of place, a refuge not only for himself but others.

In early spring a handful of men from Salem arrived and asked to join him. One of them was William Harris, who had come to America in the same ship as Williams. Williams allowed him to remain, he later said, "out of pity." He would come to regret that decision. For now, though, a tiny community began to take shape.

While living in temporary shelters, probably wigwams after the Indian fashion, the men cleared the land, planted crops, and began building homes for their families—the new arrivals had like Williams left their families in Salem. They worked communally through spring and summer.

But Massachusetts was exerting pressure on Plymouth to expel them. Plymouth Governor Edward Winslow yielded, sending him word that he had "fallen into the Edge of their Bounds, and they were loth to displease the Bay."

Winslow told him to "remove but to the other Side of the Water." They had settled on the eastern bank of a river; if they crossed to the western bank they would pass out of Plymouth's territory. Once they moved, Winslow told him, "We should be lo[ving] Neighbours togeather." More importantly, being outside any English jurisdiction he would have "the Country free before [you]."[6]

Williams had no desire to leave. He and the others had already planted a crop, and they would have to abandon it before harvest. They would have no supplies for winter. But they also had no choice.

The other side of the river was Narragansett country. The Narragansetts, rivals of the Wampanoags, were the most powerful tribe in the region—chiefly because the epidemic which had devastated most New England tribes had left the Narragansetts almost untouched. The tribe's sachem was Canonicus, an aged, tough, and wizened man whom Williams referred to as "that Old Prince," and who allowed his nephew Miantonomi to exercise considerable power. Neither of them was receptive to the English.

Soon after the Plymouth colonists arrived, Canonicus had sent them a "gift" of arrows wrapped in a snakeskin; Plymouth had taken this as a warning and returned the skin filled with powder and shot. Canonicus had refused to accept it; he would remain "most shy of all English to his last breath."[7] Miantonomi was if anything even more hostile; he considered the English a threat to the very existence of all Indians.

Williams, however, had developed an excellent personal relationship with them. He had given them frequent "tokens and presents &c. many years before" and had also advised them in conflicts both with other tribes and with the English; two years earlier he had even negotiated treaties for them. "[T]herefore," he wrote, "when I came I was welcome."

Confident of his reception, Williams climbed into a canoe with several others and began to scout out sites for a settlement. He chose a site where a broad finger of Narragansett Bay narrowed into a cove into which the Moshassuck and Woonasquatucket Rivers emptied. Tidal influences made the water in those two streams undrinkable, but a freshwater spring bubbled nearby. During salmon runs, a later writer noted, the fish "ran so thick that the English said they could walk across the river on the backs of the salmon without getting their feet wet."[8] In turn, the fish attracted swarms of birds, including thousands of migrating ducks and geese. Eels, lobster, quahaugs, and clams were there for the plucking, like berries off a bush.

The fish and game had drawn Indians of different tribes to the cove for centuries. While there, they competed in games. A trail ran past the cove, stretching up the coast north and south for many miles. (Much of it later became the Post Road, and eventually U.S. Route 1.)⁹ The land by the cove itself was also flat, but hills rose on all sides, making it defensible. It was a perfect site, better than the first.

Canonicus and Miantonomi gave Williams permission to settle there after negotiating what seemed clear boundaries. Williams later declared that Canonicus "was not I say to be stirred with mony to sell his land to let in Foreigners. Tis true he recd presents and Gratuities many of me: but it was not thouhsands nor ten thouhsands of mony could have bought of him an English Entrance into this Bay."¹⁰ He said the land was "purchasd by Love."

Massachusetts was no happier with him on that bank of the river than on the other. Ousamequin now protested. Though a friend to Williams personally, he was likely spurred to object at least partly because of pressure—and promise of support—from Massachusetts. He probably also feared that any connection between an Englishman and the Narragansetts further jeopardized his tribe. He admitted that he had ceded the land to the Narragansetts after a war—which in law made it theirs by right of conquest—but he now claimed that right of conquest did not apply because, he argued, the Narragansetts had not actually defeated him, that God "subdued us by a plague, which swept away my people and forced me to yield."¹¹ Therefore, he insisted, the cove remained Wampanoag land, and therefore still within Plymouth's boundaries.

By then Winslow, the governor who had told him simply to cross to the other side of the river, had returned to England to act as an agent for Plymouth. William Bradford had replaced him as governor.

Williams must have worried that Plymouth would force him to move once again. Yet if Bradford had warned Massachusetts authorities about him when he left Plymouth, Bradford had also called him "godly and zealous . . . a man of many precious parts." Now Bradford felt sympathy for him. He noted that Williams had already suffered the "losse of a Harvest that yeare . . . [and was] . . . as good as banished from Plymmouth, as from the Massachu." Bradford would push him no further. He pledged that even if "after due Examinacion it should be found true what the Barbarian said," still Williams "should not be molested and tost up and downe againe while they had Breath in their Bodies."¹²

Plymouth would later violate Bradford's pledge, but for now, finally, Williams had found home. If he was cut off still from Massachusetts, for now at least he enjoyed the benevolent neutrality of Plymouth. As he looked out upon the cove, knowing the ocean lay beyond, as he turned and looked inland, he must have believed he had what Winslow had promised: *the Country free before me.*

He was free, fully free, free in the wilderness, free to make of it what he would.

## ❄ CHAPTER 19 ❄

The area which eventually became Rhode Island included the lands surrounding Narragansett Bay and Aquidneck Island, a large island in the middle of the bay. All this land had a similar topography of woods, rock, and hills, although it lacked any singular great rise. Still, on the mainland one could stand atop one hill and see hill after hill beyond, soft green tree-topped ridges deep into the distance. One observer compared these hills to ocean rollers, writing, "The huge rollers stretch to the horizon in endless rise and slope . . . and over all is laid a thick mantle of woods, unbroken save . . . by a clearing so infrequent and small that it accents the ocean of forest. . . . [T]he underbrush is dense, and through vast areas all but impenetrable with such cover for quail, partridge, and woodcock . . . [and] the wildest of wild flowers. . . . Swift and pure streams pour through the valleys."[1]

The streams were, in fact, swift enough to later bring the first textile mills to America and, with them, the Industrial Revolution. The only flat area of the region lay south of Williams's purchase, along a narrow coastal plain hugging the bay in what soon became known as "Narragansett country." There a mix of rock, marsh, and sand bordered the ocean.

The central geomorphic feature of the region was Narragansett Bay itself. Verrazzano, who was the first European to explore it, reported that in it "any fleet, however large, might ride safely, without fear of tempest or other dangers." He called it "the Bay of Refuge." He particularly liked what became Newport for its "very excellent harbor."

The natives also impressed him: "[W]e saw about twenty small boats full of people, who came about our ship, uttering many cries of astonishment . . . [and] then came on board without fear. Among them were two kings more beautiful in form and stature than can possibly be described. . . . This is the finest looking tribe, the handsomest in their costumes, that we have found in our voyage.

They exceed us in size, and they are of very fair complexion; some of them incline more to a white, others to a tawny color; their faces are sharp, and their hair long and black, upon the adorning of which they bestow great pains; their eyes black and sharp, their expression mild and pleasant."[2]

(By contrast, in Maine, where the fur trade had brought Indians into more contact with Europeans, Verrazzano observed that Indians would stand "on some rocks where the breakers were most violent, while we remained on the little boat, and they sent us what they wanted to give on rope, continually shouting at us not to approach the land; they gave us the barter quickly, and would take in exchange only knives, hooks for fishing, and sharp metal. We found no courtesy in them, and when we had nothing more to exchange and left them, they made all the signs of scorn and shame that any brute creature would make.")[3]

A century after Verrazzano, the Narragansetts still survived as a powerful people outside the borders of Massachusetts and Plymouth. If Williams had had little choice but to locate there, it was indeed fortunate that he found this refuge. And from the first he intended it to be just that, a refuge, a place where one could be free. He later explained, "[H]aving made covenant of peaceable neighborhood with the sachems and natives round about us, and having, in a sense of Gods merciful providence unto me in my distress, called the place PROVIDENCE, I desired it might be for a shelter for persons distressed for conscience."[4]

He was not the first English there. William Blackstone, the man who had tired of first the Lord Bishops in England and then the Lord Brethren in Massachusetts, had already planted on the northwestern edge of Narragansett territory, near present Woonsocket, Rhode Island.

Blackstone, however, avoided others as a general rule. No one had followed him and no community had grown up around him, nor did he wish one to. Although a perfectly amiable host—even to the Puritans when they had arrived—he wanted nothing so much as to be left alone.

Williams had no desire to live by himself, to live *cut off*. To the contrary, he wanted very much to belong to and participate in a larger society. Now he had the opportunity to create one.

Now, in addition to the men who had initially sought him out and moved to Providence with him, a handful of others began straggling into what was

New England's most primitive settlement. It could not yet be called a town. He and they, without a charter or any legal authority from England, without any previous agreement as to how to govern themselves, had to determine what kind of society to build.

For guidance in defining the foundations and governance of that society, the others looked to Williams as both their natural leader and the man who owned the land. In turn, Williams needed to look no further than into himself, into the education provided by his own experience. It was a good place to begin. No one else in America had as intimate an experience with power as he, not only with the governance of Massachusetts but with the great grand power of England. If that latter experience came to him chiefly through his mentor's life, still it had brought him into the royal court, the King's Bench, Parliament, the Star Chamber, and the Tower.

Although Williams never explicitly stated that he derived his political ideas or his view of political freedom from Coke, the principles which Coke articulated clearly anchored Williams's thinking. The essence of Coke's views was encapsulated in his comment that every Englishman's home was as his castle and in Elizabeth's declaration that she sought no window into men's souls. Coke had also advanced the idea that the English constitution—not simply the written Magna Carta but all the traditions of the rights and privileges of England—prohibited arbitrary power. Williams was no anarchist. He believed in the state's authority over civil and criminal behavior. He opposed only the state's exercise of arbitrary authority—a view shared by most Puritans—and any state involvement in religion. He certainly knew Bacon's views on the royal prerogative and state power, as well as the views of Machiavelli; he rejected those views.

But Bacon may well have influenced him in other, even more fundamental ways. Bacon may have influenced the way in which Williams thought.

Williams clearly read Bacon, citing him in his own writings, but more important than any citation was an approach to evidence which he shared with Bacon. This was not the approach of Bacon as lawyer, chancellor, courtier, or interpreter of Machiavelli, but of Bacon as the great philosopher of science, the deviser of a method to seek the truth, Bacon as author of *Novum Organum*.

In this work and elsewhere Bacon called for observing nature and even experimenting upon it to find the truth. He attacked both the limitations of logic and reason itself, when relied upon alone. This was the Bacon who had dismissed Aristotle for selecting data to support his case like a litigator making an argument, instead of viewing evidence with an open mind, and for being "a mere bond-servant to his logic."

Bacon's rejection of Aristotle and scholasticism as well was not then unusual; both were commonly disparaged. But attacking logic per se *was* unusual; calling for reliance on the observed evidence of experience and on experimentation *was* unusual. Oxford and Cambridge dons still drilled the importance of logic into their students. Puritans fell under the particular influence of Peter Ramus, a French Huguenot murdered in 1572 by Catholics during the St. Bartholomew's Day Massacre. (Even the *Catholic Encyclopedia* concedes he was "singled out" for a death with "every circumstance of cruelty and brutality,"[5] and his martyrdom did not hurt his standing among Puritans.) Ramus preceded Bacon in rejecting Aristotle, but he did not attack logic. Instead he urged a closer connection between it and rhetoric, between style and argument; he built a system of categorizing knowledge and diagramming relationships between things which amounted almost to phylogeny.

Edmund Morgan, arguably the leading historian of Puritan New England, described how Ramist logic influenced Puritans using as an example Cotton, who had little interest in exploring uncertainty; he advised avoiding science because the "study of these natural things" could not "procure us settled rest and tranquility."[6] Instead, he made such statements as, "If the people be governors, who shall be governed?"[7] To Cotton, to all those following Ramist logic, this was an unanswerable argument; their training in logic and rhetoric had put blinders and straitjackets on them.

Bacon had already ripped off those blinders and shredded those straitjackets. He declared, "The logic now in use serves rather to fix and give stability to the errors which have their foundation in commonly received notions than to help the search after truth. So it does more harm than good."[8]

Bacon did not seek answers within the closed and suffocating circle of logic; he sought them in the breadth and wonder of nature. He is now too often considered simply an empiricist, despite his having warned that empiricism "gives birth to dogmas more deformed and monstrous than the Sophistical or rational school," and despite his explicit calls for experimentation, for applying "the trails and vexations of art" to nature. Because this process of experimentation took time, he called "Truth . . . the daughter of time, not of authority."

Never known for modesty, he also declared, "I am building in the human understanding a true model of the world, such as it really is, not as man's reason would like it to be."[9]

This was fully revolutionary indeed. After his death an "invisible college" of natural philosophers—scientists—began meeting regularly to discuss his ideas. Directly out of these meetings came the creation of the Royal Society.

As would become apparent in his writings, Williams, too, looked for evidence. He noted, "In the poor small span of my life, I desired to have been a diligent and constant observer." All he could do was observe; using experiments to probe the questions he contended with was and is impossible. But he observed with a fully open mind, a remarkably open mind, and his observations stretched from his personal experiences to the world—the entire known world—beyond. His analysis of different societies was ongoing, and he would voice his conclusions later, in his writings. They would prove revolutionary as well.

But before his writing, first came living.

Setting up a government for himself and the dozen or so men and their families—a total of fewer than fifty people—in Providence seemed simple. The Narragansetts had sold the land solely to him, and all English and colonial legal precedent gave him as proprietor considerable if not complete political control over the settlement. Williams, however, was willing to relinquish any special authority or power of his own to a communal society. His one requirement: that Providence remain a "common stock . . . for such as were destitute (especially for Conscience)."[10]

Initially the few heads of households in this tiny settlement made decisions by majority rule. Williams, despite the power afforded by his status as proprietor, voluntarily submitted to this majority—but he retained his ownership of the land. Yet even in this tiny settlement almost immediately interests clashed and strife and tensions developed. The key issue was the "common stock," the holding of property in common. William Harris in particular began to object to the arrangement. In fact, he objected continuously.

Harris was one of those men who can make common journey with others but while on that journey their eyes never rest; instead their gaze flicks about, searching out opportunities, determining which might be a main chance. He found such a chance in the empty lands here. He insisted to Williams that he too had left Massachusetts for reasons of conscience and began beseeching him, "wearying" him to "admit him and others into fellowship of my Purchase" and to separate out some land from the common stock and give each man title over a piece."

Williams yielded. But he would not divide the land without creating an overarching structure to link individuals together; he would not divide his holdings without creating a government. Before doing so, before translating the principles by which he hoped to govern into a formalized structure, sometime before September 1636 he wrote Winthrop, "I humbly crave your helpe . . . a word of private advise" about how to proceed.

Williams considered Winthrop a mentor and friend, which is hardly surprising given that Winthrop's warning of his impending arrest may have saved his life and certainly saved him from prison. Already, in the few months since Williams departed Salem, the two men had exchanged several letters.

How Winthrop viewed Williams is less clear, but he seemed to *like* Williams, to respect his sincerity and tenacity, and respect also his knowledge of the Indians. He also found him useful both personally—they subsequently became business partners in a venture in Narragansett Bay—and to the Bay colony. If others in Massachusetts were offended at Williams's presence just beyond their borders, Winthrop had in warning him of his imminent arrest actually suggested he "steer [his] Course to the Nahigonset Bay and Indians, for many high and hevenly publike Ends."¹² The end Winthrop had in mind was placing him in the middle of the most powerful Indian nation in the region.

Williams explained to Winthrop that so far those in Providence had governed themselves informally, with heads of families meeting every fortnight to decide issues of "our common peace, watch, and planting; and mutuall consent hath finished all matters with speede and peace."

But things were now becoming more complicated. Not only was Harris importuning Williams for change, but young men without families "of whome we had much neede" were arriving and they wanted "the Freedome of Vote allso, and aequalitie etc." Though sole owner of the land, Williams committed himself, he said, to continuing to "freely subject my selfe to Common Consent."

His letter included a draft civil compact. It stipulated "libertie of conscience," the liberty to think freely about God. He did not seek Winthrop's advice on this point, only on the political issues, adding, "I have not yet mencioned these things to my neigbours." The draft did not propose to build God's

Kingdom on earth or claim to advance God's will. It did not even ask God's blessing. Its only mention of God was to note that Williams had been "cast by the providence of the God of Heaven, remote from others of our Countriemen amongst the Barbarous in this towne of New Providence." Even this reference was a reminder that Williams had left Massachusetts over "difference of conscience."

He was awaiting Winthrop's "Councell . . . with the soonest convenience, if it may be, by this messenger." Winthrop's reply has not survived. His only reference to Providence's founding came two years later when he noted that Williams at his "first coming thither" had created a settlement in which "no man should be molested for his conscience."[13]

Whatever Winthrop advised, the final compact was virtually identical to the draft Williams sent him, except for one change. Williams—certainly not at the advice of Winthrop—excised all mention of God from the final compact. The final version did not refer to God in any way. This was extraordinary.

All comparable founding documents, whether English, Spanish, Portuguese, or French, spoke explicitly of God's purpose. Plymouth's Mayflower Compact, which governed both devout Separatists and adventurers with purely secular interests in America, stated, "Having undertaken for the Glory of God, and Advancement of the Christian Faith, and the Honour of our King and country, a Voyage to plant the first Colony in the northern Parts of Virginia. . . ."

Williams was a devout Puritan renowned for his piety. In two volumes of surviving letters, not a single one—not one—repeatedly fails to refer to God, not merely in some pro forma "God willing" but in an intimate way, citing and quoting relevant Scripture. Indeed, hardly a single paragraph in any letter fails to mention God. Faith, longing for God, and knowledge of Scripture are ingrained in his writing. Even for a seventeenth-century writer, the frequency of his religious references stands out. His life revolved around seeking God; that search informed the way he thought, the way he wrote, what he did each day.

For a man such as he to omit all mention of God underscored his absolute conviction that to assume that God embraced any state other than ancient Israel profaned God and signified human arrogance in the extreme.

All those in Providence unanimously agreed to this compact, underscoring that his views were not unique to himself. "We whose names are hereunder," they wrote, "desirous to inhabit in the town of Providence, do promise to subject ourselves in active and passive obedience to all such orders or agreements as shall be made for the public good . . . by the major consent of the present inhabitants . . . in a Towne fellowship, and others whom they shall admit unto them only in civil things."[14]

Omitting the mention of God made the document which would govern Providence utterly mundane—mundane in the most literal sense, mundane in that it dealt solely with the world. For it was hardly mundane in itself; it was revolutionary.

Williams had acquired all the land of the town but kept only a parcel equal in size to what he made available to others. He recouped his costs but declined any profit, receiving thirty shillings a lot "untill my charge be out." Once he was reimbursed, he donated all his remaining land to the town of Providence. After that, "Purchasers," as these early settlers became known, then paid "Thirtye Shillings unto a publicque stock."[15] Until land became scarce, later arrivals would also have the right to purchase land with their money also going to the town stock; this provided the town with both a small reservoir of funds and a stream of revenue. Each Purchaser had an equal voice in government. Williams's donation of land and creation of a town stock reflected his belief in both equality and social responsibility.

As the Providence government (and later Rhode Island's government also) grew and became more formalized, its essential nature remained true to the original compact Williams had written. This nature differed in important ways from that of Massachusetts, not to mention England. The most obvious difference of course involved religion. Williams was creating a haven for those whose religious views had made them outcasts. So the separation of God from the civil state continued and slowly matured: Providence would neither impose a religious test for voting nor would it require church attendance of those living there. This was a costly step, since virtually every other government in England and New England collected significant revenues from fines on those who did not attend worship.

But there were more subtle differences as well, which grew out of Williams's worldview. A comment he made to Winthrop is revealing: "I desire not to sleep in securitie and dreame of a Nest wch no hand can reach. I can not but expect changes, and the change of the last Enemie Death."[16]

One hesitates to overburden any single comment with significance, yet this stands out. It reflects a fundamental break from the more common concept of, and desire for, a fixed and immutable world, a world in which change was not embraced, a world in which stability was paramount. Clearly Puritans did not believe one simply accepted one's station; their very presence in New England spoke to this. Yet there was a qualitative difference between their view of the way society functioned—the traditional view of a calling and place for every person—and Williams's view. Williams was coming to see that individuals did not inherit a place in the world; they created it.

In addition, Williams was developing the view that governments received their authority from and were responsible to their citizens. This contradicted both the theory of the divine right of kings and the Puritan belief that they were carrying out God's plan, that they were building a City of God in New England. The fact that Massachusetts freemen elected the governor and assistants did not mean that the government's authority came from the governed. Winthrop had extended that power to freemen, but he believed that actual authority to govern came from God, not from the people, and that governors were accountable to God, not to the people. As he informed the freemen, "It is yourselves who have called us to this office, and being called by you, we have our authority from God, in a way of ordinance, such as hath the image of god eminently stamped upon it, the contempt and violation whereof hath been vindicated with examples of divine vengeance."[17]

Williams could not accept such a view. Logically, if God had extended His authority to the government of Massachusetts, then its punishment of him was also authorized by God. Because he rejected this, his punishment did not push him, as Massachusetts desired, toward conformity; instead, it drove him from it.

Everything drove him from it. His exchanges with Hooker and others at his trial had confirmed him in his analysis of Scripture, and what had happened since demonstrated the hardness of the hearts of those he had considered friends. Christian magistrates had determined not only to banish him but to send him to England, where prison and mutilation awaited him. Christians had done this. Colleagues and neighbors had done this. They had forced him to flee into the whiteness of winter.

Savages had taken him in and saved his life. He had no illusions about Indians. He was too intimate with them to have illusions and referred with disgust more than once to their "filthy smoak holes," and in moments of anger more than once denounced them as "wolves with men's minds." Yet the savages had cared for, fed, and tended to him. This fact too drove him further from conformity. And he began systematically exploring what lay beyond conformity.

His views were still maturing, but his basic principles already informed the Providence government with vitality, a vitality alive enough to flirt with chaos. The town allowed far more individual freedom than elsewhere because of Williams's developing concept—his idea was too preliminary to call it a theory—that the authority of a government derived from its citizens. Williams's views on liberty, both individual and religious, also informed the decision to build—or rather not to build—a church. In most New England towns, the building of a church and meeting place was among the community's first acts. Despite Williams's own intense religiosity, no such meeting place would be built in Providence for half a century. People worshipped in their homes, and homes in Providence were laid out not around a town common but in a straight line. This reflected an unusual, if not unique, individualism.

Roger Williams was not a loner or misanthrope. He wanted to belong to and build a society, but a society which would leave individuals within it alone, would not demand anything whatsoever of an individual's conscience. No such society existed. To live in such a society, he was creating and defining it.

But as Providence—and soon Rhode Island—grew, what he struggled with was less philosophy, or theology, or political theory, or politics itself. He struggled most with empire. For both Massachusetts and Plymouth soon began behaving imperially, and both began to move toward devouring his plantation whole, devouring also the freedom he was attempting to establish. They dwarfed him in military power, economic strength, and connections and influence in England. He countered only with an idea.

## ❧ CHAPTER 20 ❧

By the middle of the 1630s, Massachusetts had begun imposing itself upon America. As if to stamp its identity on the continent, it exercised its power both internally and externally. Indeed, one could almost say that to both define and demonstrate its power, it fought two wars, one a civil war—albeit one without bloodshed—and the other against an external enemy. It fought these wars almost simultaneously, beginning only a few months after Williams's expulsion. Both wars proved central to all that followed.

In that war against a foreign enemy, Williams provided critical assistance to Massachusetts at great personal risk. The government of the Bay did not so much as thank him, but in doing so he sealed a personal bond which ultimately proved of enormous consequence to him, to his plantation, and to his idea.

The proximate cause of the external war was the murder of John Oldham, a well-known trader who first came to New England before any Massachusetts Bay Company presence. In July 1636, another trader named John Gallop came across Oldham's pinnace adrift in the Atlantic off Block Island, which sits more than ten miles from the mainland. He could see a dozen Indians on deck but no sign of Oldham. Gallop, with a crew of only two Narragansetts and two boys—but armed with numerous guns—approached and hailed Oldham. There was no reply, but several Indians fled in a canoe filled with goods. Certain of foul play, Gallop now rammed Oldham's pinnace, knocking several more Indians into the sea, then raked the deck with shot until two Indians surrendered. Two others, armed with knives and English swords, retreated into the cabin belowdecks. Gallop boarded, bound the Indians who had surrendered, and discovered Oldham's body, "starke naked, his head clefte to the braynes, & his handes & legs cutt as if they had been cutting them off, & yet warme."[1] Gallop interrogated the bound Indians and learned that

Oldham's killer had escaped in the canoe. He then threw them overboard to drown. Judging it too dangerous to capture the Indians barricaded in the cabin, he tried to tow the pinnace to shore, but heavy seas forced him to cut it loose.

Even before this murder, relations between the English and the Indians in New England had become tense. Puritans in New England had never engaged in the kind of systematic brutality that the English in Virginia had, which had led to the wholesale slaughter of both races fifteen years before. Indeed, after Williams publicly raised concern about English rights to Indian land and in order to secure their land titles beyond any possible challenge, Puritans throughout Massachusetts began paying Indians for land which they had been using for years.

Still, as the English presence had expanded, relations with Indians had deteriorated. During the preceding few years, New England Indians had killed at least ten English. None of the killers had been caught, nor had revenge been taken. Although many of those killings may actually have been justified—for example, John Stone, who had been banished from Massachusetts and whom Plymouth was prosecuting for piracy, was killed while trying to kidnap several Indians—the English increasingly wanted revenge, increasingly wanted to teach Indians in general a lesson. This time Massachusetts was determined to find and punish the murderers and to use Oldham's death as a *casus belli*.

Contributing to this belligerency was Massachusetts's contempt for the Indians as warriors. John Underhill, the veteran of European religious wars who had been sent to arrest Williams, snorted that a battle between Indian tribes seemed "more for pastime then to conquer and subdue enemies. . . . They might fight seven yeares and not kill seven men."[2]

Williams too had observed less-than-European fury in wars between Indian tribes, noting that even large battles saw "seldom twenty slain." But he also understood that it was in the interest of Indians to avoid mass slaughter since victors often incorporated the vanquished into their own tribe, increasing their own strength. In addition, he recognized the personal nature of Indian combat and the value they placed on courage, and he saw something worthy of respect in the dance of Indian battle: "[H]aving no swords, nor guns, all that are slain are commonly slain with great valour and courage: for the conqueror ventures into the thickest, and brings away the head of his enemy."[3] Their ability "*To cut off*, or *behead*" enemies in the middle of a battle particularly impressed him: at this "they are most skilfull to doe in fight . . . tearing their head a little aside by his Locke, they in the twinkling of an eye fetch off his head though but with a sorry knife."[4] The Indians, he believed, could fight.

Regardless, Massachusetts was now determined to give example that English were not to be harmed. Some tribe was to pay dearly for Oldham's death.

It was unclear, however, whom to hold responsible for the murder. Block Island Indians belonged to the Narragansett demesne. Williams was convinced the Narragansetts had no involvement, and defended them to Henry Vane, who had just become Massachusetts governor, and Winthrop, whose political fortunes were recovering and who was now deputy governor. Vane and Winthrop investigated and agreed with Williams, telling him that Canonicus had impressed them with his "great Commande ouer his men: & a mervaylous wisdome in his answeares, . . . cleringe himselfe & his neighbors of the murder, & offering assistance for revenge of it yet upon very safe and warye Conditions."[5]

That left as possible targets several minor tribes and also the Pequot, Connecticut's most powerful tribe and mortal enemies of the Narragansett. The Pequot favored the Dutch over the English as trading partners, and, prior to Oldham's murder, the English had been warned that the Pequot were planning on "cutting off" English traders.[6] The Massachusetts magistrates decided to retaliate against Block Island Indians and the Pequot. They sent Endicott with a force of ninety men to Block Island. He was to kill all the men and remove women and children for sale into slavery, then go to Connecticut to demand of the Pequot those who had earlier killed Stone. Though Stone's death was well justified, Massachusetts was not in the mood to let it pass.

As the Massachusetts expedition readied itself, in August 1636, Williams began sending reports and his analysis of Indian activities to Winthrop, warning, for example, "The Pequots heare of your preparations."[7] This was precisely why Winthrop had advised him to settle in Narragansett country.

Endicott sailed from Boston and reached Block Island, seventy-five miles away, in late August. The Indians were prepared. As his men waded through gentle surf, flights of arrows greeted them, but they failed to pierce English armor. The Indians then evacuated the island, leaving it empty. In frustration, Endicott's force killed "their dogges in stead of men."[8] They also staved in canoes and burned empty wigwams and stocks of corn. The corn could not be replaced; its destruction meant months of hunger and the threat of starvation.

From Block Island, Endicott sailed to the mouth of the Connecticut River, where several hundred Pequots awaited him on rocks. From on board his ship, he demanded Stone's killers and a meeting with Pequot sachems. The killers had died in a smallpox outbreak, Endicott was told, and the sachems refused to appear unless the English "laye down their armes as his men should doe their bowes."[9] After hours of negotiations, he lost patience, announced that the Indians "had dared the English to come fight with them, & now they would come for that purpose."[10]

The Indians melted into the landscape, leaving several villages empty. Endicott "marched vp to their towne & . . . burnt all their wigwams & spoyled their Canoes."[11] Finally, "having burnt and spoyled what we could light on, wee imbarqued our men, and set sayle for the Bay."[12]

Although he killed few Indians—and possibly none—his behavior prompted protests to Massachusetts from Bradford, the Plymouth governor, and some of Hooker's people now living in the Connecticut interior. But most upset was Lion Gardiner, a professional soldier, who had been engaged to build and command a fort at Saybrook. Gardiner now sat exposed and isolated with Indian enemies on both sides. He complained bitterly that Massachusetts had sent Endicott "hither to raise these wasps about my ears, and then you will take wing and flee away,"[13] leaving the handful of English at Saybrook "to the Indians, whose mercies are cruelties . . . at the stake to be roasted, or for hunger to be starved."

Two groups were now eager for more war: Massachusetts considered the vengeance so far inflicted unsatisfactory, and the Pequot were inflamed.

At Saybrook the Pequot began to attack isolated English. Gardiner sent Vane an arrowhead removed from one of his own wounded men "because they had said that the arrows of the Indians were of no force."[14]

They had force. Pequots killed several of Gardiner's men "who went a mile from the house a fowling," then others who went to gather hay. They found another man and "roasted him alive." They captured a ship captain trading on the Connecticut River and "tied him to the stake, flayed his skin off, put hot imbers betweene the fleshe and the skinne, cut off his fingers and toes, and made hatbands of them."[15]

Then they besieged the fort at Saybrook, taunting Gardiner with Endicott's actions, asking if the English "did . . . kill women and children."

From behind a palisade, Gardiner shouted back that the Pequots "should see that hereafter."

The Indians "were silent a small space." Then came their reply: "We are Pequots, and have killed Englishmen, and can kill them as mosquetoes, and we will go to Conectecott and kill men, women, and children, and we will take away their horses, cows, and hogs."[16]

Of greatest concern to the English in New England was an alliance between Pequot and Narragansett. They had reason for concern. The Narragansetts numbered about twenty-five thousand then, and the Pequot population, while unknown, likely approached that. The English in New England then numbered less than ten thousand. (The Great Migration of Puritans to Massachusetts had begun, but less than half had yet arrived.) While English weaponry gave them decisive advantages over either one of these tribes, an alliance of both, especially if it included their tributary tribes, gave Indians a real possibility of success—at least temporary success. And while the English were much better armed, it was not uncommon for an Indian to have a gun—and Indians were far better marksmen, if only because they aimed. The English still used European tactics and based their training upon military manuals of the day, which instructed musketeers to "give fire breast high" and not aim.[17]

That the Narragansett and Pequot were ancient and proud enemies was the greatest obstacle to an alliance. Indeed, two years earlier, when Pequot had negotiated with Massachusetts over a treaty, their ambassadors were too proud to pay the Narragansett directly for safe passage through their territory. Instead they paid it to Massachusetts magistrates who passed it on to the Narragansetts.

But the prospect of war with the English, with their guns and iron, humbled the Pequot enough to now seek Narragansett help. As the trained bands of Massachusetts mustered and drilled, Vane learned, likely from Williams, that Pequot ambassadors were discussing an alliance with Canonicus and Miantonomi in a great war council. Immediately Vane dispatched a messenger to Williams, asking that he use his "utmost and Speediest Endeavours" to prevent it and authorizing him to negotiate a "League between [Massachusetts] and the Narigansetts."[18] The irony of asking a man banished by the Bay to become its agent at the risk of his life could not have escaped either of them.

Williams received the message in Providence. The war council was thirty miles south. By land it was a lengthy trip, especially given that he did not own a horse and traveled on foot. And so he went by canoe, into the teeth of a storm and heavy "great Seas," his canoe bobbing on jagged swells, rising on foaming white summits, falling into green troughs.

His arrival was unexpected. The village was temporary but still would have been laid out with defensible perimeters using boulders on high ground; more than a hundred wigwams would have surrounded Canonicus's. Most of the wigwams were small rounded domes of brush and animal skins covering a skeleton of easily transportable thin poles eight feet high, with a hole for smoke to escape and skins, grass, and brush covering the ground. A few larger wigwams were elongated, with two or more fires and smoke holes, elaborately decorated and colored; the largest could easily hold a hundred or more men in conference.

Williams, the only white, now was among one thousand or more Indian warriors contemplating war against whites. Yet Canonicus trusted him and allowed him access to the discussions. He was the only Puritan in the world then fluent enough in the Algonquin language to follow the conversations without a translator. (Most English traders were not Puritans, and generally even they had only rudimentary language skills.) The discussion moved deliberately. Hundreds of Indians likely sat in concentric rows. Describing another great conference, Williams later wrote, "Every man hath his pipe of their *Tobacco,* and a deepe silence they make, and attention given to him that speaketh." Some pipes were two feet long or longer, with massive wood or stone heads, "with men or beasts carved, so big or massie, that a man may be hurt mortally by one of them." Such pipes were carried slung behind a man's back. Men made their points in long speeches "with very emphaticall speech and great action."[19]

Williams remained for three days and three nights of negotiation. He did not sleep easily, fearing the Pequot ambassadors "whose hands and arms reaked with the bloud of my countrimen murthered and massacred by them on the Conecticut River, and from whome I could not but nightly looke for their bloudy Knives at my owne throat allso."[20]

The Pequots' message was simple: that the English would "overspread their country, and would deprive them thereof in time, if they were suffered to grow and increase," that "the English were minded to destroye all Indians," and that if the Narragansetts did not join with the Pequot, they would "make Way for their own future Ruin."[21]

Therefore, the Pequot ambassadors argued that the two most powerful tribes in New England must unite to drive the English out of their lands. They advised a "skulking way of war." English armor and weaponry was too strong for them, so they would "not come to open Battle with the English; only [set] Fire houses, kill Cattle, and lye in ambush for and shoot as [they] went about [their] Business; so they should be quickly forced to leave this Country."[22]

Several English sources reported that these "truly politick Arguments were upon the point of prevailing on the Narragansetts."[23] Canonicus turned to Williams for a response.

"I replied," said Williams, "that he had no cause . . . to question *English-mans, Wunnaumwauonck,* that is, faithfulnesse, he having had long experience of their friendliness and trustinesse."

Canonicus then "took a stick and broke it into ten pieces, and related ten instances (laying downe a stick to every instance)" in which the English had broken faith.

But he and his nephew Miantonomi trusted Williams. Already Miantonomi had visited him in Providence several times and "kept his barbarous court" in Williams's own home; Williams had entertained him and as many as fifty warriors there. They trusted him more than they trusted the Pequot. He explained away some of the instances Canonicus complained of and promised a response from Massachusetts magistrates regarding the others. He also spoke of English strength, of the dangers of opposing them, of the power of the Christian God. The English, he insisted, were not a people to have for an enemy. He spoke on the other hand of a treaty with the English, of the safety and security that went with it, and of all the spoils of war to be gained by joining with them. He reminded them of "how much wrong they had received from the Pequots, and what an opportunitie they now had by the help of the English to right themselves, revenge was so sweet unto them."[24]

Canonicus and Miantonomi withdrew to consider. At the least, a Narragansett-Pequot alliance would have killed certainly hundreds, possibly thousands, of whites in New England. Indians could have made farming life-threatening, cut virtually all routine land communication, and threatened all English outside of fortified areas. An alliance might even, as one Englishman worried, "in the infant State of these Colonies, have . . . accomplished their desperate Resolutions"[25] of forcing the withdrawal of the English.

The Indians could not have sustained a victory. The English would have returned and eventually taken the land. But the English crown and Laud, who were already attempting to prevent Puritans from going to New England, would not have allowed another mass Puritan emigration there. They would not have allowed another attempt to build a city upon a hill. The Indians could not have ultimately succeeded in keeping the English out of the region, but they could very well have ended the Puritan experiment.

But the Narragansetts did not join with the Pequot. Williams believed that his last argument, the prospect for revenge against their ancient enemy, "prevailed above all else."[26] Tribalism saved the English.

A few weeks after this meeting, on September 21, 1636, Vane hosted Miantonomi in Boston to negotiate a treaty. Miantonomi arrived with a retinue of several tributary sachems and twenty warriors. Vane received him with honors, assembling "most of the magistrates and ministers, to give countenance to our proceedings, and to advise with them."[27] Then Miantonomi and Vane agreed to a "Sollem League" against the Pequot. Williams did not participate because of his banishment, but the magistrates "agreed to send a copy of [the treaty] to mr. Williams, who could best interpret to them."[28]

The alliance would not last long, and it would do no good for the Narragansetts. But for now the new allies plotted war.

The Pequot, now alone, also plotted war, guerrilla war. Three miles upriver from the Saybrook fort one Englishman went onshore to hunt fowl; immediately after he fired his gun, "many Indians arose out of the covert and took him. . . . They cut off his hands and . . . cut off his feet. He lived three days afer his hands were cut off; and themselvs confesed, that he was a stout man, because he cried not in his torture."[29]

Since Endicott's provocation, Pequots had now killed or kidnapped more than twenty English. The Hooker settlement in and around Hartford now sought an Indian ally of their own and found one in Uncas, sachem of the Mohegans.

The Mohegans were a tribe in the Pequot confederation, and Uncas had recently tried to become sachem of all the Pequot. He had lost that contest to his brother-in-law Sassicus. Driven by ambition and a desire for his own empire, in maneuvering worthy of Shakespeare, Uncas now intended to use the Connecticut English to build that empire. He would get it even if it meant death to his own relatives and the destruction of his former tribe. Uncas proved his usefulness to the English when his warriors "fell upon thirty or forty of the Enemy near Saybrook Fort, and killed seven of them outright." They brought in five heads and a dying captive as proof. "This mightily encouraged the hearts of all, and we took this as a pledge of their further fidelity."³⁰

Winter was then not far away. War would wait until spring.

In March 1637, as the snows melted, Miantonomi demonstrated his fealty to Massachusetts by personally leading a punitive expedition of Narragansetts to Block Island to execute Oldham's killer. He also sent Williams a symbolic message and asked him to forward it to the Massachusetts magistrates. It was the severed hand of a Pequot. Williams did send it on, telling Winthrop, "I have alwais showne dislike to such dismembring the dead and now the more" since it was "in your name."³¹

But war between the Puritans and Indians did not begin until land-hungry English in Wethersfield, Connecticut, drove nearby friendly Indians off tribal land. This seizure was blatantly unjustified; a Connecticut court later called it theft and ordered the English to compensate the Indians, but long before that ruling the displaced victims asked the Pequot for help. The Pequot retaliated by attacking the town, killing nine, and taking two girls hostage.

Until then, the Connecticut towns upriver had preferred peace; now their hand was forced. Hooker informed Winthrop, "The Indians here our frends were so importunate with us to make warr presently that unlese we had attempted some thing we had delivered our persons unto contempt of base feare and cowardise, and caused them to turne . . . against us."³²

Another Connecticut man seconded Hooker, warning Winthrop, "Now the eyes of all the Indians in the countrey are upon the Englishe. . . . [I]f some serious and verie speedie course be not taken to tame the pride and take down the insolencie of these now-insulting Pequots . . . [w]e are like to have all the Indians in the countrey about our ears. . . . Let not Boston Roxburie &c. thinke warre is farre enough from them, for this seems to be a vniversall deluge creeping and encroaching on all the English in the land."³³

Winthrop as deputy governor now drew a reluctant Plymouth—whose leaders believed that Massachusetts had exaggerated the threat and provoked the Pequot—into war as an ally, advising them to "looke at . . . all other Indeans as a common enimie, who though he may take occasion, of the beginning of his rage, from one parte of the English, yet if he prevaile, will surly pursue his advantage, to the rooting out of the whole nation."[34]

Throughout southern New England small armies of whites and Indians gathered. Meanwhile, Williams sent constant dispatches—sometimes two a day—carrying detailed intelligence and suggestions by Indian messengers both to Boston and to soldiers in the field. The English forces prepared to do harm. They would fulfill that purpose.

The English then had relatively little outright racial prejudice against Indians. They certainly felt superiority but regarded the chief difference between themselves and Indians as Christianity. As one Englishman wrote, "We were savage and uncivill, and worshipped the divell, as now they do."[35] The English also compared Indians to "the wild Irish" and "the savage Irish."[36]

But comparing Indians to the Irish hardly meant that the English would give quarter. In Ireland, the Earl of Essex had held a banquet for two hundred Irish Catholics; once all were seated, his soldiers burst into the hall and slaughtered not only men but "women, youths and maidens" all. He also sent soldiers to track down and slaughter four hundred more women, children, and infants who had sought refuge by hiding in caves. Elsewhere in Ireland, Sir Humphrey Gilbert had ordered that "the heddes of all those . . . killed in the dai, should be cutte off from their bodies and . . . laied on the ground by eche side of the waie ledyng into his owne tente," forcing those who came to him to pass by "the heddes of their dedde fathers, brothers, children, kinsfolke, and friends."[37]

Now in Connecticut, a small English army under the command of Major John Mason, with Underhill his top lieutenant, was sent to relieve Saybrook. But the Pequots far outnumbered the English force there, had guns, and kept a "continuall Guard upon the River Night and Day . . . and being swift on foot might much impede our Landing."[38] Therefore Mason decided to sail more than thirty miles to the east, land his troops on the shore of Narragansett Bay, and march overland to outflank and "surpize them unaware."

The Pequots watched their sails disappear and mocked them. But Mason, like Underhill, had fought in the religious wars on the European continent. The Indians—both Pequot and those who had allied themselves with the English—would soon learn what it meant to war with such an enemy.

When Mason landed, Miantonomi added five hundred Narragansett warriors to the force, more than doubling its size. On foot now, they marched eighteen miles one day, twelve the next, with Narragansett guides leading Mason into Pequot country. Despite the clank of swords, corselets, and helmets moving through the woods, they were not discovered. They spent a final night with "rocks for our pillows" close enough to a Pequot fort near present Mystic, Connecticut, to hear "the Enemy Singing . . . until Midnight."

An estimated seven hundred Pequots were within the fort's palisade. At first light the English entered the fort wearing their armor and swinging their swords, catching the Pequots entirely by surprise. Even so, Pequot resistance was strong. Mason reported that "most couragiously these Pequeats behaved themselves." Only armor saved many English. Underhill wrote that but for it, "the Arrow would have pierced through me; another I received betweene necke and shoulders, hanging in the linen of my Head-peece, others of our souldiers were shot some through the shoulders, some in the face, some in the head, some in the legs." In fact, "the Fort was to hotte for us."[39]

Mason decided to make the fort too hot for the Pequot. He pulled a burning piece of wood from a fire and set a wigwam aflame. In another part of the fort Underhill set another wigwam aflame. Wind made the fires "blaze most terribly"[40] and "swiftly over-run the Fort, to the extream amazement of the Enemy, and great rejoycing of our selves." Mason wrote, "Thus now they were at their Wits End, who not many Hours before exalted themselves in their great Pride, threatening and resolving the utter Ruin and Destruction of the English, . . . but God was . . . making them as a fiery oven: Thus were the Stout hearted spoiled, having slept their last Sleep. . . . Thus did the Lord judge among the Heathen, filling the place with Dead Bodies!"[41]

The English withdrew and watched the fort burn, heard the screams therein. Underhill recounted, "[D]owne fell men, women, and children. . . . Great and dolefull was the bloudy sight to the view of young souldiers that never had been in Warre, to see so many soules lie gasping on the ground."[42]

More Indians "burnt to death then was otherwise slain. . . . Those yt scaped ye fire were slaine with ye sword; some hewed to peeces, others run threw with their rapiers, so as they were quickly dispatchte, and very few escaped. . . . It was a fearfull sight to see them thus frying in ye fyer, and ye streams of blood quenching ye same, and horrible was ye stinck & sente thereof; but ye victory seemed a sweete sacrifice, and they gave the prays therof to god, who had wrought so wonderfully for them, to inclose their inimise in their hands, and give them so speedy a victory over so proud & insulting an enemie."[43]

The lack of quarter stunned the Narragansetts, who cried out to Underhill, "It is naught, it is naught, because it is too furious, and slaies too many men."[44]

Of approximately seven hundred Pequots in the fort, seven were taken prisoner and as few as seven escaped. The rest died. The destruction of the fort at Mystic was not the only battle of the war, but it was a shattering one. English ferocity terrified Indians. And the ferocity continued.

Williams wrote Winthrop that the Narragansetts hoped that Pequots who surrendered would not be treated "like those which are taken in warr: but (as is their generall [Indian] Custome) be used kindly, have howses and fields and goods given them: because they voluntarialy chose to come in to them and if not received will . . . turne wild Irish themselves."[45]

But the English had other ideas. Two hundred Pequots surrendered to Narragansetts, who turned the captives over to the English expecting them to be treated decently. The English then slaughtered all but two of the men among them and made the women and children slaves.

Within months the Pequot nation ceased to exist. Its sachem Sassicus, brother-in-law to Uncas, sought refuge among one tribe after another. Each one, fearing English enmity, refused it. Finally he fled to the most warlike of all eastern tribes, the Mohawks—reputed cannibals whose lands were well outside English jurisdiction. They killed him and sent his scalp to Hartford.

Most surviving Pequots were divided between Mohegans and Narragansetts, and they became Mohegans and Narragansetts. The Mohegan sachem Uncas had headed a small fiefdom before the war. Now he commanded hundreds of warriors and, because of his English support, became the most powerful Indian in New England.

Dozens of Pequot captives were also enslaved. Slavery was hardly a new institution. Many an English subject had been captured by pirates—including "Dunkirkers" from Europe—and sold into slavery in the Arab world. And only a thin line separated indentured servants from outright slaves: Morton had created his Merrymount colony by convincing servants to rebel rather than be "sold for slaves"[46] in Virginia. Debtors and criminals could find themselves transformed into slaves until their debts or fines were paid off, and Irish captives of English conquerors were often sent to Barbados as indentured servants, barely removed from outright slavery.

Most of the enslaved Pequots were sent to Barbados for sale, but a few remained in New England. Winthrop kept as slaves "Monomotto, a woman of very modest countenance and behavior," and her children; she had supposedly saved the lives of the two Wethersfield girls captured at the outset of war and who survived. And Williams decided to keep a boy he had "fixed mine eye on."[47] He apparently treated him well; the boy later chose to remain with him rather than return to his mother.

The Massachusetts magistrates had wanted this war. Crushing the Pequot made clear to the Dutch in New Amsterdam the English claim to Connecticut, and it made clear to all Indians the military superiority of Massachusetts. The war had also made Uncas and the Mohegans in effect a client state of the English, especially the Connecticut English. Favoring Uncas, Massachusetts now reneged on promises that had been made to the Narragansetts in return for their support, including that they would have "free use of the pequt Country for their hunting."[48]

The rivalry between Pequot and Narragansett was dead—murdered. The rivalry between Mohegan and Narragansett was born.

With the new security for Massachusetts and Connecticut there was also born a new threat, a great threat, not only to the Narragansett but more importantly to Williams's own plantation. English from both Massachusetts and Connecticut began encroaching upon Narragansett land. When Williams or anyone else from Providence attempted to defend either the land or their own plantation's authority over the region, the General Courts of both Connecticut and Massachusetts brushed them aside.

Williams had risked his life to help Massachusetts in the war out of a sense of responsibility and loyalty, not for any reward. Winthrop did, however, try to reward him by proposing "not only [that he] be recalld from Banishmnt, but allso to be honrd with some Remarke of Favour."[49] Clergy, however, violently opposed doing so. The great victory over Indians notwithstanding, this was not a time in Massachusetts for gestures of peace, especially from clergy.

For even in the midst of this war, the plantation was riven by a dispute so bitter that many feared it could precipitate armed rebellion. The controversy was over theology, an issue that focused the mind of the colony. Indeed, one benefit of the war had been to turn the attention of the plantation outward, toward an external enemy, instead of inward, toward each other. It is likely, although it is only speculation, that at least some of Massachusetts's early aggressiveness—when both Plymouth and Connecticut were urging restraint— was prompted by a conscious desire to do just that. As one man told Winthrop after the attack on Wethersfield, God had spilled this English blood "to make us cleave more close togither, and prize each other, to prevent contentions of Brethren."[50]

But the war against a foreign enemy was over. It was time to turn back upon another in all the malice of love. It was time to turn to the question of Anne Hutchinson.

# ※ CHAPTER 21 ※

Anne Hutchinson was a brilliant, bold, forceful, and self-confident woman. She came by her self-confidence naturally. Her grandfather was a friend of Erasmus, and her father was a Puritan minister outspoken enough to be jailed for nonconformity twenty years before Laud came to power. With a knowledge of Scripture that rivaled any minister's and with practical skills as a midwife, she knew her own mind and rarely hesitated to speak it.

It was not surprising then that she brought conflict to Massachusetts. But she was not the actual source of that conflict. The source was John Cotton. She was so enamored of his preaching that in England several times a year she had journeyed twenty-five miles to old Boston to hear him. And with her husband and fifteen children, she followed him to new Boston.

In both old and new Boston, Cotton's sermons left his listeners provoked by his thought, confident of his rectitude, awed by the greatness of God, and inspired to devotion. It was the nature of that inspiration—how to interpret his preaching on inspiration—which now troubled Israel. The dispute surfaced soon after Williams fled Massachusetts; it did not involve him but it had enormous impact on the future of his colony and of his ideas.

Like his colleagues, Cotton preached awe and fear of judgment, but, more than his colleagues, he also conveyed to his listeners not just hope but exhilaration, the heady conviction that God loved *them,* had chosen *them.* He convinced them of it with his own passion, his own zeal, zeal made all the more compelling because his erudition and intelligence complemented and subsumed it. His preaching to the heart and emphasis on God's grace fitted within standard Calvinist and Puritan theology but pushed uncomfortably close to the edges of that theology. Anne Hutchinson pushed her interpretation of his preaching beyond the edge.

The theological question at issue was, as so often seemed the case with

Calvinism, predestination. Any brief summary of Puritan theology necessarily oversimplifies it and ignores nuanced views. But the essence of Puritan doctrine can be stated plainly: God would save only a tiny minority of sinners and send the rest to hell, and since all humans were corrupt nothing people did could affect their fate. Only God's grace was saving.

New England Puritans agreed that those whom God saved went through a well-defined process. The saved first received a "call," a summons to come to Christ which resonated deep within the soul.

Such persons were then "justified," chosen by God as "just." At this step God remitted all sins. They became visible saints. Next the saved were "sanctified"; the grace within them made them holy and righteous. Finally, after death the saved were "glorified."

In Massachusetts only the saved could become the stones upon which to build a New Jerusalem. Only the saved—the visible saints—could join a church. Hence, after the initial wave of settlement, new church members underwent a rigorous examination process, which helps explain why church members comprised only a small minority of the colony's population.

The discord between Cotton and nearly all other Massachusetts clergy—and between their respective followings—centered on sanctification.

One might logically expect those who believed strictly in predestination—that no human could do anything either to earn God's grace or to lose it, that salvation was in effect as random as a lightning bolt—to be fatalists who accepted what came to them and perhaps even indulged sinful desires. Yet belief in predestination had the opposite effect. As Max Weber argued in his classic study *The Protestant Ethic and the Spirit of Capitalism*, this belief drove people to demonstrate, to prove to themselves and others that they were among the saved. Since only those who had God's grace could live without sin, and since surely God gave those whom He had graced the ability to succeed, proving that one was saved required one to strive to live a virtuous life. And simple virtue was not enough. To prove God's grace required one to strive for perfection.

Puritans generally expected signs of God's grace to show themselves in the lives of the sanctified; the saved person lived a godly life full of good works, and that life was often blessed with worldly success. This was the proof of grace. This allowed others to identify the elect.

Most New England Puritans also believed—although this was not part of their theology per se—that sinners prepared themselves to receive grace, going through, as an influential Puritan professor at Cambridge said, a "process by which man becomes willing to believe . . . prior to faith, or prior to both regeneration and faith."[1] These "preparationists" worked through crises of faith, worked at understanding Scripture, worked at following God's law. Yet no matter how hard they worked, they could never know with certainty whether they were saved or not. God put even the saved through a hell of doubt and struggle, endless struggle and endless doubt, interrupted by rare moments of utter and complete surrender to God, utter and complete rapture, and utter and complete peace.

But Cotton taught, as one of his mentors had taught him, that diligently listening to the preaching of the word of God was a common way to hear the call, and to know with confidence that one has been called. One could *feel* it.

People were frightened. He reassured them. People were troubled. He brought them peace. People were alone. His words, like the Word itself, joined them to God. His words had made him hugely popular in England, and they made him hugely popular in the Boston church where he was teacher.

Cotton never directly challenged Puritan orthodoxy, but his emphasis on grace and the heart indirectly challenged both the arduous preparation most Puritans believed necessary to receiving grace and, by implication, the common view of sanctification.

Anne Hutchinson interpreted his preaching aggressively, putting ever more emphasis on his preaching about grace and less on Scripture, on written authority. She sought an inner light; she sought Christ's spirit. She led others toward that light. She began leading Bible study gatherings of like-minded worshippers in her home. As the worshippers exceeded eighty people—mostly but by no means exclusively women—the group moved to the church. She could, as one of her followers said, "show me a way, if I could attain it, even revelations, full of such ravishing joy that I should never have cause to be sorry for [abandoning] sin, so long as I live."[2]

While she was advancing a more charismatic and rapturous Christianity, she also made clear that she considered most Massachusetts clergy so focused on moral law and outward signs of sanctification that their preaching amounted to a "covenant of works"—i.e., that salvation lay in human hands and not God's, that a person could win salvation by living a good life.

No Puritan minister would admit to advocating a covenant of works; Puritans had damned such practices in the Church of England as Arminian. Puritan clergy would insist they preached only a "covenant of grace," of salvation only by God's inexplicable grace. In charging ministers with preaching a covenant of works, she was saying not only that they were wrong. She was hinting that they were damned. Unsaid but obvious to all was the implication that they might also be tools of Satan.

Her faction included the new governor young Henry Vane and it came to dominate the Boston church. But Winthrop, then deputy governor, and the pastor John Wilson did not share her views, and outside the Boston church, outside the personal reach of both Cotton's preaching and her own charismatic interpretation of it, her supporters were a distinct minority. Conflict was inevitable, and with both sides certain of the truth, deep and enraptured bitterness was inevitable as well.

Anne Hutchinson was not a quiet woman, nor one willing to watch events develop. She soon split the Boston church—and also split Vane from Winthrop—when she tried to make her brother-in-law the Reverend John Wheelwright, newly arrived from England, co-teacher with Cotton in the Boston church. This would have pushed Wilson far into the background. She proposed this in the church before its membership. Winthrop objected to him "whose spirit they knew not, and who seemed to dissent in judgment"[3] from Wilson.

Vane promptly rose in rebuttal, and the meeting became heated. Cotton himself took no position, carefully remaining neutral, trying to offend no one. In this instance, Winthrop prevailed. Wheelwright became a minister elsewhere. But this did not bring peace to the congregation. It brought hostility to it. Afterward, when Wilson "began to pray or preach" the Hutchinson faction was "rising up and contemptuously turning their backs . . . and going forth from the Assembly."[4]

These events did not pass without notice outside her church. Another minister demanded that Cotton explain—in writing—certain views he had expressed. This minister also argued that "by advancing the Spirit, and revelation of the Spirit, they destroy or weaken revelation of the Scriptures; by depending upon Christs righteousnesse and justification, without the works of the Lawe, they destroy the use of the Lawe, and make it no rule of life unto a Christian."[5]

A gathering of leading ministers overwhelmingly supported the criticism.

Pressure to patch things over was intense; as always, conformity was sought. Hugh Peter, Williams's replacement as Salem minister, told Winthrop, "I am no tolerator, but a peacemaker I will be."[6]

Peter and others convinced Cotton to yield, while also bending his critics enough to allow him to save face. The magistrates met almost immediately after this tentative reconciliation—but the magistrates were not conciliatory. Since many of the newest arrivals had favored Cotton, they forbade new settlers in the colony without their permission. The magistrates also invited Wilson to comment. He decried "these differences and alienations among the brethren . . . and laid the blame upon these new opinions risen up amongst us, which all the magistrates, except the governour"—Vane—"and two others, did confirm, and all the ministers but two"[7]—Cotton and Wheelwright.

The Cotton-Hutchinson faction, though now isolated within the Bay, still controlled the Boston church. Its members considered Wilson's words an attack on themselves and at the next service called him to account. After blistering him with abuse, they were "eager to proceed to censure"[8] him. Vane in particular "pressed it violently against him . . . [with] bitterness."[9]

Winthrop defended Wilson and appealed for a loving approach, but his voice could not cool that cauldron. Cotton finally intervened to keep the congregation from censuring its own pastor. Meanwhile, Hutchinson drew more attention to herself by accusing several ministers to their faces of preaching "the covenant of works, and that you are not able ministers of the new testament."[10]

The magistrates declared a prayerful fast to foster reconciliation. The Boston congregation invited Wheelwright to preach a sermon there. He spoke no word of peace.

Wheelwright preached as Massachusetts was preparing for its war against the Pequot, and he spoke of war—but one against their own. He preached that Massachusetts was threatened from the inside, and that keeping Christ present in Massachusetts required crushing those who disputed him. He conceded he was creating division but said, "what then?" As the plantation prepared to send a military force into combat, he told the congregation they also "must prepare for a spiritual combat" and called his opponents "antichrists." "Put on the armor of God," he urged, "kill them with the word of the Lord."[11]

The next General Court convened in the Boston meeting house, the same building used by the Boston church, the same building in which Wheelwright had preached his sermon. This court, over the protests of Vane and a few others, promptly found Wheelwright guilty of sedition but, as always hopeful of reconciliation, refrained from imposing any sentence. The court also declared that its next meeting, which would elect a governor and assistants, would not convene in Boston, home to the Hutchinson faction. It would instead convene in Newtown (soon to become Cambridge), the center of opposition to her.

That meeting occurred in May, only a few days before Mason's attack on the Pequots at Mystic. It began with ill will and ended with deep rancor. The election itself was held outdoors on the town common—no building could accommodate the crowd. As the sitting governor, Vane commenced the formal proceedings by walking with an escort of four men, each of them carrying a halberd, the medieval weapon comprised of a long-handled axe topped by a pike. Vane had instituted the escort as an honor guard, supposedly to add grandeur to the governorship—yet four burly men carrying a ferocious weapon were intimidating as well.

As Vane convened the meeting, a member of the Boston church protested the preceding court's treatment of Wheelwright. Men in the crowd began arguing, pushing, even swinging fists. Winthrop reported "great danger of a tumult that day; for those of that side grew into fierce speeches, and some laid hands on others, but seeing themselves too weak"—Wheelwright's defenders were in a distinct minority—"they grew quiet."[12]

Finally came the election. Three years earlier Winthrop had lost the governorship and barely retained his position as an assistant. He had risen back to deputy governor. Now, despite little support from Boston, from his own church, he won back the governorship.

The freemen entirely rejected Vane, not even returning him as an assistant.

Immediately Winthrop, the other officers, and the town deputies headed for the meeting house to convene the General Court, to proceed with business indoors, but the four men who had escorted Vane threw down their halberds in protest. They refused to provide an honor guard for the new governor.

The insult rankled Winthrop. And Vane himself paid Winthrop no honors. Soon after the election Winthrop invited Vane to a dinner he was hosting in honor of a prominent visitor. Vane did more than merely refuse the invitation; he convinced the guest of honor to skip Winthrop's dinner and instead dine with him and Samuel Maverick.[13] (Hostility toward Maverick after this incident drove him back to England.) That insult rankled Winthrop more.

The General Court also passed a new law increasing the magistrates' power to promote homogeneity in the church. Vane protested "against the [power] which is given by this law of rejecting those, that are truly and particularly religious, if the magistrates doe not like them."[14]

Vane was then twenty-five years old. He and Williams had become friends in the few months prior to Williams's banishment, and that friendship was cemented as they worked together against the Pequot. Now the Massachusetts ministers pushed them closer, in their views of the power of magistrates and in their fates. Eight weeks after the election, Vane returned to England. He would never see Massachusetts again, but, through Williams, he would be felt in it more than ever.

Vane's departure also brought Williams a new and personal reminder of his isolation. Ironically, that reminder came when Winthrop tried to reward his extraordinary help in the war by getting his banishment rescinded. Had Vane remained in Massachusetts, he and Winthrop together might have succeeded in accomplishing this. Without Vane, there was no possibility of it.

The other Massachusetts magistrates and its clergy, proud with victory over the Pequot, were confirmed by God in their course. Now that they were imposing orthodoxy on Cotton and the Hutchinson group, they were unwilling to show flexibility toward Williams. Indeed, perhaps to deflect the criticism for straying from orthodoxy, Cotton led the opposition to Winthrop's suggestion. The banishment remained in force.

Williams remained a nonperson in Massachusetts—even in the histories it produced. Reports about the Pequot war written in Massachusetts spoke of the lethal menace of a Pequot-Narragansett alliance, and they credited an unnamed "Agencie" of Massachusetts with preventing it. "Agencie" is an appropriate word; Vane and Winthrop had given him authority to speak for Massachusetts when he was in the Narragansett camp. That, however, had been a different moment. No official Massachusetts account of the war even mentioned Williams's name.

For Williams's own part, his confidence in the direction he had chosen had only increased. Most of his letters to Winthrop had a tone of overdone respect to them; on occasion they approached obsequiousness. But in the midst of the

Hutchinson controversy and a year into his own experiment, he felt so confident as to advise Winthrop that "the further you pass in your way, the further you wander & haue the further to come back, . . . till Conscience be permitted (though erronious) to be free amongst you."[15]

Winthrop's response, if he made one, has not survived. And Massachusetts continued to move in that further direction as it finally settled the Hutchinson matter.

Less than a month after Vane's departure, nearly all the ministers of the plantation gathered in a synod. There eighty-two specific errors were one after another condemned. Cotton, ever flexible, disowned all eighty-two of them. (Later he claimed surprise that any members of his church defended "sundry corrupt opinions, which I verily thought had been far from them.")[16]

Only Wheelwright held fast. At the next General Court, two years after banishing Williams, the court now banished Wheelwright. When a deputy from Boston protested, he too was banished. Then the court turned to Anne Hutchinson, from whom the infection which the court termed "Antinomianism" had issued. The word "antinomian" means "against law." And she did challenge the law, both in her theology and in this court. Her trial has been much discussed by historians, partly because of complete records—no record exists for Williams's trial, and, as Goethe observed, one looks where there is light—but also because it is a rare instance in early American history when a woman bested in debate a covey of intelligent and powerful male adversaries. It made no difference. Like Wheelwright, Hutchinson was banished.

Perhaps the clearest signal as to how dangerous the authorities considered Wheelwright and Hutchinson was the statement, "There is just cause of suspition that they, as others in Germany, in former times, may vpon some revelation, make some suddaine irruption vpon those that differ from them in judgment."[17]

The reference was to a rebellion in the city of Münster a century earlier. The leaders of an "Anabaptist" group which took over the city went far beyond merely rejecting infant baptism and requiring adult baptism. They used violence against those who rejected their views and argued they were ruled only by conscience, not laws. The rebellion met an inglorious end; one of its leaders, believing God would bring him triumph, attacked a far larger Catholic force besieging the city. God did not favor him; his enemies hoisted his head on a pole and nailed his genitals to the city gate. When the city fell, the remaining leaders were tortured, their bodies hung in cages from a church steeple until only skeletons remained. Ever after this rebellion, almost anyone who advocated any variation from the prevailing orthodoxy—whether that orthodoxy be Catholic or Protestant—was denounced as "Anabaptist," anarchic, and heretical, dangerous to public order and the soul.

The threat in Massachusetts from the Antinomians was not real, but the fear of it was. So the magistrates moved the plantation's armory from Boston, home to Hutchinson's supporters, to Newtown and Roxbury, home to her critics. The magistrates also ordered that all signers of a petition protesting Wheelwright's banishment hand over their "guns, pistols, swords, powder, shot and match."[18]

Seventy-six of Hutchinson's followers were disarmed. They submitted without incident. Meanwhile, unlike Williams, Wheelwright and Hutchinson were not threatened with return to England; they left in orderly fashion. Wheelwright "gathered a company, and sat down by the falls of Pascataquack, and called their town Exeter"[19] in New Hampshire. Hutchinson herself actually was required to remain in Massachusetts alone, after the departure of her family and several supporters, to submit to excommunication by her church before joining them. They planned initially to go north as Wheelwright had, "but the Winter," said John Clark, a leader of the group, "proved so cold, that we were forced to make towards the South."[20] They had several conversations with Williams, "with whom we advised about our design."

Williams had no sympathy for Antinomian theology, nor certainly for William Coddington, one of those with the Hutchinson group. Coddington, probably the wealthiest person in Massachusetts and treasurer of the Bay colony, had strongly advocated banishing him.

But Williams had every sympathy for their situation. Massachusetts had expelled them for "reason of conscience" alone, simply because of their religious views. He also sympathized with the comment of one member of their party, who said, "We were now on the wing, and were resolved through the help of Christ, to get cleer of all, and be of our selves."[21]

Also, if these refugees joined Williams in the Narragansett Bay area, it would greatly enhance his own plantation and greatly enhance the stability of the region, for they would bring not only more people but many resources to it—most of the Hutchinson group were far more wealthy than those who were settling in Providence. He brought their attention to Aquidneck Island, a large island about fifteen miles long and four miles wide, in Narragansett Bay. The Narragansetts owned it.

The group found the island much to their liking, and Williams negotiated its sale to them by Canonicus and Miantonomi. Later he declared, "It was not Price nor Money that could have purchased Rode Iland." By this he meant Aquidneck Island itself, which was also known as Rhode Island. Like the territory on the mainland which included Providence, Williams said, "Rode Iland was obtained by Love: by that Love and Favour wch that honble Gentleman Sir Hen. Vane and my selfe had with that great Sachim Miantunnomu about that Leauge, wch I procured betweene the Massachuset English etc. and the Narrigansets in the Pequt War."[22]

For now the settlement on the island had no formal or legal connection to Williams's own mainland community, although both shared the experience of flight from Massachusetts. They had close and neighborly relations, but no more.

The island settlers did not agree with Williams on separating church and state. Entirely unlike the compact Williams had written upon which the Providence government was based, those on Rhode Island agreed to "submit our persons, lives and estates unto our Lord Jesus Christ, the King of Kings, and Lord of Lords, and to those most perfect and absolute laws of His given in His Holy Word of truth." They chose only a single magistrate, Coddington, and he took the title of judge, a title representing the authority of the Old Testament judges who ruled ancient Israel, the authority of God. The freemen swore to "yield all due honour unto him according to the lawes of God" and declared that those failing "to maintaine the honour" of his position committed "a sin."[23] When a few months later they added assistants they were called not magistrates but "Elders."

Yet even they, despite having initially formed a quasi-religious government, did agree with Williams on one crucial point. They wrote into their legal compact, "It was further ordered, by the authority of this present Courte, that none be accounted a Delinquent for Doctrine"—they established freedom of religion.[24]

The Hutchinson group first settled in present Portsmouth, but friction within even this small community led Coddington and others to settle Newport, about ten miles away at the opposite edge of the island and close by the open sea. Within a year, however, shared interests caused the two settlements to form a close alliance and a joint government.

On the mainland, friction inside Providence also caused some men to settle Pawtuxet, on the northern bank of the Pawtuxet River in present Cranston but then still part of Providence. In 1638 Williams sold the territory to thirteen men for a cow, which was "then dear"—worth the enormous sum of £20 in hard coin.[25] They agreed to "propagating a public Interest, and confessed them selves but as feofees, for all the many scores" of future settlers paid thirty shillings "not to the purchasors as proprietors, but as feofees for a Town stock."[26]

Pawtuxet's chief new owners, William Arnold and William Harris, may have agreed to those terms as a condition of sale, but they had very different ideas about the future. The two men were not friends; each went his own way, and they collided as often as moved in common. But they had attributes in common. Neither cared much about either freedom of religion or any communal goals. Both cared about land. They also shared a deep antipathy toward Williams and an appetite for financial opportunity. Pawtuxet men participated in the Providence town government—both Arnold and Harris kept houses there and seem to have continued to live there—but Pawtuxet also began to develop a separate identity. It would soon become dangerously separate.

Still, English settlements on both the mainland and Aquidneck Island were now sprinkled along Narragansett Bay. Each of their populations numbered in the dozens, not the hundreds. They could barely be called towns, and they had no legal status. But they were permanent and fixed.

All the settlements owed their existence to Williams, who had purchased the land from the Narragansetts—on the mainland for himself, on the island as an agent. They also owed their existence to the fact that they lay outside the jurisdiction of Massachusetts, Plymouth, and Connecticut. They owed their existence to the fact that the laws of those colonies, and especially the laws of Massachusetts, could not reach them there. For Massachusetts had banished— not always for disagreements over religion—at least some residents in each of the four settlements.

Over the next few years, the settlements did grow. None of them thrived, but they did grow. They grew for the same reason: the people who moved to them did not find welcome in, or disliked the form of, the three established colonies. The region became a haven both for those "troubled by conscience," i.e., whose religious beliefs differed from standard Puritan doctrine, and for those who sought greater freedom than allowed elsewhere. The continuing flow of dissidents into the towns meant that, if the connection between them was initially only tenuous, nonetheless, outsiders routinely lumped them all together, generally referring to them all as Rhode Island. (And hereafter "Rhode Island" will refer to settlements on both the mainland and Aquidneck Island, although several years elapsed before the island and mainland towns formally united; "Aquidneck Island" will refer only to the island.) It also caused the other New England colonies to view Rhode Island's growth with both interest and displeasure.

Even the Dutch in New Amsterdam nearly one hundred and fifty miles away viewed Rhode Island's growth with displeasure. Compared with the Puritans, the Dutch were tolerant of religious differences, but they did not tolerate all differences. Rhode Island did. One New Amsterdam minister, speaking of people his colony expelled because of religion, remarked, "We suppose they went to Rhod island, for that is the receptacle of all sorts of riff-raff people, and is nothing else than the sewer (latrina) of New England. . . . We suppose they will settle there, as they are not tolerated in any other place. . . . All the cranks of Newe England retire thither."[27]

Meanwhile, Massachusetts in particular began to see Williams's colony as both a potential threat—fearing its pollution and corruption could spill into minds elsewhere—and, as the territory of present Rhode Island increased in value, as a potential opportunity. Winthrop saw the opportunity first and went into partnership with Williams; they bought Prudence Island in Narragansett Bay and raised cattle on it, for on this small island the livestock was safe from attack by wolves. Massachusetts, Connecticut, and Plymouth were attracted, too; that Rhode Island lay outside their boundaries yet was contiguous to them made it tantalizing. And these neighbors increasingly began behaving like hungry predators.

But Williams, having created the freest place in the world, intended to keep it free.

## Part V

# THE MISSION

# ❧ CHAPTER 22 ❧

The Massachusetts Bay colony wanted no more disturbances. To prevent them, it intended to impose itself outside its borders. It intended to bring discipline and order to what it perceived as the chaos of Rhode Island, to snuff out what it regarded as heresy there, and end the experiment Williams had embarked upon. But before doing so, it tightened discipline within its own borders.

The first town to which Massachusetts brought full order was Salem, placing Hugh Peter as minister there in 1636, as the Hutchinson controversy was beginning. Peter had called himself "no tolerator" and promptly lived up to his self-assessment. He became a large figure in history, and his views would evolve, but for now he was small, and he would always have narrowness. Unlike Cotton, Hooker, and Williams, he was no scholar nor cared to be. He had barely passed his Cambridge examinations in Hebrew and Greek and had no interest in the classics, poets, or, for that matter, Indians. What interested him was sin. In England, he had preached fervent sermons which made sin vivid and personal. "Dig up a carcass dead of the plague & go & kiss it," he told congregants who knew and recoiled from the loathsome image of a body covered by the erupted lesions of plague; "sin is more horrible."[1]

Forcing those who hungered for salvation to confront sin had proven popular. He had preached to as many as seven thousand people, and even an enemy had conceded that his "name doth echo over all the City [London] and his friends grew numerous."[2]

In Salem, he forced the church to formally excommunicate Williams, which it had never done; next, and with Endicott's full support, he wrote a new church covenant emphasizing "obedience to those that are set over us, in Church & common wealth," stating, "Members are not to reason between themselves . . . by way of opposition"[3] to the church. To remain in the church all church members had to sign this new covenant.

Then he searched out those Williams sympathizers in Salem who refused to abandon him, tried them in the church, and excommunicated them. After this he asked other Bay churches to bring down upon them all the weight of the entire plantation. "We thought it our bounden duty," he wrote, "to acquaint you with the names of such persons as have had the great censure passed upon them in this our church, with the reasons thereof, beseeching you in the Lord, not only to read their names in public to yours, but also to give us the like notice of any dealt with in like manner by you, that so we may walk towards them accordingly."[4]

His efforts brought Salem, for the first time, into real and not nominal conformity with the rest of the Bay. Other Bay churches also tightened control.

In the Boston church, Wilson and Cotton supposedly sought "unanimous concent" of the entire congregation on major decisions. But in practice that did not give individuals or even minorities power; instead it meant the majority put enormous pressure on the minority to yield. And if that failed, unanimity was achieved by simply eliminating dissenters: "If the lesser party dissenting neither can give satisfaction to the greater, nor will receive satisfaction from them, but still persist in dissenting, then doe the major part (after due forbearance, and calling in the counsell of neighbouring churches) judicially admonish them; who being thus under censure, their voyce is now extinct, and made voide. And so the rest proceed to vote."[5]

Indeed, in all Massachusetts churches, the clergy and elders moved gradually to silence not just dissent but the possibility of dissent. They silenced discussion.

Puritans both in England and in America had a tradition of lay "prophesying," of laymen preaching—their own thoughts, not reading from a text—and engaging in discourse within the church. But authorities increasingly tired of hearing lay opinion. With the support of the state, the ministry eliminated that part of the church service. Noted one observer, "It is generally held in the Bay, by some of the most grave and learned men amongst them, that none should undertake to prophesy in public, unless he intend the work of the Ministry."[6]

Lay men and women had become receivers of wisdom only; they could no longer dispense it, and even their ability to question it was limited. In church at least, they fell silent.

One Salem church member sought dismissal from Hugh Peter's congregation—one could not simply leave a church with which one had covenanted; the church had to agree to the dissolution of the covenant. He gave as his reason that he "was not suffered to ask questions in public."[7] But Cotton went to Salem and preached that it was impossible to leave a covenanted church without leaving Christ.[8] The church did not dismiss the member who complained; it excommunicated him.

Even Hanserd Knollys, a Puritan minister in New Hampshire, wrote friends in England that Massachusetts was "worse than the High Commission."[9]

He overstated. There were no pursuivants in Massachusetts, no spy system, no active effort to search out dissidents. Even individuals who were known to believe differently were generally tolerated, so long as they stayed silent, so long as they did not confront the larger polity with their differences.

But the pressure to conform was constant. The pressure to keep silent if one did not conform was constant. The pressure to yield if one's nonconformity became public was constant. The most bitter opponents in both church and civil life would speak of the "love" they had for whomever they disagreed with; their disputes were always "loving" efforts to bring someone traveling down the path of error back to the right way. Error was the one thing that was not tolerated, and the clergy and magistrates alone defined error.

And they began to use not only their own discretionary power to compel; they defined the law to compel as well.

Even among those who supported Williams's banishment, the behavior of the magistrates had caused concern about arbitrary actions by the government. As a result, the magistrates in 1636 asked Cotton—who had no legal training—to write a legal code. But if the purpose was to restrict the use of arbitrary and discretionary power, it failed, for the legal code left enormous gaps for interpretation by injecting the Word of God into it.

For Cotton based his legal code not on common law but Scripture, and he produced a draft called *Moses His Judicialls*. In it, he stated, "The more any law smells of man the more unprofitable."[10] The Bay did not adopt Cotton's draft, although the New Haven colony, founded in 1638 by John Davenport and others who felt Massachusetts lacked rigor in its religious observances, did. And Cotton's work did inform a second draft of Massachusetts laws written by a group of ministers led by Nathaniel Ward, who had practiced law prior to becoming a minister. The General Court adopted what it called the "Body of Liberties" in 1638.[11] This set of laws did borrow from Magna Carta and the Petition of Right, but it also offered the use of Scripture to both nullify any human law and go beyond it. It stated, "No custome or prescription shall ever prevaile amongst us . . . that can be proved to bee morallie sinfull by the word of God."[12] Even when the law's language hued most closely to Magna Carta and the Petition of Right it made room for Scripture. "No man's life shall be taken away, no man's honour or good name shall be stayned, no man's person shall be arrested, restrayned, banished, dismembered, nor any wayes punished," the law said, "unless it be by virtue or equitie of some expresse law of the Coun-try . . . *or in case of the defect of a law in any particular case by the word of God* [italics added]."[13]

The laws had prescribed fewer capital offenses than in England, but unlike in England some of those offenses derived directly from Scripture: "If any man, after legall conviction, shall have or worship any other god, but the Lord God, he shall be put to death. Deut. 13.6, &c. and 17.2, &c. Exod. 22. 20." "If any person shall blaspheme the Name of God the Father, Son, or Holy Ghost, with direct, expresse, presumptuous, or high-handed blasphemy, or shall curse God in like manner, he shall be put to death."

In England, laws against adultery went unenforced. Massachusetts, Con-necticut, and New Haven laws all stated, "If any person committed adultery with a married or espoused wife, the Adultere and Adulteresse shall surely be put to death. Lev. 20. 10. & 18, 20. Deut. 22. 23, 24." Although they executed adulterers only three times,[14] Massachusetts applied all the pressure of the com-munity against adultery. Adulterers of both sexes were whipped and forced to wear "Capitl Letters A.D. cut out in cloth and sewed on their uppermost gar-ments."[15] With every step, in every public place, they felt the eyes of others upon them; they felt the contempt of others toward them.

In addition, in 1638 the General Court merged offenses against church with offenses against the state. It ordered that in order to produce "good behavior" of the entire plantation, anyone who "stand excommunicate for the space of six months, without labouring . . . to bee restored" to good standing was sub-ject to "fine, imprisonment, banishment . . . as their contempt and obstinacy, upon full hearing, shall deserve."[16]

Several ministers and church elders demanded even more. They demanded that "all criminal matters concerning Church members, should be first heard by the Church." The government never granted churches that right, largely because the clergy was itself split over it, and it eventually did repeal the law which threatened an excommunicate with civil penalties. But in the meantime, the General Court, not a church, judged Hugh Bewitt "to bee gilty of heresy, & that his person, & errors are dangeros for infection of others," and that he "bee gone out of or jurisdiction . . . upon paine of death, & not to returne upon paine of being hanged."[17]

Liberty, in the view of Winthrop and his fellow magistrates, in the view of Massachusetts clergy, and in the view of most Massachusetts freemen, was the liberty to live a life which the magistrates defined as good and godly. And it was the responsibility of government to see to it that a godly life was lived. Few in Massachusetts disagreed—there is virtually no record of anything approaching widespread protest against or even discontent with this view.

Winthrop made clear his belief—a belief essentially incorporated into the Body of Liberties—that what he called "Naturall liberty," the freedom to do what one chooses, was evil and corrupt, and that true liberty meant "libertye to that onely which is good," and "to quietly and cheerfully submitt, vnto that Authoritye which is sett ouer you."[18]

This was freedom to choose, but to choose only one way, Winthrop's way, the magistrates' way, God's way. Hence it was not surprising that to avoid "heathenish and idols names," Massachusetts stopped using names for "the dayes of the weeke" and the months of the year, instead using numbers only (the first day was Sunday, the seventh Saturday; the first month was March, the twelfth was February).[19] When shortage of skilled labor drove wages up, the General Court limited wages. When fashions threatened to change, it legislated against what it regarded as too much show. When some few men began wearing their hair long, it legislated short hair (the usual depiction of Puritans with hair to their shoulders is mistaken; they despised the fashion of long-haired men).

People were to act the same, live the same, even rise at the same time. Nor was this attitude limited to Massachusetts. In Hartford the town ordered "a bell to be rung by the watch every morning, an hour before day break." It ordered further that "there should be in every house, one up, and have made some light, within one quarter hour afer the end of the bell ringing."

And in the absence of any law, even in the absence of any specific charge,

Massachusetts magistrates still felt their own liberty to act. They warned, "Mr Thomas Makepeace, because of his novile disposition, . . . wee were weary of him unlesse he reforme."[20]

In Massachusetts the prevailing forces were centripetal. In Rhode Island, and particularly on the mainland in Providence and Pawtuxet, the prevailing forces were centrifugal. As Providence grew, as individuals and families seeking refuge from Massachusetts settled there—virtually no immigrants came directly from England—Roger Williams remained the strongest voice. But he did not go uncontradicted. And he struggled to discover and define just how much government was necessary.

Williams's greatest contradictor in Providence was William Harris. Their arguments were over neither politics nor religion; they were over land, and they would last nearly half a century. Harris and some others very simply wanted more; newcomers to Providence, supported by Williams, bitterly objected that Harris was keeping them landless. Harris complained that these newcomers "rose in tumullt against the peace of Providence, order, and rule therein." Ultimately all agreed to appoint arbitrators.

The arbitration was successful enough that a town meeting declared, "[W]e apprehend, no way so suitable to our Condition as government by way of arbitration,"[21] and the government itself was reorganized along those lines. Five men, called "Disposers" and selected by a quarterly General Court, settled land claims and carried out other governmental functions, making them in effect magistrates, but their decisions could be appealed to the General Court. The new arrangement did also confirm that "as formerly hath bin the liberties of the town, so still, to hould forth liberty of Conscience."[22]

Whether Williams sought this manner of government or simply concurred in it is unknown, but he had seen enough of power. He clearly had no desire to direct other men's lives. He had even less desire to be directed by others. To him all that mattered was that he and every other person in his plantation could worship or not worship God in whatever manner he or she desired.

The new agreement did not, however, bring peace to the town. "Contention, disunion, and unquietnes" continued, even "Brawling Continually in mr williams medow" and "unnaturall flames" of anger.[23]

Williams intervened to separate contentious parties. He intervened again and again. But his own focus was internal; the prospect of governing others did not move him. He struggled instead over the questions of liturgy and worship, and his very puzzlement—the difficulty of the questions, and hence the possibility of error—confirmed him in his commitment to religious freedom.

He desired to bring himself as close to God as possible, and so he sought return to a form of worship most like early Christianity. To define this worship he turned to Scripture. Since no scriptural rule supported infant baptism, he came to reject it. When several men and women who believed in adult baptism appeared in Providence, he joined them, getting himself rebaptized and then cofounding the first Baptist church—although still no building was set aside for worship—in America in Providence. He and the others were all what became known as "Particular Baptists"; they differed from Massachusetts Puritans only in rejecting infant baptism and continued to believe that God predestined only an elect few for salvation. ("General Baptists," close kin to modern Baptists, believed that all who had faith in Christ would be saved; he did not so believe.)

Massachusetts of course had no tolerance for even Particular Baptists. Its clergy and government did not simply reject adult baptism. They attacked it violently, denigrating those who advocated it as "Anabaptists," tainting even Particular Baptists with the Münster rebellion a century earlier. Winthrop commented, "At Providence things grew still worse. . . . By these examples we may see how dangerous it is to slight the censures of the church."[24]

Meanwhile, Williams himself was questioning the apostolic succession—the idea that Christ had passed his spiritual, ecclesiastical, and sacramental authority directly to the apostles, and they had passed it on to their chosen successors, bishops who in turn passed it on to their chosen successors. The idea of the apostolic succession helped justify not only the existence of bishops but of all church discipline, and it helped prevent idiosyncratic interpretation of Scripture; the Church of England had retained this theological concept from the Catholic Church.

But Williams thought of the centuries during which the apostolic succession had passed through the Catholic Church, and then through such bishops as Laud. He concluded that the succession had passed through such corruption that it must have been broken. His reasoning and search of Scripture forced him to the position, then, that no human on earth could claim Christ's authority to gather a church, and could not again until divine intervention reestablished the succession.

He felt he had no choice. Within a few months and with the deepest of regret, he therefore abandoned the Baptist Church, casting himself loose. He would never again be a member of any church. He became simply a "Seeker."

This made him, again, alone. More than ever he was forced to confront the loneliness of freedom, the isolation of individualism. Yet it also confirmed him in his course of pursuing not only religious freedom but individual freedom, intellectual exploration. He continued to insist upon it both for himself and for what passed as a society in Providence.

And there a new dispute was developing that would test Williams personally as well as the nature of government in Rhode Island. It was a test that would force him to begin thinking more seriously than ever about the form not only of worship but of government and the state. It would also lead to an armed assault by Massachusetts on everything Williams had tried to create. That assault, prompted by Samuel Gorton, would return him to England, where he would maneuver in the greater chaos of civil war—and where he would find a voice and influence.

## ❧ CHAPTER 23 ❧

Some men will cross a street to avoid a fight; Samuel Gorton crossed an ocean to start one. Edward Winslow, a Plymouth governor and a gentle man, a man who had shown much kindness to Williams, called Gorton "this pestilent disturber of our societies."[1] Winthrop, often criticized for softheartedness, called him "a man not fit to live upon the face of the earth."[2]

Gorton arrived in Boston from England in 1637 in the midst of the Hutchinson conflict. He later observed that the plantation "had formerly banished one Master Roger Williams, a man of good report both for life and doctrine (even amongst themselves) for dissenting from them in some points about their Church government. . . . And at that time of our arrival at Boston, they were proceeding against one Master John Wheelwright, a man of like life and conversation, whom they also banished for differing from them in point of Doctrine, . . . and many others manifesting their thoughts about such points . . . were also imprisoned, fined, banished, disarmed, and cast out from amongst them. . . . Our consciences could not close with such their practices, which they perceiving, denied us the common benefit of the Country, even so much as a place to reside in."[3]

Gorton was overly modest about his own role in the Bay's decision to refuse him permission to stay. His personality made him impossible. He was charismatic and often charming and "courteous in carriage to all," but he also could be "moved to passion"[4] quickly—and it took little to move him. He was a man who could let nothing pass, an obstreperous man, and he feared nothing and no one on this earth. Confrontation in a society such as the Bay's was inevitable. This was especially so given that he arrived in America with his own theology. His ideas lacked coherence but they somewhat resembled Hutchinson's and a kind of proto-Quakerism in emphasizing an inner light. Although not formally trained as a minister, he became the first American to found an entirely new sect, and he was a harbinger of the infinity of sects that would soon bloom in England.

Unable to remain in Massachusetts, he went to Plymouth, where he hoped for a warmer welcome. He was accepted at first, but authorities there got in a dispute with his wife's servant. Gorton took up for his servant and harangued the magistrates publicly and relentlessly. So they charged him with "stirring up the people to mutynie in the face of the Court" and heresy; he was banished.[5]

Next he headed to Newport, where his religious views more closely paralleled those of the majority. But he crossed paths with magistrates over "an ancient woman's cow" which had strayed onto his land. Gorton refused to recognize the magistrates' authority because the plantation lacked a charter from England. Hauled into court, where his judge was Coddington, he also refused to recognize the court's authority and showed it such contempt that, enraged, Coddington ordered him whipped. He refused to submit. Coddington shouted, "You that are for the King, lay hold on Gorton!"

Gorton shouted back, "You that are for the King, lay hold on Coddington!"[6]

More were for Coddington than for Gorton. He was whipped and banished.

Gorton had then spent nearly four years in America. He had roiled every community he had entered. In 1641 he tried Providence, the place least able to handle him. Both Portsmouth and Newport on Aquidneck had grown larger than Providence, and Coddington had seen to it that government on the island functioned. Providence had also grown to a town of about two hundred people, but its government was comprised of nothing more than five arbitrators— chosen by the town meeting to work out disputes. Williams knew that Gorton might bring anarchy and wanted no part of it, but he granted him shelter "onely in regard of his present distresse."[7]

It was a mistake. In Providence, Gorton in his role as charismatic charmer soon drew many to him. Cotton heard of the events and mocked Williams, mocked the whole situation in Providence, noting that "friends of Mr. *Williams* were soon taken with that greater Light, which they conceived was held forth by Mr. *Gorton.*"[8]

To Winthrop, Williams complained, "Master *Gorton* having foully abused high and low at *Aquednick* is now bewitching and bemadding poore *Providence*, both with his uncleane and foule censures of all Ministers of the Country, . . .

and also denying all visible and externall Ordinances in depth of Familisme, against which I have a litle disputed and written." Williams was concerned: "[A]lmost All suck in his poyson, as at first they did at *Aquednick*. Some fewe and my selfe withstand his Inhabitation, and Towne-priviledges, without confession and reformacion of his uncivill and inhumane practices at *Portsmouth*: Yet the tyde is too strong against us, and I feare."[9]

By "Towne priviledges" Williams meant becoming a freeman of Providence. Gorton was living in Providence but he was not yet a citizen of Providence. To become that, a majority of freemen had to agree to admit him.

Gorton insisted that the only objection to his group was their religious doctrine, and they could not be excluded without violating Providence's guarantee of freedom of conscience. William Harris supported him. Of all in the colony Harris was nearly always most at odds with Williams and he taunted him by declaring, "He who can say, 'It is my conscience' ought not to yield subjection to any human order among man."[10]

Williams believed no such thing. Harris's way led to utter chaos—real chaos, not as perceived by Massachusetts—and utter disorder. It meant no state. Williams was no anarchist; he abhorred anarchy and had never doubted the legitimacy of the state or the necessity of obedience to laws governing behavior. It was freedom of thought and speech that he prized. For him the distinction was clear.

Now he found an unlikely ally in William Arnold. Arnold cared little about freedom of religion or thought. He did care about his property. He had come to Providence early because Massachusetts had banished him—for his behavior, not his beliefs—and because its cheap land made it attractive. With him had come his son Benedict Arnold (great-grandfather of the Revolutionary War figure), his son-in-law, his brother-in-law, a nephew, and their families, all of whom together formed the core of a group which had no love for Williams and had tried to undermine his relations with Winthrop. But if Arnold had little desire to support Williams, he had much desire to protect his own interest. He believed the Gortonists' "intent is . . . to get the victory over one part of the Town, but especially of those that laid the first foundation of the place, and bought it even almost with the losse of their lives, and their whole estates, and afterwards to trample them under their feet."[11]

On May 25, 1641, Arnold delivered a written brief to the town arguing that opposition to Gorton had nothing to do with religious views. It was entirely civil and political. Gorton had used "vilifying and opprobrious terms" against those trying to exercise the state's authority, and he had demonstrated a "despising and scorning of our Civill State." Gorton had been a "notoriously evill . . . trouble of Civill States where he hath lived, that are of far greater force then wee are of. . . . What may wee then expect if he could get himself in[?]. . . . Surely, first a breach of our civill peace and next a ruine of all such as are not on his side, as their daily practice doth declare; Ergo, they are not fit persons to be received into our Towne."[12]

Both Arnold and Williams feared that only a minority shared their views. But their arguments had an effect. For now the Gortonists were not admitted into town-fellowship.

Still, Gorton remained in the town. He continued preaching the inner light. He continued preaching against magistrates, against power, against the exercise of any authority by the government. In a town whose government consisted of five arbitrators, the so-called disposers, a government under constant pressure from the Gortonists, order began to break down.

Real trouble arrived when the disposers—Arnold was then one of them— issued a judgment against a Gortonist for a debt. Gortonists blocked its collection, first with their fists. Then both sides "came armed into the field, against each other." No one was killed only because Williams also came running and "Mr. Williams pacified them for the present."[13]

This virtual anarchy appalled Williams. He was still developing his views on the respective rights and responsibilities of individuals and governments, but he had never disputed the necessity of a government and the necessity for it to exercise authority. Now he worked to develop broad support for the enforcement of government decisions. He seemed to succeed. The judgment was satisfied.

The Arnold faction wanted more. Only Arnold himself had been banished from Massachusetts. The others associated with him had left to be with him and to take advantage of the land available in Providence. Contentious and determined, far more interested in property than any idea, eleven of their group petitioned the Massachusetts magistrates for help. Complaining of "no manner of honest order, or government" in Providence, charging the Gortonists with "licentious lust, like savage brute beasts" who had no respect for property, no respect for "houses, goods, lands, wives, lives blood, nor any thing will bee precious in their eyes," they asked for armed intervention.[14]

Massachusetts magistrates, despite having no legal claim to jurisdiction outside their borders, saw an opportunity to end the irritant and threat outside its border. They advised the Arnold group that if "they did submit themselves to some jurisidiction, either Plimouth or ours," that jurisdiction would "protect them."[15] The magistrates would use the submission as justification to claim the land.

Meanwhile, the Gorton problem resolved itself. Gorton had been chastened by and concerned over the armed confrontation in the field. He and his supporters therefore left Providence voluntarily. Initially they went to Pawtuxet, making Arnold very nervous. But he stayed there only a few months. Two of his sympathizers had bought land from Indians south of the Pawtuxet River, the boundary of Williams's original purchase. A tiny settlement had already developed there, outside of Providence territory, in wild country, Narragansett country. These sympathizers seem to have offered the Gortonists some land there, possibly for free. Gorton and ten supporters also purchased additional land, a total of about ninety square miles, from Miantonomi. The entire area was called Shawomet and encompassed much of present Warwick.

The area suited Gorton well. He had moved ever deeper into the wild, from England to Massachusetts, from Massachusetts to Plymouth, from Plymouth to Aquidneck, from Aquidneck to Providence. Always he had collided with authority. There was no authority here, except what he would establish. Perhaps even he had tired of fighting. Perhaps even he wanted simply to be left alone. He and his group retreated to this property and, they believed, to peace, for "by uertue of these gifts, gorton & many of his companey went & built houses"[16] on the coast, in Conimicut.

For a change, Gorton had not been banished. As soon as he removed himself from Providence, relations between him and Williams improved. Surprisingly, he began to prove himself a good neighbor. Williams was satisfied. Arnold was not.

Like the Massachusetts magistrates, Arnold saw an opportunity in Gorton. Arnold already owned considerable land in present Cranston on the northern bank of the Pawtuxet River, and some property south of the river in Shawomet, where Gorton settled. But he now also "bought" land which purported to give him title to land beginning only a few yards from the spring where Williams had founded Providence, south all the way to the Pawtuxet River. This land included a considerable part of Williams's original purchase from Canonicus and Miantonomi, land which Williams and others had occupied without challenge or dispute for years. The seller of this property was a minor Narragansett sachem named Socononoco.

Arnold's claim to the land was worse than weak. Besides the fact that the land had been occupied for years without challenge, New England colonial courts had long recognized Indian custom that the superior tribal sachem—in this case Canonicus and Miantonomi—had the right to dispose of land of lesser sachems who paid homage to them. This was well established as a matter of law. No fair-minded court would ever find Arnold's deed valid.

So he now devised a scheme to gain clear title. He got custody of Williams's original deed, cut out any references to Pawtuxet, "and pasted the said writing together againe so Cunningly that it Could hardly bee discerned."[17] (When proof later surfaced that the deed was altered while in his possession, he claimed that his wife did it accidentally.)

Arnold did not publicly declare this purported purchase, nor did he record the deed legally, nor did he assert any claim to any lands other than what he owned without dispute. But he did involve himself in other complex land purchases in Shawomet, where Gorton was.

Then, on September 8, 1642, he and several others submitted themselves and their holdings in Pawtuxet—land within the boundaries of Williams's original purchase—to the jurisdiction of the Massachusetts Bay. Before doing so, he apparently received assurances that despite having been banished by Massachusetts in the past, he could remain in this region if Massachusetts did annex the territory.

If Massachusetts accepted the submission of the Arnold group, the Bay could assert jurisdiction over any dispute involving title to land in both Pawtuxet and Shawomet, giving a judgment for Arnold the patina of proper legal procedure. Accepting the submission would also bring Massachusetts's power to Narragansett Bay in a direct way. If that also meant the destruction of Williams's dreams and the end of freedom of conscience, that seemed to Arnold a small price to pay, especially since Williams and others would be paying it. For liberty of conscience meant nothing to Arnold.

Winthrop, now back in power as governor, coldly assessed the arguments in favor of accepting the submission of Pawtuxet. He had no desire to help Arnold or those associated with him. Not only had Arnold been banished, but his colleague Robert Cole had been forced by the Massachusetts court to wear a "D" identifying him as a drunkard for an entire year. And Winthrop certainly knew that the Bay's charter did not authorize any territorial expansion.

Sometime earlier Williams had written him that "notwithstanding our differences, . . . you have bene always pleased lovingly to answer my boldness in Civill things." Implicit in the letter was a plea for help handling, or at least advice on how to handle, Arnold, "who openly in Towne meeting more than once professeth to hope and long for a better Government than the Countrey hath yet. The White"—the bull's-eye of the target—"wch such a person or persons levell at can be no other then the Raping of the Fundamentall Liberties of the Countrey, wch ought to be dearer us than our right Eyes."[18]

But Winthrop had no desire to help Williams preserve what Winthrop regarded not as fundamental liberty but as fundamental error. He did, however, desire to advance the interests of Massachusetts, and he recognized the benefits if they could "draw in . . . those parts which had become very offensive." Most importantly, he reasoned that "the place was likely to be of use to us, especially if we should have occasion of sending out against any Indians of Naragansett and likewise of an outlet into the Naragansett Bay." Accepting the submission could be the first step toward gaining full control over Rhode Island.

Pawtuxet did not even border on Massachusetts. To reach it by land, one had to pass through Providence. It could not have escaped Winthrop—nor could it escape those living in Providence—that if Massachusetts successfully absorbed Pawtuxet, it would inevitably envelop Providence, and probably take in Aquidneck Island also. He concluded, "We thought it wisdom not to let it slip."[19]

Therefore the General Court of Massachusetts extended its "government and protection" to Arnold, to those who stood with them, to those whom it had previously expelled—and to their land.[20]

Massachusetts's aggressiveness energized Plymouth, which now began exploring ways to expand into Rhode Island territory. Even Connecticut, separated from any part of Rhode Island by Indian country, began to show interest in making territorial claims that would extend its reach to Narragansett Bay.

Until now, relations between the island towns of Portsmouth and Newport and Providence on the mainland had been friendly and cooperative—for example, islanders had authorized Williams to represent them in negotiating an agreement with Miantonomi for Narragansett help in "the destruction of the wolves that are now upon the Island."[21] But in politics the towns had done nothing in concert. Keeping themselves even more apart were other scattered settlements too small to call towns.

Now, except for the thirteen men who had actually submitted themselves to Massachusetts, all those elsewhere on either the mainland or the island felt alarm. They understood what the Bay's assertion of authority over Pawtuxet meant. They understood the significance of the Plymouth and Connecticut claims to land. They recognized that their infinitely more powerful neighbors now threatened to devour the refuge Williams had created. They recognized that if that happened, then the "Fundamentall Liberties of the Countrey" would be devoured as well, and the freedoms Williams had established and they had enjoyed would quite definitely disappear.

All the settlements of Rhode Island, both on the island and on the mainland, were outcast societies. None had economic, political, or military power. They could not protect themselves. They needed the legal authority that only a patent, a charter, could give them, with a power behind it strong enough to intimidate the Massachusetts Bay colony, Plymouth, and Connecticut. Such authority and such a power could come only from England. Their only possible protection lay in England.

Eleven days after the Massachusetts court accepted the Arnold faction's submission, representatives of Portsmouth and Newport met in a General Court and "ordered, that a Committee shall be appointed to consult about the procuration of a patent for this island and Islands, and lands adjacent."[22] The mainland towns too formally authorized sending someone to England to procure a charter.

The choice was obvious. Among all these outcasts, Williams clearly had a superior understanding of the English government and superior connections to the powerful. Had he returned to England at the time of his banishment, he would soon have found himself in a prison cell, probably after an executioner had cut off his ears, bored a hole in his tongue, and taken a branding iron to his cheeks. But much had changed in the seven years since. In the spring of 1643, Roger Williams began a journey back to London for a charter—one that would guarantee freedoms that existed nowhere else in the world.

## ✥ CHAPTER 24 ✥

In the years between Williams's flight from England and his return to it, King Charles and Archbishop Laud had pushed hard on every front. The king had continued to collect taxes without parliamentary authority, and he had transformed the Star Chamber from a court of equity into a brutal arm of state power. Laud had intensified his pressure on Puritans, even briefly forbidding Puritan emigration to America—this order had prevented Oliver Cromwell from emigrating to Massachusetts. Then Charles and Laud pushed too far. In 1639 Charles tried to impose the Book of Common Prayer and other aspects of Anglican High Church discipline on Scotland. Scotland, thick with Presbyterians nearly as strong for nationalism as for Calvinism, rebelled. Insisting they were making only a "loyal protest" to the king, they demanded among other things the elimination of all bishops.

Thus two countries ruled by the same king went to war—twice. The "First Bishops War" of 1639 was essentially an armed truce in which English and Scottish armies faced each other down without much harm to either. Then, determined to impose his will, Charles launched the "Second Bishops War" a year later. It proved disastrous for him.

Against a Scottish army filled with motivated, righteous men, many of whom had fought as mercenaries on the continent, the king's ill-trained army—whose soldiers sometimes refused orders from "Popish" officers— proved worthless. One historian called it "on the King's side, a moral rather than merely a military collapse."[1]

After sweeping Charles's army aside, the Scots occupied much of northern England. Charles not only had to agree to the occupation but to pay the Scots for each day of it, and they would remain until satisfied with the peace.

More than a decade earlier, Parliament had asserted its rights. Charles had rejected that assertion, dismissed Parliament, and sworn he would not call another. Eleven years of Personal Rule, eleven years without a Parliament, had followed. But now, with no way to raise enough money for the Scots without parliamentary approval, in 1640 Charles was compelled to summon Parliament after all. It proved so unsympathetic that three weeks after it convened he dismissed this, the "Short Parliament." He next tried to raise money from Catholic nobles, and at the same time, Laud required all clergy to swear loyalty to the "discipline or government established in the Church of England as containing all things necessary to salvation, . . . *&c*"—leaving entirely undefined what one was swearing loyalty to. This became known as the "etcetera oath," and it sent more unease rippling through an increasingly distrustful country.

In London, the king's moves sparked riots. Charles, with Laud beside him, had a long history of not heeding warnings. This would be the last one.

Unable to raise enough money from Catholics, after exploring every other possible means to avoid calling another Parliament, he finally did what he had to do. For the second time in a year, he summoned a new Parliament and prepared to endure it. He would not endure it.

This new Parliament, laden with Charles's and Laud's enemies, would sit for nine years and become known as the Long Parliament. Flush with its own power and venting pent-up rage, it immediately asserted itself, requiring that Parliament meet at least every three years—even without a summons from the king—and prohibiting the crown from collecting unauthorized taxes.

It exerted enough direct pressure on Charles that in October 1640 he ordered Laud to rescind the etcetera oath. That same month Parliament abolished the High Commission—its rooms were sacked by a mob—and Laud could not persuade the Star Chamber to punish the offenders. Not long after, Parliament abolished the Star Chamber.

Then Parliament took far more personal aim at the crown. Members were still reluctant to attack Charles himself, but they had no reluctance to attack those close to him. On February 26, 1641, Henry Vane carried from Commons to Lords articles of impeachment against William Laud. The charges included tyranny, subverting the true religion, and causing the war with Scotland. On March 1 Laud was jailed in the Tower of London.

Commons had already targeted Thomas Wentworth, the Earl of Strafford and one of Charles's strongest supporters, who had raised an army in Ireland for use against the Scots. Parliament feared he planned to use it against them.

It impeached him for treason. Vane found one of the key pieces of evidence against him among his father's papers and gave it to the prosecutors.

The House of Lords acquitted Strafford. Commons, determined to kill him anyway, overwhelmingly passed a bill of attainder against him—a bill declaring him a traitor by act of Parliament and subjecting him to the death penalty. (The U.S. Constitution specifically prohibits bills of attainder or ex post facto laws.) The Lords, now fearing London mobs, did reluctantly concur, but the bill had no force without the king's signature.

Earlier Charles had promised Strafford "upon the word of the king, you shall not suffer in life, honour or fortune." Strafford released the king from his promise, advising him to sign the warrant for his death "for the preventing of such massacres as may happen by your refusal."

May 12, 1641, Strafford was beheaded.

Strafford had requested that Laud bless him from his window in the Tower as he passed by. Reportedly, Laud collapsed after he did so.

Meanwhile, with blow after blow, Parliament was striking at both the power of the crown and the changes in worship Laud had instituted. Charles accepted all these changes, watching his power erode, accepting even limits on his power to dissolve Parliament. He finally balked only at efforts to make the Church of England conform to Puritan worship. As Scotland had done, Commons wanted to remove "root and branch," to extirpate utterly, all traces of the episcopacy, and three times Parliament passed laws creating a synod to reform the Church of England. Three times Charles rejected it. In September 1641 Commons demanded—but Lords blocked—removal of "all crucifixes, scandalous pictures of one or more persons of the Trinity, and all images of the Virgin Mary . . . [and] all tapers, candlesticks, and basins."[2]

One month later Catholics in Ireland, fearing that Puritan ascendancy in England would oppress them even more, rebelled. It was no ordinary rebellion; they began it by slaughtering at least eight thousand English Protestants, most of them Puritans. Rumors in London reported 200,000 Protestants dead;[3] it was said that the Irish hated the English so much that they were torturing even English livestock.

Charles demanded money from Parliament for an army to put down the rebellion. But Puritans feared that an army raised to fight the Irish would instead be turned against them. Indeed, many believed that royalist and Irish Catholic forces were in secret alliance.

As anti-Catholic feeling intensified, a mob attacked Catholic communicants who had just worshipped in the queen's chapel. Then a monk and a priest were hanged—the priest at Tyburn, despite the queen's personal efforts to save his life. Outside London Catholic priests were tracked down as well; at least nine were executed in 1642 alone.

The most radical members of Parliament now took control. Mobs supporting them came "to the House with their swords by their sides, hundreds in companies"[4] and presented them with a petition against "popish lords and bishops." Commons passed a resolution promising to "never give consent to any toleration of the popish religion in Ireland, or in any other of his majestey's dominions."[5]

The king's hold on power seemed to be disintegrating. In January 1642, to reclaim his place and put Parliament in its, he burst into Commons with four hundred soldiers to arrest five parliamentary leaders. But, forewarned, they had already fled. His intrusion into Parliament accomplished nothing except to demonstrate his need for it—had he not needed it, he would have simply dismissed it—and to further inflame London against him. Already a haven for and hotbed of his enemies, the city responded by mustering its own trained bands to arms.

Brawls erupted in London streets between "Cavaliers," the king's supporters, and Parliament's "Roundheads." One Puritan observer stated that "many of the popish and malignant party . . . begin now to leave [London] and retire to their houses in the country, out of a panic fear of the multitude, who from all the counties come daily in thousands with petitions to the Houses."[6]

Indeed, the king himself decided London was unsafe. He withdrew to Oxford, which became his base thenceforth. Over the next months, while his wife sought financial support from Catholic royalty on the continent—she even carried the crown jewels to Holland, where she sold them—he built up an army. So did Parliament. Both sides proclaimed their determination to protect English freedom and the true Protestant religion.

Then Parliament passed the Militia Ordinance, giving itself the power to choose military commanders. Messengers from Parliament carried to the king the demand that he agree to it. He replied, "No, by God, not for an hour."

Then, in August 1642, the king formally declared war on parliamentary forces, launching the English Civil War, a war which started slowly but would ultimately become more brutal than America's Civil War. Charles began it promising to uphold "Protestant religion, the laws of England, and the liberty of Parliament."

This cauldron of an England was the destination for which Roger Williams departed Providence in early 1643, hoping to gain official sanction for his colony. But waiting for him in London would be two men representing Massachusetts already well ensconced with those in power. They had not come to England to oppose him, but they would oppose him. The men were Thomas Weld and Hugh Peter. Weld had cross-examined Williams at his trial, and Peter had replaced him at Salem, seen to his excommunication from that church, and stamped out lingering support for him in Salem.

They had come more than a year earlier as agents of the Bay, for the rise of Puritan power in Parliament had changed Massachusetts's circumstances—ironically, for the worse. The enmity of the king and Laud toward Puritans had actually prospered Massachusetts by generating the exodus of emigrants and their money to America. But as the Old World became itself new and shimmering with possibilities, English Puritans saw no reason to flee England; to the contrary, they found reason to return to it.

First a trickle, then a steady stream of Puritans began to leave America for home. Further complicating Massachusetts's situation, such men as Lord Saye and Sele, Lord Brooke, and the Earl of Warwick who had long invested in and supported New England adventures shifted their focus to Bermuda and the West Indies, where Puritans had also begun building communities and where, unlike New England, profits could be had.

As a result, Massachusetts found itself dependent solely upon its own resources for the first time in its brief history—and it abruptly discovered that those resources were grossly insufficient. In particular, immigrants had brought with them specie; without them, the money supply contracted. The General Court noted "a great stop in trade & commerce for want of money."[7] A great deflation set in throughout the colony, with Winthrop reporting, "Men could not pay their debts . . . prices of cattle soon fell the one half and less, yea to a third, and after one fourth part."[8]

The government tried to ease the money shortage by imposing controls and making all debts in the plantation payable in commodities. That eased some pressure in America, but creditors in England demanded money; without it they refused to extend more credit, setting off a downward economic spiral of contraction. The Bay considered "begging" aid from England, and friends there suggested that Parliament might give them relief, but the magistrates decided against taking that route, for "if we should put ourselves under the protection of the parliament, we must then be subject to all such laws as they should make."[9]

The need for help, however, eventually overwhelmed the arguments against seeking it. In April 1641 the General Court sent Weld, Peter, and a third man who soon returned to Massachusetts "to negotiate for us" in England. They were instructed not to compromise the Bay's independence in any way, but "to seek out some way . . . for our present supply," to raise funds "for the conversion of the benighted Indians," and to participate "in furthering the work of reformation of the churches [in England] which was now like to be attempted."[10]

Accompanied by John Winthrop Jr. on his own business, they arrived in September 1641 and, remarkably, they accomplished all their missions. Their success reflected their stature in the English Puritan community, for fundraising was then extraordinarily difficult. Even more desperate Protestants in Ireland were competing for financial support, while both Parliament and the crown were raising money for armies and demanding jewels, plate, meat, powder, and supplies of all kinds as well as cash. Nonetheless, Weld and Peter collected at least three thousand pounds and sent it to the Bay. (A considerable portion of this was diverted, and possibly embezzled, in Massachusetts, which undermined their later fund-raising efforts. For example, they raised £875 to send a hundred orphans to Massachusetts, but only a handful of children ever arrived. One hundred and fifty pounds was spent on the house of the president of Harvard College, £50 went for John Winthrop Jr.'s expenses, and other money was frittered away or embezzled, including by Winthrop's brother-in-law Emmanuel Downing.)[11] They also convinced Parliament to relieve Massachusetts of most taxes on its trade with England; later, Parliament relieved it of all such taxes.

And they involved themselves in the extraordinary events of the day in London. Peter in particular fully entered into English politics, joining an expedition authorized by Parliament to put down the Irish rebellion and becoming its spokesman in London upon his return.

He reported untruthfully—although he likely believed what he said—that the king had promised Irish Catholics freedom of religion in return for help against Parliament, and he stated that the Irish rebels declared they fought "by the Kings Order for the Kings Honour" against parliamentary forces.[12]

At the time of his report, little enthusiasm for continuing the civil war existed, and even many members of Parliament were calling for an accord with the king. His comments, injected into that conversation, galvanized and provoked; it struck the tuning fork that chilled and shook the English Protestant soul. At least partly because of his report, Commons ordered a committee "to prepare a Declaration, to set forth, that the Rebellion in Ireland, and this in England"—i.e., the king's attacks on Parliament—"spring from one Head: and are managed with concurrent Counsels to one End: for the utter Overthrow and Exterpation of the Protestant Religion."[13]

Over the next months, a time when the king's forces were routinely mauling Parliament's, Peter became one of the most vehement opponents to peace on any terms other than the king's unconditional surrender. He preached sermon after sermon, righteous sermons, justifying continued war. After one such, an angry listener remonstrated against this "new Gospell, which teacheth us (as he saies) to rebell and resist the King."[14] Peter spoke loudly enough that Charles took notice of him, charging him and several other clergy with high treason.

Yet Peter did not neglect Massachusetts. Early in 1643, he and Weld published *New Englands First Fruits;* in it they argued that Massachusetts was a great success, bragged of the conversion to Christianity of a single Indian, and excused their failure to convert more by promising to do more. This appeal raised more money for Massachusetts. Soon after, the two men injected "the New England Way"—the way in which Massachusetts was building a city upon a hill, a City of God, its way of church government and the role of its churches in civil society—directly into the debate over church reform.

Parliament had begun to act on the question. In the spring of 1643 it ordered the demolition of all religious monuments and decorations adorning Westminster Abbey; a few days later it ordered the destruction of the historic Cheapside Cross and "the obliterating of all popish monuments" in London. Then it ordered the "utter demolishing and removing of all monuments of idolatry and superstition out of all churches and chappels in England and Wales."[15]

Puritans in the Long Parliament, before civil war erupted, had also several times tried to create a great assembly of clergy to define a new path for the church and to build a godly commonwealth. Each time the king had blocked such a move. Now, with the king powerless to prevent it, on June 12, 1643,

Parliament created the Westminster Assembly of Divines, directing it to advise on the "liturgie, discipline, and government of the Church of England."[16]

William Hetherington, a nineteenth-century church historian, called the assembly "the most important event in the century in which it occurred."[17] If that assessment sounds hyperbolic, it reflects how important the assembly seemed to many contemporaries. The king issued a royal proclamation forbidding it, but his decree only kept his supporters, and most supporters of the existing worship in the Church of England, out of the assembly. That left the field entirely to those who demanded radical change.

Weld and Peter were determined to influence that change. Shortly before the assembly convened, they saw to the publication of several treatises in which Cotton and other New England ministers advanced their views and replied to questions put to them earlier by Presbyterians.

Hereafter Weld devoted more and more energy to pamphleteering, to engaging enemies with the sword of the Word. And hereafter Peter dove ever deeper into the river of revolution. He helped make that river run red.

Peter had already crusaded against peace with the king. As the Westminster Assembly convened, he ministered to a man about to be executed for plotting against Parliament. The man had insisted upon his innocence, but after one evening of Peter's ministry he confessed his guilt—and named other conspirators. Peter's usefulness was further proved as he traveled the country preaching sermons of support of Parliament.

Parliament now made him its official representative and sent him to Holland. His mission was to convince the Dutch to loan money to Parliament and withhold loans or matériel from the king. While in Holland, he also tried unsuccessfully to resolve differences over land and trade between New England Puritans and New Amsterdam.

Weld and Peter had fully engaged, and they were in full voice. While war raged in the English countryside, they had established themselves firmly in the warp and woof of London, known to all and, on the parliamentary side, well regarded by all. They knew Williams was coming, they knew his purpose, and their righteousness against him had not abated.

Roger Williams's mission was to overcome them and any others who stood in his way. For he did not simply seek a charter legitimizing the existence of his colony. His ambitions went well beyond that. He wanted the charter to specifically authorize liberty of conscience, liberty of thought in religion, and with it to authorize a government that had no role in regulating religion.

Yet enemies of his ideas and goals, men who held the precise opposite position, populated both Parliament and the Westminster Assembly of Divines. Although Williams was not entirely without potential allies, none of them shared his convictions.

To accomplish his desire seemed to require more than access to allies or an understanding of process. It required conjury.

# ❧ CHAPTER 25 ❧

Williams had all the length of his journey to devise a plan, and that journey may itself have influenced it. For on it he found another war. Massachusetts would not grant him safe passage to depart from Boston, forcing him to the Dutch colony of New Amsterdam. There, shortly before his arrival, Governor William Kieft had used the murder of a single white man as a pretext to massacre more than one hundred previously friendly Wesquaesgeek Indians—Indians who had actually sought Dutch protection from other Indians. Kieft had intended to intimidate all tribes into paying a tax for Dutch "protection" and to terrify them into abject submission. He succeeded in terrifying them. But they did not submit.

Their terror, compounded by their knowledge of the Pequots' fate at Mystic, unleashed a desperate ferocity. Williams arrived in New Amsterdam in time to "see the first breaking forth of that indian War." He offered to mediate but the Dutch, confident of easy victory, wanted the war to proceed. Williams scornfully observed, "[T]hey questioned not to finish it in a few dayes, in so much that the Name of Peace was foolish & odious to them."[1]

Time proved the Dutch foolish instead. Indians controlled the countryside and began slaughtering whites and burning their farms. The dead included Anne Hutchinson—the Hutchinson River and the eponymous parkway memorialize her—and as many as twelve members of her family, with one daughter taken captive; they had moved to the present Pelham, New York, from Rhode Island a few years before. According to one report, the Indians caught one child trying to escape "over a hedge, and they drew her back again by the hair of the head to the stump of a tree, and there cut off her head with a hatchet."[2]

(In England, when Weld heard of this he wrote, "Thus did the Lord heare our groanes to heaven and freed us from this great and sore affliction."[3]

Unrelated to her death, John Wheelwright had made peace with Massachusetts clergy, declaring himself "unfeignedly sorry" that he "did so much adhere to persons of corrupt judgment, to the countenancing of . . . evil practices."[4] His banishment was lifted. The Hutchinson episode was over.)

Indians fired houses and farms close enough outside the walls of New Amsterdam itself that refugees and residents huddled inside the walls could taste the smoke, feel the grit of ash in their nostrils, hear the war whoops. Williams himself "saw the flames at their Townes end . . . their Bowries were in Flames."[5] The name of peace was no longer foolish and odious to the Dutch, who now waited in terror defended by a weak garrison. According to Winthrop—unfortunately no details are extant—"by the mediation of Mr. Williams" several tribes "were pacified, and peace re-established between the Dutch and them."[6]

The peace was not total—that would not come for several years—and New Amsterdam remained in panic. Williams reported "the Flights and Hurries of Men, Women and children and the present removall of all that could"[7] into ships leaving America. Williams stayed a few months before finding crowded passage to London. Thoughts of Indians were fresh in the minds of everyone aboard. Thoughts of Indians would consume him during that voyage. And thoughts of Indians would lead him to his strategy in London.

None of Williams's correspondence from this period survives, so we cannot know why he chose his strategy—or even if it was a conscious choice. But the path he followed reflected either extraordinary good luck or a brilliant analysis of the fabric that made up English political and intellectual life.

He had never lost contact with that life. The latest English books and pamphlets routinely circulated throughout New England, reaching even Providence. Both travelers and correspondence carried great lodes of news and political gossip, which was widely disseminated as well. And Williams personally remained in close touch with London: a few months after one of his children was born—barely enough time for news of the birth to make it to England—his mother died and she recognized the child in her will.

At any rate, whether analysis or serendipity first carried him to his strategy, he discovered that the key to his success lay in Indian country. Indians would become his route to the center of power in London. This was his conjury. He began his conjuring on board ship.

By now, having routinely traveled along the coast by pinnace and canoe, he was at home with the sea, and spring was a fine time to sail. Compared with his winter voyage of twelve years earlier, when violent storms had lashed his ship and made the ocean "the terrible Atlanticke" to him, this was a peaceful journey. Crossing the ocean generally took six to eight weeks. As day supplanted day, as the sea swells and the bob and groan of the ship incorporated themselves into his own rhythms, Williams had nothing to do but think.

In that time it could not have escaped him, with his nuanced and sophisticated understanding of the colliding intellectual, political, and religious forces in England, that the subject of Indians highlighted his own strength and exploited Massachusetts's weakness, for the level of the Bay's hypocrisy in regard to Indians exceeded that in all else. Nor could it have escaped him that both England's security and Scripture made Indians of tremendous importance to those men active in English political and religious life—especially to those Puritans actively supporting Parliament in the civil war. To them, the failure to advance Protestant Christianity among Indians was the greatest disappointment of America.

The Spanish and Portuguese had imposed Catholicism upon millions with the sword. Although the French had less success because they had eschewed force, French priests had proselytized with considerable return throughout the Mississippi valley. But what results had the English achieved? They had achieved nothing. They had achieved nothing because, despite all their rhetoric, they had tried nothing. Not the Virginia Company, not Plymouth, not the Massachusetts Bay, not the Connecticut or New Haven colonies—all of whose founding documents claimed to justify colonization because it advanced Christ's kingdom among Indians—had made the slightest effort to convert Indians. Yet Weld and Peter were soliciting money for just that purpose.

Besides the security provided by adding millions of Protestants to the struggle against the so-called Whore of Babylon, Puritans had a second reason to concern themselves with the conversion of the Indians. Many believed the Gospel had to be spread around the world and the conversion of the Jews must occur before Christ would return, and a growing number believed that "these Indians in America may be Jewes (especially of the ten Tribes)"—i.e., the Lost Tribes of Israel—"[a]nd therefore to hope that the work of Christ among them, may be as a preparatory to his own appearing."[8]

All this Williams knew. As early as 1635, English minister Thomas Thorowgood had asked his opinion on whether the Indians were the Lost Tribes, and Thorowgood later wrote a book making this argument. Williams had wondered about but doubted the theory. Williams also knew that Weld and Peter in *New Englands First Fruits* had excused Massachusetts for failing to convert Indians by arguing that the Indians were so wild, so far removed from behaving in a civilized way, that they first had to be tamed before they could be converted.

Williams had a very different view of Indians. He intended to prove his view correct.

On that voyage, while the sea rocked him in its rhythms, he poured that different view and much of his own soul into a book which would have impact immediately upon its publication. Its title described it well: "A KEY into the LANGUAGE of AMERICA: or, An help to the *Language* of the *Natives* in that part of AMERICA, called NEW-ENGLAND. Together, with briefe *Observations* of the Customes, Manners and Worships, &c., of the Aforsesaid *Natives*, in Peace and Warre, in Life and Death . . . By ROGER WILLIAMS of *Providence* in *New-England*."

Reading it today, one sees the work of an open-minded, intellectually curious, and close observer. The book's stated purposes were to provide a dictionary to allow the English to converse with Indians and to describe Indian life. It fulfilled those purposes. It was neither the first attempt at a dictionary of a native language nor the first attempt to describe the culture and life of the Indians; nearly all of the many books about America published in the preceding century included sections about Indians. But in both areas, it was the best by far published in English. It offered detailed descriptions of how Indians bound their babies to a board, how they dried corn, how they made war, what they valued, what excited their curiosity. He reported, for example, "They hold the band of brother-hood so deare, that when one had committed a murther and fled, they executed his brother; and tis common for a brother to pay the debt of a brother deceased."[9]

If there was an underlying theme to the book beyond its stated purpose, it was its identification of commonalities between all peoples. Going beyond such simplistic pieties as "God having of one blood made all mankind," he noted, "Their desire of, and delight in newes, is great, as the Athenians, and all men, more or lesse; A stranger that can relate newes in their own language, they will stile him *Manitoo*, a God."[10] And, consistent with many views that had been expressed in England, he reminded his readers that the English had not so long before resembled them: "They have no *Clothes, bookes,* nor *Letters,* and therefore they are easily perswaded that the *God* that made *English* men is a greater *God,* because he hath so richly endoweed the *English* above *themselves*: But when they heare that about sixteen hundred yeeres agoe, *England* and the *Inhabitants* thereof were like unto *themselves,* and since have received from *God, Clothes, Bookes* &c. they are greatly affected with a secret hope concerning *themselves.*"[11]

Poems interspersed in the text all make a similar point: that Europeans should not assume superiority. As poems they are weak. As statements of values, they were, in the seventeenth century, unusual and provocative. In one he notes that upon hearing of "the horrid filths, Of Irish, English men" and their slaughter of each other, the Indians say to the English, "You are Barbarians, Pagans wild, Your Land's the Wildernes." Another poem went further down the same path, warning the "proud English" that Indians were "by birth as Good," and that the English might well find "Heaven open to Indians wild, but shut to thee."[12]

To suggest that God might draw Indians close while rejecting Christians was extraordinary; for a Calvinist, it had considerable theological implications.

Readers of this book well knew that Massachusetts had expelled Williams. In *Key* he reminds his readers, "Let none distrustfull *be;* / *In* wilderness, *in great* distresse / *These* Ravens *have fed me.*"

Williams arrived in London in early summer 1643. Likely he reconnected quickly with Henry Vane, with whom he had worked so closely during the Pequot War. The two men's "great friendship"[13] was commented on by Robert Baillie, a member of the Westminster Assembly and close observer of London politics, and Williams later lived in Vane's household, both in Whitehall Palace and at Vane's country estate. He may have done so during this period as well.

Vane was a good friend to have. He had become one of the most influential members of Parliament, and he was on his way to even greater power and influence. He likely also introduced Williams to John Milton. Although the actual evidence for a Milton-Williams friendship at this time—later they definitely developed one—is only circumstantial, David Masson, in his magnificent and massive biography of Milton, concluded the two "almost certainly"[14] knew each other in this period. Milton was extremely close to a grandson of Coke, moved in the Cromwell-Masham-Barrington circle as did Williams, and knew Vane well, even writing a sonnet to him. So it does seem likely the two met and started their friendship now.[15]

This matters for two reasons. First, Williams may have influenced Milton's views on the freedom of religion. Historians are virtually unanimous that Williams did significantly influence Vane's views on this subject, and between 1641 and 1644 Milton's position on toleration also changed dramatically, from opposition to a view close to Williams's. Williams almost certainly played some role in this change, but it is impossible to say how much.

Milton may also have introduced him to his printer, Gregory Dexter, who became Williams's printer. In those days the relationship between a writer and a printer was often close; it had to be. Newspapers did not yet exist. Books and pamphlets carried the public debate and they were then censored and licensed, so printers took risks publishing controversial writers and positions. As Dexter's biographer notes, "Dexter followed an extremely hazardous course . . . [and] operated when the printing trade was fighting for the liberties of Englishmen as well as for its own freedom. . . . [He] could make the press a weapon and never hesitated to use it as such when a particularly domineering conscience told him that was the right thing to do."[16]

Whether Milton introduced them or not, Williams did find Dexter, and Dexter became his confidant and supporter; he would print all of Williams's publications until he himself was "obliged to fly" London for printing an "offensive"[17] publication—almost certainly one of Williams's—and followed Williams back to Providence.

*Key* appeared in September 1643 and became immediately and broadly popular, enough to be reprinted. With it, Williams also published a "little additional discourse" which addressed "the great inquiry of all men, What Indians have been converted? What have the English done in those parts? What hopes of the Indians receiving the knowledge of Christ?"[18]

In this pamphlet, he rebutted Peter's and Weld's insistence that Indians were not yet ready to consider Christ. He also stated, "I can speak it confidently, I know it to have been easie for my selfe, long ere this, to have brought many thousands of these natives, yea, . . . I could have brought the whole Countrey to have observed one day in seven: I adde, to have received Baptisme, to have come to a stated Church meeting, to have maintained Priests, and Forms of Prayer."[19]

He had not done so because, he explained, convincing Indians to merely observe the forms of worship did not advance the kingdom of Christ, for mere forms were "indeed the subversion of the souls of millions in Christendom." This argument resonated with Puritans in and out of Parliament, who had long decried Laud's emphasis on form and practice. So did his two books resonate inside the intellectual, political, and religious communities of London, and his talk of potentially thousands of Indian conversions was far more often remembered than the limitation he placed upon it. That promise also mocked the utter inaction by Massachusetts.

His books created excitement in the most exciting of times. They made him a man talked about, a man whose ideas were talked about. He had already developed friendships with men whose influence was growing, particularly Vane and Cromwell, and he knew well at least three of the five parliamentary leaders whom Charles had sought to arrest when he had burst into Parliament. His book made him a man of substance in his own right, a man his powerful friends could perceive as a near equal, a man worth introducing to others, a man worth listening to. And his friends were becoming more powerful.

Vane was not in London to enjoy his friend's new celebrity. He was in the north, on the most urgent business, representing Parliament in negotiations with the Scots that would determine the outcome of the war. Parliament's own soldiers had yet seen little but defeat, and Parliament needed to reassure London that the king would not march into it, needed good news to beat back those who wanted peace, peace now, peace by surrender. Therefore Parliament needed the Scottish army, which had crushed the king's forces three years earlier. It was Vane's mission to secure that army. London tracked the negotiations closely; one finds almost daily references to them in the Commons journal.

Vane quickly resolved all issues but one, church governance. The Scots, in exchange for sending their army against Charles, insisted upon imposing their Presbyterian system on England and Wales. John Knox had carried this system from Calvin's Geneva to Scotland in the previous century. In it, individual churches sent representatives to a synod, where church issues were defined and agreed upon. But the individual church had to conform to whatever the synod decided. The Scots demanded this. They believed Scripture, the very Word of God, required it, and one could not compromise on God's Word. They wanted a covenant with Parliament on it.

Parliament wanted only a military alliance, a league. And Vane personally abhorred, found stifling, the Presbyterian system; he had watched and suffered five years before as such a system expelled Antinomians in Massachusetts. He had devoted much energy to efforts to destroy the Church of England hierarchy; he was unwilling now to create a new system giving some clergy the authority to discipline others.

Late in September, Vane found a way around the problem and convinced the Scots to agree to the Solemn League and Covenant with Parliament. The covenant stipulated that church government should be "according to the Word of God" and "the practices of the best reformed churches"—language open to interpretation. It also allowed Scotland to have representatives in the Westminster Assembly.

This agreement soon sent an army of twenty thousand Scots marching to Parliament's relief, enormously increasing its military might. It also elevated Vane's stature even higher in Parliament, transforming him into one of its very most powerful members. For Williams, Vane's ascension would become important.

Also, at precisely this time, in September 1643, Weld and Peter had been due to return to Massachusetts. But they did not return. Weld explained to the General Court that "very many godly persons" were importuning them to stay because "we by or presence doe more good here, then we orselves dare imagine." But they did not expect to stay much longer. "The prsent condition of this kingdome, yt is now upon the Verticall point. . . . Things can not long stand at this passe here, as now, but speedily will be better or worse. If better, we shall not repent us to have bene spectatours & furtherers of or Dear Countries good. . . . If worse, we are like to bring thousands wth us to you."[20]

Williams and his plantation in America stood upon a vertical point as well. For events there had moved fast forward, and they seemed inclined toward spiraling past all control.

Earlier, while Roger Williams was at sea, on May 19, 1643, the four Puritan colonies—Massachusetts, Plymouth, Connecticut, and New Haven—joined in permanent alliance. This was a military alliance only, formed in response to perceived external threats, primarily from Indians but also from the Dutch to their south and the French to the north.

The agreement establishing "the United Colonies" states, "Whereas we all came into these parts of America with one and the same end and aim, namely, to advance the kingdom of our Lord Jesus Christ, and to enjoy the liberties of the Gospel in purity with peace; and whereas, . . . the natives have formerly committed sundry insolences and outrages . . . and, seeing, by reason of the sad distractions in England, (which they have heard of) and by which they know we are hindered . . . we, therefore, do . . . enter into a present consociation . . . that, as in nation and religion, so in other respects, we be and continue one."

That the Indians followed events in England closely enough to understand that New England was now isolated indicates how efficiently information flowed across the Atlantic. And the members of the United Colonies understood that. The statement—"in nation and religion . . . we be and continue one"—also mattered. The agreement pointedly excluded Rhode Island, although many there wanted to join the alliance.

By September, Williams certainly would have learned of this alliance. He would also soon learn of two other events which occurred fast upon it. Both made his plantation's plight utterly desperate, and both involved Miantonomi.

An accusation had been made to the United Colonies that Miantonomi was trying to organize all Indian tribes for a general uprising against the English. He had supposedly told the Montauks on Long Island much what the Pequot had told the Narragansetts six years earlier: his accuser quoted him as saying, "For so are we all Indians . . . and Say Brothr to one another; So must we be one as the English are, othrwise we shall be all gone shortly. . . . The Indians beyond the Dutch, and all the Northern and Eastern Indians [are] . . . Joyning with us, and we are all resolved to fall upon them all, at one apoynted day . . . [and] kill men, women, and children."[21]

Miantonomi denied any such plans, as he had denied previous accusations. Convinced that Uncas was the source of the report, he went to war against him. Far from triumphing, he found himself a captive. Uncas demanded a ransom from the Narragansetts for their prince. They paid it. But Uncas did not release him. Instead, he asked for guidance from the United Colonies. The commissioners met on the matter in Boston in September 1643.

On several occasions in the past, Williams had intervened with Winthrop to protect the Narragansetts in general and Miantonomi in particular; more than once he had proven accusations against them false. When accused of being gullible, he had even shown uncharacteristic sharpness, telling Winthrop, "I am not yet turned Indian, to believe all barbarians tell me." He had gone on to say, "[Y]ou have received many accusations and hard conceits of this poor native Miantunnomu." They were, Williams had demonstrated at the time, "malice and falsehood. . . . I am as confident of the truth, as that I breathe."[22]

But from across the sea Williams could now neither know the truth nor help Miantonomi if he did.

The United Colonies commissioners concluded unanimously that "it would not be safe to set [Miantonomi] at liberty, neither had we sufficient grounds for us to put him to death."[23] They then sought the opinion of five clergy who decided that he should be killed—but not by them. And so the commissioners told Uncas to kill him.

Uncas, a party of Mohegans, and two Englishmen escorted Miantonomi into the forest, and an Indian came up behind him and "clave his head with a hatchet."[24] According to one report, Uncas then cut out a piece of Miantonomi's shoulder, ate it, and pronounced it "the sweetest meat he ever ate; it made his heart strong."[25]

No record survives of Williams's reaction to the news of the death of this man who had provided a refuge to him, who had for him refused to join with the Pequot against the English, who had for him instead led the Narragansetts into alliance with the English. They had entertained each other in their respective homes, had taught each other foreign ways; they had tested each other and, the tests passed, relied upon each other, leaned upon each other, gone to war beside each other. They had become comrades. Even more, Williams, the Englishman who had met kings and knew the royal court, and this "barbarian" had become friends.

And now Williams's countrymen had seen to Miantonomi's death. Perhaps Williams thought of his poem in *Key*, his warning to the English that "thou shalt see / Heaven open to Indians wild, / but shut to thee."

Miantonomi's death was more than a blow to Williams personally. His death threatened the very existence of Rhode Island and, more importantly, of the freedom of thought which Williams was seeking to secure. For William Arnold used the death as a wedge to split off another part of the plantation, and in doing so threatened to shatter the entire colony, leaving small pieces lying about for members of the United Colonies to plunder.

Arnold had always recognized Miantonomi's ownership of lands south of the Pawtuxet River, beyond the boundaries of Williams's original Providence purchase, and had himself bought property in the region from him. Miantonomi had also sold land in this area to Gorton and his followers. But in the wake of Miantonomi's death, Arnold paid two lesser Narragansett sachems, Pomham and Socononoco, goods and liquor to claim that they owned the land which Miantonomi had sold to the Gortonists.

Arnold next bought a vast tract of land from the two sachems which included the Gortonists' prior purchases; he added this to the land north of the Pawtuxet which Williams had bought from Canonicus and Miantonomi in the original sale of Providence, but which Socononoco also claimed to own. Next he had Pomham and Socononoco submit themselves to the authority of Massachusetts.

Having got hold of Williams's original deed and cut out references in it to Pawtuxet, having gotten Pomham and Socononoco to submit to the Bay's authority and declare Gorton's deed invalid, Arnold was now prepared to take his case to Massachusetts courts. The Bay immediately asserted its jurisdiction over all the territory in dispute. And the territorial integrity of all Rhode Island seemed about to unravel.

When Williams had first settled in Providence, the Wampanoags in Plymouth, old rivals of the Narragansetts, had claimed to own it. Plymouth had promised Williams that even if the very questionable Wampanoag claims were investigated and found valid, it would never disturb him. Now, without any investigation, Plymouth asserted ownership of the land the Wampanoags had claimed, including much of the town of Providence and Aquidneck Island.

Connecticut—upon no grounds whatsoever—also claimed parts of Rhode Island and much of Narragansett land.

At a meeting in Boston of the United Colonies, the commissioners did not resolve their competing claims. They did, however, agree that Massachusetts should deal with Gorton, whom they all found abhorrent.

The next Massachusetts General Court informed Gorton that the Bay had taken "into our Jurisdiction and Protection two Indian Sachims, whose names are Pumham and Soccononoco, who have lately complained to us of some injurious and unjust dealing [by you]." The court therefore demanded his presence immediately, "in the Generall Court now assembled at Boston."[26]

Gorton was not intimidated. He and his supporters replied that they had "wronged no man," and rejected Massachusetts's claim to jurisdiction in words certain to infuriate the magistrates, calling the Bay full of "pride and folly" and "the kingdome of darknesse and the devill."[27]

The magistrates replied not with words but force, sending forty soldiers to arrest all the Gortonists. The troop passed through Providence on its way south, inflaming all there at the insult to their sovereignty. Although Providence had no military force capable of halting this expedition, several Providence men had enough courage to accompany it, simultaneously deriding the soldiers and warning them that they would bear witness to their behavior.

Gorton met them in a fortified house with nine other men. Their families had fled. To avoid a pitched battle, the commander listened as Gorton objected that "our professed adversaries should be our Judges." He also protested that the Massachusetts soldiers were to be paid out of "our goods"—the troops were to be paid by plundering the Gortonists' possessions, thus proving that the Massachusetts court had already concluded they were guilty. Gorton suggested arbitration. The commander agreed to a truce while waiting for an answer to Gorton's proposal from Boston. But a committee appointed by the General Court and advised by clergy rejected arbitration as "neither seasonable nor reasonable."[28]

The truce ended and the Gortonists withdrew into their fortified house. Gunfire was exchanged, but Gorton had successfully made their house "musket-proof." A siege lasted for days. Finally the soldiers closed upon the house by digging trenches; then they hurled burning torches onto the roof. Fortunately for those inside, the wind defeated the attempt to fire the house. But the Gortonists were worn down. Not long after, under constant stress, having nearly been burned alive, and without possibility of prevailing, Gorton and six men surrendered, while three others escaped.

The victorious army arrived in Boston in triumph, their prisoners in tow, on October 13. Although Gorton had been arrested on civil charges relating entirely to property, he was now charged with blasphemy because of his letters to the General Court. This made that court the offended party, the prosecutor, the judge, and the jury.

Gorton demanded the right to appeal to England. The court told him to "never dream or think any such thing." It then explored many of Gorton's theological writings and demanded explanations for them. He and his colleagues refused to recognize the court's jurisdiction and did not explain. The court ordered them to answer on pain of death. They remained silent. The court persisted, laying a kind of siege against their silence, sending ministers to talk to them, but still they remained silent. Winthrop complained, "They would acknowledge no error or fault. . . . After divers means had been used both in public and private to reclaim them, and all proving fruitless, the court proceeded to the sentence."[29]

As to the property issue, although New England land law clearly recognized the right of a superior sachem to dispose of land held by his inferiors, the court dispossessed the defendants and declared Arnold's claims valid. Soon settlers from Massachusetts were moving into Shawomet, onto the lands the Gortonists had cleared and planted. Then the court moved on to the charges of blasphemy and sedition.

Winthrop had often been accused of being soft. He was not soft now. He and nearly all the other magistrates believed "that Gorton ought to die." A slim majority of the town deputies, however, considered death too harsh. The court sentenced Gorton and others "to be confined to Charlestown, there to be set on work, and to wear such bolts and irons as may hinder his escape. . . . If he shall break his said confinement, or publish, declare, or maintain any of the blasphemous or abominable heresies wherewith he hath been charged . . . upon conviction thereof [he] shall be condemned to death and executed."[30] Their imprisonment would last for "the pleasure of the court."[31]

The sentence was imposed in October 1643. It seemed to presage the dismemberment of Rhode Island. Massachusetts through Arnold was already claiming jurisdiction over Shawomet and Pawtuxet, and Arnold had manufactured a deed which would allow Massachusetts to claim much of the town of Providence itself. As Gorton's close escape from a death sentence demonstrated, in none of those territories would freedom of thought be allowed. And Plymouth and Connecticut were watching, watching and waiting, eager to wolf down any morsels of territory left over from the Bay's dismembering of the colony.

At the time, Williams was enjoying the enthusiastic reception in London of his two books, a reception which, with his old friendships, was winning him an opportunity to present his case. It would be a few weeks before he would hear all this news from America, before he learned that the colony he was attempting to make secure was being rendered and devoured.

When he did learn, perhaps he recognized the irony: Indians had saved his life and provided him the key to securing his plantation; through Pomham and Soconoco, Indians were now destroying all that he had tried to achieve. Or perhaps he was too desperate to see anything but the absolute necessity of success.

For if he did not succeed, if he did not bring to bear the intervention of a more powerful force, then Massachusetts would succeed. He knew also that that meant his experiment in free thought, unique in all the world, would be snuffed out. He had, somehow, to keep it alive.

There was one other thing. In the wake of Massachusetts's aggression, he was developing views on power and government which he had not yet articulated. These views would prove as revolutionary as his conception of the proper relationship of church and state.

Part VI

# SOUL LIBERTY

# ✣ CHAPTER 26 ✣

Desperate though he was, Roger Williams nonetheless had no plan he was following to get a charter. He could have none, for in London he faced a kind of vacuum. A Parliament preoccupied with questions about its own survival had not yet claimed authority over colonies, and Royalists did not exercise any. No entity could give him a charter even if its members had been inclined to do so. He had to wait. But he did not wait idly.

There could hardly have been a greater contrast between life in Providence and life in London: of the one, the spare homes and barns, the single rutted street, the open fields, the swells of the sea, and the isolation; of the other, the jumble of grandeur and squalor and pickpockets and plague, streets cut so narrow between buildings that the sun never penetrated them, the cool thick stone of the Inns of Court, the grand magnificence of Vane's homes, the fetid open sewer of the Thames. Yet Williams was immediately and once again at home, home in the city where he grew up, home in the city which his uncle James Pemberton had served as mayor, home in the lobbies and alcoves of Whitehall and Westminster Palace.

In any society, even in normal times, underground frictions develop as institutions and interests grind together, but now, here, in these most extraordinary of times, it must have seemed that all English history was coming together upon this moment and upon this place. Much of that history he had watched: Coke and Bacon disputing the power of the king, the Petition of Right, Laud's rise. Now, added to that was Parliament in rebellion, the Star Chamber abolished, Laud in the Tower, the reform of the church. Grand great things were moving all about him. He could feel it, feel that movement.

He was determined to participate in that movement, and immediately engaged in the debate over the future of the English church. Not only would the outcome of the debate in England affect America, but he believed that his views had enormous ramifications in England. If his ideas were valid, they were valid everywhere; if his ideas had use, they had use everywhere.

Virtually all who participated in this debate believed that man's eternal salvation was at stake, as was the fate of England itself. Williams did not so believe. Further, he considered those who did so believe self-inflated and dangerous, and he prepared to say so. He began working on more books and pamphlets, publications which would speak directly to these questions.

Then, abruptly, he found himself engaged in two seemingly unrelated problems, yet both would bear indirectly upon his mission. First, he joined his brother Sydrach in a lawsuit against his other brother Robert over their mother's estate. Ultimately Roger lost because he refused to take an oath before testifying. Still, his family reunion was apparently a happy one. Robert later followed him to Providence and would prove extremely supportive over the years. And Sydrach, a merchant who traveled throughout the Mediterranean, informed him of his personal experiences in Islamic countries, which tolerated his religion, while some Catholic states had not: he had been imprisoned "by the Inquisition at Milan."[1]

The second problem had nothing to do with his beliefs. It had to do with coal. The king controlled Newcastle, the primary supplier of London's coal. As winter arrived with unusual severity, a coal shortage became more than an inconvenience; it became demoralizing and dangerous. There was hope that the Scottish army, moving through deep snow in the coal regions, would make Newcastle's supplies available, but in the meantime the cold bit into the city with sharp teeth, and then ground up those caught up in them. The cold made many of the poor burn a mixture of dung and sawdust despite its noisome smell, made "some turn thieves that never stole before—steal posts, seats, benches from doors, rails, nay, the very stocks that should punish them."[2] The lord mayor promised that supplying any "manner of Fewell . . . shall be taken as a very acceptable service to this City, not to bee forgotten."[3]

So Williams devoted much of that winter in "service of Parliament and City, for the supply of the poor of the City with wood,"[4] hoping his efforts would not be forgotten. At the same time he continued to write. Even during his searches outside London for fuel supplies, he wrote, wrote furiously, wrote wherever he found himself, wrote "in change of rooms and corners, yea . . . in variety of strange houses, sometimes in the fields, in the midst of travel."[5]

He wrote with the fever of a man with much to say and little time in which to say it. Always he had been someone who had engaged with others, who had spoken loudly, but he had been isolated and silenced for seven years. In the wilderness he had carved out a society and translated his experiences there into a view of how the world worked, and how he thought the world should work. But in the wilderness, no matter how loudly he shouted he could not be heard. Now others could hear him, and he intended that his words would move him ever closer to the very quick of the moment.

They would do more than that. He was drafting one of the most remarkable and revolutionary documents about freedom ever written. And one of the most remarkable aspects to it was its originality. What he believed, for now, he believed alone.

Meanwhile, Parliament established a Committee on Foreign Plantations and made Robert, Earl of Warwick, governor-in-chief of all American plantations. This committee had the power to "assign . . . their aforementioned authority and power; and in such manner, and to such persons, as they shall judge to be fit, for the better governing and preserving of the said plantations and islands."

Immediately upon the committee's creation and without waiting for instruction from Boston, Thomas Weld sought a charter which would bring Massachusetts control of Providence, of Newport and Portsmouth, of Pawtuxet and Shawomet, of all the occupied areas in and around Narragansett Bay. This would not only crush Williams's experiment in freedom, it would push him out into the wilderness once again.

Weld lobbied hard, approaching members of the committee individually. In his conversations he did not simply present his case. While Williams was away from London trying to find fuel supplies, Weld was asking for the signatures of committee members on a proposed charter for Massachusetts. (Hugh Peter was then in Holland representing Parliament.) Weld convinced Warwick and eight others to sign it. Weld then dated the document, making it seem as if the committee had voted on it. This document would become known as the "Narragansett patent."

But for any charter to be legal, it had to "pass the table," i.e., a majority of the entire committee had to approve it during a committee meeting. The majority also had to include Warwick, the chair; even if the rest of the committee was unanimous against him, his opposition would defeat any proposal. The charter then had to be formally signed and enrolled and appropriate seals placed upon it.

Weld's charter had no force. The total of nine signatures fell short of a majority. In dating the document Weld had clumsily selected a sabbath; members would never have desecrated the sabbath to discuss such an issue, or any issue short of a major emergency. The date was also one on which at least one signatory was not in London; he was commanding an army engaged with Royalist forces far from the city. The signatures clearly had been collected one at a time, not at a committee meeting when the charter was discussed. Finally, the document was never enrolled, and it bore no seals whatsoever.

Weld's purported charter was not exactly a forgery, but neither was it valid. It did not do what Weld and subsequently Massachusetts claimed that it did; it did not authorize Massachusetts to take control of Rhode Island. As with Arnold's title to Shawomet, no court but the Massachusetts General Court would ever have found it valid. Nonetheless, it did give Massachusetts a claim it could attempt to enforce in New England, three thousand miles from an English court. Weld had stolen a march on Williams. Warwick, without whose support no charter could be issued, was now on record in opposition. So was almost half the committee. Weld had made Williams's task more difficult than ever.

There was only one way to accomplish his task. He had to fit Providence into context. The context that mattered most had nothing to do with events in America. The context that mattered most was developing right then in England. And that context did not favor him.

Parliament was moving away from rather than toward any toleration of religious differences. If the bull's-eye of suppression were Catholics, all who differed were in the target. In February 1644, Parliament required every man above the age of eighteen to swear to the Solemn League and Covenant. A Scottish observer nonetheless complained that the "penalty to them that refuse, [is] not death, which is warranted." The penalty was merely "confiscation of estates, . . . the least penalty that we have any example of in Scripture."[6]

Four members of Parliament refused to take the oath and were expelled. To the chagrin of the Scots, they did not even lose their estates; enforcement of the new law proved lax.

But more context was found in each day's debate in the Westminster Assembly of Divines. Parliament had created the assembly to advise it on reforming the Church of England, and Parliament had selected the approximately one hundred and fifty English members, roughly thirty of whom also served in Parliament. Vane, who headed a parliamentary committee on religious affairs, was one of them. The other members of the assembly were clergy. Parliament allotted fifteen seats to Scotland and also named Cotton, Hooker, and John Davenport, founder of New Haven, to the assembly. None of the three ever attended a meeting, but naming them testified to their importance and to the importance of their views, as expressed in pamphlets, treatises, and sermons they had published explaining church government in Massachusetts, which became known as "the New England Way."

The assembly was virtually unanimous on several points: church attendance would remain mandatory; the theology would be Calvinist; and England would have "a Nationall church," i.e., there would be a state church for all England. As in Massachusetts, the assembly believed the model should be ancient Israel, in which state and church were intimately interwoven. The only real point of contention in the assembly was over church governance, church discipline.

Many members of Parliament—but few in the assembly—preferred to keep the episcopacy, but those who demanded its abolition were relentless and fought hard. The bishops' defenders did not. As Lord Falkland observed, "Those who hated the bishops hated them worse than the devil and those that loved them loved them not so well as their dinner."[7]

Bishops were abolished. But who and what would replace them? At issue was power. The blending of church and state—and the precedent in England, in the absence of a governmental bureaucracy, of using the bureaucracy of the church to carry out governmental functions—made the issue power. Would the state dictate to the church, the church to the state, or neither?

Parliament would decide this, but the Westminster Assembly would advise upon it. Members of the assembly reflected several viewpoints, but the overwhelming majority wanted a church government identical to Scotland's Presbyterian system, with local churches sending elders and ministers to synods which could discipline individual congregations. They believed that Scripture, the Word of God, dictated it. A solid majority of English members believed this, and they were stiffened in their belief by the Scottish representatives, with the power of Scotland's armies behind them. Nothing made that point better than a comment by Robert Baillie, a Scot and a leader of the Presbyterians in the assembly who wrote penetratingly about the events and personalities. Baillie said he would conciliate opponents "till it please God to advance our armie, which we expect will much assist our arguments."[8]

Eventually, the Presbyterians would win their point in the assembly. But if the Scottish army supported this system, the English parliamentary army did not. And the English army would eventually have its say on this subject.

As to "toleration," the word itself seemed dirty both to the assembly and to Parliament. It also seemed impossible. Where would one draw the line? Was toleration to be offered only those who agreed on all fundamentals of Calvinist theology? Was it to be toleration for the plethora of sects just beginning to emerge? That opened the way to chaos, error, and sin. Was toleration even to allow worship by Catholics, Turks, and Jews? That seemed utterly abhorrent. And atheists? That went beyond blasphemy. One shuddered at the idea.

Not only did toleration appall nearly all in the assembly. It appalled Parliament, which sent two Baptists to prison in early 1644 and demanded to know what Cromwell would do about an "Anabaptist" officer in his army. Cromwell defiantly replied, "Sir, the state, in choosing men to serve them, takes no notice of their opinions."[9]

Williams was of course not a member of the assembly. But he was determined to have his views heard. He began attending its sessions regularly. In the hallways and lobbies in Westminster Palace, in the rooms and lobbies outside Parliament itself, in taverns, in homes, he spoke passionately and earnestly for full freedom of conscience, citing experience, history, logic, and Scripture to support his position.

Williams's "great friendship" with Vane helped him. Vane would certainly have introduced him to all those who mattered, and Vane—whose star, already high, was still rising and who was personable, physically attractive, and as intense as any youth—saw everyone who mattered. For example, though he and Baillie agreed on almost nothing about church governance, they dined together often, and in private letters Baillie called him "a very gracious youth"[10] and considered him "our most intime friend."[11] Williams went through openings Vane made for him and also found his own.

Baillie gradually came to know him, referring to him as "my good acquaintance Mr. Roger Williams."[12] The two men were violently opposed to each other's principles. Baillie condemned his "extreme mistakes," but also came away impressed by Williams's character, commenting on "the man's great sincerity though in a very erroneous way, and of his disposition which is without fault as I conceive." Baillie noted Williams's "great averseness from reporting known lies." He concluded, "I would be loath in any point of fact to call his testimony into question, . . . and have thought him fitted with many good endowments for eminent service to Christ."[13] Baillie also noted with concern that Williams had become an influential voice, that others had begun to listen, that he was a "Seeker," outside of a church but seeking one. He seemed even to have unintentionally founded a sect of Seekers.

One man listening to him was Vane himself. Vane had earlier called for state control of churches but he had abandoned that plan and moved in Williams's direction, asking Parliament, "Why should . . . any bee supprest" if they "seek God"?[14] Williams had heard him say this and called it a "heavenly speech." Now Williams urged him to advance even further down that path. He did.

But Vane had not yet arrived where Williams stood. No member of the assembly accepted what Williams preached, nor did a single member of Parliament or the assembly embrace the position he was preparing to assert explicitly and publicly: the utter and complete removal of the state from church business. He wanted not toleration, but freedom. And by now he had also come to understand the full implications of freedom—not just religious freedom but political freedom, including the necessary limitations upon it in order that a society could function. By now his thought was fully developed, and he was about to begin expressing it.

It was not clear whether doing so would advance or retard his cause, but for all his boldness he knew he had a foil to use to win his point. He had John Cotton.

## ❧ CHAPTER 27 ❧

At about the same time that Weld was obtaining the fraudulent charter authorizing Massachusetts to absorb Rhode Island, an old letter from Cotton to Williams appeared in print as a pamphlet. The letter had been written immediately after Williams's banishment, while he was literally wandering in the wilderness; it was published now without Cotton's knowledge or consent, most likely by either a supporter of Williams or by a Presbyterian who thought it would embarrass the "Independents," those who agreed with Presbyterians on theology but who wanted no organization superior to and able to impose discipline upon the individual church. (Massachusetts churches were considered Independents. Cotton introduced the word "Congregationalist" as a substitute for "Independent," but Cotton's word had not yet taken hold.) The letter's tone was harsh—Cotton told Williams that "you have banished yourself" and that, if he died, "your bloode had been on your owne head"—and it did not support the position of English Independents who wanted toleration for themselves.

In early February 1644, Williams published his own pamphlet—pamphlets were then used like artillery in public debates—entitled *Mr. Cotton's Letter Examined and Answered*. Without question, he understood the context in which his words would be read and the larger significance of what he had to say. Already well known for *Key*, already a regular observer in Parliament and in the assembly, already a man who dined with those who were creating a new world, he knew his comments would be read by men engaged in the issue. Certainly members of the Committee on Foreign Plantations would read his pamphlet with particular interest.

Williams tried to make his readers live through and feel his own personal experiences, make them understand the reasons for his differences with Massachusetts, make them see the hypocrisy of Massachusetts. As always, he had an ally in this: Massachusetts itself. By then every person in London who had the slightest interest in America knew that Massachusetts soldiers had marched contemptuously through Providence to Shawomet, besieged Gorton and his followers, and pillaged their possessions; London knew too of Gorton's trial, his close escape from the death sentence, and the refusal of Massachusetts to allow him an appeal to England.

Williams attempted to lead readers to the inevitable conclusion that, rather than allowing Rhode Island to be absorbed by Massachusetts, the behavior of Massachusetts in matters of both church and state not only justified but required sanctioning Rhode Island's existence as an independent colony. Thus he spoke of his astonishment and outrage that he himself had been "denied the common aire to breath in, and a civill cohabitation upon the same common earth; yea and also without mercy and humane compassion be exposed to winter miseries in a howling Wildernes?"[1]

Cotton had claimed that Williams received a "civill sentence from the civill state," but Cotton had conceded this also meant "a banishment from the Churches." Therefore, Williams argued, Cotton did "silently confesse" that Massachusetts had, despite its denials, blended its civil state with its church. He continued, "[O]therwise why was I not permitted to live in the world, or Common-weale, except for this reason, that the Common-weale and Church is yet but one, and hee that is banished from the one, must necessarily bee banished from the other also."[2]

He also reminded his readers that Massachusetts had never allowed anyone to "set up any other Church and Worship."[3] The plantation had expelled even those who had tried to worship privately using the Book of Common Prayer. And he charged that Cotton "publickly taught, and teacheth . . . persecuting all other consciences and wayes of worship but his own in the civill state, and so consequently in the whole world, if the power . . . were in his hand."[4]

Williams described the true church as a beautiful and magnificent garden, unsullied and pure, resonant of Eden. The world he described as "the Wildernesse." That word too had resonance with him, a personal resonance. Then he charged that Massachusetts had mixed the two, and he used for the first time a phrase which he would use again in the future, a phrase which although not attributed to him has echoed through American history. "[W]hen they have opened a gap in the hedge or wall of Separation between the Garden of the Church and the Wildernes of the world," he wrote, "God hathe ever broke down the wall it selfe, removed the Candlestick, &c. and made his Garden a Wildernesse, as at this day."[5]

He was saying that mixing church and state corrupted the church. He was saying that when one mixes religion and politics one gets politics. At that place at that time, in London amid both civil war and ongoing meetings of the Westminster Assembly, he knew perfectly well that his argument for what he began calling "Soul Libertie" had enormous political and secular implications.

Williams's ambitions for liberty started with Rhode Island, but they went beyond Rhode Island. He would soon expand his argument to explicitly examine all that he implied.

Mr. *Cotton's Letter Examined* had immediate repercussions. Since Independents were seeking toleration from the Presbyterians, the dramatic account of how Massachusetts had refused to tolerate a man who differed not one whit on theology embarrassed them in Parliament. It also eroded support for Massachusetts on the Committee on Foreign Plantations, and undermined its efforts to acquire Rhode Island. The fresh evidence of Gorton's treatment provided an exclamation point to Williams's account.

Now Williams pressed his advantage and turned directly to the committee and to the Earl of Warwick, trying to convince them not only to grant the charter but to explicitly warrant its existing "Soul Libertie" with all its implications. He could be both relentless and charming; he was a man with reasoned arguments who advanced them with passion. In lobbies and hallways and taverns, in the great homes and palaces of London, he wore at his listeners with his persistence, his argument, and his character.

On March 4, 1644, a month after Williams published his reply to Cotton, Hugh Peter returned from Holland and likely joined Weld in attempting to block Williams. But events had begun now moving Williams's way.

Williams had one final argument on his side. Rhode Island could be a test, an experiment. It was safely isolated from England. If the committee granted a charter and allowed an experiment in soul liberty, all England could watch the results.

Vane, a member of the committee, was helping. Both Vane's stature in Parliament and his special provenance on colonial issues gave him particular influence. His committee colleagues knew he had not merely lived in America but had served as governor of Massachusetts; they trusted his assessment of both the situation and Williams himself. Together Vane and Williams were slowly pushing Warwick and the committee in their direction.

Finally Warwick agreed to reverse himself, then convened the committee to consider Williams's petition. Unlike Weld's document, this charter did pass the table. The signatures were in proper order and properly sealed, and all appropriate legal procedures were adhered to.

On March 14, 1644, Williams had his charter.

Some of the most powerful men in England signed this charter—not only Warwick and Vane but Lord Saye and Sele and Arthur Haselrig, both of whom were much involved in New England. They well knew that those in other American plantations—even the Dutch in New Amsterdam—referred to Rhode Islanders as "scumme" and "riff-raff" and the colony as a "sewer" and "latrina."

Yet the charter granted these outcasts in Rhode Island the dignity of calling them "well Affected and Industrious English" and named the agglomeration of Providence, Portsmouth, and Newport "Providence Plantations in the Narragansett Bay." (Not for eighteen years would the name officially become "Rhode Island and Providence Plantations.") The charter placed the plantation's southern border at the "Pequot river," present New London, Connecticut, thus granting it control of territory including Pawtuxet and Shawomet, but it did not explicitly reject Massachusetts's claims to either.

The charter itself was remarkable both for what it did say and what it did not. The committee could have responded to the numerous complaints it had heard of disorder in the colony by imposing a governor or defining a structure of government. Instead, it gave the colony "full Powre & Authority to Governe & rule themselves, and such others as shall hereafter Inhabite within any part of the said Tract of land, by such a form of Civil Government, as by voluntary consent of all, or the greater Part of them shall find most suteable to their Estates & Conditions." The only limitation was "that the said Laws, Constitutions and Punishments . . . be conformable to the Laws of England, so far as the Nature and Constitution of the place will admit."[6]

By allowing "the greater Part" of the inhabitants, i.e., a majority, to establish any form of government and laws which they chose, the committee explicitly authorized a fully democratic government. This marked an extraordinary liberty.

More extraordinary was the fact that the committee left all decisions about religion to this majority, knowing full well that it wanted to completely and utterly remove the state from the issue of worship. The charter mentioned God only once, in stating that the settlers efforts "may in time by the blessing of God upon theire endeavors Lay a surer foundation of hapines to all America."[7] Even this mention referred to the colony's role as an experiment from which to learn, rather than a confirmation of a received truth or godly purpose.

Williams had succeeded. Providence Plantations thus exceeded any other known state in the world in its freedoms. Holland tolerated different religions, but its toleration had limits and each province still had a state church; the Dutch government had even paid the salaries of some of the Puritan ministers who had fled to the Netherlands. The Committee on Foreign Plantations by not interfering, by leaving its status up to those living there, had now given official sanction to Williams's soul liberty.

Williams had created the only such society in the civilized world. But this did not mark the end of his quest or influence. Nor did it mark the end of efforts by Massachusetts, Plymouth, and Connecticut to swallow his plantation whole, and to snuff out that freedom. It marked another beginning.

It marked a beginning for Williams as well. He could feel history moving on the land; he could feel it, a tangible thing, like a tremor in the ground. No letters of Williams from this period survive, but based on his correspondence during another extended absence,[8] he missed his wife terribly. He yearned for the company of his family, the sanctuary of home. But he was not ready to return to America. First he intended to leave his mark upon the debate in England, indeed, upon England itself.

For months he had been working on two manuscripts explaining his views on the proper relationship between church and state, and between the state and the individual—on power. He had observed power closely beside Coke, and he had endured its exercise to the risk of his life. A few weeks after receiving the charter, he published what was in effect an outline of his position in the pamphlet *Queries of the Highest Consideration*.

The pamphlet was addressed "To the Right Honourable Both Houses of the High Court of Parliament," and it directly and forcefully attacked the premises upon which members of the Westminster Assembly based their debate. But first it attacked the Parliament itself, for arrogating to itself the power to censor books. This it had done in June 1643, when it passed a Licensing Ordinance for "suppressing the great late abuses and frequent disorders in printing many false, forged, scandalous, seditious, libelous Papers, Pamphlets, and Books to the great defamation of Religion and Government."[9]

No censor would ever have authorized a printer to publish *Queries,* so Williams published it anonymously, though it became quickly and widely known that Williams had written it. Dexter printed it. Williams began by stating, "It is a wofull Priviledge attending all great States and Personages, that they seldome heare any other Musick but what is Known will please them. . . . For who can passe the many Locks and Bars of any of the severall Licensers appointed by you with such a Message? By such Circumscribing . . . it is rarely possible that any other Light . . . shall ever shine on your Honours Souls, though ne're so sweet, so necessary, and though it come from God, from Heaven."[10]

After this plea for free speech, Williams proceeded to ask twelve "queries" of the Westminster Assembly. He began by questioning its very right to exist, asking, "First, what Precept or Pattern hath the Lord Jesus left you in his last Will and Testament for your Synod or Assembly of Divines, by vertue of which you may expect his presence and assistance?"[11]

From there he went on to point out, "Whereas you both"—Independents and Presbyterians—"agree . . . that the Civill Magistrate must Reform the Church, establish religion, and so consequently must first Judge, and Judicially Determine which is True, which is False. . . . Is this not to subject the Wife and Soule of Jesus"—i.e., the church—"to the vain uncertain and changeable Mutations in this present evill world?"[12]

He went on to question the assembly's reasoning, methods, and direction, provoking it by asking, "[W]hy even the Papists themselves and their Consciences may not be permitted in the World?"

Finally he cited Scripture, including Luke 9:56 (*I came not to destroy Mens Lives, but to save them*), John 18:36 (*My kingdome is not of this world*), and 2 Timothy 3:12 (*all that will live godly in Christ jesus must suffer persecution*). Then, with a biting sarcasm, he quoted King James's comment that it was "a true mark of a false church to Persecute."[13]

His tract incited swarms of hornets in response. Williams was too busy to rebut them. At the moment his pamphlet was published, he was a few weeks away from departing England and working feverishly to complete a much longer manuscript. He had to have known its importance, and he had only those few weeks to finish it and oversee its being set into type. In it he looked at the issue of soul liberty comprehensively. In fact, it would be one of the most comprehensive treatises not just on the freedom of religion but on the freedom of thought, political freedom, and the foundation of democracy ever written.

# ❧ CHAPTER 28 ❧

While Williams prepared to leave London for Rhode Island, Samuel Gorton prepared to leave Rhode Island for London. And he intended to go there well armed.

He and his colleagues had been released from their imprisonment after only a few months, for they proved a great trouble. Despite warnings to remain silent about their beliefs or be put to death, they had not remained silent. Gorton in particular had, while performing forced labor in chains outside the jail, ignored the order and preached his beliefs. Fearing he might seduce new followers, the magistrates had to choose between execution, cutting out his tongue, and banishment. Having already heard intense criticism from England for their treatment of him, they hesitated to do worse, so early in 1644 they banished him and his colleagues from "any part of our jurisdiction, . . . includ[ing] the lands which you pretended to have purchased . . . be the place called Shawomet or otherwise, so as you are not to come there, upon peril of your lives."[1]

Evidence suggests that Gorton went to live on Aquidneck Island, but he and several followers did visit the Shawomet area. They did not attempt to displace those who now lived on and worked what had been their property. Instead, Gorton decided to employ the same strategy Massachusetts had employed against him. He intended to use Indians to destroy their claims.

Canonicus and Pessicus, Miantonomi's son and now Canonicus's chief lieutenant, invited him to discuss his plans. Gorton was already a friend of and to the Narragansetts; he had even tried to save Miantonomi's life. And he understood the rhythms of a meeting with the two leading sachems of this once formidable tribe: the precision with which procedures were followed, the formality of address, the smoking of long pipes passed one to another, all as if the meeting's purpose was to preserve and protect each other's dignity. It seemed perhaps that dignity was all any of them, Indian or white, had left, for they were all of them, Indian and white, destitute and bitter. The Narragansetts had impoverished themselves to pay the great ransom for Miantonomi; Uncas had kept the ransom and killed him anyway. The Gortonists had even less; they were propertyless vagabonds, breaking the law simply by coming within the vicinity of land which had once been theirs.

So when Gorton presented his proposal, he had little difficulty convincing Canonicus and Pessicus of it. Massachusetts had manufactured the submission of two minor sachems of the Narragansetts to themselves and stolen Gorton's holdings. Gorton now proposed that the most powerful sachems of the Narragansetts submit themselves to Charles Rex, King of England, Scotland, Wales, and Ireland. In questions of sovereignty, from the king there was no appeal; even those fighting the civil war against him still recognized his sovereignty.

Canonicus and Pessicus immediately understood the usefulness of allying themselves with a power whom even Massachusetts must obey. They knew their great ally and friend Roger Williams had gone to England for this purpose. And they were impressed that Gorton had survived the Massachusetts court, impressed enough to believe Gorton's claim that "however farre off from our King and State, yet we doubted not but in due time, we should have redresse."[2] Or perhaps they were simply so desperate that they were willing to reach so far.

Massachusetts heard rumors that Gorton and Canonicus were negotiating and sent two representatives to inquire of the sachems why they would "countenance and take counsel from such evil men." Canonicus, aware of the Bay's involvement in Miantonomi's death, kept them waiting outside in a rainstorm for two hours, then referred them to Pessicus, who kept them waiting four hours more and received them in an "ordinary wigwam" where they made their protest.[3]

Canonicus ignored it. Instead he called a great assembly of Narragansetts, attended likely by thousands. No legal claim by two isolated minor sachems could stand against the authority of such an assembly endorsing an act of Canonicus. On April 19, 1644, this assembly declared, "Know all men, Colonies, Peoples, and Nations, . . . that we the chiefe Sachims, princes or Governours of the Nanhyganset together with the joynt and unanimous consent of all our people and subjects, . . . bendeth our hearts with one consent, freely, voluntarily, and most humbly, to submit, subject and give over our selves, Peoples, lands, Rights, Inheritances, and Possessions whatsoeevr, in our selves and our heires, successively and for ever, unto the protection, care, and government of that WORTHY AND ROYAL PRINCE, CHARLES, KING OF GREAT BRITAIN AND IRELAND, his heirs and successors for ever, to be ruled and governed according to those ancient and honourable Lawes, and customs established in that so renowned realme and Kingdome of Olde-England."[4]

The assembly also chose Gorton and three others of his party to convey their submission to the king. The ramifications of this submission would not be seen for years, but they would come.

While Gorton and the Narragansetts met, in London Williams was delivering two manuscripts—a book of more than four hundred pages and a short pamphlet. The book would be published in July, shortly after his departure, the pamphlet six months later. Like *Queries*, the book was not submitted to the censor for approval and was not licensed. The author and printer pretended anonymity, although again it was quickly known that Williams had written it. Dexter almost certainly also printed it; he supported Williams to the extent that he soon gave up his profession and, seeking freedom, followed Williams to Providence, never to return to London.

The book is extraordinary for its comprehensiveness, for its synthesis, for its courage, and—in the area not of religion but of political philosophy—for its originality. His conclusions demonstrated his willingness to follow wherever evidence and logic took him. Those conclusions were far in advance of and went well beyond the thinking of his day, far in advance of and beyond leading contemporary spokesmen for toleration, including John Milton, and far in advance of and beyond most of those who came later, including John Locke, who was also fully cognizant of and strongly influenced by his work.

In Geneva, the International Monument to the Reformation (generally known as Reformation Wall), built to commemorate the four hundredth anniversary of Calvin's birth, has statues of just ten men deemed important enough to justify their inclusion. At the center is Calvin. Because of this book, to the right stands a statue of Roger Williams.

Williams titled it *The Bloudy Tenent, of Persecution, for cause of Conscience,* *discussed in A Conference betweene Truth and Peace.** He had to know it was the work of his life.

*The Bloudy Tenent* called for true freedom of religion and absolute separation of church and state. It was by no means fully original in either plea. Calls for toleration of different sects had been made with some regularity for half a century, almost always by a member of a persecuted sect. Calls for separating church and state were far less frequent—most who sought toleration also sought the continued intertwining of state and church—but Williams certainly knew of such calls going back at least to Arnold of Brescia, who was burned at the stake in Rome in 1155 for insisting upon it.

Still, mainstream European intellectual and political tradition rejected tolerance. As historian Henry Lea observed, "[U]niversal public opinion from the thirteenth to the seventeenth century" demanded death for heretics. Lea noted that even Saint Dominic, Saint Francis of Assisi, and other "men of the kindliest tempers, the profoundest intelligence, the noblest aspirations" concurred out of a "sense of duty."[5]

The intellectual tradition derived from Augustine, who had justified death for unyielding heretics, and Aquinas, who had argued that the sin of heresy was so great that heretics "deserve not only to be separated from the Church by excommunication, but also to be shut off from the world by death."[6] Once in power, neither Luther nor Calvin had disputed this.

As a result, by the time Williams wrote, hundreds of thousands of Christians had been slaughtered by other Christians because of the way they worshipped Christ. The slaughter had itself compelled some grudging and slight movement toward accommodation. The first significant formal agreement came in 1555: the Peace of Augsburg allowed the local ruler in each principality of the Holy Roman Empire to determine whether his subjects be Lutheran or Catholic; it also allowed subjects who balked at conforming to the religion of their prince to emigrate to another territory. But even that agreement applied only to Catholics and Lutherans and excluded Calvinists. Calvin returned the favor, hunting down and burning those he perceived as heretics.

---

*The first edition was titled *The Bloudy Tenet,* the second *The Bloudy Tenent.* The book is actually better known by the second title.

And every step toward tolerance of "error" seemed matched by a step back from it both in philosophy and in actuality. In the early 1500s Thomas More in his *Utopia* wrote that residents of his fictional world "count this principle among their most ancient institutions, that no one should suffer for his religion." Yet in *A Dialogue Concerning Heresies* he insisted that in the real world burning heretics at the stake was legal, necessary, and beneficial, and he personally persecuted heretics.

Among states, the story was the same. In the late sixteenth century, Polish king Stephen Bathori allowed real freedom of worship, saying, "I am King of Men, not of Consciences, a Commander of Bodies, not of Soules."[7] But his successors withdrew this freedom.

In 1598, Henry IV of France issued the Edict of Nantes, granting Calvinist Huguenots limited legal worship—effectively ending a civil war. But Henry had been a Huguenot, converting to Catholicism in order to become king—supposedly saying, "Paris is well worth a Mass." He was later assassinated by a Catholic. His successor Louis XIII honored Huguenot rights in the breach, and Louis XIV formally revoked the edict.

The Dutch had moved consistently toward toleration, but only because they had to. In the 1570s, Low Country provinces rebelled against Spain, but Spain soon reconquered the Catholic south. Protestant provinces in the north continued the rebellion and formed a federated state, the United Provinces, which had as a main goal the establishment of so-called pure religion. To this end, each province banned the Catholic Church and recognized the Calvinist Dutch Reformed Church as the state church. The state managed church property, selected and paid ministers—including English Puritans who had fled to Holland—and intervened in theological disputes. But much of the population remained Catholic and pressure from Spain was omnipresent, forcing northern provinces to, as one writer stated, "choose between two things: we can live in peace . . . or we can all die together."[8]

Preferring to live, the United Provinces chose de facto toleration. But even the Dutch persecuted Arminians after their theology was formally rejected in 1609, and even Arminians believed the state should intervene in church affairs.

Only occasional, isolated voices called for anything other than toleration based on pragmatism. One such voice was Sebastian Castellio, who had once been so close to Calvin that he had lodged with him and who was a major intellectual force in Europe. The auto-da-fé of Michael Servetus in 1553 in Geneva caused Castellio to say *enough*.

Servetus was a polymath, a brilliant mathematician, a meteorologist, and the first European to describe pulmonary circulation—the oxygenation of the blood. After he questioned the scriptural basis of the Trinity and suggested that the Father, Son, and Holy Ghost were all manifestations of a single being, Calvin promised that should Servetus ever come to Geneva, "I will never permit him to depart alive." Catholics agreed with Calvin on this one point, and the French Inquisition sentenced Servetus to be burned at the stake along with his books. He escaped the French, who were left to burn only his books and his effigy. Then, hunted, living under an assumed name, he did come to Geneva. Calvin kept his pledge. Servetus accepted death but begged to be beheaded and not burned at the stake. Calvin personally rejected his plea. Servetus was burned at the stake along with his books.

What made Servetus different from hundreds of others killed were his scientific achievements, his personal gentleness, the fact that he did not attempt to convert others to his beliefs, and Calvin's personal involvement in his death. After it, Calvin published a justification for killing heretics.

In response, Castellio published *Concerning Heretics and Whether They Should Be Persecuted, and How They Should Be Treated*. In it, he selected twenty texts by twenty prominent authors decrying persecution—and he included Saint Augustine, Luther, and Calvin, all of whom were known for advocating death for heretics. In the cases of Luther and Calvin, Castellio implicitly charged that they had denounced persecution, speaking of "the meekness and mercy of Christ," until they achieved power; only after achieving power had they abruptly "converted true religion into force and violence."[9] He also stated, "I can discover no more than this, that we regard those as heretics with whom we disagree."[10]

In his final book, *The Art of Doubting,* he wrote, "Nothing is too monstrous to teach the people when to doubt is prohibited, since if you doubt or do not believe, you are put to death."[11]

Castellio, forced to publish many of his works anonymously or risk being branded heretic himself, was easily the most important voice for toleration in the sixteenth century. His influence ran deep, but it did not reach broadly and should not be overstated. Only a tiny, isolated minority echoed his views. And, giant that he was, even he asserted that the state could and should execute the impious, whether they be blasphemers or atheists.

Perhaps the greatest influence, though, was Hugo Grotius, who was also an Arminian. A giant of the seventeenth century, he had enormous impact on international law, starting with the concept of the freedom of the seas. In 1613 he also called upon the Dutch church to tolerate dissent. Even the Dutch were not ready for this: his book led indirectly to the execution of a mentor and a life sentence for himself. He escaped prison stuffed into a book chest and spent the rest of his life in exile in France. When John Milton toured the continent, the two met.

In 1625, Grotius wrote the masterpiece *De Jure Belli ac Pacis,* i.e., *On the Law of War and Peace,* which defined a just war and argued that natural law bound all peoples and nations even in war. Other writings defined individual rights, and said that rights "come to the state from private individuals; and similarly, the power of the state is the result of collective agreement."[12] That did not, however, suggest to him limits on power; he defined sovereignty as "that power . . . whose actions are not subject to the legal control of another."[13]

Yet Grotius too, like virtually everyone else, believed in a state church and admired the simplicity of the Church of England, with the monarch as head of the church.

The very few who did call for both freedom of religious thought and separating church and state were either isolated intellectually or outcasts or both. On the continent the Mennonites favored, along with adult baptism, toleration and the separation of church and state—to the extent they preferred having no dealings at all with the state—but, themselves a hunted and fugitive group, their views had little impact.

In England it was no different. Thomas Helwys, minister to a congregation of Baptists who had fled to Amsterdam and then returned to London, wrote a confession of faith in 1611, stating that "the Magistrate is not to meddle with religion or matters of conscience, nor to compel men to this or that form of religion." Helwys died in Newgate prison, near Williams's home, in 1616. His position was too extreme for the time and all but died with him. Even John Goodwin, who was regarded as radical on toleration, conceded that heresy presented a threat to society and the state should consider it criminal.[14] While men of influence—Francis Bacon among them—denounced zealotry and urged acceptance of differences over issues that were not "fundamental," those fundamentals went undefined.

Thus W. K. Jordan, author of the classic multivolume study *The Development of Religious Toleration in England,* noted that on the eve of Williams's return to London, "No voice had yet been raised in Parliament for a toleration of all Protestant groups. Men's hearts were attached by the tuition of conviction and by habits to the ideal of a national Church which would permit of no dissent. One inflexibility was to be replaced by another, one uniformity by another quite as rigorous and infallible."[15] Jordan also noted, "It was clearly the intention of Parliament to destroy Catholicism in England."[16]

Williams knew all this. He knew the literature of toleration, and he knew its history. That was not all he knew. Bacon had taught him a methodology, and an intellectual honesty. His time with Coke and his own experiences with Massachusetts had burned into him an understanding of the law and of the power of the state; this sparked ideas beyond the question of religion. He knew what he thought. He knew what he believed to be right. And he did not flinch before the implications of his evidence and his logic. He was now to have his say.

In June 1644, immediately upon finishing his manuscript and before its publication, he boarded ship for America. His book he left behind.

# ❧ CHAPTER 29 ❧

*The Bloudy Tenent, of Persecution, for cause of Conscience, discussed, in A Conference betweene Truth and Peace* suffers from prolixity and in spots is difficult to follow. Yet it is extremely direct, too. The term "truth and peace" in the title was itself direct, if ironic, for "truth and peace" was a catchphrase of the revolution. The supposed purpose of the Solemn League and Covenant was, for example, to "establish these Churches and kingdoms in truth and peace." Later, to celebrate military victories, Parliament struck a coin bearing the figures Truth and Peace.

Williams was direct in his approach. Before any preface, before any dedication, in the first page and a half of his book, he promised to prove twelve specific assertions, each one a variation of his theme: "It is the will and command of God, that since the comming of his Sonne the Lord Jesus, a permission of the most Paganish, Jewish, Turkish, or Antichristian consciences and worships, bee granted in all Nations and Countries."

Next, in the dedication itself, Williams engaged his subject as directly as if he had slapped his reader in the face, telling "the Right Honourable both houses of the High Court of Parliament" that while their task as Christians was the saving of their own souls and the souls of others, their task "as Magistrates" was limited to protecting "the Bodies and Goods of others." He pledged that "Arguments from Religion, Reason, [and] Experience" would prove that the state had no business involving itself in any way in religion and that those, including Calvin himself, who supported "the Doctrine of persecution for cause of Conscience" erred and erred grievously. He also stated that Parliament, by using "Civill force and violence to [worshippers'] Consciences" to compel a particular worship, "hath committed a greater rape, then if they had forced or ravished the bodies of all the women in the world."

Williams then drew upon both Coke and Bacon in cautioning Parliament:

"[T]he greatest yoakes, yet lying upon English necks . . . are of a spirituall and soule nature." He implores them "to ease the Subjects and Your selves from [this] yoake." He then quotes "that learned Francis Bacon," who warned that those who used religion to advance a state policy often " 'are guided therein by some private interests of their owne.' "

He cited Bacon in the dedication. He cited Coke on the second page of the book proper. Williams did not cite either of them often in this book, but they appear at this, the very beginning, as if to say they lay at the beginning of his book, subsuming the rest, as they lay at the beginning of his thought, subsuming his thinking.

Their names could not have escaped the notice of a single reader of *The Bloudy Tenent*, and their placement at the beginning of the book signaled from whence Williams came. Most readers would have known something of Bacon's approach to evidence. His views on scientific method lived after him and made many admirers, including among those, like Williams, who rejected his political views. Coke's name, particularly in the context of this great conflict between the crown and Parliament, meant even more.

The writings of Bacon had helped frame the way Williams evaluated what he observed in the world. Coke's influence was more direct. He had heard Coke argue in Star Chamber that it was the state's obligation, not the church's, to maintain public peace and civil stability; Coke had gone so far as to suggest that the state should assist the church only insofar as to keep worship peaceable and protect church property. Coke had never pursued the implications of such judgments. Williams would.

His experiences drove home those lessons. His personal interactions with two kings had left the taste of contempt in his mouth; both James and Charles seemed utterly unsuitable for any role in church leadership. And of course his dealings with Massachusetts, the bitterness he still felt and would always feel over his banishment, had left its imprint upon him.

All this combined in a way that led him to challenge the fundamental order in the world, not only in religion, not only in politics, but on the question of power. In this book Williams took a great leap, and no contemporary or near contemporary leaped so far.

The structure of *The Bloudy Tenent* is simple. After its blunt opening, it reprinted a plea for tolerance written anonymously—reputedly in invisible ink—by a prisoner jailed for rejecting infant baptism and smuggled out of Newgate prison, the prison a few hundred yards from where Williams grew up. It had originally been published in 1620 as four chapters in *An Humble Supplication of the Kings majesty's Loyal Subjects . . . who are persecuted (only for differing in Religion)*. This supplication accepted the need for a state church and asked only for toleration, citing Scripture to argue that "Persecution for Cause of Conscience" was "against the Doctrine of Jesus Christ."

This document had circulated widely enough that Cotton had written a rebuttal several years earlier. Williams reprinted Cotton's rebuttal. This was typical of his presentations: he allowed his opponents their own voice and did not distort their views; he wanted readers to see an argument whole, both his opponents' and his own, and come to their own conclusions.

Williams then wrote, "A Reply to the Aforesaid Answer of Mr. Cotton." This is the body of the book, and unlike both the anonymous prisoner in Newgate and Cotton, Williams was not brief. He took four hundred pages to expand upon the subject.

Over the next years Cotton would reply in *The Bloudy Tenent, Washed, and made white in the bloode of the Lambe*, and Williams would respond in *The Bloudy Tenent Yet More Bloudy*. These two volumes would add hundreds of pages more to the debate.

Williams addressed religious, political, and economic questions involving toleration. Some he dispensed with quickly; as Jordan notes, he "bent the economic argument to his larger thesis in a few detached but brilliant paragraphs."[1] He did this chiefly by pointing out that Amsterdam had been "a poor fishing Town," until it became a haven for "dissenting consciences. . . . [T]his confluence of the persecuted drew Boats, drew Trade, drew Shipping so that mightily in so short a time, that Shipping, Trade, Wealth, Greatnesse, Honour (almost to astonishment in the Eyes of all Europe, and the world) have appeared to fall as out of Heaven in a Crown or Garland upon that poor Fisher Town."[2]

But the overwhelming majority of the book is devoted to interpreting Scripture. Upon that rested his case for separating the civil power and religion. He had to cite Scripture, for all those who sought to compel a single mode of worship—whether in England or on the continent, whether they be Puritans, High Church Anglicans, other Protestants, or Catholics—justified their position by insisting that the Word of God required it. Only a rebuttal also based upon the Word of God could answer. And his interpretation of Scripture supported, indeed required, the utter separation of church and state.

His use of Scripture was not simply a tactic. He was not an early Spinoza, attempting to separate philosophy and intellectual analysis from religion. Yet his thinking did represent at least one step in Spinoza's direction, for what was truly new in Williams's book was precisely the divorce of the material world from the spiritual world, and the conclusions he drew about politics and religion from that divorce.

Historians have disagreed on how to see Williams, and whether to place him in a religious or political context (see the Afterword for a discussion of this); the very difficulty historians have had in defining Williams as primarily either a religious or political figure speaks to the intertwining of church and state at the time. In reality, it makes no difference how one categorizes him. What matters is what he said, what conclusions he reached, and, equally, how he thought. He thought originally.

The argument of those—of whatever religion—who sought to blend church and state rested upon three assertions.

First came the claim that even governments which imprisoned and even killed "blasphemers" and "heretics" actually did grant full liberty of conscience.

Second came the assertion that Scripture called for separating the godly from, or killing, enemies of God. The Word of God, those who believed this argued, not only allowed but required them to do so.

The third argument, which is most relevant in the twenty-first century, was that the state must be "the nursing father or mother" to the church. This was necessary, advocates declared, to protect and preserve not only the church but to create a moral society. From this last premise in particular, it also followed inevitably that church and state were inextricably linked.

Regarding the first assertion, even Cotton declared, "No man is to be persecuted for conscience."[3] And, "It is not lawfull to persecute any for *Conscience* rightly informed; for in persecuting such, Christ himselfe is persecuted in them, *Acts*, 9.4."[4]

But if that sentiment seemed to agree with Williams's position, Cotton also said that "in fundamentall and principall points of Doctrine or Worship, the Word of God is so clear, that hee cannot but bee convinced in Conscience of the dangerous Errour of his way, after once or twice Admonition, wisely and faithfully dispensed. And then, if anyone persists, it is not out of Conscience, but against his Conscience. . . . So that if such a Man after such Admonition shall still persist in the Errour of his way, and be therefore punished: He is not persecuted for cause of Conscience, but for sinning against his Owne Conscience."[5]

The Jesuits whom Bacon and Coke had interrogated in the Tower would have taken pride in Cotton's circuitous, if not quite tautological, argument. He was saying—no, not saying but insisting—that Scripture was so clear on fundamental points that an authority such as himself could not be mistaken. Further, such clergy as himself could present this "truth" in so compelling a fashion that no listener could withstand the argument. And once unanswerable arguments were presented, then the offender's conscience had been "rightly informed." Anyone who still disagreed could not be disagreeing out of conscience; the offender knew what was right, but chose error anyway. Continued resistance was then coming from pure arbitrary stubbornness at best, Satanic directives at worst. Such a person "is subverted and sinneth, being condemned of Himselfe, that is, of his owne Conscience."[6]

Even for the seventeenth century Cotton's argument sounded absurd. Certainly Williams found it absurd. In hundreds of pages, it is the only assertion of Cotton's which Williams did not so much rebut as simply dismiss. If Scripture was so clear, how was it possible there were so many interpretations of it? Using a rare exclamation point to show his astonishment at the nature of the argument, he noted Cotton's "Pretences of not persecuting men for conscience, but punishing them only for sinning against conscience!"[7] Cotton's position also astonished Williams because it presumed that "so many thousands in the Nations of the World all the world over"[8] who disagreed were, simply and entirely, wrong; Cotton refused to consider the possibility, any possibility, that it might be he who was wrong.

Williams damned this as a "monstrous Partiality."[9] He truly considered such partiality to one's own beliefs, such conviction of one's own correctness and of others' errors, monstrous. Precisely such a monstrosity, such a partiality to one's own beliefs, had killed "so many hundred thousand soules of Protestants and Papists . . . in the Wars of present and former Ages."[10] And he noted that in England itself efforts at "inforced uniformity" had sparked the bloodletting of the present "civill Warre."

Williams was not simply astonished at Cotton's reasoning and presumption. He was appalled and outraged by it. It maddened him that anyone could be so partial to his or her own belief as to reject "all the consciences in the world"[11] but one's own, so presumptuous as to force one's views upon others.

This reaction reflected his ability to step outside of himself, step back and see both another's position and the implications of one's own. It was an ability central to his character. It also enabled him to maintain a balancing act; he never lacked conviction that his own course was right—never—yet always seemed cognizant of the possibility of error.

The second premise of those seeking to create a New Jerusalem was that Scripture required the destruction of heretics and blasphemers. Williams disputed this interpretation of Scripture as well.

He willingly conceded that in the Old Testament, "It is most true that blasphemers in Israel and blasphemers against Israel and the God of it, were put to death."[12] However, he rejected the position of those who claimed that this meant Scripture made it right and proper for a modern state to do the same. His rebuttal rested on a manner of interpreting the Bible called "typology."

Typology reconciled the Old Testament and the New, helping both to explain inconsistences between them and to link them more closely. It identified "types" in the Old which prefigured "anti-types" in the New. An anti-type was in no way in opposition to the original type. Far from it. An anti-type complemented and fulfilled the type. For example, in typology, Jonah's experience in the whale's belly was the type, prefiguring its anti-type, which was considered to be Christ's entombment. Typology obviously left much to the interpreter.

Williams was hardly alone in employing typology; many theologians, and certainly Puritan theologians—including Cotton—routinely used it. But Williams did go further than most, and he interpreted the Old Testament in a particularly allegorical or, to use his word, "figurative" way. His reading of Scripture also convinced him that the appearance of Christ not only fulfilled but supplanted much of the Old Testament, and that whenever the New and Old Testaments conflicted, the New trumped the Old. Therefore, he declared that ancient Israel was not a model for a modern society. As early as July 1637 he had sent Winthrop a treatise explaining the differences between Israel and all other states. He conceded that church and state had in Israel been melded, but he argued that Christ's appearance and teaching had utterly altered this, making Israel a unique entity, a "onesuch" and no precedent. After many pages of analysis and scriptural citation, he concluded, "The Pattern of the Nationall Church of Israel, was . . . unimitable by any Civill State."[13]

Thus he rejected any use of the Old Testament to justify persecution of religious differences.

But his disputants also used passages from the New Testament to justify their position. Cotton used Revelation 16, for example, in which seven angels are told, "Go your ways, and pour out the vials of the wrath of God upon the earth," interpreting this to mean that magistrates had the authority to sentence believers in false religion "to be put to death as traitors against the state." Thus Cotton insisted, "And so in the New Testament as in the Old, He condemns all such to death, and he is most righteous in so doing."[14]

Williams rejected any such interpretation. Line by line, he deconstructed and reinterpreted New Testament passages which Cotton and others had used in their arguments. Almost always, his alternate interpretation seemed more straightforward.

Perhaps the single key passage representing the different views was Matthew 13:24–30, a parable in which a sower planted wheat but "his enemy came and sowed tares among the wheat." When the sower's servants asked if they should gather up the tares, they were told not to lest "ye root up also the wheat with them. Let both grow together until the harvest; and in the time of harvest I will say to the reapers, gather yet together first the tares, and bind them in bundles and burn them; but gather the wheat into my barn."

The message of this parable seemed to be that until Judgment Day all would live together. Augustine reversed this meaning, arguing that when one knew which was the wheat and which the tares, it was right to uproot the tares. It was right to kill heretics and blasphemers. Over the centuries his views on this and other passages took seed themselves.

Williams returned to the text itself and emphasized "Let both grow together until the harvest." Whatever happened at the harvest, he declared that this parable required toleration—including for error—in this world. He was not the first to make this argument; indeed, the *Humble Supplication* reprinted in *The Bloudy Tenent* made it. But he applied enormous scholarly effort and many pages of analysis and citation to buttress this more obvious interpretation. He also examined other New Testament passages which he considered to have been similarly misinterpreted, and he cited numerous passages which explicitly and repeatedly separated church and state. Christ's message was, he said, for the state to let people alone.

For example, Romans 16:17—"mark them which cause divisions and offences contrary to the doctrine which ye have learned, and avoid them"—had been used to justify the destruction of those who caused divisions. Williams said this and similar passages only justified a church's policing itself, and that it extended no such power either to the church in the larger society or to the government.

Similarly, Cotton and his allies on this issue, including Presbyterians, all cited Matthew 15:13 to justify their position: "Every plant, whch my heavenly Father hath not planted, shall be rooted up." But they stopped their citation of Scripture there. Williams continued with Matthew 15:14: "Let them alone: they be blind leaders of the blind. And if the blind lead the blind, both shall fall into the ditch."

He conceded that any who seduced a soul away from God did more harm than "if he blew up Parliaments, and cut the throats of Kings and Emperours, so pretious is that invaluable Jewell of a Soul," and that "a firme Justice" demanded "eye for eye, tooth for tooth, life for life . . . also soule for soule."

But he pointed out that only Christ could inflict this eternal punishment: "Such a sentence no Civil judge can passe, such a Death no civill sword can inflict."[15]

Finally, the question came back to the idea of *monstrous partiality*. If people were to suffer punishment—even death—for their errors of belief, of conscience, "Who shall judge in this case?"[16]

A human had to be the judge, and all humans erred. Worse, if the state was to impose the punishment, "It must needs . . . follow that the Civill State must judge of the truth of the Spirituall."[17]

Williams reviewed biblical, European, and English history, and reminded his readers that magistrates were not necessarily even Christians, much less godly Christians. England itself had had magistrates who by definition erred, since in the space of a few decades England had turned from Catholic to Protestant to Catholic to Protestant. In just the preceding few years an English king and the Church of England had hunted down Puritans, while now a Parliament controlled by Puritans was extirpating the episcopacy and had imprisoned Laud, the archbishop of Canterbury—and it would behead him a few months later.

Williams now pointed out that, despite all the errors made by English magistrates in spiritual matters, Cotton believed that, except for those who believed as he believed, "in plaine English . . . millions of millions of blasphemers, idolaters, seducers, throughout the wide world, ought corporally to be put to death."[18]

Williams called this "directly contrary to the nature of Christ Jesus, his Saints and Truths, that throats of men should be torne out for his sake, who most delighted to converse with the greatest sinners."[19] He was certain that "against this Christ Jesus was, who professed in answer to the rash zeal of his disciples (Luke. 9). That he came not to destroy mens lives, but to save them."[20]

## ❧ CHAPTER 30 ❧

Roger Williams's departure into first original, then revolutionary thought began with logic and observation. He had already distinguished between the "Garden" of purity in the real church and the "Wildernesse" of the world. Indeed, to him the words "wilderness" and "world" were almost interchangeable, and they connoted corruption. He observed, "The truth is the great Gods of this world are God-belly, God-wealth, God-honour, God-pleasure, &c"[1]—greed, status and power, and pleasure.

Government was comprised of people in the world. He recoiled at the idea of allowing this worldly wilderness to intrude upon the Edenic garden of the church, and he was convinced that any breach of the wall between them—any involvement either of a magistrate in churchly things or of the church in government—would bring the wilderness into the garden.

Therefore, the heart of his disagreement with his critics and enemies, the axis upon which all else turned, was their conviction that the state was and must be "nursing father" to the church. For the Word of God, Isaiah 49:23, said, "And kings shall be thy nursing fathers, and their queens thy nursing mothers: they shall bow down to thee with their face toward the earth, and lick up the dust of thy feet; and thou shalt know that I am the LORD; for they shall not be ashamed that wait for me."

Virtually all of England, all of the Puritan colonies in America, and all of Europe—Catholic or Protestant—believed that, and believed also that without it not only could society not be moral but that it would not survive. For the next passage, Isaiah 49:25, continued, "I will contend with them that contendeth with thee, and I will save thy children."

The proximity of the two passages to each other seemed to support an intimate connection between church and state. It also seemed to support a covenant between God and the state: that in return for being a nursing father, God would look after the state. Upon these and other passages—in Acts 25, for example, Paul, after being sentenced to death, appealed to Caesar for help—rested nearly the entire argument.

It was thus seen as an axiom that if government compelled a civil society to behave in closer accord with Christ, that society would prosper. And if magistrates allowed a civil society to drift from Christ's teachings, God would punish and possibly even destroy it. History, they believed, proved this. As Edmund Morgan said of New England Puritans, "Seldom has a people been so well supplied with historians, and the lesson they drew was always the same: that God rewarded the obedience of His chosen covenant people with prosperity and their disobedience with adversity."[2]

Cotton exemplified that view, noting, "For if the church and people of God fall away from God, God will visit the city and country with public calamity, if not captivity, for the church's sake."[3]

Williams began his attack upon the concept of nursing father deliberately, as usual examining the key scriptural passages and interpreting them differently or citing contradictory Scripture. He of course cited such obvious passages as Mark 12:17, "render to Caesar the things that are Caesar's, and unto God the things that are God's." And regarding Paul's calling upon Caesar, he pointed out that Paul wanted the government to intervene not in spiritual or church affairs but to protect his corporal body and enforce human law, since according to human law the charges against Paul did not warrant death.

But as Williams advanced his argument, as he used one example, then another, as he made one analogy, then another, as he forced his readers to confront not simply logic but the evidence of experience and universally accepted fact, he pushed beyond Scripture, raising questions not only about the relationship between the state and the church but about the nature of the state, and society, itself. And in doing this, he moved from original to revolutionary.

He did so by examining the evidence for the axiom that God judged how godly or sinful a civil society was and showered material blessings and material punishments upon it accordingly. He found the evidence wanting.

First he looked at several past rebellions against the papacy in which "after mutuall slaughters and miseries to both sides, the final successe of victory fell to Popedome and . . . utter extirpation"[4] of the rebels. Then he noted that in conflicts going on at that very moment in Europe, both in diplomacy and on the battlefield, Catholics had "victory and dominion." He pointed out that "if successe be the measure," then all evidence suggested that God had chosen Catholics and renounced Protestants.[5]

He went on to examine events and societies elsewhere in the world and pointed out how not only many Catholic states but many "Turkish," i.e., Islamic, ones were thriving: "Men of no small note, skilfull in the state of the World, acknowledge, that the World is divided into 30 parts, 25 of that 30 have never yet heard of the name of Christ,"[6] yet many of those Christ-less places were "glorious and flourishing cities of the world."[7]

Thus "all Reason and Experience" left no choice but to recognize, "First, event and successe come alike to all, and are no Arguments of [God's] love or hatred, &c."[8] Of the belief that God only blessed godly Christian societies and punished others, he concluded, "Divers ages of temporal prosperity to the Antichristian kingdoms, prove that common Assumption or maxime false."[9]

He also believed that laws designed simply to create a moral society—as when Calvin outlawed playing cards, dice, or ninepins in Geneva—breached the wall between the garden of the church and the wilderness of the world. Massachusetts would outlaw shuffleboard, bowling, and gambling; Cotton abhorred all card playing, and the Reverend Increase Mather called the waste of time in such games as "cards, and Dice, and Tables, haynously sinfull."[10]

In Williams's view, such laws invaded the garden with weeds and corruption by confusing good works with salvation. Such laws "may cast a blush of civility and morality" on a society, but they allowed "unrepentant persons . . . dreams of ther owne blessed estate"; therefore they sent "millions of soules to hell in a secure expectation of a false salvation." In rejecting such moralistic legislation, he stated, "I confidently deny . . . that Christs Ordinances and administrations of Worship are appointed and given by Christ to any Civill State, Towne or City as is implied by the instance of Geneva."[11]

Then he made an analogy astounding in the seventeenth century, especially for a man so devout. "The Church or company of worshippers," he wrote, "is like unto . . . a Corporation, Society, or Company of East-Indie or Turkie-Merchants, or any other Society of Company in London: which Companies may hold their Courts, keep their Records, hold disputations; and in matters concerning their Societie, may dissent, divide, breake into Schism and Factions, sue and impale each other at the Law, yea wholly dissolve and breake up into pieces, and yet the peace of the Citie not be in the least measure impaired or disturbed; because the essence or being of the Citie, and so the well-being and peace thereof is essentially distinct from those particular Societies; the Citie-Courts, Citie-Lawes, Citie-punishments distinct from theirs. The Citie was before them, and stands absolute and intire, when such a Corporation is taken down."[12]

The shock of that assessment, of asserting that the church was not the center of human society from which all else flowed but merely an entity like other entities within society, was little softened by his citing a precedent from the New Testament: "The City or Civill State of Ephesus was essentially distinct from . . . the Church of Christ in Epheses (whiche were Gods people, converted and call'd out from the worship of that City unto Christianity or worship of God in Christ)."[13]

His view of the "city," the civil state, and of the church could hardly have differed more from Winthrop's "citty upon a hill." Yet Williams and Winthrop shared the identical theology, the identical belief that the Bible was the Word of God, the identical religiosity, the identical devotion to Christ, the identical conviction that Christ could be returning soon.

In short, his belief in both the purity of the church and the sinfulness of man compelled him to demand absolute separation, "a wall of separation" as he had written earlier, between the Edenic garden of the church and the corrupt world of the state.

And he was only beginning.

It was then generally believed that Scripture said subjects owed their allegiance to their government; by definition, that government's very existence meant that God had ordained it. Rebellion against it was rebellion against God, except in certain very limited circumstances. The pope claimed power to release Catholic subjects from their obligation to obey a secular ruler by excommunicating that ruler. Luther denied that a king was divine, but he authorized only lesser magistrates—not subjects—to disobey an evil king. Calvin declared that if a ruler issued an order against God, it should not be obeyed. But like Luther, Calvin authorized only lesser magistrates to resist, not individual subjects.

Not surprisingly, however, King James rejected even those options for resistance. He argued that to disobey a monarch was to disobey God, and that the subject's only recourse against a poor or even evil ruler was not rebellion but "serious repentance" for whatever sins brought the affliction of a bad ruler upon them, and more prayer since God "guideth the hearts of princes."

The idea of democracy was entirely foreign. The idea that authority and sovereignty came from below, from the governed, as opposed to from above, from God, was entirely foreign.

In England, despite the fact that Parliament was waging a civil war against the king, no member of Parliament was advocating democracy. Creating rule from below was neither the announced nor unannounced goal of Parliament. The predominant view of the relationship between the state and the subjects was that the state held sovereignty over and was separate from its subjects—hence the use of the word "subject" as opposed to "citizen." And although the theory of the divine right of kings—which as advanced by James and Charles gave them virtually dictatorial powers—was much disputed, the idea that authority came from God was not disputed.

New England Puritans differed not at all. The goal of creating a democracy had never stirred the leadership of Massachusetts—except to opposition. Winthrop believed that the magistrates, even though "being called by you [freemen], we have our authority from God."[14] Therefore they must be obeyed. He compared electing a governor not to a freeman's right to control his government but to a woman choosing a husband. That husband "being so chosen he is her Lord, & she is to be subiecte to him . . . & a true wife acconts her subiection her honer & freedome. . . . Euen so brethren, it will be between you & your magistrates . . . so shall your Libertyes be preserved, in vpholding the honor & power of Authoritye amongst you."[15] And he declared, "Democracy is, amongst most civil nations, accounted the meanest and worst form of government." He called it a "manifest breach of the 5th commandment," and noted that "history records that it hath always been of least continuance and fullest of troubles."[16]

Similarly, Cotton wrote, "Democracy, I do not conceyve that ever God did ordeyne as a fitt government eyther for church or commonwealth. If the people be governors who shall be governed? As for monarchy, and aristocracy, they are both of them clearly approved, and directed by scripture."[17]

Williams believed differently. In Providence no gap separated the governed and the governors. Aquidneck Island settlers had followed suit; they had initially organized a government based on Scripture (although allowing for disagreement over religion) but in 1641 in a General Court, they had "ordered and unanimously agreed upon, that the government . . . is a democracie, or popular government."[18]

In his book, Williams now made what in the seventeenth century was indeed an original and revolutionary claim—that the people were sovereign— writing, "I infer that the sovereign, original, and foundation of civil power lies in the people."

This echoed Grotius and similar-sounding statements by others. Coke of course had said of Parliament, *We serve here for thousands and ten thousands.* Robert Phelips had talked about a contractual relationship between monarch and subject, with privileges reserved to both. And in 1642 Henry Parker declared that Parliament was "the whole kingdome it selfe" and "the State it self."[19]

But there was an important difference between what Williams said and what they or anyone else had said. Parker, for example, had placed sovereignty in Parliament without a nod to the people, and Parliament was a particular estate of men of great title and great wealth—it had been said that Commons could buy Lords.

Williams asserted that sovereignty remained wholly in the people and called that sovereignty "distinct from the government set up. And if so, that a people may erect and establish what form of government seems to them most meet for their civil condition. It is evident that such governments as are by them erected and established have no more power, nor for longer time, than the civil power or people consenting and agreeing shall betrust them with."[20] He continued, "All true civill Magistrates have not the least inch of civill power, but what is measured out to them from the free consent of the whole: even as a Committee of Parliament, cannot further act then the power of the House shall arme and enable them. . . ."[21]

"All lawfull Magistrates in the World, both before the comming of Christ and since," Williams wrote, "are but Derivatives and Agents. . . . Hence they have and can have no more Power, then fundamentally lies in the Bodies or Fountaines themselves, which Power, Might or Authority, is not Religious, Christian &c. but naturall, humane and civill."[22] And just as religion was utterly irrelevant to a person's performance as a soldier, physician, lawyer, ship captain, merchant, or any other civil profession, since government was civil, a Christian magistrate was "no more" a magistrate and no better than one "of any other Conscience or Religion."[23]

This conclusion obviously undermined the concept of the state as nursing father to the church. If one believed that the state's authority came from God, much less if one believed in the divine right of kings, then it was reasonable to link church and state and to expect the state to play a nursing-father role to the church, to believe that somehow and in some way God would invest the state with divine guidance, much as Catholic orthodoxy decrees that the pope is incapable of error when acting in the religious realm. But if one believed that the state derived its authority and power from the people, then the state was invested with all the errors of humanity. And it should refrain in any way—in any way—from involving itself in matters of religion. For giving *any* power to the magistrate over the church meant giving power to the people over the church. "If no Religion but that which the Commonweal approves," he argued, "then no Christ, no God, but at the pleasure of this world."[24]

But this was impossible. This would "turne the World upside-down . . . turne the Garden and Paradise of the Church and Saints into the Field of the Civill State of the World."

It meant the violation of the garden by the wilderness of the world. It meant forced worship, and "forc't Worshpp stincks in Gods Nostrills."[25] It meant in fact "a Soule or Spirituall Rape, more abominable in Gods eye, then to force and ravish the Bodies of all the Women in the World."[26]

He concluded therefore, "The government of the civill Magistrate extendeth no further then over the bodies and goods of their subjects, not over their soules."[27]

# CHAPTER 31

When *The Bloudy Tenent* appeared in London, Williams was a thousand miles distant, aboard ship rolling in the thick green swells of the mid-Atlantic, the sea to all points of the compass. There is something infinitely serene about sail; the wind billowing the sail, the depth of the sea beneath, the only sounds the creaking and yawing of wood and the wash of the bow cutting water, while one is propelled across surface as if by divine compulsion. All of it humbles, all of it brings a man, if he is inclined to, closer to God.

If he found peace aboard ship, however, he left no peace behind him in London. There his book generated stunned outrage, and it sold rapidly—so rapidly that a second edition appeared no more than three weeks after the first.[1] Still, the outrage outpaced the book, developing with such extraordinary speed that it spread far beyond those who actually read it.

Even those who had paid a heavy price for their own religious views were outraged, among them William Prynne, the same man whom the High Commission had singled out for brutal treatment first in 1634, then even worse in 1637. He had had his ears cut off, suffered being pilloried, and had two life sentences imposed. Parliament had eventually freed him, paid him reparations, and gave him the sweetest revenge: a commanding role at Laud's trial. He failed to win a conviction, so by bill of attainder Parliament declared Laud a traitor anyway and in January 1645 he was beheaded. Prynne's repaying butchery with greater butchery demonstrated that his own persecution had not made him receptive to diverse opinions, nor did he doubt that the state should control the church. He condemned Williams's "dangerous Licentious Booke"[2] for suggesting that each person "be left free to his owne free liberty of conscience" which might include "false, seditious, detestable" beliefs. And he blamed Williams, along with Milton for his *Doctrine and Discipline of Divorce* and Richard Overton for his *Mans Mortalitie,* for the "dangerous increase of many

Anabaptistical, Antinomian, Heresiacall, Atheisticall opinions . . . which I hope our Grand Council will speedily and carefully suppress."[3]

Almost simultaneously, Herbert Palmer, a member of the Westminster Assembly and master of Queens College at Cambridge, preached a sermon before both houses of Parliament and demanded they act "against the ungodly Toleration pleaded for under the pretence of LIBERTY of Conscience."

On August 9, Parliament turned directly to Williams's book. One after another, members attacked it, insisting that toleration of error was dangerous to the state, for it could bring God's wrath down upon England. Toleration of blasphemy was worse, a heinous evil in itself, and failure to act against it was itself a sin. Williams's own former Pembroke College tutor Edmund Calany rose, not to defend his pupil but to condemn him. No more than eight weeks after the publication of *The Bloudy Tenent,* Parliament "Ordered, that Mr. White do give Order for the Publick Burning of one *Williams* his booke . . . [for] the Tolerating of All Sorts of Religion."[4]

"Mr. White" was the public hangman. He would likely have carried out the order in Smithfield, where Williams grew up. A large and noisy crowd would have attended, for this was spectacle. They would have watched a very considerable bonfire, for the hangman and his assistants would have searched out every copy of the book they could find to add to the fire, and they would have sought the typeset as well. For burning a book was not a symbolic act of disapproval; it was a concerted attempt to extirpate the thought which that book contained.

Six weeks after the burning, both houses of Parliament gathered for a sermon delivered by Lazarus Seaman. He too spoke of the role the state had over religion, condemned toleration, and damned dangerous books, specifically Williams's. And he warned of *The Bloudy Tenent's* possible resurrection: "The shell is sometimes throwne into the fire, when the kernell is eaten as a sweet morsel."[5]

Few initially had the taste to find the kernel of Williams's book sweet, but that taste was developing. The book helped develop it.

It did not bring the questions of toleration and separation of church and state to England. They were already there. Members of persecuted sects had initially raised them, and, in the increasing upheaval of the times, sects were multiplying rapidly enough to cause tumult and distress among Presbyterians,

Independents, and Anglicans alike, as the vote to burn Williams's book indicates. But Williams moved the question forward and brought it into sharp focus, like a magnifying glass concentrating the sun's rays on a focal point, both bringing brilliant light to it and setting it afire.

He did so partly by presenting the rationale for his position cogently and provocatively, thereby convincing some and arming them and others with reasons and justifications to use in argument. His position as a man of consequence also mattered; he was not a despised felon smuggling words out of prison; he was respected and godly, an associate of such men as Cromwell and Vane.

Slowly some of his views had begun resonating. Baillie had already noted with dismay, "Mr. Williams has drawn a great number after him."[6] Now, soon after the book was burned, Baillie complained that Vane was "joyning with a new faction to procure liberty for sects."[7] Shortly after making that observation, Baillie seemed both astounded and worried: "Sir Henry Vane, whom we trusted most, had given us many signs of his alteration; twyce at our table . . . [he] earnestlie, and passionatelie had reasoned for a full libertie of conscience to all religions, without any exceptions."[8]

All of Vane's biographers credit Williams as a major influence on him. Williams's direct impact on others, including John Milton, is more difficult to assess. And Milton was emerging as an influential voice.

Two years earlier in *The Reason for Church-Government* he had expressed the consensus view opposing toleration and arguing for uniform church discipline: "[T]here is not that thing in the world of more grave and urgent importance throughout the whole life of man then is discipline. . . . He that hath read with judgment, of Nations and Commonwealths, of Cities and Campes, of peace and warre, sea and land, will readily agree that the flourishing and decaying of all civill societies, all the moments of turnings of humane occasions are mov'd to and fro as upon the axle of discipline."[9] Yet Milton had moved from that position and, though devout, like Williams he would cease belonging to any church. The two men had several commonalities, including the fact that Milton's treatise on divorce was published at the same time as *The Bloudy Tenent* and the two works were often condemned together. (Back in Rhode Island, Williams wrote the most liberal divorce law in the English-speaking world.)

Over the next years, Williams's influence ran both deep and wide. Between 1644 and 1649, at least sixty pamphlets directly addressed Williams and at least one hundred and twenty more quoted him.[10] Still more indirectly reflected his ideas.

More than two years after Williams left England, Baillie blamed his concept that sovereignty lay in the people as the "masters of our mis-orders"[11] and the rise of "Levellers," the most radical of the groups which emerged as civil war dragged on. Three years after Williams's departure, John Lilburne, a founder of the Levellers, called the citizenry "the true fountains . . . of all just power." That became an axiom of the Leveller program and their pamphlets routinely quoted Williams verbatim. Other pamphlets simply reprinted Williams "even to the periods and commas and parentheses,"[12] noted historian James Ernst, though without attribution. And in 1649, five years after *The Bloudy Tenent* was published, opponents of religious freedom were still aiming most of their denunciations directly at his work. That after all that had happened in those five years—the beheading of the king, Cromwell's rise—his enemies still aimed their fire at him testified to his importance.

Only a minority called for toleration. Presbyterians did triumph both in the Westminster Assembly and in Parliament, and Parliament attempted to impose a Presbyterian system on England. But they could not stop the growth of sects, some of them wild with such names as "Ranters." In turn the sects pushed Parliament to extremes; it went so far in 1648 as to pass a law punishing blasphemy with death.

But Parliament could not silence either the sects or the calls for toleration. For the army, where the power was, was home both to religious and political radicalism. Most of those seeking toleration still wanted only Protestant dissent allowed—they wanted to prohibit Catholic worship and often Anglican worship as well. Virtually all but Williams still condemned atheism as a serious crime. And Williams still remained largely isolated in calling for the utter separation of church and state—the complete disengagement of one from the other. Williams still stood apart.

Roger Williams had accomplished all that he had set out to do in England, and more. There was the charter, of course, the signatures of the mighty upon it; he must have carried it in his luggage with enormous satisfaction. But there was the personal, too, if revenge meant anything to him. He had sent Cotton and Massachusetts reeling. In addition, as a young man he had clearly aspired to join the higher ranks of English society. His attempt to elevate himself by marrying into that rank had left him humiliated, slapped down for his presumption, peremptorily dismissed as unsuitable. It had rankled him, and he had lashed out in return. Now he had elevated himself to that rank by his own accomplishment, moving easily in the circle of Warwick, Vane, and even Cromwell. How much more gratifying that must have been.

The idea of remaining in England must have tempted him. He had always aspired to play on the large stage, and, now counted and courted as a man of influence himself, he had been doing that—and doing it during the most tumultuous years of English history. Had he remained, he could easily have brought his family over and found a prominent post, having already injected himself into and left a mark on the tremendous ferment that was London. He would hardly have been alone in remaining. His antagonists Weld and Peter never returned to America. They had left England to build a new society, but now England itself seemed the place where that glorious and godly new society would emerge. Many others were coming back to England from America to join in the struggle for it. Nearly half the university-trained emigrants returned. Noted one, "Since the year 1640, more persons have removed out of New England, than have gone thither."[13] Winthrop's own son Stephen returned—and became a senior officer in Cromwell's army—and Winthrop's friends in England would soon try to convince Winthrop himself to come back.

Yet Williams chose to return to Providence, even though it remained one of the crudest and most primitive settlements in New England. It was no Boston. It was not even Newport, which had become prosperous.

To return marked a kind of defiance, an assertion of his own freedom, a renunciation of his own weaknesses for rank, a further commitment to the ideas he had articulated in his book. In Rhode Island a man could be free. Williams would not abandon the plantation, and more importantly the concept, he had created.

As Baillie was complaining of Vane's embrace of toleration, Williams's ship was finding Cape Ann on the Massachusetts coast. This was the land which had been withheld by the General Court from Salem as both a punishment for the town's support of Williams and a bribe for it to abandon him. He had spent years in Salem, had been welcomed there, had made a home there, had been loved there. Perhaps the sight of this cape from the deck of his ship embittered him anew with the memory of all that had happened. Perhaps those memories gave him a sense of present triumph and further defiance. And perhaps as well he had a naïve hope of being welcomed there again.

On September 17, 1644, his ship was warped into position in Boston harbor and he landed. There he presented two letters to the Massachusetts magistrates. One letter ordered them not to molest him and to provide safe passage. The other urged a reconciliation. Signed by such influential men as the Earl of Northumberland, mayor of London Isaac Pennington, war leaders Cornelius Holland, Oliver St. John, and the increasingly influential William Masham, it read:

"To the Right Worshipful governor and Assistants and the rest of our worthy friends in the plantation of Massachusetts bay, in New England. . . .

"Taking notice, some of us of long time, of Mr. Roger Williams his good affections and conscience, and of his sufferings by our common enemies and oppressors of God's people, the prelates, as also of his great industry and travail in his printed Independent labours in your parts, the like whereof we have not seen extant from any part in America, and in which respect it hath pleased both houses of Parliament freely to grant unto him . . . absolute charter of civil government for those parts of his abode: and withal sorrowfully resenting that amongst good men (our friends) driven to the ends of the world, exercised with the trials of the wilderness, and who mutually give good testimony each of other, as we observe you do of him, and he abundantly of you, there should be such a distance; we thought it fit . . . to profess our great desires of both your utmost endeavours of nearer closing."[14]

The governor of Massachusetts was then John Endicott, Williams's old colleague and friend, and once his most loyal of supporters. The deputy governor was Winthrop, whom despite their many collisions Williams still considered a close friend and mentor—indeed, almost a father. The Reverend William Hubbard recorded their response: "The governour and magistrates of the Massachusetts found, upon examination of their hearts, no reason to condemn themselves for any former proceedings against Mr. Williams." And, unless and until he abandoned his beliefs, they could "see no reason why to concede to him, or any so persuaded, free liberty of ingress and egress, lest any should be drawn away with his erroneous opinions."[15]

Far from reconciling themselves to him, they refused Williams freedom even to move about. He was free only to depart the jurisdiction—quickly. He was banished again.

To be expelled from Massachusetts anew, to have Endicott join against him, could only have reminded him of his first expulsion, layered by a fresh pulse of bitterness, humiliation, and pain. But this time he was not fleeing for his life with only the unknown before him. This time he was not fleeing at all. He was returning in some triumph to his home—a home created entirely of his mind, his heart, and his hands, a home that of all the world was where he chose to be. Matching his humiliation and anger depth for depth must have been his sense of gratification and achievement.

From Boston he traveled by land to Seekonk in the Plymouth colony, near the site where he had first settled, and from there he climbed into a canoe to paddle the last few miles. Then, as he pushed off from shore, he encountered a fleet of fourteen canoes.

The canoes carried his English neighbors of Providence. If the flotilla sounds small, so was Providence small, and the canoes—some of them likely large war canoes holding a dozen or more each—seemed to have contained most of the town's male population. They had come to pay tribute. Even some of his most bitter enemies had come. They surrounded him, embraced him, greeted him with, huzzah! huzzah! huzzah!

This embrace by neighbors was the first such greeting he had ever received, and emotion overcame him. Even a man who counted himself an enemy of Williams had come this day to pay him tribute, and he noted that Williams was "Elevated and Transported out of himself."[16]

He was, finally, home.

Perhaps the treatment he received from Massachusetts did not surprise him. Certainly word of his views had preceded him; copies of his attacks on Cotton and the Bay would have long since reached Boston. News of his accomplishment and Rhode Island's charter also would have reached Boston weeks before he did, along with *Queries of Highest Consideration*. A fast ship, one that caught the wind, might even have beaten him to Boston with word of *The Bloudy Tenent*. In all this, he had challenged the axioms upon which Massachusetts was constructed, the propositions that the state must nurse the church and its corollary that the church informed and infused the state with its spirituality.

Those propositions lay at the heart of the decision of most Puritans to emigrate to New England. They lay at the heart of the covenant Winthrop believed God had made with those emigrants. And they lay at the heart of what they intended to do in America. Yet Williams was denying those propositions and undermining those axioms.

Winthrop and Cotton and most other emigrants to Massachusetts had come to America with purpose and mission; they believed that God blessed that mission, which was the furtherance of God's design and not simply civil government. In order to succeed in their purpose, they believed that the entire community must conform and that their government must use compulsion if necessary to ensure conformity.

That sense of community, of communal effort, also lay at the heart of their mission. As one historian has pointed out, in England on the eve of the Great Migration, "If the Puritan movement stood for anything . . . beyond simple opposition to the Church of England, it was the proposition that individual godliness is attained and practised in company. Man was not meant to live, to be saved, or to serve his God alone."[17]

Once in America that sense of a commonwealth and the common weal, of the group, only intensified. Massachusetts and Plymouth even passed laws prohibiting adults from living alone. Every element of church and government was to contribute to the creation of the godly commonwealth.

Williams also sought a commonwealth in which all shared. To benefit the larger community, he had voluntarily relinquished any political power which these landholdings could have given him. He had forgone profit and donated the bulk of his original land purchase from the Narragansetts to the town stock of Providence. And he was as godly as any Puritan in Massachusetts, as devout as any, as committed to Christ as any. But he did not share their view of a godly commonwealth in which government advanced a biblical message, much less one which imposed such biblical strictures as Cotton's Mosaic legal code.

Williams also saw conformity in a different way than did Winthrop and Cotton, or for that matter than did any of the members of the Westminster Assembly or of Parliament. Conformity is a function of the desire for certainty; the greater or lesser that desire, the greater or lesser the demand for conformity. This was an age both believing in and seeking certainty, certainty of everything from the infallibility of Scripture to one's place in God's plan. The very sense of society as a body, with each person in a fixed place and performing a fixed task, reflected that view, and that view was not limited to Puritans. Whether one was a New England Puritan, a Westminster Assembly Presbyterian, or fighting for the king—and by no means were those on the king's side limited to High Church Anglicans, nor were all his enemies Puritans—the loosing of centrifugal forces caused by the civil war did nothing to change that desire. It increased it. The chaos threatened by the war only strengthened the desire for certainty and stability.

Roger Williams had never conformed—not even as a child, for even his father had persecuted him for his beliefs as a young boy. Yet for all his conviction, for all his commitment to his own way, it was not certainty he had clung to much of his life. Quite the contrary, he had a remarkable willingness to live with doubt and uncertainty. As he had told Winthrop so many years before, *I desire not to sleep in securitie and dreame of a Nest wch no hand can reach.*

His ability to live without security matched his willingness to live with error—including the possibility of his own error. He lived in a way that was the antithesis of Cotton's *monstrous partiality*, a partiality to one's own views that appalled him, that he found repulsive. By contrast, he urged the asking of questions and argued that without doing so a society could not advance. He warned that if "it shall be a crime, humbly and peaceably to question . . . what ever is publickly taught and delivered, you will most certainly find your selves . . . enslav'd and captivated in the Chains of those Popish Darknesses, (to wit, Ignorance is the mother of Devotion, and we must believe as the church believes, &c.)."[18]

Error was key. His experiences had made him conscious of both the power of the state and the state's willingness to use power even when in error. He had also come to see the church as tainted; he had earlier concluded that centuries of Catholicism had so corrupted the church that the apostolic succession had been broken; that forced him to conclude that until Christ reestablished that authority no church could be gathered. Seeing both state and church as corrupt vessels, he had therefore, and with great reluctance, come to see that his own worship must be personal and individual, and not communal.

This individualism was reflected in the physical layout of Providence. As noted earlier, most New England towns built meeting houses soon after their founding to use both for worship and other community purposes. In many towns, homes were also built around a central common. Both the meeting house and the centrality of the common mirrored the sense of community. But the town Williams founded, Providence, built no meeting house until half a century after its founding, and houses there were initially laid out along what is now North Main Street in linear fashion, single file, where each was alone.

The words "Conformist" and "Nonconformist" had a specific and limited meaning in England, defined by whether one did or did not adhere to Church of England practice. In America the words took on a more general and unlimited social and cultural meaning.

Williams wished to conform in this more general sense, but he could not. He simply could not. He abhorred any power which would force conformity, and he championed a new kind of individualism almost by default: he had been forced to it. His views of individualism, freedom, and nonconformity, in both the specific and general sense, were rooting themselves in both England and for now in that small parcel of America that was Rhode Island.

Yet Williams's ideas nonetheless became quintessentially American. So did Winthrop's. Williams saw the individual standing alone with God, in glorious isolation, and so independent of the state as to almost be outside it. Winthrop saw a state committed to Christian ideals, demanding conformity and imposing community standards upon individuals. Between Williams's views on one side and those of Winthrop on the other was a tension, and that very tension was also quintessentially American. It was in that tension that the American soul was being created.

*Part VII*

# THE TEST

# ❧ CHAPTER 32 ❧

Roger Williams had returned to America with a charter. He had convinced the Committee on Foreign Plantations to authorize the plantation at least partly as an experiment in freedom of conscience. Now he had to make the experiment succeed. He had no visions of creating a utopia; he knew human frailties too well for that. Yet he began trying to build more than just a stable government. Over the next few years, he began trying to build a new kind of society. The task almost overwhelmed him—and it almost overwhelmed that society for it forced a test of his principles.

The pressure on him and on the colony became relentless, not only from without but from within. Its survival and the survival of his ideas became more than ever a question of power, and of politics.

Immediately after news of the charter arrived in America but before Williams returned with it, from Newport, William Coddington—easily still the wealthiest man in the colony—tried to prevent any colony-wide government from being established by warning Winthrop that Rhode Island would become "an enemye lying in the heart of" the United Colonies. He proposed that Newport and Portsmouth be incorporated into Massachusetts or Plymouth.[1] Several weeks later, a Plymouth magistrate went to Newport and declared that its "supposed Government is within" Plymouth's "ancient limits,"[2] i.e., within Plymouth's territory. The magistrate then did "forbid them and all and every of them to exercise any authority or power of Government."[3] The town ignored the order. While Plymouth did nothing in America to enforce its claim to the land, it petitioned the Committee on Foreign Plantations to grant it Aquidneck Island.

Winthrop too now changed toward Williams. Williams had so much looked up to him, so much always sought his approval, felt so close to him, and certainly Winthrop had reciprocated at least some warmth. They trusted each other, did favors for each other, conducted business for each other, had even partnered in one enterprise. But Winthrop had had quite enough of liberty.

Even in Massachusetts he believed too much liberty prevailed. In July 1645, he addressed the question at a General Court where he defined two kinds of liberty. One was "Naturall" liberty, which he denounced as doing what one wants, "a Libertye to evill . . . that wilde beaste which all the ordinances of God are bent against." He contrasted that with "moral liberty . . . the Covenant betweene God & man, . . . & the Politicall Couenantes & constitutions, amongst men themselues. . . . [I]t is a libertye to that onely which is good, iust & honest."[4]

Clearly he saw in Rhode Island the "natural" kind of liberty. It was one thing for Winthrop to suffer Williams to survive in a pitiful colony where he might provide important intelligence on Indian affairs. It was quite another for Williams to now have parliamentary authorization for the obstrepery, defiance, and chaos which had spawned such devils as Samuel Gorton. To have such a plantation legitimized, to have it just beyond the Massachusetts border, mocked the Bay's very existence, and mocked the vision of the city upon a hill which Winthrop had articulated. Winthrop's indulgence of Williams now ended. Henceforth he gave Williams only a cold cliff of silence, rising stiff and white above Williams's entreaties.

Williams felt the change, felt it deeply. And he could not understand it. He wrote Winthrop an extraordinary and distraught letter. "Much honoured Sir," he began. "Though I should feare that all the Sparkes of former love are now extinct &c. Yet I am confident that your large Talents of Wisedome and Experience of the Affaires of Men will not lightly condemne my endeavour to give Informacion and Satisfaction as now I have done in this poore Apologie." He then tried to rebuild the relationship by replicating his old service to Massachusetts, providing intelligence on two of its potential enemies, the Dutch in New Amsterdam and Indians. He closed with the assurance, "Sir . . . you have not a truer friend and Servant to Your worthy person."[5]

Winthrop's reply came a few weeks later. It came not from him personally but from the Massachusetts magistrates, who viewed Rhode Island with such enmity that they prohibited sale of guns or powder to anyone there even while allowing sales to Indians. Now the magistrates claimed all of Rhode Island under Weld's fraudulent charter and ordered Williams and all others in his plantation to "forbeare to exercise any Jurisdiccion therein."[6]

Williams wrote a "Righteous and Waighty" response. It has not survived, but it surely denounced Weld's charter, detailed many flaws, and used Warwick's name to warn the Bay not to attempt to exercise jurisdiction itself. Williams later noted, "I never recd the least Reply" from the Massachusetts General Court, its magistrates, or Winthrop.[7] Between Williams and Winthrop there was now only silence.

In silence, then, Williams served as "chiefe officer" of his colony and managed to hold Massachusetts and Plymouth at bay. Despite their unrelenting antagonism, in the next two years Rhode Island began to stabilize, and Williams tried to build the political and social structure he had envisioned. Here too it looked radically different than in Massachusetts.

Later Williams recalled that he had often been "charged with folly for that freedom and liberty I have always stood for; I say liberty and equality, both in land and government."[8] His comment was not merely rhetorical.

In Massachusetts, Cotton called for giving "men of eminent quality and descent . . . large and honorable" landholdings.[9] The General Court had done so, routinely rewarding such men as Winthrop, Dudley, Endicott, and John Wilson thousands of acres. In total, the General Court granted thirty-two men 57,214 acres; individual towns also gave most of these same men large additional land grants.[10] Through these and related actions, noted one historian, "The settlement was gradually converted from a communal enterprise to a system of land companies exclusive in membership and keen for speculation."[11]

Nor did Massachusetts towns welcome new residents. In Taunton, which lay close by the Rhode Island line, the minister persuaded members of his church—and only church members could vote—to allow only those "as might be fit for Church-members" to acquire land. The town would allow other settlers, but only "to be but as Gibeonites, hewers of wood and drawers of water for the service of them that were of the Church."[12] Williams protested that this led to "Breaches of Civill and humane Societie . . . [and] the spoile and hindrance of a most likely and growing Plantation."[13]

In Providence, by contrast, he fought to extend property rights. The town owned the large reserve of land that he had donated to it. Consistent with the agreement Williams had reached with the first settlers, new arrivals who paid thirty shillings to the town stock got a hundred acres and voting rights. But young, single men who lacked thirty shillings were settling in the town. With neither voting rights nor prospect for improving their lot, they grew restive. One town meeting controlled by William Harris passed "an Order to receave no more" such men. An outraged Williams charged that Harris intended "Monopolizing" all the land. The two men had already feuded, and their feud would last four decades. Harris then issued "Challenges to fight, yea with Pistol and Rapier."[14] No duel occurred, but Williams reminded the next town meeting that Providence was a refuge for all and convinced it to rescind the order. He also worked out a compromise, creating so-called 25 acre men who for ten shillings got that much land, along with the promise of admission as freemen in the future.[15]

Then, in 1646, the Earl of Warwick and the Committee on Foreign Plantations granted Rhode Island and Gorton complete victory. They declared Shawomet "wholly without the bounds of the Massachusetts," prohibited the Bay from interfering with the Gortonists' religious practices or their "civill peace," ordered that those who occupied their old property "be removed," and warned "to these orders of ours we expect a conformity, not only from [Massachusetts], but from all other governours and plantations in New England."[16] The Gortonists reclaimed their property, and Gorton subsequently returned from England to join them. They renamed Shawomet "Warwick," not only to honor their deliverer and perhaps cause Warwick to hold the town close to his heart, but in the hope that the name would itself deter any of the United Colonies from making further claims or incursions.

The ruling marked a tremendous legal triumph for Rhode Island, with implications for Pawtuxet as well. Providence continued to claim jurisdiction over that area but, fearful of offending Massachusetts, did not exercise it. And now the Rhode Island government reorganized itself. In May 1647, representatives from Providence, Newport, Portsmouth, and Warwick/Shawomet met for three days and produced a sixty-one-page constitution and legal code. Williams led the Providence delegation, which included his brother Robert and his former printer Gregory Dexter.

This document created the freest society in the world, built around a structure of law, endorsing every man's "peaceable and quiet enjoyment of his lawful right and Libertie." It of course confirmed that the government established freedom of religion, and decreed that legally "a solemn profession" would have "as full force as an oath."[17] It even included a divorce law clearly influenced by Milton's treatise that was, for its time, liberal. And the government was reaffirmed as "Democraticall; that is to say, a Government held by ye free and voluntarie consent of all, or the greater parte of the free Inhabitants."

This assembly was well aware of the common belief that magistrates received their authority from God, no matter who selected them. It was well aware of the fear of mob rule engendered by democracy. Determined to prevent this form of government from becoming, "as some conjecture it will, an Anarchie, and so a common Tyranny," and determined "to preserve every man safe in his person, name and estate and to show ourselves, in soe doing, to be vnder authoritie," the assembly stipulated, almost certainly through Williams's influence, that they would follow "the common Law of the Realme of England, the end of which is, as is propounded, to preserve every man safe in his person, name and estate."[18]

The colony now seemed stable and growing. Williams had been chief officer for three years, and he was tired. He became the assistant governor and began spending most of his time at his trading post in present Wickford, Rhode Island, twenty miles south of Providence along the coast. Canonicus had "with his own hande" laid out the land there for him. Sometimes his wife or one of his children joined him there. It was his retreat. He discovered he now relished solitude, relished his "beloved privacie." He had become weary, weary of politics, weary of criticism, weary of dispute. In one particularly important and acrimonious confrontation—one in which he was not personally involved—he called upon all parties to accept arbitration; Coddington, one of the parties, asked him to serve as arbitrator, but he declined. His trading post also made him, for the first time in his life, financially successful, generating £100 a year—enough that he now owned several small canoes, a "great Canow," a pinnace, a shallop.

But the victory the Earl of Warwick had handed Gorton also proved Pyrrhic—in the extreme. It took time for the damage to become apparent but when it did, it nearly shattered Rhode Island. And it sent Williams back to England one more time.

In the end this trip forced him to confront both in England and at home the shape of liberty; it forced him to define the limits of state power and the limits of individual freedom.

The problem was Coddington. Coddington could not forget the disrespect Gorton had shown him so long before; he despised him enough that he literally would not live in the same colony and told Winthrop he "abhorred [Rhode

Island's] course" and "abstained from their meetings."[19] And Coddington's wealth gave him influence and connections, and made him dangerous. Rhode Island tried to appease him by electing him president, a position he had not sought, hoping the office would placate him. He spurned the position. (Williams seems to have served as acting president.)

Instead, he again tried to convince Plymouth and Massachusetts to absorb the Aquidneck Island towns of Newport and Portsmouth. He was seconded in that by William Arnold from Pawtuxet. Threatened by Gorton's return, asking that "my name may be conceled, lest they . . . be enraged against me," Arnold tried to provoke the Massachusetts magistrates by charging that Rhode Island hosted "professed enemies against all the united colonies," and that some Rhode Islanders "say there be no other witches upon earth nor devils, but your own pastors and ministers."[20] This amounted both to blasphemy by those making the charge and an accusation against Massachusetts of murder, for three Massachusetts towns had executed women as witches in 1648 alone. (Rhode Island had a law prohibiting witchcraft—the only intrusion of religion into its legal code—but never prosecuted anyone for it, and many women accused of it took refuge from the United Colonies in Rhode Island.) He suggested that Massachusetts simply seize the colony.[21]

Nonetheless, all the United Colonies declined to act, declaring seizure "full of confusion and Dangr."[22]

So Coddington went to London himself. In 1651, after two years' effort and telling outright lies, he received a charter for a new plantation of Aquidneck Island and the towns of Newport and Portsmouth. The charter also made him governor for life. But when he attempted to rule there, the overwhelming majority of islanders refused to recognize his commission and an assembly of island freemen affirmed "unanimously to stand imbodyed and incorporated as before, by virtue of our Charter."[23] First there was chaos as two governments ruled, with fistfights breaking out in the streets. Then a Coddington lieutenant tried to enforce a particularly offensive decree, and an angry crowd armed with "guns and swords and stafs" beat him and lynched him.[24] Coddington fled to Boston and disavowed any special rights on the island. (He later returned as a private citizen.)

But Coddington had opened a legal crack and the United Colonies pried it wide apart, declaring that his grant invalidated Williams's charter and authorizing Plymouth to occupy Warwick/Shawomet—by force. For now, Plymouth made no attempt to do so. Massachusetts continued to exert pressure through the open sore of Pawtuxet. And now even Connecticut prepared to claim lands south of Warwick, all the way to Narragansett Bay. Legal chaos gripped the plantation.

When a lawsuit advanced in a Providence court against a Boston man, Massachusetts magistrates demanded of Providence "to know a reason of their proceeding in the said suit," and threatened to send in reply "a Sword if anything."[25]

Rhode Island lacked the strength to make any of the United Colonies retreat. There was only one power Massachusetts, Plymouth, and Connecticut would respect: England's power.

When Coddington left for England, the Rhode Island General Assembly had asked Williams to return to England to counteract his efforts, offering "to pay the hundred pound dew him"—unpaid reimbursement for his earlier trip—"and a hundred pound more."[26] Probably because he expected Coddington to fail and unwilling to make further personal sacrifice, Williams refused. Now, asked again, he agreed to go. He had to go. Providence and Warwick sent him, and Portsmouth and Newport sent as their representatives John Clarke, a physician and Baptist minister in Newport, and the colony's attorney general, William Dyer, who took his wife, Mary.

The trip would prove enormously important, not only to Rhode Island but in generally advancing the concept of separation of church and state. Williams intended as much. At least four months before leaving for London, he sent the manuscript of *The Bloudy Tenent Yet More Bloudy* ahead, continuing his argument with Cotton and replying to Cotton's 1647 book *The Bloody Tenent, Washed, and made white in the bloude of the Lambe.*

Then, shortly before they departed, possibly in a deliberate attempt to create an incident that would help in London, Clarke and fellow Baptist Obadiah Holmes visited a coreligionist in Massachusetts. Clarke preached a sermon. The three men were arrested and tried before the General Court. Prior to sentencing, Cotton preached that "denying Infants Baptism . . . was a capitall offence; and therefore they were soul-murtherers."

Winthrop had died in 1649. Endicott was governor, and he would remain governor for all but one of the next fifteen years until his death in 1665. He listened to the sermon, then told the men, "You deserve to dye."[27] Holmes spoke out. John Wilson stepped forward, slapped him across the face, and declared, "The curse of God and Jesus go with thee."[28]

The court sentenced them, however, only to heavy fines, which were paid anonymously. Holmes refused to accept it and he was brutally whipped, viciously enough to scar him for life. A spectator who shook his hand after his scourging was arrested, fined, and threatened with whipping. A few weeks later, Williams, Clarke, Dyer, and Dyer's wife sailed for England.

In their absence, Rhode Island demonstrated that the seeds Williams had planted had taken deep root, and that the plantation believed in freedom as a principle. It outlawed slavery—an extraordinary action, likely the first in the world, and a reflection of the beliefs of both Williams and Gorton. On May 23, 1652, the Rhode Island General Assembly passed the following law: "Whereas, there is a common course practised amongst English men to buy negers, to that end that they may have them for service or slaves forever; for the preventinge of such practices among us, let it be ordered, that no blacke mankind or white being forced by covenant bond, or otherwise, to serve . . . longer than ten yeares. . . . And at the end of ten yeares to sett them free, as the manner is with the English servants."[29] (The law was never repealed but in the next century it was ignored; Rhode Islanders, including the family after whom Brown University is named, would become prominent slave traders.)

While Rhode Island moved toward freedom, Williams, Clarke, and Dyer arrived in an England moving toward a military dictatorship. The civil war had ended, but Parliament had not triumphed. Cromwell's New Model Army had. On December 6, 1648, Colonel Thomas Pride had stood at the doors of Parliament, refused entry to all but army supporters, and arrested forty-five known army opponents. Of parliament's 471 members, "Pride's Purge" left only about eighty to form the initial "Rump Parliament."

Even this Rump had only reluctantly, by a tiny majority, acceded to the army's demand to try the king for treason. During the trial, Hugh Peter had preached to the court, demanding conviction and a death sentence: "Let the saints be joyful in glory . . . [t]o execute vengeance upon the heathen."[30]

On January 30, 1649, King Charles was taken to the scaffold after being allowed to take a last walk in St. James's Park with his dog. The day was bitterly cold. Concerned that spectators would think any shivering came from fear, the king wore heavy underclothes. He did not shiver. On the scaffold he was forced to listen as Hugh Peter prayed. Then he bent over the block and held out his hands, a signal to the executioner. A clean stroke beheaded him. From the basket the executioner reached down and pulled up the head, held it high, and proclaimed, "Behold the head of a traitor!"

The monarchy and the House of Lords were abolished on February 6 and 7. The army had taken England into the deepest water, where none had ever been before. On February 14 the Council of State was established to carry out the executive responsibilities of government. Cromwell chaired it; second in power on it was Vane; William Masham and others of Williams's friends also sat on it.

A tiny minority of Commons had authorized the trial of the king; in the end only a minority of the court had endorsed the king's death sentence. Now a smaller minority still held real power.

This bothered few in government. Milton, who joined this government, justified it: "Is it just or reasonable, that most voices against the main end of government should enslave the less number that would be free? More just it is, doubtless, if it come to force, that a less number compel a greater to retain . . . their liberty, than that a greater number, for the pleasure of their baseness, compell a less . . . to be their fellow-slaves."[31]

This was the England to which Williams was returning. Even three years after the king's execution, it was not a quiet England.

The king's death launched a period of horrifying uncertainty. The only good was that the Civil War was over; one estimate puts its death toll at 190,000 in England alone, a staggering 3.7 percent of the entire population,[32] with a higher proportion killed in Scotland and a far higher proportion in Ireland. Any respite from such slaughter was welcome, under almost any government. So if a majority of the English did not embrace the minority rule of Cromwell and the Rump Parliament, they endured it, going about their lives while in the center of their being they felt a deep unsettling.

But some few men and women found in the king's death a great freeing, a great enlargement of the world. Suddenly anything was possible. It was the glorious end of the world. It was the even more glorious beginning of the world. This end and beginning unleashed enormous passions and enormous expectations. "Fifth Monarchists" believed Christ's return was at hand. Millenarianism infected not simply a tiny fringe; a broad swath of London to greater or lesser degree became millenarians. The rule of bishops was overthrown; a king was overthrown; a kingdom was overthrown; the House of Lords was overthrown. All was ending, so how could the end times not be near? Into all this was injected, just after Williams's arrival, war with Holland.

Politics was tumultuous. Levellers and other political radicals wanted, demanded, and expected the revolution to proceed further. This truly was "the world turned upside down."

Yet in all this tumult Williams at first made rapid progress. He could report that on October 2, 1652, only three months after his arrival, the Council of State acted on "the petition Sir Henry Vane and myself drew up."[33] It revoked Coddington's charter and reaffirmed Williams's original one. But the council, even with Vane pressing it, did not resolve all the territorial claims of Plymouth and Connecticut. One member of the Council of State whose son-in-law was a commissioner of the United Colonies blocked a final decision, so the council gave Rhode Island jurisdiction over the disputed territory only "for the present and until further direction."

Still, it was good news and Dyer returned to Rhode Island with it. Williams and Clarke waited for a final determination. Meanwhile, Williams engaged men at the highest levels. During most of his time in England he lived as Vane's houseguest, seeing him daily. Williams had ready access to Cromwell as well; he partly bragged and partly just noted, "It hath pleased the Generall himselfe to send for me and to entertaine many Discourses with me."[34]

And there were others: his old friends Masham and Barrington; his new friend Major General Thomas Harrison, a radical whom Cromwell later imprisoned despite his having been so involved in Charles's execution that he was hung, drawn, and quartered after the restoration of the monarchy; even his old antagonist Hugh Peter, who had climbed high among the revolutionaries, high enough that his lodgings in Whitehall had once been Laud's, high enough that he also would later be hung, drawn, and quartered for his role in the king's death. All these, even including Peter, now supported religious toleration, although they stopped short of Williams's own views. And there was

Stephen Winthrop, who had fought beside Cromwell; Williams wrote John Winthrop Jr. that "your bro. Stephen is a great man for Soule Libertie."[35] Williams and Milton also became close. Milton was Secretary for Foreign Tongues, an important post since it involved translating foreign documents during war. Williams taught Milton Dutch and they began to spend much time together.

With all these men, in all their circles and in more, Williams reentered the debate about the future of England. He was eager to do so, had planned to do so. As Milton's biographer Masson said, "Was he not the man in the whole world who had done most to propagate the theory of Absolute Voluntaryism in Religion, or No State-Church of any kind; and might it not be said that the controversy he now found going on was the result in great part of the ideas he himself had sown in the English mind in his former visit . . . , and that the Voluntaries he now found so numeorus in England were his pupils?"[36]

He engaged his subject in his person, in homes and in Westminster, and he engaged his subject in print, not only with his books but with pamphlets.* Most provocative was *Hireling Ministry None of Christs,* in which he denounced tithes, noting with disdain that the Westminster Assembly had "first made sure of an Ordinance of Parliament for Tithes and Maintenance, before any ordinance for God himself. . . . He that makes a Trade of Preaching, that makes the care of Souls, and the charge of mens eternall welfare, a trade, a maintenance, and a living, . . . the Son of God never sent such a one to be a Labourer in his Vineyard."[37]

He continued, "Humane learning and the knowledge of Languages, and good Arts, are excellent and excell other outward gifts, as far as light excels darknesse," and that such studies "ought to be maintained and cherished." But to the extent that universities became "the pretended Seed plots and Seminaries for the Ministry" he called them "great mistakes."[38]

Yet for all his involvement, for all its intensity and excitement, he was wearing down. He routinely sent letters and more formal reports to Providence of his progress. They show a tired man. After nine months in England—six months after Coddington's charter was rescinded and Rhode Island's tentatively reaffirmed—he wrote his friend Gregory Dexter, "[B]y my publike Letters you will see how We Wrastle and how we are like Yet to Wrastle, in the hopes of an

---

*These pamphlets were: *Experiments of Spiritual Life and Health, The Examiner Defended, The Fourth Paper Presented by Major Butler,* and, the most interesting, *Hireling Ministry None of Christs.*

End. For my selfe I had hopes to have got away by this ship but I see now the mind of the Lord to hould me here. . . . The Determinacion of . . . the Controversie . . . Sir, I feare will be a worck of Time, I feare longer than we have Yet bene here."[39] He spoke of his wife, of missing her, asking Dexter to tell her "how joyfull I should be of her being here with me until our Affaires were ended."[40] But he left the decision to make the voyage to her.

She declined. The memory of the fearful ocean on her trip to America was too strong.

Then, in March 1653, the Council of State submitted a report favoring Rhode Island to Parliament. On April 1, he wrote to the town of Providence to remind them that they had already achieved "the confirmation of the charter." He and their opponents, he explained, "stand as two armies ready to engage, observing the motions and postures each of other, and yet shy of each other."[41] He added that Vane, "the sheet anchor of our ship, . . . faithfully promised me" to protect the plantation.[42] Then he made a personal plea to be released: "Remember I am a father and an husband; I have longed earnestly to return with the last ship, and yet I have not been willing to withdraw my shoulders from the burthen lest it . . . fall heavy upon all." He asked for "discharge" from this task, and continued, "If you conceive it necessary for me still to attend this service, pray you consider if it be not convenient that my poor wife be incouraged to come over to me. . . . I write to my dear wife, my great desire of her coming while I stay; yet left it to the freedom of her spirt, because of the many dangers; truly at present the seas are dangerous." He closed the letter, "P.S. My love to all my Indian friends."[43]

Nineteen days after Williams wrote this letter, the world changed. He could not return.

Williams remained on good terms with both Vane and Cromwell, but the two had become enemies to each other. Vane had become a champion of Parliament, Cromwell its most bitter critic. On April 20, 1653, Cromwell took the floor of Parliament. He began to speak, calmly at first, then passion filled his words, passion expressing revulsion. "Drunkard!" he called one member, and another, "Whoremonger!" He denounced them, walked up and down spewing rage, declared that Parliament was "dishonoured by your contempt of all virtue, and defiled by your practice of every vice; ye are a factious crew, and enemies to all good government; ye are a pack of mercenary wretches. . . . Ye are grown intolerably odious to the whole nation; . . . your country therefore calls upon me to cleanse the Augean stable."⁴⁴

Most members sat silent, frozen and intimidated, but Vane shouted a protest. Cromwell turned on him in fury and charged, "You might have prevented this extraordinary course, but you are a juggler, and have not so much as common honesty."

Then Cromwell thundered, "But now begone! You are no Parliament!"

Vane shouted, "This is not honest, yea, it is against morality and common honesty!"

"O Sir Henry Vane, Sir Henry Vane," Cromwell bellowed, "the Lord deliver me from Sir Henry Vane!"

Soldiers swarmed in. Parliament was dissolved. Cromwell was now become Oliver Cromwell, Lord Protector of the Commonwealth of England, Scotland, and Ireland.

W‍illiams was confident Cromwell would confirm the charter, for Cromwell favored not only him personally but toleration. Williams pressed his wishes upon both him and the new Council of State, frequently seeing "divers of the chiefe of our Nation, and especially his Highnes, in many discourses I had with him."⁴⁵ But Cromwell also had other priorities, which meant more delay.

Nearly a year passed. With each day's passing, his desire to return home grew. He was not only homesick. He was also running out of money. Rhode Island had promised him £200; it had given only £18, with another £5 to his family. Anticipating this failure of supply, Williams had sold nearly everything he owned—his trading post, guns, fields, fencing—to pay for his trip, retaining only his home and lot in Providence. But his resources were becoming exhausted. And most important, disorder had invaded Rhode Island, "the noyse whereof Ecchoes into the Eares of all, as Well Friends as Enemys by Every returne of ships from those parts."⁴⁶ Now that disorder threatened Rhode Island more than did anything in London. Williams could have ignored the problems in America. Once again he could have stayed in England, brought his family over, made a fine life there. He relished the easy familiarity he had attained with such men as Vane and Cromwell and said, "I humbly acknowledge (as to Personal worth) I deal with men, for many excellent gifts, elevated above the common rank of men." A man who had long been his enemy judged him arrogant, egotistical, superficial, and snorted, "That which took him and was his life, was to get honour among men, especially amongst the Great Ones."[47]

But if that was entirely true, it was an odd kind of arrogance. The same critic had earlier complained in astonishment that Williams "put his hat off to every Man or Boy, that puts off his Hat to him."[48]

Williams was in fact eager for America. He had confidence that Clarke, who had personal reasons to remain in England, could by himself pursue a final, definitive confirmation of the charter. Williams left London and was waiting to board a ship when the head of the Council of State, Henry Lawrence, sent him good news. The Council had decided. Its decision was still not absolutely final. But Lawrence personally sent Williams three documents to take home with him. They were nearly all he could have hoped for. The first reaffirmed the original charter. The second warned the United Colonies "not to molest" him—a permanent safe passage through all their territories. The third was a statement of policy: "that Liberty of Conscience should be maintained at all American plantations etc."[49]

Williams had done what he could. It was enough. A few months after this action of the Council of State, Cromwell himself wrote to Williams and the colony to personally apologize for the delay in resolving the issue and to tell them "to proceed in your Governmt according to the Tenor of your Charter formerly granted."[50] In doing so, he changed the equation. Massachusetts magistrates had never yielded to Vane's support of Williams; they knew Vane, knew him as one who had sided with Anne Hutchinson, knew him as one whom they had turned out of office. But Cromwell—they had to heed Cromwell.

All the United Colonies ceased all direct depredations against Rhode Island. Indirect efforts to gain control of Rhode Island territory by land companies in Connecticut and Massachusetts soon began and continued for decades, chiefly by targeting the Narragansetts. But that was a far less serious threat and Rhode Island would fight nearly all of them off as well.

No doubt with a defiant satisfaction, upon landing in Boston Williams had the order granting him permanent safe passage entered in Bay records so no future magistrate could bar him. Then, "saluting the wilderness" again, he headed on foot back to Providence.

This time no happy crowd greeted him. Chaos did. The plantation had splintered. Ironically, Dyer's return with the earlier confirmation of the charter had caused the split, for he also carried authorization to make war on the Dutch of New Amsterdam by licensing privateers and he was eager for the profit he believed privateering would yield. The mainland wanted no part of such a scheme, warning it would "set all New England on fire."[51] Rival governments organized; one in Newport claimed to represent the entire colony, while one on the mainland claimed authority over Providence and Warwick.

Gorton had served one term as plantation president but refused reelection, saying that the chief qualification for office was the ability to take abuse. Williams tried to bring peace. He asked Vane to write a letter to the colony, and Vane remonstrated with it, denouncing "such divisiens amongst you, such headinesses, tumults dissorders Injustice."[52] But Vane's criticisms only incited more resentment.

Williams followed with his own plea, a long letter, a personal letter, a pained letter. "Well beloved Friends and Neighbours," he began, "I am like a Man in a great Fog. I know not well how to steere. I feare to run upon the rocks at home." He lamented that "words have bene so sharpe betweene my selfe and some lately . . . the contentions of brethren are the bars of a castle, and not easily broken." He recited complaints against himself: that he had given away the town's land, that he had given up advantages in negotiations. "I have been censured," he wrote, even "called Traitour . . . and as good as banished by Your Selves and therefore it is said allso that both sides wisht I might never have landed."

Was that really what they wanted? Bickering? Enmity? Accusation? Then he stepped back and reminded them what had been achieved: "Such peace, such security, such liberties for the Soule and Body as were nevere enjoyed by any English men, nor any in the world," "Libertie and Equalitie both in land and government," and "that grand cause of TRUTH and FREEDOME OF CONSCIENCE, hath been upheld to this day."[53]

They had what others wanted, dreamed of, aspired to. Did they not know that? Had they not come to Rhode Island for that? Finally, he warned that all that could yet be undone and urged a reconciliation of all, and a reuniting of the colony.

His personal plea succeeded in bringing about a semblance of unity. Within a month of his writing it, representatives of all the towns on both Aquidneck Island and on the mainland met in Warwick. They agreed to reunite under the terms of the original charter, and less than two weeks later a special election was held.

When Williams was in London, the town of Providence had urged him to have the Council of State name him governor. He had declined. But now it seemed that only he could hold the plantation together. Williams confided that they "haled me out (sore agst my Spirit) to publike Service."[54] This was not false modesty; he had had enough public service.

Nonetheless, he accepted the office of president. But reunion did not end the contention. At every attempt to exercise authority, there was protest. Frustrated, he complained privately to John Winthrop Jr., "We enjoy Liberties of soule and body, but it is license we desire."[55]

The greatest protest came over the ultimate power that any state had: the use of force. Rhode Island was the weakest New England colony by far, weaker than New Haven. He and the colony government attempted to make military training compulsory. Providence, his own Providence, was the center of opposition, and his own brother led this opposition. They had become pacifists, yet there was rumor that these pacifists were incensed enough for "taking up of armes to the opseing [opposing] of authoritie."

As his frustrations grew, as the plantation teetered toward anarchy, he wrote another public letter, a letter which has been reprinted literally hundreds of times.[56] In this letter, in a succinct but comprehensive way, Williams laid out his understanding of how individual freedom fitted into a political order.

He said he had always "disclaimed and abhorred" any interpretation of his views which suggested that "Liberty of Conscience" led to anarchy. To explain himself, he used an analogy: "There goes many a Ship to Sea, with many a Hundred Souls in one Ship . . . a true Picture of a Common-Wealth, or an human Combination, or Society. . . . *Papists* and *Protestants, Jews* and *Turks,* may be embarqued into one Ship. . . . [A]ll the Liberty of Conscience that ever I pleaded for, turns upon these two Hinges, that none of the *Papists, Protestants, Jews or Turks* be forced to come to the Ships Prayers or Worship; nor, secondly, compelled from their own particular Prayers or Worship. . . . I never denied, that notwithstanding this Liberty, the Commander of this Ship ought to command the Ship's Course; yea, and also. . . . If any Seamen refuse to perform their Service, or Passengers to pay their Freight; . . .—if any refuse to obey the common Laws and Orders of the Ship, concerning their common Peace and Preservation; . . .—if any shall preach or write, that there ought to be no Commanders, nor Officers, because all are equal in CHRIST, therefore no Masters, nor Officers, no Laws, nor Orders, no Corrections nor Punshments—I say, I never denied, but in such Cases, the Commander or Comanders may judge, resist, compel, and punish such Transgressors."[57]

Slowly, in response to his letter and with a grudging and reluctant recognition of the necessity of some authority, order did come to the colony. Stability was achieved.

There were two proofs of this increasing order and stability. First, Benedict Arnold, who with his father and others had once subjected Pawtuxet to Massachusetts, abandoned that position, moved to Newport, and supported full unity of Rhode Island.

Then, after Williams was reelected president, the General Court of Trials met in Warwick, Gorton's home. To that court came Coddington, the man who rather than live in the same colony as Gorton had once preferred to destroy it. He came now as a representative of Newport to participate in government side by side with Gorton, who represented Warwick. Coddington had changed his views, for he was soon to become a Quaker, and the treatment of Quakers in the rest of the world gave him a new appreciation for religious liberty. Therefore, on March 11, 1656, he "publickly professed"—he did not swear, for there were no oaths in Rhode Island—that "I, William Coddington, doe freely submit to ye authoritie of . . . this Colonie as it is now united, and that with all my heart."[58]

# ❦ CHAPTER 33 ❦

Roger Williams despised the Quaker religion. He despised Quaker theology, he despised what he regarded as Quaker presumptuousness and egocentrism, he despised the behavior of Quakers, and he despised the implications of Quaker beliefs for government. In all this he was, for a change, one with the United Colonies—with one exception. On the question of Quakers, the United Colonies would not merely make violent threats; they would carry through on them.

If Quakers had brought Coddington into Rhode Island's fold, they were also about to put both Williams personally and the entire colony to the test: to reject what they already despised—and be accepted for the first time as full and equal partners with neighboring colonies—or to protect what they despised—and risk their own destruction.

The strife between Puritans and Quakers was inevitable. Quaker doctrine, particularly as advanced in the early days of the sect's founding, seemed to mock all established Christian theologies, but none more than Puritans'. It mocked their effort and struggle and, even worse, mocked their doubt and torment. For Quakers had their own confident certainty, their own monstrous partiality.

Puritans believed in predestination, that God elected saints for reasons beyond understanding, and that no human action had any bearing on election. Yet they also saw great personal struggle and living a godly life as symptomatic of—although not the cause of—salvation. Those who were saved worked, they did the hardest of work, and Puritans no matter how confident of their own fates had to live with the terror of doubt. They saw Christ as an historic figure and an individual, indivisible like other individuals. They believed God was rational, and that the world was an ordered place. They believed that careful, scholarly study of Scripture was necessary to understand God's desires and their own tasks in the world.

Quakers rejected every element of those beliefs. They believed in universal redemption, and they denied that mankind was forever burdened with original sin. They discarded all outward forms of worship, and they turned their thoughts inward, seeking the "light within," the "inner light," which they believed came from and was part of God and lay within themselves. Indeed, in effect they raised humans nearly to divine status because they believed that Christ was *inside* them. They substituted human judgment for Scripture and the rule of law. They eliminated the ministry and all forms of worship. They considered men and women virtually equal and allowed women to speak in worship. They also justified riotous behavior and even disobedience to the law. If the word "antinomian" derives from "against law," this was Antinomianism raised by orders of magnitude. Any one of these beliefs was, to Calvinists, blasphemy; taken together they certainly justified a death sentence.

Organized in northern England in 1652 largely by George Fox, initially the sect made little progress there; it was too extreme even for most of those who shared its revulsion at tithes. Williams was in England when Quakers virtually invaded and disrupted church services; the disruptions received enormous attention and made the Quakers notorious. It also sent thousands of Quakers to English prisons—more often for refusing to pay tithes than for outrageous behavior—over the next several decades. And by 1656 the Quakers were focusing on the New World, which they regarded as "an exceeding wicked place" but a "vineyard" for a "master builder" to "stablish and build up what is already planted, and pull down all that is of the old foundation."[1]

To do that, Quakers established a small community in Barbados; although their numbers were tiny, likely no more than a dozen at first, it became a base of Quaker activity. Next they deliberately sought confrontation. And if there was one place in the English world which felt itself capable of dealing with deliberate confrontation, it was Massachusetts.

That confrontation began in 1656 when two Quaker women arrived in Boston from Barbados to preach. Magistrates seized and burned their books, stripped them to look for evidence that they were witches, and kept them in prison before deporting them. Two days after their departure, eight other Quakers arrived. Magistrates seized their writings and imprisoned them for eleven weeks. Samuel Gorton wrote them to offer refuge in Warwick, but Massachusetts wanted no "infection" so close to itself and deported them to England.

Few as the Quakers yet were, the Bay considered them a real threat. Its

General Court, at its first meeting after this initial confrontation, decided that existing laws were insufficient to address this heresy. It declared, "[T]here is a cursed sect of heretickes lately risn vp in the world, which are commonly called Quakers, who take vpon them to be immediatelie sent of God . . . despising gouernment & the order of God in the church & comon wealth."² So the court passed new laws. Any ship commander who knowingly landed a Quaker would be fined £100. Anyone who imported any Quaker writings would be fined £5. Any Quaker discovered in the colony would receive twenty stripes with a corded whip and then be imprisoned, and while a prisoner their windows would be boarded up to prevent their communicating with anyone. Any Massachusetts resident who voiced a Quaker opinion would be fined 40 shillings; if upon correction he or she defended the opinion the fine rose to £4.³

Nonetheless, the infection spread; if not quickly and widely, still it spread insidiously. It took special root in Salem, as always a trouble spot, and parts of Cape Cod.

Meanwhile, Quakers used outrageous behavior to draw more attention to their beliefs and provoke a response. A Quaker man walked into a Boston church holding a bottle in each hand, then smashed them to the floor; he shouted, "Thus will the Lord break all to pieces!" A Quaker woman stripped herself naked and paraded through the Newbury church during worship. Another Quaker woman paraded nude through the streets of Boston.⁴

When expelling Quakers did not stop them, Massachusetts grew harsher. A third Quaker woman blackened her face and walked the streets of Boston proclaiming that the world was ending; she was flogged. A fourth Quaker woman went "barbarous and inhuman going naked through the town"; she was tied naked to a cart and sentenced to be "whipped from Mr. Gidney's gate till she come to her house, not exceeding thirty stripes."⁵ Another woman was stripped to her waist and whipped so hard the whip split her nipples.⁶

Plymouth, Connecticut, and New Haven all also hardened toward the Quakers, imprisoning, whipping, and deporting them, sometimes after cutting off their ears, and fining any who harbored them. Not even "tolerant" New Amsterdam tolerated Quakers. Those who tried to disembark there were not allowed to land. One Quaker youth did manage to land and was imprisoned, fined, and sentenced to hard labor with Africans for two years. He refused to work. The court had him whipped, and promised to continue whipping him each time he refused to work. Eventually he did work, but so poorly that the

Lord Director was asked "whether it be not best to send him to Rhode Island, as his labor is hardly worth the cost"[7] of feeding him.

Massachusetts had always worried that blasphemy, corruption, error, and heresy would find a refuge in Rhode Island, from which it would seep into the Bay. The Quakers now made those fears concrete. Many of them found refuge in Rhode Island and from there were invading Massachusetts and Plymouth in small boats or on foot.

On the abhorrent nature of the Quakers, the United Colonies and Roger Williams agreed. As a theologian, he responded much as Cotton would, arguing that the disorder Quakers brought could not be godly, "For we all know that the Spirit of God was most purely Rational, and a Spirit of pure order."[8] He rejected their assertions that their emotionalism, their responses to the movement of a spirit within, their extreme and disruptive behavior all emanated from God. Such an assertion, he argued, was not proof. Proof could come only from intellectual rigor, from, as Williams said, his "Reason, or some Testimony of unquestionable Witnesses satisfying my Reason, or some heavenly inspired Scripture or Writing which my Reason tells me came from God."

The United Colonies turned now to Williams, then president of the colony, and demanded that Rhode Island cease providing refuge. In God's name, the United Colonies demanded it.

More than the question of the Quakers was involved in Williams's response. Coincidentally, just before the arrival of Quakers in New England, Williams had written an unrelated and extraordinary letter to the Massachusetts General Court. Many times before he had written to this court, always from a position of great weakness, always to protest or to plead. This time, after Cromwell's endorsement, he wrote from a position approaching equality.

In this letter Williams showed himself as he must have been in London— subtle, charming, gracious, and yet determined. It is one of the few surviving documents that shows him as a courtier, almost a protégé of Francis Bacon.

He began by making the self-interest of Massachusetts clear, offering to help Massachusetts solve a major problem of its own, reminding the Bay that Gorton's suit against them for £2,000 in damages was awaiting a decision by Cromwell and the council. He did not have to remind them of his and Gorton's prior victories there, or his closeness to Cromwell. He implied that he could help "friendly and easily determine that affaire between you." He also reminded them that "with the people of [Rhode Island] your commerce is as great as with any in the countrey."

But the heart of his letter dealt with Pawtuxet. He turned gracious, so much so as to "cordially professe" that if "ourselves and all the whole country, by joint consent, were subject to your government, it might be a rich mercy."[9]

It is inconceivable that he actually thought that. He could not have endured the persecution of Baptists and all other sects, which continued, or the burning of books, which continued. Indeed, he and John Winthrop Jr., then in Connecticut, routinely traded new books arriving from England, often ones which the Massachusetts court "burnt in the market place at Boston," or "2 of Mr Dells books lately burnt at the Massachusetts . . . of which I brought one over." He could not have endured any of this, any of what it showed of the condition "Libertie of Conscience hath in this land."[10]

But his graciousness smoothed the way for him to raise the issue of Pawtuxet. He informed the General Court that because of Cromwell's endorsement of the Rhode Island charter, those who had earlier submitted to Massachusetts "lately have professed a willingness" to rejoin Rhode Island, but they hesitated to do so because they feared "offending of yourselves."

He reminded the Massachusetts magistrates that several of these English were Baptists who would be "banished by you," while others were "very far allso in religion from you." He also pointed out that "insolent and defiant" Indians in Pawtuxet "live as barbarously if not more than any in the country" and steal from English yet "pretend your name" to escape Rhode Island law. Since Massachusetts was not actually exercising any authority there, Pawtuxet had become a sanctuary for both Indian and English criminals. He appealed "to your own wisedome and experience" to settle this matter.[11]

In response, Massachusetts invited Williams to Boston—for the first time since his banishment twenty years earlier—to discuss the issue. Williams also reported to the Rhode Island General Assembly that "for the Ending of all such Contraversies amongst us," Massachusetts had agreed "to Arbietration of some Indifferent and Juditious men, muttulie Chossen," rather than demand adjudication in a Massachusetts court as it always had in the past. In the interim, "the saied Inhabitants of Patucett may Injoy the Benefitts of this Jurisdiction"[12]— i.e., of Rhode Island.

Then an incident occurred, complicated by his own misjudgment, which seemed at first likely to prove disastrous and which unseated Williams from any role in government. But it turned into a victory sweeter than he could have imagined.

Richard Chasmore was a ruffian of ill repute, a rounder who traded liquor and guns to Indians, a randy man known as "Long Dick"—a nickname which meant the same thing four hundred years ago as today. And he was observed by several Indians buggering a heifer in Pawtuxet, a crime with a potential death sentence in every jurisdiction in England or New England.

Williams hesitated to assert jurisdiction over Pawtuxet now by arresting Chasmore. He did not want to risk provoking the Bay, not at the very moment he was nearing success in convincing it to abandon its own claims to jurisdiction there. So he asked John Endicott, then Massachusetts governor, what Massachusetts intended to do about the crime.

Chasmore first fled, then, recognizing that his chances of escaping a severe penalty—including death—were greater in Rhode Island than in Massachusetts, returned and gave himself up to Williams personally. Williams arrested him. Chasmore posted bond to appear at trial and in the meantime remained free.

But shortly before that trial was to commence, Endicott decided to assert the Bay's jurisdiction after all. Two Massachusetts marshals crossed into Rhode Island, arrested Chasmore in Pawtuxet, then stopped at a tavern in Providence for the night. Word quickly spread in Providence. So did outrage.

Arthur Fenner, once a lieutenant in Cromwell's army, was an elected official of the town and called an immediate town meeting. Williams did not attend. Fenner sent four men to bring the marshals and Chasmore to the meeting, and there demanded of the marshals "in his Hinesses name"—i.e., Cromwell—"to answer for the affront you have put uppon us by takeing away our prisner from us: he beinge bound over to answr in our Collonie." Fenner demanded the warrant. The chief marshal refused to produce it and instead challenged the town's authority to question him. Dexter, Williams's close friend, rose and declared, "Pawtucksitt is in our liberties and not in the bays." William Harris seconded him, repeating that Massachusetts "had noe right to seaze a man att Pawtucksitt. . . . [Chasmore] was there prisoner and had given in bayle for to answer in there Collony." Then Dexter spoke again: "I stand for our libertye. Deliuer him to the cunstabl."[13]

The marshals did not resist and a Providence constable took custody of Chasmore. Everything had been peaceable and orderly. But the incident had explosive repercussions.

Several times in the past, Massachusetts had marched its armed men through Providence to compel obedience of Rhode Islanders to its orders; most egregiously it had seized Gorton, his followers, and all of what was now Warwick. Armed men representing Massachusetts had never been opposed. Several times in the past, the Rhode Island government had tried to exercise some authority in Pawtuxet. The Massachusetts court had always demanded it "forbeare," warning that if Rhode Island did so, Massachusetts would "seek satisfaction . . . in such manner as God shall put into theire hands."[14] Such warnings had frozen Rhode Island into inaction.

This time, those who participated in the emergency town meeting had not only defied an order of the Bay backed up by its armed officers, they had threatened violence to those officers. They had done so not over anything that had occurred in the town of Providence itself, but outside it. They had demonstrated a sense of sovereignty and a willingness to fight for that sovereignty.

Yet the act incensed Williams. In an angry letter, he called Fenner and other participants "rioters" and condemned them for holding "an unlawful Towne meeting" because they had failed to give proper notice. He saw no difference between it and mob action. Few non-lawyers appreciated the importance of procedure more than Williams. His years with Coke, his own banishment, had taught him that due process was no mere technicality. In it lay freedom. He knew what three centuries later Felix Frankfurter would say: "The history of liberty has largely been the history of the observance of procedural safeguards."

Williams charged that they did "arrogate a power over the Colony."[15] And he did not simply write an angry letter. He charged the ringleaders, including his longtime friend and comrade Gregory Dexter, the man who had risked prison for him in printing *The Bloudy Tenent* and whom he had relied upon to look after his family during his second stay in London, with treason.[16]

Two weeks later Williams, as president of the colony, presided over a trial court. Chasmore's case came first. No witness to his act appeared. He was acquitted. The charges against Fenner, Dexter, and others were tried the next day. Williams failed to appear in court. He had made his point by charging them; to proceed further would have divided a suddenly united colony. He was the complaining witness; without him, those charges also were dismissed.

But charging them had two consequences. The first was positive. No damage was done to his effort to convince Massachusetts to renounce its claims to Pawtuxet. In fact, the Massachusetts General Court responded with the most courteous treatment it had ever extended to Williams, writing him of "Our good acceptance of his readyness to applye himselfe to what may conduce to peace and righteousnes, . . . [so] peace and amitie may be mayntayned between the two jurisdictions."[17]

The second consequence was not so positive for him. He had founded the colony, donated a fortune in land to it, established the freest society on earth, and won the charter, then convinced two different Councils of State and Cromwell personally to confirm it. He had served three consecutive terms as president, during which the colony had enjoyed the greatest prosperity, stability, and security in its history. He was about to reestablish his colony's unquestioned jurisdiction over Pawtuxet; Massachusetts soon did abandon all claims to it.

Yet in the next election, May 1657, he was not reelected president, nor was he elected to any other post whatsoever in either the town or colony government. Other than his time in England, this was the first time he held no place in government. Fenner, who had organized the seizure of Chasmore, took over leadership of Providence, while Benedict Arnold of Newport became president of Rhode Island.

There was something else, something symbolic. Williams had always kept the charter in his personal possession. The legislature ordered him to deliver it to Arnold.

Yet most concerning was the fact that this new government, without Williams, was about to feel all the weight of Massachusetts, all the weight of Plymouth, all the weight of Connecticut, and all the weight of New Haven in combination. For the question of the Quakers was on the table.

To build its city upon a hill, to build a New Jerusalem, Massachusetts had always tried to cleanse itself of error and protect itself from contamination and infection. It had proscribed and banished Anglicans, it had proscribed and banished Antinomians, it had proscribed and banished Baptists. It had proscribed and banished any individual who dared challenge its theology, moral code, or political dominion. But no prior challenge represented, in its view and that of the other United Colonies, the vileness and corruption of the Quakers.

The United Colonies, Massachusetts especially, had always feared that Rhode Island would become a sanctuary for the corrupt, a pesthole, and that from it corruption and pestilence would spread to godly plantations. Preventing that had always been part of the justification for territorial ambitions in Rhode Island. Now Quakers had established a refuge in Rhode Island, and they were entering Massachusetts and Plymouth, and to a lesser extent Connecticut, with the deliberate purpose of proselytizing, of drawing people away from Puritan worship.

In Puritan eyes, this threatened to undermine the very foundations of those societies, turning them from godly to at best error-prone and at worst Satanic. If enough people turned to error, they could breach the covenant between Massachusetts and God. God would then send not blessings but curses upon the land.

The United Colonies no longer had to worry about Williams. Williams had no role in the new Rhode Island government. Not long after Arnold became the plantation's president, the commissioners of the United Colonies wrote him a letter, informing him that they could not allow the "the danger that might befale the Christian religion" from the "pernicious opinions" of the Quakers and therefore had passed laws that "all Quakers, Ranters, and such notorious heretiques might be prohibited coming among vs."

However, they feared their efforts would fail since Quakers were "at Rode Island, and entertained there, . . . from whence they may have opportunitie to creep in amongst us, or meanes to infuse and spread their accursed tenates. . . . Noe care [is] too great to preserve us from such a pest, the contagion whereof (if received) . . . were dangerous. . . . We therefore make it our request that you . . . take such order herein that your neighbours may be freed from that danger; that you remove those Quakers that have been receaved, and for the future prohibite theire cominge amongst you."

They closed with a warning: "Wee apprehend that it will bee our dutie seriously to consider what further provision God may call us to make to prevent the aforesaid mischiefe."[18]

If the United Colonies commissioners believed that the new government, without Williams, would yield to them on this matter, they were quickly disappointed.

The reply from Rhode Island came not from the president. It came from him and every officer in the plantation and reflected their unanimity. The reply is significant in itself, and it is more significant because it did not come from Williams.

With great tact, they assured their neighbors, "Our desires are, in all things possible, to pursue after and keepe fayre and loveing correspondence and entercourse with . . . all our countreymen in New England." They stipulated that the government of Rhode Island shared the concern of the United Colonies that Quaker doctrines "tend to very absolute cutting downe and over-turninge relations and civill government among men." They went so far as to promise that the signatories would recommend to the next session of the Rhode Island legislature laws to "prevent the bad effects of theire doctrines and endeavours."

But this promise was carefully worded: any new laws would address "the bad effects" only; they would be limited to civil disruptions, actions, and not to Quaker worship itself. As to that, every officer of the Rhode Island government stated, "[W]e have no law among us, whereby to punish for only declaring by words, &c., theire mindes and understandings concerning the things and ways of God."[19]

The United Colonies did not accept this response. They intensified the pressure, both on Quakers and on Rhode Island. As usual, Massachusetts took the harshest line: it imposed fines of ten shillings for attending a Quaker meeting, forty shillings for speaking at one, and forty shillings for every hour someone allowed a known Quaker to remain in his home. Quakers themselves upon first conviction, if a man, lost an ear, upon second conviction, the other ear; if a woman, severe whippings for first and second offenses; for men and women both, upon third conviction the tongue would be bored with a red-hot iron. Banishment went without saying. Then, one month after cutting off the ear of one Quaker, Massachusetts specifically legislated death for Quakers who returned after banishment.

There could be no mistake about the seriousness of the United Colonies. All of them would treat Quakers with violence. Massachusetts would later hang several Quakers, including Mary Dyer, who had accompanied her husband

and Roger Williams to England. She joined two men on the gallows in 1659, the rope was tied around her neck, and the drum rolled. The men were then hanged. But she was released and warned not to return to Massachusetts. Haunted by her escape, she did return, refused another offer of release in exchange for her promise not to reenter Massachusetts, and was executed.

To Rhode Island, the United Colonies now offered a concession and issued a threat. Each would have enormous consequences. If Rhode Island cooperated, the United Colonies promised to, finally, admit Rhode Island into the alliance as an equal partner. And Rhode Island must yield, "or else" it would be "cut . . . off from all commerce and trade with them."[20]

In the eyes of the United Colonies, virtually every person who moved into Rhode Island was an outcast and an outsider. The colony itself had been called a "sewer," the people there "scumme," so reviled that Massachusetts still refused to sell Rhode Islanders arms and ammunition even while selling them to Indians. Yet the United Colonies was now offering this reviled colony and its people full acceptance if only it cooperated against the Quakers—an indication of how grave the United Colonies considered the threat.

Membership in the United Colonies carried tangible benefits for Rhode Island. For one thing, it meant security. The plantation had trained bands, but they were inadequate to defend against either a concerted Indian attack or the Dutch. The colony had always survived on a knife's edge of concern. Now the alliance was offering to place it under the umbrella of its vastly more powerful military forces.

Economic benefits would be of even greater consequence. Lacking either a coinage or access to English money, citizens of the plantation generally used wampum between themselves and with colonials elsewhere. This gave Boston merchants great advantages. As one Rhode Islander complained, "[I]n effect they make the prices, both of our comodities and theire own also, because wee have not English coyne."[21] Membership in the alliance would bring Rhode Islanders equal treatment and fair dealing; a sudden readjustment in prices favoring Rhode Island would create an economic boom there.

Perhaps even more important was the question of respect—the emotional impact of membership. Those in Rhode Island would be outcasts no longer. They would be rejected no longer. They would be welcomed as equals. This had to have been extraordinarily tempting and extraordinarily gratifying.

Then came the "or else," the threat of having "all commerce and trade with" the United Colonies cut off. This would surely strangle the life out of the colony. Rhode Island was not self-sufficient; it was too small, had too few resources and too few people. It could not attract ships direct from England; virtually all of its trade went through Massachusetts or Plymouth. Isolation would also make the colony a target for the Dutch and for Indians.

The enticement of membership in the United Colonies then would bring enormous economic, military, and psychological benefits. The "or else" was an existential threat.

The full General Assembly now considered Rhode Island's response. Williams was, again, not a member. Any answer was not his answer; he had no authority and no right to participate in the drafting of an answer.

But on March 13, 1658, the assembly responded much as the officers had, tactfully noting "our truly thankful acknowledgements of the honourable care of the honored gentlemen commissioners of the United Colonies, for the peace and welfare of the whole country, as is expressed in their most friendly letter." And it promised to see "to our utmost" that Quakers "perform all duties requisitt" to maintain order in Rhode Island.

The General Assembly was referring to civil order only. It offered nothing more than that. It reminded the United Colonies that "freedom of different consciences, to be protected from inforcements was the principle ground of our Charter, both with respect to our humble sute for it, as also to the true intent of the Honourable and renowned parlement of England in grantinge of the same unto us; which freedom we still prize as the greatest hapines that men can posess in this world." It could not allow "infringement of that chiefe principle in our charter concerning freedom of consciences."

Lest the United Colonies carry out its threats, the assembly also reminded the United Colonies that, thanks to Williams, Rhode Island "is most happily . . . and graciously taken into the protection" of Cromwell. Therefore it intended to present the matter to the single authority which even Massachusetts feared to offend: "the Lord Protector, his highness and government aforesayd."[22]

No government or society in the world offered as much freedom as the colony which Roger Williams had founded. Now, without him, that colony had confronted a threatening power. Refusing enticement and defying a threat, it had stood its ground.

In doing so, the assembly embraced what fifteen years earlier he wrote: "Having bought Truth deare, we must not sell it cheape, nor the least graine of it for the whole World, no not for the saving of Soules, though our owne most precious; least of all for the bitter sweetning of a little vanishing pleasure."[23]

Soul liberty had become popular, if only in one small corner of the English world.

## ❦ CHAPTER 34 ❦

In May 1660, Charles II, who had been eighteen years old when his father was beheaded, was restored to the English throne. The way to the Restoration was opened by Cromwell's death and the widespread discontent which greeted his son Richard's efforts to rule.

Restored with the king was the Anglican Church and High Church practices, including the use of the Book of Common Prayer. But Charles did not seek revenge. He wanted to unify the nation and offered an amnesty. John Milton was freed from prison under its terms. Exempted from the amnesty were only a handful of regicides directly involved in killing his father.

Three regicides fled to New England, first to Boston and then to New Haven. One of them was Edward Whalley, nephew of Lady Joan Barrington and brother to the girl Williams had so long ago hoped to marry. Their presence in New Haven was an open secret. They were never apprehended.

Only thirteen men were executed. All of them were known to Williams, and he had long and intimate personal history with two of them, Hugh Peter and Henry Vane. Peter went to the gallows with John Cook, who had prosecuted the king for treason. Cook was taken first. After hanging him, then cutting him down still alive to disembowel and then behead him, the hangman reportedly taunted Peter by rubbing his bloody hands together, asking, "How do you like this, Mr. Peter, how do you like this work?" Peter replied, "I am not, I thank God, terrified at it, you may do your worst."[1]

He too was hung, cut down alive, disemboweled alive, then beheaded, drawn, and quartered. The crowd enjoyed each twist of the torture. One report said, "[N]ever was a person suffered death so unpitied and whose Execution was the delight of the people. . . . When his head was cut off, and held up aloft upon the end of a Spear, there was such a shout, as if the people of England had acquired a victory."[2]

The regicides' heads were placed on poles on London Bridge.

Vane had played no role in the king's execution and refused afterwards to approve of it, which helped make the king's return easy. He had opposed Cromwell's dictatorship and had rebelled against Cromwell's son. He had done nothing worthy of death. But he had played an important role during the time of the Commonwealth, and he had participated in drafting—and perhaps personally drafted—a petition which called "the people . . . the original of all just power,"[3] a position Williams had articulated before him.

This made him, in the new king's eyes, too dangerous a man to let live, if it was possible to, Charles said, "put him out of the way."[4] So he was taken to the Scilly Islands, out of reach of habeas corpus. Not until his trial did he learn the charge against him: treason not against the dead king, but against the live king. Yet he had done nothing. He was granted one grace: he would only be beheaded and not suffer torture and humiliation.

On the scaffold he tried to read a long speech, denouncing the fact that his arrest and trial violated Magna Carta and affirming he had done no wrong. Trumpets played so no one could hear him, and the lieutenant of the Tower tried to seize his notes but, Samuel Pepys reported, he tore them into pieces "with more choler than could be expected in a dying man. . . . One asked him why he did not pray for the King. He answered, 'Nay,' says he, 'you shall see I can pray for the King: I pray God bless him!' " He was to be beheaded and "had a blister, or issue, upon his neck, which he desired them not hurt . . . and in all things appeared the most resolved man that ever died in that manner, and showed more of heat than cowardize, but yet with all humility and gravity. . . . [A]nd so to the Trinity-house all of us to dinner."[5]

One would have expected Charles II to look unkindly on Williams and Rhode Island, with their close connections to Vane and Cromwell and their democratic government. Indeed, during his reign the Clarendon Code was enacted, reinstating High Church practices and even forbidding any unauthorized worship by five or more people not of one household. But Charles personally favored toleration; raised of a Catholic mother, ever sympathetic to that religion, and a convert to it on his deathbed, he inclined toward those few English who would allow it.

John Clarke had never left England; Rhode Island formally submitted itself to the king and Clarke petitioned him for final resolution of the charter. John Winthrop Jr., governor of Connecticut continuously from 1659 until his death in 1676, was in London to oppose him; Winthrop represented both his colony and his own private interests, for he was a partner in a land company claiming ownership of much of Narragansett territory. But in 1663, the king confirmed what so many of his enemies—Parliament, two Councils of State, and Cromwell—had done. He granted a royal charter to "Rhode Island and Providence Plantations," still the official name of the state today.

In doing so, Charles ignored his own advisers and defied his own Clarendon Code, for the charter stated, "Whereas . . . they have freely declared that it is much on their hearts (if they may be permitted) to hold forth a lively experiment, that a most flourishing civil state may stand and be best maintained, and that among our English subjects, with a ful liberty in religious concernments. . . . No person within the said colony, at any time hereafter, shall be any wise molested, punished, disquieted, or called in question, for any differences in opinion, in matters of religion, who do not actually disturb the civil peace of Our said colony."[6]

Surprisingly, rather than impose a royal governor, the new charter also confirmed that "the form of government established is Democratical." The king's endorsement of a democratic society, even if only as an experiment, was extraordinary—especially given that he, like his father and grandfather, believed in the divine right of kings and that he took power after revolutionaries had beheaded his father. A Royal Commission of three men investigated the remaining territorial disputes between the United Colonies and Rhode Island. One commissioner was Samuel Maverick, the same man who had preceded the Puritans in Boston but had been pushed aside by them. Another was Sir Thomas Temple, an Anglican who had once tried to establish settlements in Nova Scotia. The greatest dispute was land claimed by Connecticut south and west of Warwick. This was Narragansett country. The commissioners, largely because the Narragansetts, at Gorton's urging, had in 1644 submitted themselves to the king, voided any agreements the king had not authorized. This area became "King's County" (Washington County today). Nonetheless, disputes over the border there dragged on.

Once, in Westerly, Rhode Island, on the Connecticut border, the tensions erupted into an armed skirmish. In an attempt to resolve the problem, Williams used personal diplomacy, writing to "my honred deare and ancient friend" John Mason, his comrade-in-arms from the Pequot War. Mason had served as deputy governor of Connecticut and a commissioner of the United Colonies, but he was a friend who had told Williams he longed to see his face once more before he died.[7] Now Williams asked, "What are all the Contentions and Wars of this World about (generally) but for greater Dishes and Bowles of Porridge?"[8] He reminded Mason that God "provided this Countrey and this Corner as a shelter for the poore and persecuted according to their Severall perswasions," and that the king "hath vouchsafed his Royall promise under his Hand and Broad Seale, that no person in this Colony shall be molested or questioned for the Matters of his Conscience to God. . . . Sir we must part with Lands and Lives before we part wth such a Jewell."[9]

The letter convinced Mason to urge Connecticut authorities to abandon all claims to Rhode Island.[10] But when it came to a larger dish of porridge, it would take more than a letter from an ancient soldier to convince Connecticut to desist. It did not abandon its claims, nor did Plymouth. Rhode Island's boundaries were not fixed until 1747, but in the end it won on nearly every point.

Roger Williams returned to government soon after he left, and, as his letter to Mason suggests, for years he remained active as an elder statesman. He performed his last major public act in 1672. By then the Quaker presence in Rhode Island had expanded, particularly in Newport. George Fox, the leader of the sect, was visiting there.

Williams still held Quaker theology in contempt and challenged Fox to a public debate. He explained his reasons: "I had in mine eye the vindicating of this colony for receiving of such persons whom others would not. We suffer for their sakes, and are accounted their abettors. That, therefore, . . . I judged it incumbent upon my spirit and conscience to . . . give a public way against their opinions."[11]

By the time his challenge reached Newport, however, Fox had departed. Three other Quakers accepted the challenge. At age sixty-nine Williams canoed twenty miles to Newport to engage in an all-day debate with all three.

The debate lasted nearly ten hours. It moved no one, for audience members had already formed their opinions. And in Newport, the audience was hostile. His opponents interrupted him constantly. When he tried to make a point, audience members mocked him, shouting, "Old man! Old man!"

Perhaps what frustrated and enraged Williams the most was that these

Quakers had the same monstrous partiality to their own views that Cotton had. " 'I was commanded this work from heaven,' " he quoted Quakers as saying, to justify their position in unanswerable fashion. But he asked, "Why should not this argument be good for me and others as well as the Quakers?"

A second day of debate took place in Providence; the audience had fewer Quakers but the result was the same. There was no movement. His last book was *George Fox Digg'd Out of His Burrowes,* which recounted the exchanges. (Indication of how fairly Williams represented his opponents' views is that the Quaker rebuttal did not accuse him of misquoting them.)

For confronting the Quakers, Massachusetts for the first and only time publicly congratulated him. The Bay had by then made good its threats against Quakers. It had by then hanged four Quakers on Boston Common; drummers had marched them to the gallows, beating a constant rat-tat-tat so nothing they said could be heard. The executions ended only when Charles II sent orders forbidding them.

Williams may well have despised the Quakers as much as did Massachusetts clergy and magistrates. But he sought no law to constrain them, much less did he seek to have them killed. Instead, he debated them.

He ever remained true to his statement on the very first page of *The Bloudy Tenent:* "It is the will and command of God, that since the comming of his Sonne the Lord Jesus, a permission of the most Paganish, Jewish, Turkish, or Antichristian consciences and worships, bee granted in all Nations and Countries: and they are onely to bee fought against with that *Sword* which is onely in Soule matters able to *conquer,* to wit the *Sword of Gods Spirit,* the *Word* of God."[12]

Roger Williams lived another decade. He continued his life of ideas, continued exchanging books with John Winthrop Jr. and others. Williams would cite in a single letter Erasmus, Luther, and Calvin, quote Latin phrases, place current events in the context of history, analyze the latest news of Indians. Winthrop would reply in kind, thanking him "for that kindnesse, and that little volume of poetry therewh. Pictoribus atque Poetis, quid libet audendi semper fuit aequa potestas ["To poets and painters alike there has always been a capacity for daring anything," from Horace, *De Arte Poetica* IX]. Yours according to ancient friendship. Semper idem [Always the same]."[13]

He continued his preaching, usually in Narragansett country, particularly in the area where he had once had his trading post. When Winthrop, who owned land in the vicinity, offered to send a minister to the area, one of his partners told him it was unnecessary, for "Mr Williams doeth exaceys [exercise] amongst us and sayeth he will contuny itt: he precheth well and abell, and much peopell comes to here him to theyr good satisfacion."[14]

Williams also continued his involvement in government; as late as 1677 he was elected to the legislature but, as Coke once did, he declined to serve, pleading infirmity. Williams did, however, remain active in the town of Providence. Approaching eighty years of age, he addressed it in two public letters.

Both were brief, reproachful, and to the point. Both reflected his years with Coke and his deep understanding of power, of the importance of procedure, and of the law itself. As in the Chasmore controversy, one letter "Protest[ed] agnst the Legalitie or Lawfullnes of this abovesaid Meeting as not being Lawfully Called . . . at three dayes warning: and Consequently . . . all Acts and Orders" made were "illegal, factious, and [upon] dangerous Foundation."[15]

The next letter spoke of government itself and his understanding of the rights and responsibilities of individuals. He wrote it after a town meeting erupted into rancorous shouting over "Rates," i.e., taxes, and he addressed the stated refusal of some to pay. "Mankind can not keepe together without some Government," he said. "One of these 2 great lawes in the World must prevaile, either that of Judges and Justices of peace, in courts of peace: Or the Law of Arms, the Sword and Bloud. . . . No Govrment is maintaind without Tribute Custome, Rates Taxes &c." Those in Providence, he reminded his readers, had freedom, greater freedom than in "the Whole World." Every man had a vote and thus "hath a hand in making the Rates by himselfe or his Deputies." It was irresponsible and utter selfishness to refuse to pay one's taxes. To do so was another example of monstrous partiality, for "if one [refused] why not more?" If freemen did not meet their responsibilities, then came anarchy. He was ever for freedom, but ever also the enemy of anarchy.

He closed, "Your old unworthy Srvant. Roger Williams."[16]

These two letters to the town dealt only with civil matters; in that, they complement one of his earliest letters to the elder Winthrop, a letter which dealt with the soul. He always saw the soul as uncertain searcher, and it was always the difficulty in finding the truth which underlay his revulsion at those who proclaimed certainty, whose monstrous partiality left no room for the possibility of their own error.

He wrote the letter in response to several questions Winthrop asked him. Possibly Winthrop desired an explanation of what Williams had meant in saying, *I desire not to sleep in securitie and dreame of a Nest wch no hand can reach. I can not but expect changes, yet dare I not despise a Libertie, wch the Lord seemeth to offer me if for mine owne or others peace.*

Winthrop's questions included, "What have you gayned by your new-found practices &c.?" and, "From what spirit and to what end do you drive?"

To the first, Williams conceded, "I confess my Gaines cast up in mans Exchange are Losse of friends, esteeme, maintenance, etc." But he went on to say he hoped to gain "the excellencie of the knowledge of Christ Jesus my Lord." Later in the letter he spoke for freedom in saying "your case is the worst by farr: because . . . your very Judgment and Conscience leads you to Smite and beate your fellow Servants, expell them [from] your Coastes &c."

To the second query, he answered, "Whether the Spirit of Christ Jesus, for whose visible Kingdome and Ordinances I witnes etc. or the spirit of Antichrist . . . doe drive me, let the Father of Spirits be pleased to Search."

Even then, though he had sacrificed everything for his beliefs, he recognized the possibility of his own error, and of all human error. For he concluded, "I hope you will finde that as you Say you doe, I allso seeke Jesus who was nayled to the Gallowes."[17]

Roger Williams last played a major public role in 1675 and 1676, during King Philip's War, the bloodiest of all the New England Indian wars.

King Philip was sachem of the Wampanoags in Plymouth. Watching all New England tribes grow weaker by the day, and the English stronger, Philip sought to bring all the tribes into an alliance against the English. The Pequot had attempted this so many decades before, when Williams had sat in a war council, the only white among thousands of Indians, and convinced the Narragansetts not to join. The Pequot had been crushed; the tribe had vanished from the earth. Seven years later, still many decades ago, the United Colonies had accused Miantonomi of attempting to do the same; for this they had set Uncas to murder him. But Philip succeeded; he forged an alliance of several tribes and launched a war of extermination. In the end, of course, it was the Indians who were all but exterminated, yet his success in killing and putting fire to the English in New England showed how dangerous those earlier alliances would have been, when Indians were far stronger and the English far weaker.

As usual, Williams tried to keep the Narragansetts out of this war. This time he failed. Also as usual, he conveyed intelligence to several governors and military leaders of the United Colonies.

In one of the last acts of the war, Indians attacked Providence itself. The residents, those who had not fled, retreated to fortified houses, their musket fire keeping the attackers at bay. But they could not protect the town. Providence then had 120 houses; by one report only thirty survived. The rest burned.

With the town in flames, with Indians still whooping in triumph, the assault against the fortified buildings ceased. An odd peace settled over the town. The Indians shouted that they wanted to speak with Williams. They wanted him to come unarmed, as they promised to do, to a point at the southern tip of the settlement in present Fox Point. He later recounted to his brother, "I Heard them ask for me." He and a second man decided to go out. "The Towne cried out to us not to Ventur. My Sonns came crying aftr me."

The second man changed his mind and returned to the fortification. But Williams felt he had no choice. "My Heart to God and Countrie forced me to go on." At the edge of town he found "about 1500" warriors from several tribes. "I asked them Whither they were bound. They said to all the Towns about Plimoath. . . . I asked them Why they assaulted us With burning and Killing who ever were Neighbours to them. . . . This House of mine now burning before mine Eyes hath Lodged kindly some Thousands of You."

They said, "[W]e were their Enemies Joyned with Masathusets, and Plimoth."

Williams disputed that: "nither Wee nor this Colloney had acted Hostilitie against them. I told them they were all this while Killing and burning themselves Who had forgot they were Mankind, and ran about the Countrie like Wolves tearing, and Devouring the Innocent."

They replied, "You have driven us out of our own Countrie and then pursued us to our Great Miserie, and Your Own, and we are Forced to live upon you."

"I again offered my Ser[vices] In A Way of peas. . . . I told them Planting time was a coming for them and Us."

The Indian commander told him they would talk peace "a month hence after we have bin on Plimouth Side."[18] Williams knew that attacking Plymouth would be suicidal at this late point of the war. As the Indians and Williams talked on, it seemed that they all understood this, that they would not be coming back to talk peace. Williams reported, "They Confessed they were in A Strang Way . . . [but] we had forced them to it."[19]

"We parted and they were so Civill that they calld after me and bid me not goe bear the Burned Houses for there might be Indians [who] might mischiefe me, but goes by the Water Side."

And so they left one another. The Indians would not return to talk peace. There would be no talk at all, only English victory. The Narragansetts, like all the tribes who participated in this war, would be nearly wiped out.

A few weeks later a wounded Indian came out of the forest at the edge of the ruined Providence seeking mercy. According to the town records, "Capt. Roger Wms. Caused ye Drum to be beat, ye Town Councell & Councell of War called." The town was in no merciful mood. "[Y]e Councell of War gave sentence & he was shot to death, to ye great satisfaction of ye Towne."[20]

Williams's own home had been burned in the attack, and its loss plunged him into poverty. Connecticut voted him £10 and a letter of appreciation. Massachusetts offered to lift his banishment so long as he was "not disseminating and venting any of his different opinions." He stayed in Providence, in poverty. Although the destruction of his home made these years difficult, his last surviving letter, written at a time he felt his mortality—describing himself as "old and weake and bruised . . . and lameness on both my feete"[21]—showed no bitterness toward Indians. Far from it. He recalled, "When the hearts of my countrymen and friends and brethren failed me, [God's] infinite wisdom and merits stirred up the barbarous heart of Canonicus to love me as his son to his last gasp, by which means I had not only Miantonomo and all the lowest sachems my friends, but . . . my enjouyment of . . . Providence itself, and all the other lands I procured . . . and I never denied him or Miantonomo whatever they desired of me as to goods or gifts or use of my boats or pinnace, and the travels of my own person, day and night, which, though men know not, nor care to know, yet the all-seeing Eye hath seen it, and his all-powerful hand hath helped me, Blessed be his holy name to eternity."[22]

Decades earlier he had told Winthrop, *I have not yet turned Indian.* He still had not. But neither was he anymore English. He was an American.

# ❧ AFTERWORD ❧

This book was supposed to be about the home front in World War I, culminating in the events of 1919, the most tumultuous peacetime year in American history. My plan was to use several major figures as narrative vehicles to explore the enormous changes then occurring in the country. One of those figures was Billy Sunday, the first evangelist to visit big cities, the model for Sinclair Lewis's *Elmer Gantry,* and a man who did not hesitate to inject himself into politics. I intended to use him to investigate the role of religion in American public life as part of a larger story, but the more I thought about it, the more I was drawn to that subject itself, and specifically to the source of the debate over it, to the debate's origin.

That origin was the conflict between John Winthrop and Roger Williams and between two visions: the one embodied in Winthrop's city on a hill with its authoritative and theocentric state, the other in Williams's call for utter separation of church and state and individual rights. The First Amendment did not come from any abstruse theory. It came from history. This book has detailed an important part of that history.

King James died in 1625, Sir Edward Coke in 1634, King Charles and Winthrop in 1649, and Williams in 1683. Nonetheless, the disputes which this book describes, and I hope illuminates, could not be more relevant today.

King James used "reason of state" to justify expanding state power in a time of terrorism. In the Justice Department of George W. Bush, John Yoo essentially repeated the arguments made by James's lawyers and asserted not only that in war the president could ignore congressional mandates but that, in confronting terrorism, sections of the U.S. Constitution prohibiting such things as warrantless searches "would *not* apply."[1] The italics are Yoo's.

By contrast, Coke fought to establish the power of habeas corpus and declared, "Reason of state lames Magna Carta," and "Every Englishman's home is as his castle." The question of whether the end of national security justifies extraconstitutional means is as alive now as it was four hundred years ago.

In even more obvious ways, nearly every day brings a new conflict over defining the proper spheres of church and state.

When Roger Williams died, his fellow citizens in Providence marked his death with "a considerable parade" and "guns fired over his grave."[2] Throughout the rest of New England, he was not missed. That is hardly surprising, since from his very arrival in America he had ignited antagonism and controversy. He and his legacy have remained controversial ever since.

Williams created the first government in the world which broke church and state apart. Because those who had linked the two believed that political authority came from God, this led to a fission whose fallout included the new and equally explosive concept that the state derives its authority from and remains subject to its citizens.

Given the importance of both these ideas and Williams's centrality to their development and spread, it is unremarkable that historians have demonstrated intense interest in him. Although his is not a household name, academics in several fields have made him certainly one of the very most studied figures of pre-Revolutionary America. Nor is it surprising, given the controversy in which he engaged, that academics have formed no consensus about him.

Some academics have denigrated his role. A few do not even recognize Williams for achieving much of anything because, they argue, his success in Rhode Island was isolated. William McLoughlin, for instance, credits religious toleration not to him but to Baptists who, particularly in the 1700s, endured persecution in other colonies; he calls Williams only a "magnificent failure . . . because of the inability of Rhode Islanders to shape, by example or evangelism, the destiny either of New England or any of the other colonies."[3]

But Rhode Island did shape other colonies. One example: after granting Rhode Island its charter, Charles II copied the concept and some of the language on religious freedom—no one was to be "molested, punished, or disquieted or called in question" for their religion—from it into the charters of New Jersey and Carolina, even while establishing the Anglican Church there.

Others have argued that Williams's justifications for religious freedom derived too much from Scripture, implying that they therefore had less value than secular thought. Emil Oberholzer concluded, "Williams was no forerunner of the Enlightenment of Jefferson. When Jefferson advocated religious liberty, he did it as a child of the Enlightenment; his motive was political and social. With Williams, the child of a theological age, the motive was wholly religious."[4] Alan Simpson asserted, "There is no trace whatever in Roger Williams of that gradual secularization of interest which is a marked feature in the history of the Levellers. . . . There is every evidence that his principle of religious liberty was derived both formally and emotionally from his sense of what was due to God."[5]

That view is hard to reconcile with many of Williams's positions, such as that a church was "like unto a Corporation, Society, or Company of East-Indie or Turkie-Merchants" within but distinct from the larger society.

Most academics have viewed Williams more generously than these critics. Even Perry Miller, who dismissed Williams's analysis as dependent entirely upon his typological interpretation of the Bible and placed him exclusively in the religious sphere, conceded, "For the subsequent history of the United States, Roger Williams possesses one indubitable importance: that he stands at the beginning of it. Just as some great experience in the youth of a person is ever afterward a determinant of his personality, so the American character has been molded by the fact that in the first years of colonization there arose this prophet of religious liberty. . . . [A]s a figure and a reputation he was always there to remind Americans that no other conclusion but absolute religious freedom was feasible in this society."[6] And Miller admired him as "an explorer into the dark places, of the very nature of freedom."[7]

Others credited Williams with infinitely more. They argued that he played a direct role in separating church and state in the United States, and that he recognized the full implications of his position and of his view of individual rights vis-à-vis the state—i.e., that he understood the meaning of freedom. James Ernst went so far as to assert, "His theory of religious liberty came out of his unique theory of the individual and the state."[8] Vernon Parrington called Williams "primarily a political philosopher rather than a theologian . . . , one of the notable democratic thinkers that the English race has produced."[9] Parrington concluded that he was "a forerunner of Locke and the natural rights school" as well as of Benjamin Franklin, Thomas Paine, and Thomas Jefferson, and stated that his "theory of the commonwealth must be reckoned the richest contribution of Puritanism to American political thought."[10]

Edmund Morgan, perhaps the best of America's colonial historians, noted that Williams "wrote most often, and most effectively, most significantly about civil government."[11] Morgan pointed out that Williams concerned himself with theology only when theology became intertwined with institutions, be those institutions the Massachusetts magistracy or Laud's High Commission. Morgan also recognized that Williams had "the rare simplicity of an original mind. . . . [H]e put human society in new perspective; and he demolished, for anyone who accepted his premises, some of the assumptions that encumbered the statesmen of the day and still haunt our own."[12] Finally, Morgan stated that if Williams had an intellectual successor it was Thoreau, although Williams had more use for government than did Thoreau.

Outside the United States, Williams has often been viewed with enormous respect. As previously noted, he is one of only ten men honored in Geneva's Reformation Wall for their contribution to the Reformation. The German legal philosopher Georg Jellinek argued that he was a major contributor to the ideals emerging from the French Revolution: "What has been held to be a work of the [French] Revolution was in reality a fruit of the Reformation and its struggles. Its first apostle was not Lafayette, but Roger Williams."[13] Another European scholar, Michel Freund, called Williams "the ripest fruit of the Renaissance and the Reformation movements."[14] Those are just some indicators of that respect.

Only a few of the generation of Jefferson and Madison read Williams, but they learned the English history which Williams had lived through and helped make. They did read Coke and revered common law, and many American lawyers, including several members of the Constitutional Convention, studied at the Inns of Court.[15] And there are four routes through which Williams influenced the generation of the Founding Fathers.

First, Williams was a symbol. He symbolized both religious and political liberty. He was not forgettable. His place at the very beginning of American history and the positions he argued for were, as Miller said, "always there to remind Americans that no other conclusion but absolute religious freedom was feasible in this society."

Second, two publications which appeared on the eve of or during the Revolution reminded Jefferson's generation of that. Both reprinted Williams's "Ship of State" letter and both made much of the question of religious and political freedom. The lesser work was by Stephen Hopkins. It was probably not read beyond New England, but he personally carried his views outside it, including to Philadelphia where he signed the Declaration of Independence.

The second work, by Isaac Backus, was widely read. One of the founders in 1764 of Rhode Island College—now Brown University—which came into being as a Baptist school committed to free inquiry, Backus incorporated a biography of Williams into a larger history of the Baptists in New England. This book was in essence a history of the struggle for religious freedom. At the same time that American colonies were fighting a war for their own freedom, Backus thus brought Williams and his views on freedom to the fore, calling him "[t]he first founder and supporter of any truly civil government upon earth."[16]

For all that Backus said of Williams, to make the case for religious liberty he leaned less upon Williams than upon John Locke, which brings up the third route of Williams's influence—through his impact on thought in revolutionary England, which in turn influenced Americans. Much of this influence did flow through Locke. The prominent religious historian Winthrop Hudson concluded, "The parallels with the thought of Roger Williams are so close that it is not entirely implausible conjecture to suggest that Locke's major contribution may have been to reduce the rambling, lengthy, incoherent exposition of the New England 'firebrand' to orderly, abbreviated, and coherent form. . . . [I]t is impossible to discover a single significant difference between the argument set forth by Williams and later advanced by Locke. They scarcely differ even in the details of its practical application."[17] Similarly, David Little determined that on the question of religious toleration "Locke's ideas are . . . simply restatements of the central arguments in favor of freedom of conscience developed by Roger Williams in the middle of the seventeenth century, when Locke's opinions on these subjects were being shaped."[18]

That is why W. K. Jordan, in his classic multivolume study *The Development of Religious Toleration in England*, could conclude that not Locke's but Williams's "carefully reasoned argument for the complete dissociation of church and State . . . may be regarded as the most important contribution made during the [seventeenth] century in this significant area of political thought. No contemporary figure could command such attention as this remarkable and accomplished leader."[19]

Williams and Locke differed only in that Williams believed Catholics and atheists deserved the same rights to freedom of conscience as others, and Locke excluded them because he feared they would undermine the civil state. Catholics gave themselves, he wrote, to "the service of another prince," hence were unreliable (he later retreated somewhat from this position), and Locke did not believe that atheists would honor a moral code. Locke in turn exerted tremendous and oft-acknowledged influence on the thinking of the entire generation of Founding Fathers and particularly on Jefferson and Madison.

Williams's final route of influence on Jefferson's generation came, ironically, through the restoration of Charles II to the throne. As noted above, he not only confirmed Rhode Island's charter with its separation of church and state, but he also used language from Rhode Island's charter to guarantee freedom of conscience in the new colonies of Carolina and New Jersey, although he established the Church of England there. Such freedom of conscience was not then available in England.

Thus Williams's ideas entered America's bloodstream.

American thinking about freedom did not, of course, end with Jefferson's generation. It continued, and still continues, to evolve. And in the decades and centuries since Jefferson, Americans have used Williams as they have used other historical figures: for their own purposes. Gradually Williams began to inform, directly and not merely through Locke, American views on liberty. To many, particularly on the left, Williams came to represent an ideal.

In 1834 George Bancroft, one of America's first great historians, made a hero of Williams, declaring him the first person "to assert in its plenitude the doctrine of the liberty of conscience, the equality of opinions before the law."[20] That same year one of the first and best biographies of Williams appeared. In it James Knowles wrote that a "better knowledge of the principles of Roger Williams will have a salutary tendency . . . [because] [t]he position in which this country is placed, as the great exemplar of civil and religious liberty, makes it inexpressibly important, that the true principles on which this liberty rests, should be thoroughly understood." The United States would demonstrate to the world, a world then undecided whether democracy could work, "that man can govern himself. . . . If civil liberty fail here, or if religion be overwhelmed with error or worldliness, the great cause of human happiness will suffer a disastrous check."[21] In 1860, on the eve of America's Civil War and as abolitionists attempted to rally the north, Francis Wayland, president of Brown University, injected Williams into contemporary debate when he wrote that the Pilgrims and Puritans had sought liberty for themselves in coming to America. But Williams sought "liberty for humanity."[22]

Rhode Island itself, at least historically, was always willing to go its own way. It declared independence from England on May 4, 1776, two months before the rest of the colonies. And the statue atop the state capitol represents not any person but an idea; it is of the Independent Man.

I started this book in order to examine the origins of the debate over the role of religion in public life. I wanted to understand how Winthrop and the Puritans envisioned their city upon a hill and what they intended to accomplish. I wanted to understand Williams's objections. I did not then know anything about Coke's influence on him, much less Bacon's. I did not then realize how intimately connected—the interplay between—the question of religion's role was to the debate over individual rights. Particularly since the rise of Christian conservatives beginning in the 1970s, the debate over these issues has sounded much like the one Williams first engaged in with Winthrop and Cotton in Massachusetts. That has never been more true than in 2012 when, almost simultaneously with the publication of this book, every Republican candidate for president—even libertarian-minded Ron Paul—embraced the idea that the United States was a Christian nation. Rick Santorum went furthest, sounding much like Winthrop. Four hundred years ago Winthrop declared his belief in "a liberty to do only that which is good," to be maintained by "subjection to authority." As I write this, a few months ago, Santorum said, "[L]ibery is not what you want to do, but what you ought to do. That's what liberty really is about," and, "The founders said we have the right to happiness. Well, happiness as defined at the time of our founders . . . wasn't doing what you want to do, it isn't doing things that please you. . . . Happiness at the time of our founders was to do the moral, right thing . . . doing God's will in your life."²³

Cultural commentators and anthropologists speak of the "myths" which inform and define a society. But it is no myth that the Puritans who founded Massachusetts came to build a Christian country, a city on a hill that would shine for all the world to see. They believed themselves and this nation to be chosen and blessed by God. That belief is not myth but reality.

But it is also not myth but reality that those Puritans fled England because they would not submit to forced prayer: they would not submit to the use of the Book of Common Prayer. They would not even sit silently as nonpartici- pants while others listened to prayers from it.

It is also not myth but reality that another informing principle runs like a great river through American history and culture. That principle was first articulated when Roger Williams declared that the state must not enforce those of the Ten Commandments which defined the relationship between humanity and God. It matured when he further separated himself from the dominant view of the day and declared a citizenry "distinct from the government set up. . . . [S]uch governments as are by them erected and established have no more power, nor for longer time, than the civil power or people consenting and agreeing shall betrust them with."[24]

And it is not myth but reality that the U.S. Constitution is an entirely secular document, with no reference to any entity that can be considered divine. It does ask for a blessing, but only for "the blessings of liberty." Then it prohibits a religious test for office, equates an "affirmation" with an "oath," and, in the First Amendment, it establishes absolute religious freedom—the first freedom, the freedom to think—and its corollary, the freedom to express thought. They understood that infringing upon that in any way limited not only religious freedom but *all* freedom. As Justice Robert Jackson wrote, "This freedom was first in the Bill of Rights because it was first in the forefathers' minds; it was set forth in absolute terms, and its strength is its rigidity."

In 1797, the Senate explicitly separated government from religion when it unanimously approved a treaty drafted under George Washington and signed by John Adams, which stated, "The government of the United States is not in any sense founded on the Christian Religion."

If before his time, Roger Williams was not entirely a man out of time. In most ways, he did still belong to the seventeenth century, and to Puritans in that century. Yet he was also one of the most remarkable men of his century.

With absolute faith in the Bible, with absolute faith in his own interpretation of it, he nonetheless believed it "monstrous" to compel another person to believe what he or anyone else believed, or to compel conformity to his or anyone else's beliefs. His enemies called him a "firebrand." They feared the conflagration free thought might ignite. They lacked faith in the "Sword of God's Word." They feared being challenged, and having their world, under challenge, disintegrate. They feared the chaos of freedom, and they feared the loneliness of it.

Williams embraced all that. Freedom, he believed, was worth it, worth his life and worth far more than his life. The courage to risk one's life is a rare commodity, but not so rare that such courage does not show itself on many battlefields. Roger Williams, this devout Puritan, this man of faith who loved God, was willing to risk more than his life. For of all the remarkable things he said, the most remarkable was this: "Having bought Truth deare, we must not sell it cheape, nor the least graine of it for the whole World, no not for the saving of Soules, though our owne most precious."

For he knew that to believe in freedom and liberty required faith in the freedom of thought, of conscience. And that was soul liberty.

# Acknowledgments

For all my other books I have had long lists of people to thank. For this book the list is relatively short. The reason: for earlier books I spent much time in archives, and archivists were generous with their advice and time. Much to my surprise, for this book I spent relatively little time in archives because nearly everything which still survives from the seventeenth century has been transcribed and published. All of Roger Williams's surviving published work and correspondence sits on bookshelves in my office. I did go to archives to read enough of the original correspondence in his and others' hands to validate that the transcriptions were reliable. After doing that, I considered the transcriptions primary sources.

The fact that the list of people to thank is shorter for this book than for my earlier ones certainly does not mean those who helped me are any less important. Let me start by thanking those who read part of my manuscript, with the usual disclaimers that they are absolved from responsibility for any problems that remain in the book. For that matter, they are absolved from any suggestion that they agree with everything (or anything?) that's in it. But they devoted quite a bit of time, and I much appreciate the efforts of Edmund Morgan, Glenn LaFantasie, and Sylvia Frey. I also want to thank Larry Powell for offering his help in convincing Morgan, the preeminent historian of this period, to read the manuscript. Glenn LaFantasie still knows as much about Williams as anyone, even though he himself has switched fields. And Sylvia Frey was one of the first people I spoke to when I started the book, and she helped guide my initial research.

The entire staff of Tulane's Rudoph Matas Medical Library has been extraordinarily gracious and helpful during the course of this book, starting with Sue Dorsey, Mary Holt, Millie Moore, and especially the people in Interlibrary

Loan, Josie Patton and Isabel Altamirano. (One may ask why the medical library, but that's too long a story.)

I would like to thank the archivists at the John Carter Brown Library of Brown University, especially former director Norman Fiering. This library is the largest repository in the world of early writings and maps about the Americas, and it sits in a mausoleum-like building on the campus green. I might add that there is a legend that any undergraduate who entered that library would never graduate; I went to Brown and did not challenge that legend, so I was very happy to finally go inside.

I thank Pat Bowdish for alerting me to some letters of her ancestor William Harris. And the people at the Rhode Island Historical Society were also helpful whenever I visited there, as were those at the Massachusetts Historical Society.

Everyone at Viking seemed understanding about the delay in getting them the book. They never put any pressure on me to hurry it. Maggie Riggs and Roland Ottewell did more probably than their job description (this is the first time I've ever acknowledged a copy editor; generally my relationship with copy editors is a hostile one). Thanks also to Gabriel DeVries, Donald Homolka, John Jusino, and Lisa Thornbloom for their close reading of the material and to Barbara Campo for her thoughtful suggestions and meticulous attention to detail and for shepherding the book to completion. No one at my publisher has put more effort into this book than Yen Cheong, and I thank her for it; also, thanks to Meghan Fallon. Most important at Viking, of course, is my editor Wendy Wolf. She and I have spent many years together at this point. It was quite evident that she put in considerably more effort on this manuscript than editors normally do. She's been committed to this book, and she edits the old-fashioned way. She works at it. And I appreciate it.

Finally, I want to thank my wife, Margaret Anne Hudgins. When I first met her one of her friends remarked, "She is so brilliant you want to follow her around with a notebook and write down everything she says." That was an astute assessment. No one ever said that about me, and never will. She is a great reader and is particularly good when she offers insights into character which would otherwise escape me. In addition to Margaret Anne, I of course also need to thank the beloved cousins and the travelers whose love and support was always there for me. My wife and they make it all worthwhile.

# *Notes*

## Prologue

1. Edward Coke, *Third Institute*, 162.
2. Henry Dexter, "As to Roger Williams, and his 'banishment' from Massachusetts Plantation . . . : a monograph" (Boston: Congregational Publishing Society, Franklin Press, 1876), 88. See also John Quincy Adams, "Address Before the Massachusetts Historical Society," 1843, in *Proceedings of the Massachusetts Historical Society* 2 (1835–1855) (Boston: The Society, 1880).

## PART I: THE LAW

### Chapter 1

1. Alan Simpson, *Puritanism in Old and New England* (Chicago: University of Chicago Press, 1955), 61.
2. J. E. Neale, *Elizabeth I and Her Parliaments, 1584–1601* (New York: St. Martin's Press, 1958), 1:42.
3. Catherine Drinker Bowen, *The Lion and the Throne: The Life and Times of Sir Edward Coke, 1552–1634* (New York: Little, Brown, 1990 [1957]), 100.
4. Roger Lockyer, *The Early Stuarts: A Political History of England, 1603–1642* (London and New York: Longman, 1989), 283.
5. William Cobbett, *Cobbett's Complete Collection of State Trials and Proceedings for High Treason and Other Crimes and Misdemeanors from the Earliest Period to the Present Time*, ed. Thomas Bayley Howell (London: T. C. Hansard, 1809), 2:183.
6. Mark Kishlansky, *A Monarchy Transformed: Britain, 1603–1714* (New York: Penguin, 1997), 72–73.
7. Ernest Law, *History of Hampton Court* (London: Bell and Sons, 1888), 45.
8. Kishlansky, *A Monarchy Transformed*, 72–73.
9. Law, *History of Hampton Court*, 40.
10. Ibid., 45. The italics are in the original.
11. Joseph R. Tanner, ed., *Constitutional Documents from the Reign of James I, 1603–1625* (London and New York: Cambridge University Press, 1960), 55.
12. Quoted in Lockyer, *The Early Stuarts*, 96.
13. Larzer Ziff, *The Career of John Cotton: Puritanism and the American Experience* (Princeton, NJ: Princeton University Press, 1962), 34.
14. Conrad Russell, *The Crisis of Parliaments* (Oxford: Oxford University Press, 1971), 258.
15. "The House of Stuart: James I and VI, 1603–1625," http://www.englishmonarchs.co.uk/stuart.htm.
16. Quoted in Roger Lockyer, *Buckingham: The Life and Political Career of George Villiers, First Duke of Buckingham, 1592–1628* (London and New York: Longman, 1981), 20.
17. Quoted in Bowen, *The Lion and the Throne*, 394.
18. Numerous sources, including http://internetshakespeare.uvic.ca/Library/SLT/history/james.html.
19. Quoted in Lockyer, *Buckingham*, 22.
20. Quoted in Kishlansky, *A Monarchy Transformed*, 86.
21. Alan Stewart, *The Cradle King: James VI & I, the First Monarch of a United Great Britain* (New York: St. Martin's, 2003), 243.
22. Jonathan Scott, *England's Troubles: Seventeenth-Century English Political Thought in European Context* (Cambridge: Cambridge University Press, 2000), 83.
23. Quoted in Kishlansky, *A Monarchy Transformed*, 34.

24. Quoted in Lockyer, *The Early Stuarts*, 37.
25. http://history.wisc.edu/sommerville/367/mocketGK.htm.
26. William Stubbs, *The Constitutional History of England* (Oxford: Oxford University Press, 1897), 1:291, 300.
27. Ibid., 1:574.
28. Ibid., 2:332.
29. Ibid., 2:331.
30. F. W. Maitland, *The Constitutional History of England* (Cambridge: Cambridge University Press, 1968 [1908]), 188; for a full discussion, see W. S. Holdsworth, *A History of English Law*, 5th ed. (London: Methuen, 1942), 3:458–469.
31. Maitland, *The Constitutional History of England*, 17.

## Chapter 2

1. Roger Williams to Mrs. Anne Sadleir, ca. April 1652, in *The Correspondence of Roger Williams*, ed. Glenn W. LaFantasie (Hanover, NH, and London: Brown University Press, 1988), vol. 1.
2. Ibid.
3. Sir Edward Coke, *The Selected Writings of Sir Edward Coke*, ed. Steve Sheppard (Indianapolis: Liberty Fund, 2003), Bonham's case, 1:264.
4. The Online Library of Liberty, http://oll.libertyfund.org. The quotation is found at http://oll.libertyfund.org/?option=com_staticxt&staticfile=show.php%3Ftitle=678&chapter=53274&layout=html&Itemid=27.
5. Allen D. Boyer, *Sir Edward Coke and the Elizabethan Age* (Stanford, CA: Stanford University Press, 2003), 196.
6. Catherine Drinker Bowen, *The Lion and the Throne: The Life and Times of Sir Edward Coke, 1552–1634* (New York: Little, Brown, 1990 [1957]), 417, 411.
7. Quoted in Boyer, *Sir Edward Coke and the Elizabethan Age*, 192.
8. Quoted in Charles Gray, "Reason, Authority, and Imagination: The Jurisprudence of Sir Edward Coke," in *Culture and Politics from Puritanism to the Enlightenment*, ed. Perez Zagorin (Berkeley: University of California Press, 1980), 26.
9. Bowen, *The Lion and the Throne*, 108.
10. F. W. Maitland, *The Constitutional History of England* (Cambridge: Cambridge University Press, 1968 [1908]), 115.
11. Quoted in Roger Lockyer, *The Early Stuarts: A Political History of England, 1603–1642* (London and New York: Longman, 1989), 60.
12. Bowen, *The Lion and the Throne*, 300.
13. Pauline Croft, *King James* (London: Palgrave MacMillan, 2003), 17.
14. Quoted in Roland Usher, "James I and Edward Coke," *English Historical Review* 18, no. 72 (1903): 671.
15. The following account of this meeting synthesizes several sources: Coke's own, in his *Reports*, 12:65, and letters or notes from three others present: John Hercy, Sir Fare Boswell, and Sir Julius Caesar; see also Coke, *Selected Writings of Sir Edward Coke*, "Prohibitions del Roy," vol. 1, paragraph 1280 (from Coke, *Reports, Part XII*, 65); Usher, "James I and Edward Coke," 664–676. Usher agrees on the essential points here but believes Coke's own version exaggerates his defiance.
16. Coke, *Reports*, Edwards case, 13:9–12, quoted in Bowen, *The Lion and the Throne*, 310.
17. J. H. Hexter, "Property, Monopoly, and Shakepeare's *Richard II*," in Zagorin, ed., *Culture and Politics from Puritanism to the Enlightenment*, 12.
18. Quoted in Alden T. Vaughan and Virginia Mason Vaughan, "England's 'Others' in the Old and New Worlds," in *The World of John Winthrop: Essays on England and New England, 1588–1649*, eds. Francis Bremer and Lynn Botelho, *Massachusetts Historical Society Studies in American History and Culture* 9 (Boston: Massachusetts Historical Society, 2005).
19. Coke, *Reports*, 12:74; see also Coke, *Selected Writings*, vol. 1, paragraph 1311.
20. Conrad Russell, *The Crisis of Parliaments* (Oxford: Oxford University Press, 1971), 286.

## Chapter 3

1. Perez Zagorin, *Francis Bacon* (Princeton, NJ: Princeton University Press, 1998), 4.
2. Ibid., 162.
3. Ibid., 132.

4. Ibid., 144, 142.
5. Catherine Drinker Bowen, *The Lion and the Throne: The Life and Times of Sir Edward Coke, 1552–1634* (New York: Little, Brown, 1990 [1957]), 77.
6. Quoted in Roger Lockyer, *The Early Stuarts: A Political History of England, 1603–1642* (London and New York: Longman, 1989), 255.
7. Francis Bacon, "Sir Francis Bacon His Apologie, In Certaine Imputations, Concerning the Late Earle of Essex," http://hiwaay.net/~paul/bacon/misc/apology.html.
8. Ibid.
9. Roger Lockyer, *Buckingham: The Life and Political Career of George Villiers, First Duke of Buckingham, 1592–1628* (London and New York: Longman, 1981), 70.
10. Francis Bacon, *The Works of Francis Bacon, Lord Chancellor England*, ed. Basil Montagu (Philadelphia: Carey and Hart, 1842), 2:497.
11. Quoted in *Encyclopedia Britannica*, 1888 edition, 3:204.
12. Sir Edward Coke, *Selected Writings*, ed. Steve Sheppard (Indianapolis: Liberty Fund, 2003), "Commendams and the King's Displeasure," vol. 3, chapter B, paragraph 577.
13. See Joseph R. Tanner, *Constitutional Documents from the Reign of James I, 1603–1625* (London and New York: Cambridge University Press, 1960), 193–195.
14. In addition to Tanner, for an account of this meeting told from Bacon's perspective see William Dixon, *Personal History of Lord Bacon from Unpublished Papers* (Leipzig, 1861), 230–233; for Coke's perspective, see Bowen, *The Lion and the Throne*, 372.
15. Tanner, *Constitutional Documents from the Reign of James I*, 19.
16. Quoted in Bowen, *The Lion and the Throne*, 379.
17. See Alan Cromartie, *The Constitutionalist Revolution: An Essay on the History of England, 1450–1642* (New York: Cambridge University Press, 2006), 207.
18. P. B. Waite, "The Struggle of Prerogative and Common Law in the Reign of James I," *Canadian Journal of Economics and Political Science* 25, no. 2 (May 1959): 144–152.
19. Bowen, *The Lion and the Throne*, 396.

## Chapter 4

1. Mark Kishlansky, *A Monarchy Transformed: Britain, 1603–1714* (New York: Penguin, 1997), 14.
2. Thomas Fuller, *Church History of Britain* (1655), Book X, 63–64.
3. Roger Williams to Gov John Winthrop, between July & Dec 1632/from Plymmouth [*sic*], in *The Correspondence of Roger Williams*, ed. Glenn W. LaFantasie (Hanover, NH, and London: Brown University Press, 1988), vol. 1.
4. Roger Williams, *The Complete Writings of Roger Williams* (New York: Russell and Russell, 1963), 6:345.
5. Roger Williams to Anne Sadleir, winter 1652/53, in *Correspondence of Roger Williams*, vol. 1.
6. Catherine Drinker Bowen, *The Lion and the Throne:The Life and Times of Sir Edward Coke, 1552–1634* (New York: Little, Brown, 1990 [1957]), 444.
7. Anne Sadleir's note was attached to Williams's correspondence to her, winter 1652/53. Williams, *Correspondence of Roger Williams*, vol. 1.
8. David Benedict, *A General History of the Baptist Denomination in America* (Boston: Lincoln & Edmonds, 1813), 1:474, quoted in Raymond L. Camp, *Roger Williams: God's Apostle of Advocacy* (Lewiston, NY: Edwin Mellen Press, 1989), 34.
9. Kishlansky, *A Monarchy Transformed*, 92.
10. *Commons Debates, 1621*, ed. Wallace Notestein, Frances Helen Reif, and Hartley Simpson (New Haven, CT: Yale University Press, 1935), 6:370.
11. Bowen, *The Lion and the Throne*, 415.
12. Ernest Law, *History of Hampton Court Palace* (London: Bell and Sons, 1888), 67.
13. Kishlansky, *A Monarchy Transformed*, 24.
14. For the price of titles see Conrad Russell, *The Crisis of Parliaments* (Oxford: Oxford University Press, 1971), 280, also 259.
15. Quoted in Bowen, *The Lion and the Throne*, 418.
16. Francis Bacon, *The New Organon*, http://www.constitution.org/bacon/nov_org.htm.
17. Ibid., author's preface.
18. Bowen, *The Lion and the Throne*, 424.

19. Ibid., 424; see her footnote, 549–550.
20. Chris Kyle and Jason Peacey, eds., *Parliament at Work: Parliamentary Committees, Political Power and Public Access in Early Modern England* (Woodbridge, UK: Boydell Press, 2002), 4–10.
21. Brennan Pursell, "James I, Gondomar and the Dissolution of the Parliament of 1621," *History* 85, no. 279 (July 2000): 433.
22. Edward Nicholas (attributed), *Proceedings and Debates of the House of Commons, in 1620 and 1621, Collected by a Member of that House* (London: Clarendon Press, 1766), 1:308; see also 2:155; see also Bowen, *The Lion and the Throne*, 420, 436.
23. Stephen White, book review of Colin Tite, *Impeachment and Parliamentary Judicature in Early Stuart England, Harvard Law Review* 89, no. 8 (June 1976): 1934–1945.
24. Ibid.
25. Bowen, *The Lion and the Throne*, 429.
26. Quoted in Perez Zagorin, *Francis Bacon* (Princeton, NJ: Princeton University Press), 4.
27. Bowen, *The Lion and the Throne*, 446.
28. *Historical Collections of Private Passages of State: Volume 1, 1618–1629* (1721). http://www.british-history.ac.uk/report.aspx?compid=70138.
29. Bowen, *The Lion and the Throne*, 449.
30. Ibid., 450.
31. James to the Speaker of the House of Commons, December 3, 1621, in *Historical Collections of Private Passages of State, Volume 1, 1618–1629* (1721). http://www.british-history.ac.uk/report.aspx?compid=70138.
32. Bowen, *The Lion and the Throne*, 452.
33. *Parliamentary History of England from the Earliest Period to 1803*, vol. 1, *1066–1625* (London: Hansard, 1806), 1563.
34. Ibid., 1555; see also C. H. McIlwain, "The House of Commons in 1621," *Journal of Modern History* 9, no. 2 (June 1937): 206–214.
35. Bowen, *The Lion and the Throne*, 453.
36. Ibid.; Coke, *The Selected Writings of Sir Edward Coke*, ed. Steve Sheppard (Indianapolis: Liberty Fund, 2003), 1194.
37. Bowen, *The Lion and the Throne*, 454.
38. Coke, *Selected Writings*, 1329.
39. Lord Calvert to Buckingham, December 17, 1621, in *Commons Debates, 1621*, ed. Wallace Notestein, Frances Helen Reif, and Hartley Simpson (New Haven, CT: Yale University Press, 1935), 7:626–627.
40. Bowen, *The Lion and the Throne*, 456.
41. Henry Chupack, *Roger Williams* (New York: Twayne, 1969), 31.
42. Thomas Fuller, *Church History of Britain*, Book X, 108–110, quoted in Ola Winslow, *Master Roger Williams: A Biography* (New York: Macmillan, 1957), 66.
43. George Schochet, ed., *Religion, Resistance, and Civil War* (Washington, DC: Folger Institute, 1990), 131.
44. Raymond L. Camp, *Roger Williams: God's Apostle of Advocacy* (Lewiston, NY: Edwin Mellen Press, 1989), 46.
45. Ibid., 48.
46. Winslow, *Master Roger Williams*, 55.
47. Howard Chapin, *Roger Williams and the King's Colors* (Providence: Rhode Island Historical Society / E. A. Johnson, 1933), 31.
48. Williams, *The Bloudy Tenent*, in *The Complete Writings of Roger Williams* (New York: Russell and Russell, 1963), 3:306.
49. Thomas Hobbes, *Leviathan*, chapter XI, 70.

## Chapter 5

1. Catherine Drinker Bowen, *The Lion and the Throne: The Life and Times of Sir Edward Coke, 1552–1634* (New York: Little, Brown, 1990 [1957]), 465.
2. Simonds D'Ewes, *The Autobiography and Correspondence of Sir Simonds D'Ewes*, ed. J. O. Halliwell (London: Richard Bentley, 1845), 1:166.
3. Chris Kyle, "Prince Charles and the Parliaments of 1621 and 1624," *Historical Journal* 41, no. 3 (September 1998): 620.

4. Alan Simpson, *Puritanism in Old and New England* (Chicago: University of Chicago Press, 1955), 6.

5. Ola Winslow, *Master Roger Williams: A Biography* (New York: Macmillan, 1957), 65.

6. Quoted in William Hunt, *The Puritan Moment: The Coming of Revolution in an English County* (Cambridge, MA: Harvard University Press, 1983), 228.

7. Quoted in Roger Lockyer, *The Early Stuarts: A Political History of England, 1603–1642* (London and New York: Longman, 1989), 96.

8. Samuel Rawson Gardiner, ed., *Debates in the House of Commons in 1625* (London: Camden Society, 1878), 85–87; see also 110–115. Bowen, *The Lion and the Throne*, 470.

9. George Johnson, ed., *The Fairfax Correspondence: Memoirs of the Reign of Charles I* (London: Michael Bentley, 1848), 1:92.

10. Ibid., 3:65.

11. Bowen, *The Lion and the Throne*, 483.

12. William Cobbett, *Cobbett's Complete Collection of State Trials and Proceedings for High Treason and Other Crimes and Misdemeanors from the Earliest Period to the Present Time*, ed. Thomas Bayley Howell (London: T. C. Hansard, 1809), 3:63–64.

13. Lockyer, *The Early Stuarts*, 228.

14. Bowen, *The Lion and the Throne*, 489.

15. Ibid.

16. *Journal of the House of Lords*, vol. 3, *1620–1628*, April 25, 1628, 768–770. British History Online, http://www.british-history.ac.uk/report.aspx?compid=30576.

17. Coke, *The Selected Writings of Sir Edward Coke*, ed. Steve Sheppard (Indianapolis: Liberty Fund, 2003), 1628 Petition of Right, vol. 3, chapter D, paragraph 346.

18. William Stubbs, *The Constitutional History of England* (Oxford: Oxford University Press, 1897), 1:55.

19. *Journal of the House of Lords*, 3:729, 731.

20. Conrad Russell, *Parliaments and English Politics, 1621–1629* (New York: Oxford University Press, 1979), 348.

21. John Forster, *Sir John Eliot: A Biography* (London: Chapman and Hall, 1872), 2:44. http://www.archive.org/stream/sirjohneliotbiog02forsuoft/sirjohneliotbiog02forsuoft_djvu.txt.

22. http://www.constitution.org/eng/petright.htm.

23. http://www.statutelaw.gov.uk/content.aspx?activeTextDocId=1518333.

24. Coke, *Selected Writings*, 1628 Petition of Right, vol. 3, chapter D, paragraph 447.

25. Bowen, *The Lion and the Throne*, 496.

26. Ibid., 499.

27. John Rushworth, *Historical Collections of Private Passages of State, Weighty Matters in Law, Remarkable Proceedings in Five Parliaments* (London: Tho. Newcomb for George Thomason, 1659–1701), 1:609–610; see also Bowen, *The Lion and the Throne*, 500.

28. Roger Lockyer, *Buckingham: The Life and Political Career of George Villiers, First Duke of Buckingham, 1592–1628* (London and New York: Longman, 1981), 467.

29. John Hostettler, *Sir Edward Coke: A Force for Freedom* (Chichester, UK: Barry Rose Law Publishers, 1997), 136.

30. Russell, *Parliaments and English Politics*, 379.

31. Coke, *Selected Writings*, 1628 Petition of Right, vol. 3, chapter D, paragraph 468.

32. Russell, *Parliaments and English Politics*, 380.

33. Quoted in Jim Powell, "Edward Coke: Common Law Protection for Liberty," *Freeman* 47, no. 11 (November 1997).

## Chapter 6

1. Conrad Russell, *Parliaments and English Politics, 1621–1629* (New York: Oxford University Press, 1979), 383.

2. Roger Lockyer, *Buckingham: The Life and Political Career of George Villiers, First Duke of Buckingham, 1592–1628* (London and New York: Longman, 1981), 457–458.

3. Roger Lockyer, *The Early Stuarts: A Political History of England, 1603–1642* (London and New York: Longman, 1989), 309.

4. Ibid.

5. Darrett B. Rutman, *John Winthrop's Decision for America* (Philadelphia: Lippincott, 1975), 23; Jonathan Scott, *England's Troubles: Seventeenth-Century English Political Thought in European Context* (Cambridge: Cambridge University Press, 2000), 123.

6. Stephen D. White, *Sir Edward Coke and "The Grievances of the Commonwealth," 1621–1628* (Chapel Hill: University of North Carolina Press, 1979), 203.

7. Larzer Ziff, *The Career of John Cotton: Puritanism and the American Experience* (Princeton, NJ: Princeton University Press, 1962), 54.

8. Scott, *England's Troubles*, 110.

9. Ibid., 122.

10. Ibid., 103, 123.

11. Conrad Russell, *The Crisis of Parliaments* (Oxford: Oxford University Press, 1971), 308.

12. Egerton Ms. 2650, folio 314; quoted in James Ernst, *Roger Williams: New England Firebrand* (New York: Macmillan, 1952), 52.

13. Quoted in Raymond L. Camp, *Roger Williams: God's Apostle of Advocacy* (Lewiston, NY: Edwin Mellen Press, 1989), 100.

14. Russell, *Parliaments and English Politics*, 405.

15. Scott, *England's Troubles*, 111.

16. Russell, *Parliaments and English Politics*, 405.

17. Ibid., 407.

18. Ola Winslow, *Master Roger Williams: A Biography* (New York: Macmillan, 1957), 80.

19. Russell, *Parliaments and English Politics*, 404.

20. Scott, *England's Troubles*, 95–96.

21. Quoted in Camp, *Roger Williams: God's Apostle of Advocacy*, 101.

22. Quoted in ibid.

23. William Cobbett, *Cobbett's Complete Collection of State Trials and Proceedings for High Treason and Other Crimes and Misdemeanors from the Earliest Period to the Present Time*, ed. Thomas Bayley Howell (London: T. C. Hansard, 1809), 3:61–63.

24. Camp, *Roger Williams*, 102.

25. Quoted in ibid.

26. Russell, *Parliaments and English Politics*, 415.

27. Russell, *Crisis of Parliaments*, 309.

28. Quoted in Camp, *Roger Williams*, 104.

29. Samuel Rawson Gardiner, ed., *The Constitutional Documents of the Puritan Revolution, 1625–1660* (Oxford: Oxford University Press, 1906), 82–83; Lockyer, *The Early Stuarts*, 350.

30. Camp, *Roger Williams*, 104.

31. Ibid., 102.

32. Ibid.

# PART II: THE COVENANT

## Chapter 7

1. Jonathan Scott, *England's Troubles: Seventeenth-Century English Political Thought in European Context* (Cambridge: Cambridge University Press, 2000), 111.

2. Roger Lockyer, *The Early Stuarts: A Political History of England, 1603–1642* (London and New York: Longman, 1989), 317–318.

3. John Milton, *Eikonoklastes*, 534–535.

4. Daniel Neal, *The History of the Puritans* (New York: Harper, 1844), 2:210; Will Durant, *The Age of Reason Begins* (New York: MJF Books, 1997), 189–190.

5. George H. Williams, Norman Pettit, and Sargent Bush, eds., *Thomas Hooker: Writings in England and Holland, 1626–1633* (Cambridge, MA: Harvard University Press, 1975), 3.

6. George Schochet, ed., *Religion, Resistance, and Civil War* (Washington, DC: Folger Institute, 1990), 132.

7. Conrad Russell, *Unrevolutionary England, 1603–1642* (London: Hambledon Press, 1990), 179.

8. Ibid., 191.

9. Ibid., 200.

10. Scott, *England's Troubles*, 111.

11. Richard Rogers, *Seven Treatises* (1603), 490, quoted in Francis J. Bremer, *John Winthrop: America's Forgotten Founding Father* (New York: Oxford University Press, 2003), 60.

12. Lockyer, *The Early Stuarts*, 6.

13. Mark Kishlansky, *A Monarchy Transformed: Britain 1603–1714* (New York: Penguin, 1997), 27.

14. Robert Cushman, "The Lawfulness of Removing out of England," in *A Relation, or Journal of the Beginning and Proceedings of the English Plantation settled at Plymouth, in New England . . .* (1622), reprinted in Darrett B. Rutman, *John Winthrop's Decision for America* (Philadelphia: Lippincott, 1975), 84–85.

15. Lockyer, *The Early Stuarts*, 2.

16. Kishlansky, *A Monarchy Transformed*, 29.

17. Lockyer, *The Early Stuarts*, 273.

18. Cushman, "The Lawfulness of Removing out of England," reprinted in Rutman, *John Winthrop's Decision for America*, 84–85.

19. Scott, *England's Troubles*, 99.

20. Rutman, *John Winthrop's Decision for America*, 8.

21. John Milton, *Areopagitica: A Speech for the Liberty of Unlicensed Printing*, in *Harvard Classics* (1909), 3:223.

22. *Thomas Hooker: Writings in England and Holland*, 67–69.

23. Ibid., 202–205.

24. Quoted in Rutman, *John Winthrop's Decision for America*, 13.

25. *Thomas Hooker: Writings in England and Holland*, 92.

26. Ibid., 67–69.

27. Ibid., 55n.

28. Ibid., 47–49.

29. Ibid., 76.

30. Ibid., 24.

31. Quoted in Rutman, *John Winthrop's Decision for America*, 11.

32. *Thomas Hooker: Writings in England and Holland*, 24.

## Chapter 8

1. Karen Ordahl Kupperman, *The Jamestown Project* (Cambridge, MA: Belknap Press of Harvard University, 2007), 200.

2. Quoted in William Heath, "Thomas Morton: From Merry Old England to New England," *Journal of American Studies* 41, no. 1 (2007): 135–168.

3. Kupperman, *The Jamestown Project*, 83.

4. Francis Jennings, *The Invasion of America: Indians, Colonialism, and the Cant of Conquest* (Chapel Hill: University of North Carolina Press, 1975), 45.

5. Ibid., 75.

6. David Cressy, *Coming Over: Migration and Communication Between England and New England in the Seventeenth Century* (Cambridge: Cambridge University Press, 1987), 2.

7. Ibid., 3.

8. Kupperman, *The Jamestown Project*, 242.

9. Allison Games, *Migration and the Origins of the English Atlantic World* (Cambridge, MA: Harvard University Press, 1999), 215.

10. Ibid., 16.

11. Kupperman, *The Jamestown Project*, 310.

12. Ibid., 125.

13. Sidney Perley, *The History of Salem Massachusetts* (Salem: Sidney Perley, 1926), 1:54.

14. John Donne, *Sermons of John Donne* (Berkeley: University of California Press, 1959), 9:38.

15. Quoted in Ola Winslow, *Master Roger Williams: A Biography* (New York: Macmillan, 1957), 26.

16. Kupperman, *The Jamestown Project*, 238.

17. William Bradford, *Of Plimoth Plantation* (Boston: Houghton Mifflin, 1912), 1:53.

18. Quoted in Perley, *The History of Salem Massachusetts*, 1:39.

19. Neal Salisbury, *Manitou and Providence: Indians, Europeans, and the Making of New England, 1500–1643* (New York: Oxford University Press, 1982), 103.

20. Richard Gildrie, *Salem, Massachusetts, 1626–1683: A Covenant Community* (Charlottesville: University of Virginia Press, 1975), 3.

21. Alexander Young, ed., *Chronicles of the First Planters of the Colony of Massachusetts Bay, 1623–1636* (Boston: Little, Brown, 1846), 26.

22. Thomas Fuller, *Worthies of England*, 2:233.

23. Perley, *The History of Salem Massachusetts*, 1:67.

24. Joseph Felt, *Annals of Salem* (Salem: W. & S. B. Ives, 1845), 1:39–40.

25. Perley, *The History of Salem Massachusetts*, 1:97.

26. Lawrence Shaw Mayo, *John Endecott: A Biography* (Cambridge, MA: Harvard University Press, 1971 [1936]), 179–180.

27. Thomas Morton's observation quoted in Mayo, *John Endecott*, 29; see also Michael Zuckerman, "Pilgrims in the Wilderness: Community, Modernity, and the Maypole at Merrymount," *New England Quarterly* 50, no. 22 (1977): 255–277.

28. Gildrie, *Salem, Massachusetts*, 7.

29. John White, *The Planters Plea* (London, 1630); see Gildrie, *Salem, Massachusetts*, 9.

30. Francis J. Bremer, *John Winthrop: America's Forgotten Founding Father* (New York: Oxford University Press, 2003), 153.

31. Roger Williams to Lady Joan Barrington, April 1629, in *The Correspondence of Roger Williams*, ed. Glenn W. LaFantasie (Hanover, NH, and London: Brown University Press, 1988), vol. 1. Williams's letter does not specify that the offer was for Salem, but Salem had the only church in the colony at the time.

32. Perley, *The History of Salem Massachusetts*, 1:156.

33. Higginson to his friends in England, July 24, 1629, in Everett Emerson, ed., *Letters from New England: The Massachusetts Bay Colony, 1629–1638* (Amherst: University of Massachusetts Press, 1976), 21.

34. Ibid.

35. Mayo, *John Endecott*, 25.

36. Quoted in ibid., 26.

## Chapter 9

1. Darrett B. Rutman, *John Winthrop's Decision for America, 1629* (Philadelphia: Lippincott, 1975), 37.

2. *Records of the Governor and Company of the Massachusetts Bay in New England*, ed. Nathaniel Shurtleff (Boston: Wm White, 1853), 1:49.

3. Iain Murray, "Thomas Hooker and the Doctrine of God," *Banner of Truth*, issue 195 (December 1979): 19–29; http://www.puritansermons.com/banner/murray5.htm.

4. William Hunt, *The Puritan Moment: The Coming of Revolution in an English County* (Cambridge, MA: Harvard University Press, 1983), 196–197.

5. George H. Williams, Norman Pettit, and Sargent Bush, eds., *Thomas Hooker: Writings in England and Holland, 1626–1633* (Cambridge, MA: Harvard University Press, 1975), 3.

6. Quoted in Hunt, *The Puritan Moment*, 196.

7. *Thomas Hooker: Writings in England and Holland*, 3.

8. Larzer Ziff, *The Career of John Cotton: Puritanism and the American Experience* (Princeton, NJ: Princeton University Press, 1962), 52.

9. Ibid., 55.

10. Ibid., 58.

11. Quoted in ibid., 28.

12. Ibid., 80.

13. Roger Williams to Lady Joan Barrington, April 1629, in *The Correspondence of Roger Williams*, ed. Glenn W. LaFantasie (Hanover, NH, and London: Brown University Press, 1988), vol. 1.

14. "Mr. Cottons Letter Lately Examined," in *The Complete Writings of Roger Williams* (New York: Russell and Russell, 1963), 1:324; see also *The Bloudy Tenent Yet More Bloudy*, in ibid., 4:65.

15. John Smith, "Advertisements for the Unexperienced Planters of New England, &c." (London, 1631), 16.

16. Allison Games, *Migration and the Origins of the English Atlantic World* (Cambridge, MA: Harvard, 1999), 45–47.

17. Sidney Perley, *The History of Salem Massachusetts* (Salem: Sidney Perley, 1926), 1:186.

18. Nathaniel Morton, *New Englands Memoriall*, 5th ed., edited by John Davis (Boston: Crocker and Brewster, 1826 [1669]), 144. See also Larzer Ziff, "The Salem Puritans in the 'Free Aire of a New World,'" *Huntington Library Quarterly* 20, no. 4 (1957): 373–384.

19. Edmund Carpenter, *Roger Williams: A Study of the Life, Times, and Character of a Political Pioneer* (New York: Grafton Press, 1909), xxix.

20. W. Clark Gilpin, *The Millenarian Piety of Roger Williams* (Chicago: University of Chicago Press, 1979), 23.

21. David D. Hall, *The Faithful Shepherd: A History of the New England Ministry in the Seventeenth Century* (Chapel Hill: University of North Carolina Press, 1972), 78.

22. Quoted in Walter F. Terris, "The Right to Speak" (PhD dissertation, Northwestern University, 1962), 72.

23. Morton, *New Englands Memoriall*, 147; see also William Bradford, *Of Plimoth Plantation* (Boston: Houghton Mifflin, 1912).

24. Richard Gildrie, *Salem, Massachusetts, 1626–1683: A Covenant Community* (Charlottesville: University of Virginia Press, 1975), 17.

25. Ibid.

26. Perley, *The History of Salem Massachusetts*, 1:168.

27. Rutman, *John Winthrop's Decision for America*, 31.

28. This version of Winthrop's *Experiencia* comes from the *Winthrop Papers*, http://muweb.millersville .edu/winthrop/jwexp.html.

29. Israel Stoughton to John Stoughton, 1635, reprinted in Everett Emerson, ed., *Letters from New England: The Massachusetts Bay Colony, 1629–1638* (Amherst: University of Massachusetts Press, 1976).

30. John Winthrop Jr. to John Winthrop, January 15, 1627, *Winthrop Papers*, 1:341.

31. Francis J. Bremer, *John Winthrop: America's Forgotten Founding Father* (New York: Oxford University Press, 1994), 144–45.

32. Winthrop to Margaret Winthrop, June 5, 1629, *Winthrop Papers*, 2:94.

33. Winthrop to Margaret Winthrop, June 22, 1629, *Winthrop Papers*, 2:100.

34. Winthrop to Margaret Winthrop, May 15, 1629; see *Documents* in Rutman, *John Winthrop's Decision for America*, 81.

35. This is the title of the document in the *Winthrop Papers;* other versions have slightly different titles. Some historians have speculated that John White or even Higginson was the author.

36. Robert Cushman, "The Lawfulness of Removing out of England," part of pamphlet *A Relation, or Journal of the Beginning and Proceedings of the English Plantation settled at Plymouth, in New England . . .* (1622), reprinted in Rutman, *John Winthrop's Decision for America*, 82–84.

37. Richard Eburne, *A Plaine Path-way to Plantations*, quoted in Rutman, *John Winthrop's Decision for America*, 32.

38. John Bellamy, *An Historical Discoverie and Relation of the British Plantations in New England*, quoted in Rutman, *John Winthrop's Decision for America*, 33.

39. Quotes in this version are taken from a handwritten copy in the Library of Congress, available at http://www.loc.gov/exhibits/british/images/vc15p1.jpg, and also from http://Winthropsociety.com/ doc_reasons.php.

40. "The Agreement at Cambridge," *Winthrop Papers*, 2:151–152.

41. *Records of the Governor and Company of the Massachusetts Bay in New England*, 1:59.

42. John Winthrop, "Particular Considerations in the Case of J:W:" (1629), *Winthrop Papers*, 2:126.

43. Ibid.

44. Address of Winthrop to Massachusetts Bay Company, *Winthrop Papers*, 2:174–176.

45. *Records of the Governor and Company of the Massachusetts Bay*, 1:26–27; see also *Winthrop Papers*, 2:171–172.

46. Winthrop and others to Wm Gager (undated), *Winthrop Papers*, 2:199.

47. Higginson to His Friends in England, July 24, 1629, in Emerson, ed., *Letters from New England*, 29–38.

48. J. Franklin Jameson, ed., *Johnson's Wonder-Working Providence* (New York: Scribner, 1910 [1653]), 33.

49. John Smith, "Advertisements for the Unexperienced Planters of New England, &c.," 16.

50. Francis Higginson, quoted in Perley, *The History of Salem Massachusetts*, 1:185.

51. Rutman, *John Winthrop's Decision for America*, 47.

## Chapter 10

1. Winthrop to Sir William Spring, February 8, 1630, *Winthrop Papers*, 2:205.

2. This and all other quotes from his sermon come from John Cotton, *Gods Promise to His Plantation . . . As it was delivered in a sermon* (London: Wm Jones & John Bellamy, 1630), passim.

3. Andrew Delbanco, *The Puritan Ordeal* (Cambridge, MA: Harvard University Press, 1989), 72.

4. Peter Gomes, *New York Times Magazine,* April 18, 1999.

5. William Perkins, *A Treatise of the Vocations, or Callings of Men . . .* (London: I. Legatt, 1612), reprinted in Darrett B. Rutman, *John Winthrop's Decision for America, 1629* (Philadelphia: Lippincott, 1975), 57–59.

6. Many versions of this sermon exist. I have chosen to use a scanned version of a text in the Collections of the Massachusetts Historical Society, http://history.hanover.edu/texts/winthmod.html.

7. http://digitalcommons.unl.edu/cgi/viewcontent.cgi?article=1003&context=scottow.

8. John Winthrop, *Journal of John Winthrop,* ed. Richard Dunn, James Savage, and Laetitia Yeandle (Cambridge, MA: Belknap Press of Harvard University Press, 1996), 6.

9. Ibid., 13.

10. Ibid., 23.

11. Ibid., 20.

12. Ibid., 33.

13. Thomas Dudley to the Countess of Lincoln, March 12 and 28, 1631, in Everett Emerson, ed., *Letters from New England: The Massachusetts Bay Colony, 1629–1638* (Amherst: University of Massachusetts Press, 1976).

14. Ibid.

15. Ibid.

16. Quoted in W. Clark Gilpin, *The Millenarian Piety of Roger Williams* (Chicago: University of Chicago Press, 1979), 28.

17. Winthrop to wife Margaret, July 16, 1630, *Winthrop Papers,* ed. Samuel Eliot Morison (Boston: Massachusetts Historical Society, 1931), 2:301–302.

18. *Journal of John Winthrop,* 38–39.

19. J. Franklin Jameson, ed., *Johnson's Wonder-Working Providence* (New York: Scribner, 1910 [1653]), 65–66.

20. Downing's letter of December 1630, quoted in Emerson, ed., *Letters from New England,* 87.

21. Downing to Winthrop, 30 April 1631, *Winthrop Papers,* 3:31.

22. Quoted in James Knowles, *Memoir of Roger Williams* (Boston: Lincoln and Edmands, 1834), 36.

23. Winthrop to John Winthrop Jr., March 28, 1631, in Emerson, ed., *Letters from New England,* 87.

24. Quoted in Edmund Morgan, *The Puritan Dilemma: The Story of John Winthrop* (New York: Little, Brown, 1958), 81.

25. Jameson, ed., *Johnson's Wonder-Working Providence,* 64.

26. William Bradford, *Of Plimoth Plantation* (Boston: Houghton Mifflin, 1912), 1:208; William Heath, "Thomas Morton: From Merry Old England to New England," *Journal of American Studies* 41, no. 1 (2007): 135–168.

27. Michael Leroy Oberg, *Dominion and Civility: English Imperialism and Native America, 1585–1685* (New York: Cornell University Press, 1999), 93.

28. Ibid.

29. Michael Zuckerman, "Pilgrims in the Wilderness: Community, Modernity, and the Maypole at Merrymount," *New England Quarterly* 50, no. 2 (1977): 255–277.

30. Quoted in Oberg, *Dominion and Civility,* 94.

31. Oberg, *Dominion and Civility,* 94.

32. John Noble, ed., *Records of the Court of Assistants, 1630–1692* (1901), 1:33–50.

33. *Journal of John Winthrop,* 56–57.

34. Ibid., 52.

35. Winthrop to wife Margaret, September 9, 1630, *Winthrop Papers,* 2:313.

### Chapter 11

1. Raymond L. Camp, *Roger Williams: God's Apostle of Advocacy* (Lewiston, NY: Edwin Mellen Press, 1989), 107.

2. Roger Williams to Lady Joan Barrington, May 2, 1629, in *The Correspondence of Roger Williams,* ed. Glenn W. LaFantasie (Hanover, NH, and London: Brown University Press, 1988), vol. 1.

3. Camp, *Roger Williams,* 87.

4. Emily Easton, "Mary Bernard," *Collection of the Rhode Island Historical Society* 29 (1936): 65–80.

5. William Laud, *The Works of the Most Reverend Father in God, William Laud, D.D.* (London: R. Chitwell, 1694; reprinted Oxford: John Henry Parker, 1843), vol. 6, 327, quoted in Camp, *Roger Williams,* 106.

6. Ibid., vol. 6, 268–69, quoted in Camp, *Roger Williams,* 106.

7. Benjamin Brook, *Lives of the Puritans* (London: J. Black, 1813), 380–383. Camp, *Roger Williams,* 109.
8. Egerton Ms. 2645, folio 77, quoted in Camp, *Roger Williams,* 107.
9. Thomas Shepherd, *A Memoir of His Own Life,* in Alex Young, ed., *Chronicles of the First Plantation of the Colony of Massachusetts Bay* (Boston: Little, Brown, 1846), 519–520; William Hunt, *The Puritan Moment: The Coming of Revolution in an English County* (Cambridge, MA: Harvard University Press, 1983), 256.
10. Richard Rogers, *Certaine Sermons Preached and Penned by Richard Rogers* (1612), 189, quoted in Francis J. Bremer, *John Winthrop: America's Forgotten Founding Father* (New York: Oxford University Press, 2003), 109.
11. Hunt, *The Puritan Moment,* 256.
12. George H. Williams, Norman Pettit, and Sargent Bush, eds., *Thomas Hooker: Writings in England and Holland, 1626–1633* (Cambridge, MA: Harvard University Press, 1975), 231.
13. Ibid., 80.
14. Ibid., 88.
15. Roger Williams to Mrs. Anne Sadleir, ca. April 1652, in *The Complete Writings of Roger Williams* (New York: Russell and Russell, 1963), vol. 1.
16. Ibid.

# PART III: THE NEW WORLD

## Chapter 12

1. John Winthrop, *Journal of John Winthrop,* eds. Richard Dunn, James Savage, and Laetitia Yeandle (Cambridge, MA: Belknap Press of Harvard University Press, 1996), 45.
2. This description actually comes from Francis Higginson for his otherwise peaceful voyage in July 1629. Williams's voyage, being "verye tempestuous," would have been considerably worse. "Higginson to his friends in England, July 24, 1629," in Everett Emerson, ed., *Letters from New England: The Massachusetts Bay Colony, 1629–1638* (Amherst: University of Massachusetts Press, 1976), 17.
3. Charlestown Records, 385, quoted in Francis J. Bremer, *John Winthrop: America's Forgotten Founding Father* (New York: Oxford University Press, 2003), 194.
4. *Journal of John Winthrop,* 45.
5. Thomas Dudley to Countess of Lincoln, March 28, 1631, reprinted in Emerson, ed., *Letters to New England,* 75.
6. Patrick Malone, *The Skulking Way of War: Technology and Tactics Among the New England Indians* (Lanham, MD: Madison Books, 1991), 63.
7. Thomas Dudley to Countess of Lincoln, March 12 and 13, 1631, reprinted in Emerson, ed., *Letters from New England,* 68.
8. Edmund Carpenter, *Roger Williams: A Study of the Life, Times, and Character of a Political Pioneer* (New York: Grafton Press, 1909), 3.
9. Thomas Weld to his former parishioners at Tarling, June or July 1632, reprinted in Emerson, ed., *Letters from New England,* 93.
10. Roger Williams to John Cotton Jr., March 25, 1671, in *The Complete Writings of Roger Williams* (New York: Russell and Russell, 1963), vol. 2.
11. See *The Complete Writings of Roger Williams,* 3:10–14.
12. Hugh Spurgin, *Roger Williams and Puritan Radicalism in the English Separatist Tradition* (Lewiston, NY: Edwin Mellen Press, 1989), 70, 71.
13. Lawrence Mayo, *John Endecott: A Biography* (Cambridge, MA: Harvard University Press, 1971), 3–4.
14. *Journal of John Winthrop,* 50.
15. Endecott to unidentified correspondent, April 12, 1631, quoted in Mayo, *John Endecott,* 61.
16. Ibid.

## Chapter 13

1. William Bradford, *Of Plimoth Plantation* (Boston: Houghton Mifflin, 1912), 2:161.
2. Quoted in Edmund Carpenter, *Roger Williams: A Study of the Life, Times, and Character of a Political Pioneer* (New York: Grafton Press, 1909), 124.
3. Roger Williams, *The Complete Writings of Roger Williams* (New York: Russell and Russell, 1963), ed. Glenn W. LaFantasie (Hanover, NH, and London: Brown University Press), 7:14.

4. Bradford, *Of Plimoth Plantation,* 2:162.
5. Williams to Winthrop, between July and December 1632, in *Complete Writings,* 1:8–9.
6. Ibid.
7. "A True and Sincere Declaration of the Purpose and Ends of the Plantation" (1609), quoted in Michael Leroy Oberg, *Dominion and Civility: English Imperialism and Native America, 1585–1685* (Ithaca, NY: Cornell University Press, 1999), 51.
8. Ibid., 51.
9. Roger Williams to Assembly of Commissioners, 17 November 1677, in *The Correspondence of Roger Williams,* ed. Glenn W. LaFantasie (Hanover, NH, and London: Brown University Press, 1988), vol. 2.
10. Patricia Rubertone, *Grave Undertakings: An Archaeology of Roger Williams and the Narragansett Indians* (Washington, DC: Smithsonian Institution Press, 2003), 83.
11. Williams, *Complete Writings,* 1:141.
12. Quoted in Oberg, *Dominion and Civility,* 10.
13. Quoted in ibid., 21.
14. Williams, *Complete Writings,* 1:267.
15. Williams, "A Key into the Language of America," in *Complete Writings,* vol. 1, passim, esp. 81, 218. For an excellent discussion of Williams's views on the equality of Indians, see also David Read, *New World, Known World: Shaping Knowledge in Early Anglo-American Writing* (Columbia, MO: University of Missouri Press, 2005), 120–127.
16. Williams, *Complete Writings,* 1:147.
17. Neal Salisbury, *Manitou and Providence: Indians, Europeans, and the Making of New England, 1500–1643* (New York: Oxford University Press, 1982), 34.
18. Williams, *Complete Writings,* 1:19.
19. Ibid., 1:180.
20. Edward Winslow, *Good Newes from New England* (1624), 57.
21. Bradford, *Of Plimoth Plantation,* 2:161.
22. Nathaniel Morton, *New Englands Memoriall,* 5th ed., edited by John Davis (Boston: Crocker and Brewster, 1826 [first published 1669]), 78. See also Bradford, *Of Plimoth Plantation,* 1:163n.
23. Bradford, *Of Plimoth Plantation,* 2:163.
24. Quoted in Cotton Mather, *Magnalia Christi Americana* (Hartford, CT: S. Andrus & Son, 1855), 1:263.
25. Ibid.
26. Larzer Ziff, *The Career of John Cotton: Puritanism and the American Experience* (Princeton, NJ: Princeton University Press, 1962), 65.
27. George H. Williams, Norman Pettit, and Sargent Bush, eds., *Thomas Hooker: Writings in England and Holland, 1626–1633* (Cambridge, MA: Harvard University Press, 1975), 31.
28. Ibid.
29. Cotton to unidentified clergyman, December 3, 1634, reprinted in Everett Emerson, *Letters from New England: The Massachusetts Bay Colony, 1629–1638* (Amherst: University of Massachusetts Press, 1976), 127.

## Chapter 14

1. Allison Games, *Migration and the Origins of the English Atlantic World* (Cambridge, MA: Harvard University Press, 1999), 25–29.
2. Edward Howes to John Winthrop Jr., June 22, 1633, in Samuel Eliot Morison, ed., *Winthrop Papers* (Boston: Massachusetts Historical Society, 1931), 3:132.
3. John Winthrop, *Journal of John Winthrop,* eds. Richard Dunn, James Savage, and Laetitia Yeandle (Cambridge, MA: Belknap Press of Harvard University Press, 1996), 102.
4. Ibid., 102.
5. Ibid.
6. Ibid., 107.
7. John Winthrop to John Endecott, January 3, 1634, in *Winthrop Papers,* 3:146–149.
8. Ibid.
9. *Journal of John Winthrop,* 107.
10. Ibid.
11. Ibid., 107–108.

12. Ibid., 109.
13. Quoted in James Ernst, *Roger Williams: New England Firebrand* (New York: Macmillan, 1932), 90.
14. Quoted in Oscar Straus, *Roger Williams: The Pioneer of Religious Liberty* (New York: Century Co., 1894), 67.
15. *Journal of John Winthrop*, 345.
16. Emil Oberholzer, *Delinquent Saints: Disciplinary Action in the Early Congregational Churches of Massachusetts* (New York: Columbia University Press, 1955), 220.
17. William Gouge, *Of Domesticall Duties* (London, 1622), quoted in John Demos, *A Little Commonwealth: Family Life in Plymouth Colony*, 2nd ed. (New York: Oxford University Press, 2000), xxvii.
18. Demos, *A Little Commonwealth*, 78.
19. Ibid., 134–135.
20. Ibid., 136.
21. George H. Williams, Norman Pettit, and Sargent Bush, eds., *Thomas Hooker: Writings in England and Holland, 1626–1633* (Cambridge, MA: Harvard University Press, 1975), 115–116.
22. Ibid., 117.
23. Quoted in Darrett B. Rutman, *Winthrop's Boston: Portrait of a Puritan Town* (Chapel Hill: University of North Carolina Press, 1965), 124; see also Everett Emerson, *John Cotton* (Boston: G. K. Hall, 1990), 61.
24. Quoted in Thomas Lechford, *Plain Dealing, or News from New England*, introduction by Darrett Rutman (New York: Johnson Reprint Corporation, 1969), 32n.
25. Oberholzer, *Delinquent Saints*, 113–114.
26. Ibid., 228.
27. *Journal of John Winthrop*, 63. See also Francis J. Bremer, *John Winthrop: America's Forgotten Founding Father* (New York: Oxford University Press, 2003), 211.

## Chapter 15

1. Edward Howes to John Winthrop Jr., November 27, 1632, in Samuel Eliot Morison, ed., *Winthrop Papers* (Boston: Massachusetts Historical Society, 1931), 3:100–101.
2. Francis Kirby to John Winthrop Jr., March 26, 1633, in ibid., 3:117.
3. John Winthrop Jr. to Sir Simonds D'Ewes, July 31, 1634, in ibid., 3:172.
4. Edward Howes to John Winthrop Jr., March 18, 1633, in ibid., 3:112.
5. John Bluett to John Winthrop Jr., in ibid., 3:108.
6. Francis Kirby to John Winthrop Jr., March 26, 1633, in ibid., 3:117.
7. Richard Saltonstall Jr. to John Winthrop Jr., early 1634, in ibid., 3:145.
8. Allison Games, *Migration and the Origins of the English Atlantic World* (Cambridge, MA: Harvard University Press, 1999), 18.
9. Ibid.
10. *Journal of Richard Mather, 1635, Coll. of Dorchester Antiquarian and Historical Society* (Boston, 1850), quoted in Games, *Migration and the Origins of the English Atlantic World*, 65.
11. *Records of the Court of Assistants, 1630–1692*, ed. John Noble (1901), 1:42–44, quoted in Francis J. Bremer, *John Winthrop: America's Forgotten Founding Father* (New York: Oxford University Press, 2003), 217.
12. *Records of the Governor and Company of the Massachusetts Bay in New England*, ed. Nathaniel Shurtleff (Boston: Wm White, 1853), 1:117; quoted in Bremer, *John Winthrop*, 217.
13. Games, *Migration and the Origins of the English Atlantic World*, 139.
14. Quoted in Bremer, *John Winthrop*, 216.
15. Quoted in Edmund Morgan, *The Puritan Dilemma: The Story of John Winthrop* (New York: Little, Brown, 1958), 95.
16. *Records of the Governor and Company of the Massachusetts Bay*, 1:151–152, 160–161; see also Samuel Brockunier, *The Irrepressible Democrat: Roger Williams* (New York: Ronald Press, 1940).
17. William Wood, *New England's Prospect*, quoted in *The Correspondence of Roger Williams*, ed. Glenn W. LaFantasie (Hanover, NH, and London: Brown University Press, 1988), 1:11n.
18. Roger Williams to Assembly of Commissioners, November 17, 1677, in LaFantasie, ed., *The Correspondence of Roger Williams*, vol. 2.
19. Roger Williams, *The Complete Writings of Roger Williams* (New York: Russell and Russell, 1963), 7:164.

## Chapter 16

1. John Winthrop, *Journal of John Winthrop*, ed. Richard Dunn, James Savage, and Laetitia Yeandle (Cambridge, MA: Belknap Press of Harvard University Press, 1996), 124.
2. Ibid., 126.
3. Ibid., 127.
4. Israel Stoughton to John Stoughton, in Everett Emerson, ed. *Letters from New England: The Massachusetts Bay Colony, 1629–1638* (Amherst: University of Massachusetts Press, 1976), 145.
5. *Journal of John Winthrop*, 127.
6. Israel Stoughton to John Stoughton, in Emerson, ed., *Letters from New England*, 144–155.
7. Roger Williams, "Mr. Cottons Letter Lately Printed and Answered," in *The Complete Writings of Roger Williams* (New York: Russell and Russell, 1963), 1:321.
8. Ibid., 4:461–462.
9. Ibid.
10. *Journal of John Winthrop*, 136–137.
11. Ibid., 137.
12. Ibid., 140.
13. Ibid., 142.
14. Act of General Court of Massachusetts, March 4, 1634, *Massachusetts Colonial Records*, 1:142, quoted in *The Complete Writings of Roger Williams*, 3:viii.
15. John Cotton, "Reply to Mr. Williams," in ibid., 2:62–63.
16. Roger Williams, *The Bloudy Tenent Yet More Bloudy*, in ibid., 4:461.
17. John Cotton, "A Reply to Mr. Williams His Examination," quoted in ibid., 2:22.
18. John Cotton, "A Reply to Mr. Williams His Examination," reprinted in Theodore P. Greene, *Roger Williams and the Massachusetts Magistrates* (Boston: D. C. Heath, 1964).
19. Ibid.
20. Ibid.
21. *Journal of John Winthrop*, 144.
22. Ibid.
23. John Cotton, "A Reply to Mr. Williams His Examination," reprinted in Greene, *Roger Williams and the Massachusetts Magistrates*.
24. Ibid.
25. *The Complete Writings of Roger Williams*, 1:22.
26. "Cottons Answer," in *The Complete Writings of Roger Williams*, 2:6–12.
27. Ibid., 2:14.
28. John Winthrop, *History of New England* (1853 edition), 1:188–189.
29. Ibid.
30. Quoted in John Marshall, *Life of George Washington*, 2nd ed. (Philadelphia: J. Crissy, 1832), 1:96.
31. Quoted in James Ernst, *Roger Williams: New England Firebrand* (New York: Macmillan, 1932), 110.
32. *Journal of John Winthrop*, 149, 151.

## Chapter 17

1. John Winthrop, *Journal of John Winthrop*, ed. Richard Dunn, James Savage, and Laetitia Yeandle (Cambridge, MA: Belknap Press of Harvard University Press, 1996), 150.
2. Roger Williams, *The Complete Writings of Roger Williams* (New York: Russell and Russell, 1963), 1:24.
3. Ibid.
4. John Cotton, "A Reply to Mr. Williams His Examination," in ibid., 2:48.
5. *The Complete Writings of Roger Williams*, 1:324.
6. *Journal of John Winthrop*, 150.
7. Ibid.
8. Ibid.
9. "Cotton's Answer," in *The Complete Writings of Roger Williams*, 2:47.
10. Quoted in James Ernst, *Roger Williams: New England Firebrand* (New York: Macmillan, 1932), 118.
11. "Cottons Answer," in *The Complete Writings of Roger Williams*, 2:14.
12. *Journal of John Winthrop*, 151.

13. John Cotton, "A Reply to Mr. Williams His Examination," in Theodore P. Greene, *Roger Williams and the Massachusetts Magistrates* (Boston: D. C. Heath, 1964), 10.

14. "Cotton's Answer," in *The Complete Writings of Roger Williams*, 2:47.

15. *The Complete Writings of Roger Williams*, 1:23.

16. Irwin H. Polishook, *Roger Williams, John Cotton, and Religious Freedom: A Controversy in New and Old England* (Englewood Cliffs, NJ: Prentice Hall, 1967), 71.

17. *Journal of John Winthrop*, 144.

18. Quoted in Lawrence Mayo, *John Endecott: A Biography* (Cambridge, MA: Harvard University Press, 1971 [1936]), 91.

19. *The Complete Writings of Roger Williams*, introduction, 26.

20. *Records of the Governor and Company of the Massachusetts Bay in New England*, eds. Nathaniel Shurtleff (Boston: Wm White, 1853), 1:156, September 3, 1635.

21. *Journal of John Winthrop*, 153.

22. Ibid., 156.

23. Ibid., 157.

24. Ibid., 158.

25. As with the preceding General Court, there are somewhat conflicting accounts concerning what transpired, and at precisely what point the Salem church abandoned Williams. As before, where there is a discrepancy between accounts, I have relied upon Winthrop's version since his journal comes closest to a contemporaneous account—although parts of his journal were clearly not written at the time. None of the sources are perfect.

26. *Journal of John Winthrop*, 158.

27. Quoted in Samuel Brockunier, *The Irrepressible Democrat: Roger Williams* (New York: Ronald Press, 1940), 67.

28. Quoted in *The Complete Writings of Roger Williams*, 1:52.

29. *The Complete Writings of Roger Williams*, 1:53.

30. *Journal of John Winthrop*, 158.

31. John Cotton, "Reply to Mr Williams," in *The Complete Writings of Roger Williams*, 2:39.

32. *The Complete Writings of Roger Williams*, 1:329.

33. Ibid., 2:64.

34. *Massachusetts Bay Records;* see also Ola Winslow, *Master Roger Williams: A Biography* (New York: Macmillan, 1957), 119.

35. Quoted in James Knowles, *Memoir of Roger Williams* (Boston: Lincoln and Edmands, 1834), 73.

36. *The Complete Writings of Roger Williams*, 1:339.

37. Sir Edward Coke, *The Selected Writings and Speeches of Sir Edward Coke*, ed. Steve Sheppard (Indianapolis: Liberty Fund, 2003), vol. 1, chapter "*Semayne's Case*"; accessed from http://oll.libertyfund.org/title/911/106328.

38. "Cotton's Answer," in *The Complete Writings of Roger Williams*, 2:51.

39. *Journal of John Winthrop*, 1:163–164.

40. Roger Williams to John Cotton Jr., March 25, 1671, in *The Correspondence of Roger Williams*, ed. Glenn W. LaFantasie (Hanover, NH, and London: Brown University Press, 1988), vol. 2.

41. *Journal of John Winthrop*, 1:163–164.

42. Ibid.

43. Ibid., 1:163.

44. Ibid., 1:163–164.

## PART IV: THE WILDERNESS

### Chapter 18

1. Roger Williams to Major John Mason [copy to Thomas Prence, governor of Plymouth], June 22, 1670, in *The Correspondence of Roger Williams*, ed. Glenn W. LaFantasie (Hanover, NH, and London: Brown University Press, 1988), vol. 2.

2. Roger Williams, "Mr. Cottons Letter Lately Printed, Examined and Answered," in *The Complete Writings of Roger Williams* (New York: Russell and Russell, 1963), 1:313.

3. Roger Williams to an Assembly of Commissioners, November 17, 1677, in *The Correspondence of Roger Williams*, vol. 2.

4. Roger Williams to Major John Mason [copy to Thomas Prence, governor of Plymouth], June 22, 1670, in ibid.
5. "Cottons Letter Answered," in *The Complete Writings of Roger Williams*, 315.
6. Roger Williams to Major John Mason [copy to Thomas Prence, governor of Plymouth], June 22, 1670, in *The Correspondence of Roger Williams*, vol. 2.
7. Ibid.
8. "Roger Williams: Founding Providence," http://www.nps.gov/rowi/historyculture/founding providence.htm.
9. Ibid.
10. Roger Williams to an Assembly of Commissioners, November 7, 1677, in *The Correspondence of Roger Williams*, vol. 2.
11. Howard Chapin, ed., *Documentary History of Rhode Island* (Providence: Preston and Rounds, 1916), 1:55.
12. Roger Williams to Major John Mason [copy to Thomas Prence, governor of Plymouth], June 22, 1670, in *The Correspondence of Roger Williams*, vol. 2.

## Chapter 19

1. Irving Richman, *Rhode Island: A History* (Boston and New York: Houghton Mifflin, 1905), 4.
2. Kathleen Bragdon, *Native People of Southern New England, 1500–1650* (Norman: University of Oklahoma Press, 1996), 4.
3. Neal Salisbury, *Manitou and Providence: Indians, Europeans, and the Making of New England, 1500–1643* (New York: Oxford University Press, 1982), 54.
4. *The Correspondence of Roger Williams*, ed. Glenn W. LaFantasie (Hanover, NH, and London: Brown University Press, 1988), 2:526. See also *Confirmatory deed of Roger Wiliams, 20 Dec. 1661*, in John Russell Bartlett, ed., *Records of the Colony of Rhode Island and Providence Plantations, 1636–1792* (Providence, 1856–62), 1:22–25.
5. New Advent, "Peter Ramus," http://www.newadvent.org/cathen/12638b.htm.
6. John Cotton, *A Briefe Exposition with Practicall Observations upon the Whole Book of Ecclesiastes* (London, 1654), 13, quoted in Larzer Ziff, *The Career of John Cotton: Puritanism and the American Experience* (Princeton, NJ: Princeton University Press, 1962), 12.
7. Quoted in Edmund Morgan, *The Puritan Family: Religious and Domestic Relations in Seventeenth-Century New England*, 3rd ed. (New York: Harper & Row, 1966), 25.
8. Francis Bacon, *The New Organon*, Author's Preface, http://www.constitution.org/bacon/nov_org.htm.
9. Quoted in Perez Zagorin, *Francis Bacon* (Princeton, NJ: Princeton University Press, 1998), 89, 223.
10. Roger Williams to an Assembly of Commissioners, November 17, 1677, in *The Correspondence of Roger Williams*, vol. 2.
11. Ibid.
12. Roger Williams to Major John Mason [copy to Thomas Prence, governor of Plymouth], June 22, 1670, in ibid.
13. John Winthrop, *Journal of John Winthrop*, ed. Richard Dunn, James Savage, and Laetitia Yeandle (Cambridge, MA: Belknap Press of Harvard University Press, 1996), 1:340.
14. August 20, 1636, in Howard Chapin, ed., *Documentary History of Rhode Island* (Providence: Preston and Rounds, 1916), 1:14.
15. Chapin, ed., *Documentary History of Rhode Island*, 1:28. See also Roger Williams to an Assembly of Commissioners, November 17, 1677, in *The Correspondence of Roger Williams*, vol. 2.
16. Roger Williams to John Winthrop, before August 25, 1636, in *The Correspondence of Roger Williams*, vol. 1.
17. *Journal of John Winthrop* (1908 edition), 2:237–239.

## Chapter 20

1. John Winthrop, *Journal of John Winthrop*, ed. Richard Dunn, James Savage, and Laetitia Yeandle (Cambridge, MA: Belknap Press of Harvard University Press, 1996), 180.
2. John Underhill, *Newes from America* (London, 1638), 37.
3. Patrick Malone, *The Skulking Way of War: Technology and Tactics Among the New England Indians* (Lanham, MD: Madison Books, 1991), 23.
4. Roger Williams, *The Complete Writings of Roger Williams* (New York: Russell and Russell, 1963), 1:138.
5. *Journal of John Winthrop*, 182.

6. Jonathan Brewster to John Winthrop Jr., June 18, 1636, in Samuel Eliot Morison, ed. *Winthrop Papers* (Boston: Massachusetts Historical Society, 1931), 3:270–271.

7. Roger Williams to John Winthrop, before August 25, 1636, in *The Correspondence of Roger Williams*, ed. Glenn W. LaFantasie (Hanover, NH, and London: Brown University Press, 1988), vol. 1.

8. Underhill, *Newes from America*, 7.

9. *Journal of John Winthrop*, 185.

10. Ibid.

11. Ibid.

12. Underhill, *Newes from America*, 13.

13. *Massachusetts Historical Society Collections*, 3rd ser., vol. 3, 140; also quoted in Michael Leroy Oberg, *Dominion and Civility: English Imperialism and Native America, 1585–1685* (Ithaca, NY: Cornell University Press, 1999), 106.

14. Ibid., 106, 108.

15. Underhill, *Newes from America*, 20.

16. Oberg, *Dominion and Civility*, 106, 108.

17. Brown, *Skulking Way of War*, 58.

18. Roger Williams to Major John Mason [copy to Thomas Prence, governor of Plymouth], June 22, 1670, in *The Correspondence of Roger Williams*, vol. 2.

19. *The Complete Writings of Roger Williams*, vol. 1, 142.

20. Roger Williams to Major John Mason [copy to Thomas Prence, governor of Plymouth], June 22, 1670, in *The Correspondence of Roger Williams*, vol. 2.

21. *Journal of John Winthrop*, 187; John Mason, *A Brief History of the Pequot War* (Boston, 1736), iv; see also Neal Salisbury, *Manitou and Providence: Indians, Europeans, and the Making of New England, 1500–1643* (New York: Oxford University Press, 1982), 212.

22. Mason, *A Brief History of the Pequot War*, iv.

23. Ibid.; see also Oberg, *Dominion and Civility*, 106.

24. Oberg, *Dominion and Civility*, 106.

25. Mason, *A Brief History of the Pequot War*, 7.

26. Oberg, *Dominion and Civility*, 106.

27. *Journal of John Winthrop*, 190–191.

28. Ibid.

29. Ibid., 193.

30. Oberg, *Dominion and Civility*, 109.

31. Roger Williams to John Winthrop, September 9, 1637, in *The Correspondence of Roger Williams*, vol. 1.

32. *Winthrop Papers*, 3:407–408.

33. John Higginson to John Winthrop, May 1637, ibid., 3:404–407; see also Thomas Hooker to John Winthrop, May 1637, ibid., 3:407–408.

34. *Journal of John Winthrop*, 213.

35. Ibid., 53–54.

36. Ibid.

37. Nicholas Canny, "The Ideology of English Colonization," *William and Mary Quarterly*, 3rd ser., 30, no. 4 (1973): 582.

38. Mason, *A Brief History of the Pequot War*, 2.

39. Underhill, *Newes from America*, 34.

40. Ibid., 35.

41. Mason, *A Brief History of the Pequot War*, 9.

42. Underhill, *Newes from America*, 35.

43. William Bradford, *Of Plimoth Plantation* (Boston: Houghton Mifflin, 1912), 2:250–252.

44. Underhill, *Newes from America*, 38.

45. For more information on enslaving Indians, see Almon Wheeler Lauber, *Indian Slavery in Colonial Times within the Present Limits of the United States* (New York, 1913), especially 109–125.

46. Salisbury, *Manitou and Providence*, 157.

47. Roger Williams to John Winthrop, June 30, 1637, in *The Correspondence of Roger Williams*, vol. 1.

48. Roger Williams to John Winthrop, August 1638, in ibid.

49. Roger Williams to Major John Mason [copy to Thomas Prence, governor of Plymouth], June 22, 1670, in ibid., vol. 2.

50. *Winthrop Papers*, 3:404–407.

### Chapter 21

1. For more on this see Teresa Toulouse, *The Art of Prophesying: New England Sermons and the Shaping of Belief* (Athens: University of Georgia Press, 1987), 20.
2. Edward Johnson, *Johnson's Wonder Working Providence*, ed. J. Franklin Jameson (New York: Scribner, 1910 [1653]), 134.
3. Quoted in Edmund Morgan, *The Puritan Dilemma: The Story of John Winthrop* (New York: Little, Brown, 1958), 125.
4. John Winthrop, "The Short Story of the Rise, Reign, and Ruine of the Antinomians, Familists, and Libertines that Infected the Churches of New England," in Charles Francis Adams, *Antinomianism in Massachusetts* (Boston: The Prince Society, 1894), 82.
5. Thomas Shepard, *New Englands Lamentations . . .* (London, 1645), 4, quoted in Philip Gura, *A Glimpse of Sion's Glory: Puritan Radicalism in New England, 1620–1660* (Middletown, CT: Wesleyan University Press), 240.
6. Quoted in Francis J. Bremer, *John Winthrop: America's Forgotten Founding Father* (New York: Oxford University Press, 2003), 281; Samuel Eliot Morison, ed., *Winthrop Papers* (Boston: Massachusetts Historical Society, 1931), 5:146–147.
7. John Winthrop, *Journal of John Winthrop*, ed. Richard Dunn, James Savage, and Laetitia Yeandle (Cambridge, MA: Belknap Press of Harvard University Press, 1996), 204.
8. Ibid., 203–205.
9. Ibid.
10. Bremer, *John Winthrop*, 285.
11. Quoted in ibid., 290.
12. Ibid., 215.
13. Morgan, *The Puritan Dilemma*, 130
14. Thomas Hutchinson Collection of Papers, vol. 1, 84–85, quoted in Gura, *A Glimpse of Sion's Glory*, 187.
15. Roger Williams to John Winthrop, July 21 1637, in ibid., vol. 1.
16. John Cotton, *Way of the Congregational Churches Cleared*, quoted in Bremer, *John Winthrop*, 296.
17. *Records of the Governor and Company of the Massachusetts Bay in New England*, ed. Nathaniel Shurtleff (Boston: Wm White, 1853), 1:211.
18. Ibid.
19. Thomas Lechford, *Plain Dealing, or News from New England*, introduction by Darrett Rutman (New York: Johnson Reprint Corporation, 1969), 106n.
20. Relation of John Clark, in Howard Chapin, ed., *Documentary History of Rhode Island* (Providence: Preston and Rounds, 1916), 2:17.
21. Ibid.
22. Roger Williams to Court of Commissioners, August 25, 1658, in *The Correspondence of Roger Williams*, vol. 2.
23. John Russell Bartlett, *Records of the Colony of Rhode Island and Providence Plantations in New England, 1636–1792* (Providence, 1856–65), 1:52.
24. Ibid., March 16, 1641, 1:112–113.
25. See Chapin, ed., *Documentary History of Rhode Island*, 2:80.
26. Harris papers (Providence: RIHS Collection, 1902), 2:237; see also Chapin, ed., *Documentary History of Rhode Island*, 2:80.
27. *Letter of Johannes Megapolensis and Samuel Drissius, Aug 14, 1657, Ecclesiastical History of State of New York* (Albany, 1901), 1:400, 410, quoted in Ola Winslow, *Master Roger Williams: A Biography* (New York: Macmillan, 1957), 259.

# PART V: THE MISSION

### Chapter 22

1. Raymond Stearns, *The Strenuous Puritan: Hugh Peter, 1598–1660* (Urbana: University of Illinois Press, 1954), 36.
2. Ibid.
3. Thomas Lechford, *Plain Dealing, or News from New England*, introduction by Darrett Rutman (New York: Johnson Reprint Corporation, 1969), 23, 38, 42.
4. James Knowles, *Memoir of Roger Williams* (Boston: Lincoln and Edmands, 1834), 176.

5. W. Rathband, *Brief Narration of Some Church Courses in N.E.*, in Lechford, *Plain Dealing*, 39.
6. Quoted in Richard Gildrie, *Salem, Massachusetts, 1626–1683, A Covenanted Community* (Charlottesville: University of Virginia Press, 1975), 77.
7. Letter of Weston (no first name cited), Essex Institute Historical Collections, 1:42–43; see also Stearns, *The Strenuous Puritan*, 126.
8. *A sermon . . . deliver'd at Salem, 1636*, in Ziff Larzer, *John Cotton on the Churches of New England* (Cambridge, MA: Belknap Press of Harvard University Press, 1968), 41–68.
9. Quoted in Stearns, *The Strenuous Puritan*, 144.
10. Vernon Parrington, *Main Currents in American Thought* (New York: Harcourt Brace and Co., 1927), 1:32.
11. For more on this see Michael Ditmore, "Laws and Liberties," in Francis J. Bremer and Tom Webster, *Puritans and Puritanism in Europe and America: A Comprehensive Encyclopedia* (Santa Barbara, CA: ABC-Clio, 2006), 1:445.
12. http://oll.libertyfund.org/title/694 on 2011-08-29.
13. Ibid.
14. Edmund Morgan, *The Puritan Family: Religious and Domestic Relations in Seventeenth-Century New England*, 3rd ed. (New York: Harper & Row, 1966), 41.
15. Alan Taylor, *American Colonies: The Settling of North America* (New York: Viking Penguin, 2001), 96.
16. See Lechford, *Plain Dealing*, 32n.
17. Howard Chapin, ed., *Documentary History of Rhode Island* (Providence: Preston and Rounds, 1916), 121.
18. John Winthrop, *Journal of John Winthrop*, eds. Richard Dunn, James Savage, and Laetitia Yeandle (Cambridge, MA: Belknap Press of Harvard University Press, 1996), 589.
19. Lechford, *Plain Dealing*, 54.
20. *Records of the Governor and Company of the Massachusetts Bay in New England*, ed. Nathaniel Shurtleff (Boston: Wm White, 1853), March 13, 1639, 1:252.
21. John Russell Bartlett, *Records of the Colony of Rhode Island and Providence Plantations, 1636–1792* (Providence, 1856–65), July 1640, 1:28–29.
22. Ibid.
23. *The Correspondence of Roger Williams*, ed. Glenn W. LaFantasie (Hanover, NH, and London: Brown University Press, 1988), 1:211.
24. *Journal of John Winthrop*, March 16, 1638/39, 286.

## Chapter 23

1. Edward Winslow, *Hypocrisie Unmasked, a true Relation of the Proceedings of the Governor and Company of the Massachusetts against Samuel Gorton* (Providence: Club for Colonial Reprints, 1916), ii.
2. Samuel Gorton, *Simplicities defence against Seven-headed Policy . . .* (London, 1646 [from 1846 reprint]), 22.
3. Ibid., 18.
4. Nathaniel Morton, *New Englands Memoriall*, 5th ed., ed. John Davis (Boston: Crocker and Brewster, 1826 [1669]), 138.
5. *The Correspondence of Roger Williams*, ed. Glenn W. LaFantasie (Hanover, NH, and London: Brown University Press, 1988), 1:218n.
6. Thomas Lechford, *Plain Dealing, or News from New England*, introduction by Darrett Rutman (New York: Johnson Reprint Corporation, 1969), 94–96.
7. Howard Chapin, ed., *Documentary History of Rhode Island* (Providence: Preston and Rounds, 1916), 133.
8. *The Correspondence of Roger Williams*, 1:210.
9. Roger Williams to John Winthrop, March 8, 1640/41, in ibid.
10. Quoted in Bruce Daniels, *Dissent and Conformity on Narragansett Bay: The Colonial Rhode Island Town* (Middletown, CT: Wesleyan University Press, 1983), 102.
11. Chapin, ed., *Documentary History of Rhode Island*, 130.
12. Ibid.
13. John Winthrop, *Journal of John Winthrop*, eds. Richard Dunn, James Savage, and Laetitia Yeandle (Cambridge, MA: Belknap Press of Harvard University Press, 1996), 383.
14. Letter to Governor Richard Bellingham, November 17, 1641, quoted in Winslow, *Hypocrisie Unmasked*, 54–56.

15. *Journal of John Winthrop*, 384.
16. Chapin, ed., *Documentary History of Rhode Island*, 144.
17. William Field's testimony, Providence Town Papers, 01293. See also Chapin, ed., *Documentary History of Rhode Island*, 63.
18. Roger Williams to John Winthrop, early May 1638, in *The Correspondence of Roger Williams*, 1:153.
19. *Journal of John Winthrop*, 413.
20. *Records of the Governor and Company of the Massachusetts Bay in New England*, ed. Nathaniel Shurtleff (Boston: Wm White, 1853), 2:26, 27.
21. John Russell Bartlett, *Records of the Colony of Rhode Island and Providence Plantations, 1636–1792* (Providence, 1856–65), 1:124.
22. Ibid.

## Chapter 24

1. David Masson, *The Life of Milton* (1858–80), 2:141.
2. Quoted in Roger Lockyer, *The Early Stuarts: A Political History of England, 1603–1642* (London and NY: Longman, 1989), 321.
3. Gordon Schochet, ed., *Religion, Resistance, and Civil War* (Washington, DC: Folger Institute, 1990), 8.
4. W. K. Jordan, *The Development of Religious Toleration in England* (Cambridge, MA: Harvard University Press, 1932), 3:38, 3:19.
5. Quoted in ibid., 3:33.
6. State Papers, Dom. Charles I, cccclxxxix, 14, quoted in Jordan, *The Development of Religious Toleration in England*, 3:40.
7. Quoted in Raymond Stearns, "The Weld-Peter Mission to England," *Publications of the Colonial Society of Massachusetts* 32 (1934): 190.
8. John Winthrop, *Journal of John Winthrop*, ed. Richard Dunn, James Savage, and Laetitia Yeandle (Cambridge, MA: Belknap Press of Harvard University Press, 1996), 339.
9. Ibid., 346.
10. See ibid., 346, and Stearns, "The Weld-Peter Mission to England," 193.
11. Stearns, "The Weld-Peter Mission to England," 216.
12. Ibid., 209.
13. Quoted in Raymond Stearns, *The Strenuous Puritan: Hugh Peter, 1598–1660* (Urbana: University of Illinois Press, 1954), 201.
14. Quoted in Stearns, "The Weld-Peter Mission to England," 213.
15. Jordan, *The Development of Religious Toleration in England*, 3:43.
16. Quoted in ibid., 3:44.
17. Quoted in editor's comment by Reuben Guild, in Roger Williams, *The Complete Writings of Roger Williams* (New York: Russell and Russell, 1963), 2:244.

## Chapter 25

1. Roger Williams to Massachusetts General Court, October 5, 1654, in *The Correspondence of Roger Williams*, ed. Glenn W. LaFantasie (Hanover, NH, and London: Brown University Press, 1988), vol. 2.
2. Quoted in Eve Laplante, *American Jezebel: The Uncommon Life of Anne Hutchinson, the Woman Who Defied the Puritans* (San Francisco: Harper San Francisco, 2003), 237.
3. Quoted in Jonathan Beecher Field, *Errands into the Metropolis: New England Dissidents in Revolutionary London* (Hanover, NH: Dartmouth College Press, 2009), 53.
4. John Winthrop, *Journal of John Winthrop*, ed. Richard Dunn, James Savage, and Laetitia Yeandle (Cambridge, MA: Belknap Press of Harvard University Press, 1996), 505–507.
5. Roger Williams to Massachusetts General Court, October 5, 1654, in *The Correspondence of Roger Williams*, vol. 2.
6. *Journal of John Winthrop*, 428.
7. Roger Williams to Massachusetts General Court, October 5, 1654, in *The Correspondence of Roger Williams*, vol. 2.
8. See Philip Gura, *A Glimpse of Sion's Glory: Puritan Radicalism in New England, 1620–1660*

(Middletown, CT: Wesleyan University Press, 1984), 132–135; see also W. Clark Gilpin, *The Millenarian Piety of Roger Williams* (Chicago: University of Chicago Press, 1979), 127–131.

9. Roger Williams, *The Complete Writings of Roger Williams* (New York: Russell and Russell, 1963), 1:117.
10. Ibid., 1:142.
11. Ibid., 1:81.
12. Ibid., 1:106, 227, 141.
13. Robert Baillie, *A Dissuasive from the Errors of the Time* (1645), 63.
14. David Masson, *The Life of Milton: Narrated in Connexion with the Political, Ecclesiastical, and Literary History of His Time* (1858–80), 3:189.
15. For a discussion of this evidence see George Potter, "Roger Williams and John Milton," *Collection of the Rhode Island Historical Society* 13, no. 4 (1920): 113–129.
16. Bradford Swan, *Gregory Dexter of London and New England* (Rochester, NY: Leo Hart, 1949), 1.
17. Ibid., 51.
18. *The Complete Writings of Roger Williams*, 1:72.
19. The actual pamphlet has not survived, but was quoted by Baillie in *Dissuasive*; see *The Complete Writings of Roger Williams*, 1:220n.
20. Weld to General Court, September 25, 1643, quoted in Raymond Stearns, "The Weld-Peter Mission to England," *Publications of the Colonial Society of Massachusetts* 32 (1934): 221.
21. Lion Gardiner, "Leift Lion Gardiner His Relation of the Pequot Warres," in *Appendix to the History of the Wars of New England with the Eastern Indians*, ed. Samuel Penhallow (Cincinnati: Wm Dodge, 1859), 26.
22. Roger Williams to John Winthrop, June 14, 1638, in *The Correspondence of Roger Williams*, vol. 1.
23. *Journal of John Winthrop*, 472.
24. Ibid., 473.
25. See *Journal of John Winthrop*, 473, footnote.
26. Howard Chapin, ed., *Documentary History of Rhode Island* (Providence: Preston and Rounds, 1916), 1:172–173.
27. Ibid., 1:173.
28. Ibid., 1:188.
29. See *Journal of John Winthrop*, 480–489, passim, especially 486; Samuel Gorton, *Simplicities defence against Seven-headed Policy . . .* (London, 1646 [from 1846 reprint]), passim; see also Gura, *A Glimpse of Sion's Glory,* 194.
30. *Records of the Governor and Company of the Massachusetts Bay in New England,* ed. Nathaniel Shurtleff (Boston: Wm White, 1853), 2:52.
31. *Journal of John Winthrop,* 487.

## PART VI: SOUL LIBERTY

### Chapter 26

1. Quoted in Samuel Brockunier, *The Irrepressible Democrat: Roger Williams* (New York: Ronald Press, 1940), 142.
2. Quoted in David Masson, *The Life of Milton: Narrated in Connexion with the Political, Ecclesiastical, and Literary History of His Time* (1858–80), 3:37.
3. Ola Winslow, *Master Roger Williams: A Biography* (New York: Macmillan, 1957), 184.
4. Roger Williams, *The Complete Writings of Roger Williams* (New York: Russell and Russell, 1963), *The Bloudy Tenent Yet More Bloudy,* 4:103.
5. Ibid.
6. Quoted in W. K. Jordan, *The Development of Religious Toleration in England.* (Cambridge, MA: Harvard University Press, 1932), 3:52n.
7. Quoted in Mark Kishlansky, *A Monarchy Transformed: Britain, 1603–1714* (New York: Penguin, 1997), 168.
8. Robert Baillie, *Letters and Journals of Robert Baillie* (Edinburgh, 1882), 2:111.
9. Oliver Cromwell, *The Letters and Speeches of Oliver Cromwell,* ed. S. C. Lomas (London: Methuen, 1904), 1:171.
10. Baillie, *Letters and Journals of Robert Baillie,* 1:345.
11. Ibid., 2:231.

12. Ibid., 2:212.
13. James Ernst, "Roger Williams and the English Revolution," *Collections of the Rhode Island Historical Society* 24 (1931): 1–58, esp. 51–53.
14. Vane is not explicitly identified as the speaker, but it was almost certainly he; see "Answer," in *The Complete Writings of Roger Williams*, 1:313.

## Chapter 27

1. Roger Williams, *The Complete Writings of Roger Williams* (New York: Russell and Russell, 1963), 1:319.
2. Ibid., 1:326–327.
3. Ibid., 1:393.
4. Ibid., 1:328.
5. Ibid., 1:392.
6. Howard Chapin, ed., *Documentary History of Rhode Island* (Providence: Preston and Rounds, 1916), 1:215–217; note this copy is from State Paper Office, London; several other copies exist with some variation.
7. Ibid.
8. See for example Roger Williams to Gregory Dexter, October 7, 1652, in *The Correspondence of Roger Williams*, ed. Glenn W. LaFantasie (Hanover, NH, and London: Brown University Press, 1988), vol. 1.
9. Licensing Ordinance quoted in Sharon Achinstein and Elizabeth Sauer, eds., *Milton and Toleration* (New York: Oxford University Press, 2007), 66.
10. *The Complete Writings of Roger Williams*, 2:253.
11. Ibid., 2:257.
12. Ibid., 2:259–260.
13. Ibid., 2:274.

## Chapter 28

1. Quoted in Jonathan Beecher Field, *Errands into the Metropolis: New England Dissidents in Revolutionary England* (Hanover, NH: Dartmouth College Press, 2009), 55.
2. Howard Chapin, ed., *Documentary History of Rhode Island* (Providence: Preston and Round, 1916), 1:202.
3. *The Correspondence of Roger Williams*, ed. Glenn W. LaFantasie (Hanover, NH, and London: Brown University Press, 1988), 1:22
4. Chapin, ed., *Documentary History of Rhode Island*, 1:203–204.
5. Quoted in Perez Zagorin, *How the Idea of Religious Toleration Came to the West* (Princeton, NJ: Princeton University Press, 2003), 17.
6. Ibid., 43.
7. Quoted in Roger Williams, *The Complete Writings of Roger Williams* (New York: Russell and Russell, 1963), 3:32.
8. Zagorin, *How the Idea of Religious Toleration Came to the West*, 153.
9. Quoted in ibid., 103.
10. Quoted in ibid., 107.
11. Quoted in ibid., 111.
12. Quoted in *Stanford Encyclopedia of Philosophy*, http://plato.stanford.edu/entries/grotius/.
13. Hugo Grotius, *On the Law of War and Peace*, in ibid.
14. Sharon Achinstein and Elizabeth Sauer, eds., *Milton and Toleration* (New York: Oxford University Press, 2007), 56.
15. W. K. Jordan, *The Development of Religious Toleration in England* (Cambridge, MA: Harvard University Press, 1932), 3:29.
16. Ibid., 3:32.

## Chapter 29

1. W. K. Jordan, *The Development of Religious Toleration in England* (Cambridge, MA: Harvard University Press, 1932), 4:341.
2. Roger Williams, *The Complete Writings of Roger Williams* (New York: Russell and Russell, 1963), *The Bloudy Tenent Yet More Bloudy*, 4:9.

3. Quoted in ibid., 4:90.
4. Quoted in ibid., *The Bloudy Tenent,* 3:42.
5. Quoted in ibid.
6. Quoted in ibid.
7. Ibid., *The Bloudy Tenent Yet More Bloudy,* 4:24.
8. Ibid., 4:44.
9. Ibid.
10. Ibid., *The Bloudy Tenent,* 3:3–4.
11. Ibid., *The Bloudy Tenent Yet More Bloudy,* 4:44.
12. Ibid., 4:28.
13. Ibid.
14. John Cotton, *The Pwring out of the Seven Vials: or an Exposition of the 16. Chapter of the Revelation, with an Application of it to our Times* (London, 1642), Part 3, quoted in Irwin H. Polishook, *Roger Williams, John Cotton, and Religious Freedom: A Controversy in New and Old England* (Englewood Cliffs, NJ: Prentice Hall, 1967), 68.
15. *The Complete Writings of Roger Williams, The Bloudy Tenent,* 3:125.
16. Ibid., 3:213.
17. Ibid.
18. Ibid., *The Bloudy Tenent Yet More Bloudy,* 4:154.
19. Ibid., *The Bloudy Tenent,* 3:421.
20. Ibid., *The Bloudy Tenent Yet More Bloudy,* 4:154.

## Chapter 30

1. Roger Williams, *The Complete Writings of Roger Williams* (New York: Russell and Russell, 1963), *The Bloudy Tenent Yet More Bloudy,* 4:206.
2. Edmund Morgan, *Roger Williams: The Church and the State* (New York: Norton, 1967), 82.
3. From John Cotton, *Bloudy Tenet Washed,* quoted in Irwin H. Polishook, *Roger Williams, John Cotton, and Religious Freedom: A Controversy in New and Old England* (Englewood Cliffs, NJ: Prentice Hall, 1967), 73.
4. *The Complete Writings of Roger Williams, The Bloudy Tenent,* 3:190.
5. Ibid., 3:189.
6. Ibid., 3:414.
7. Ibid., 3:73.
8. Ibid., 3:189.
9. Ibid., *The Bloudy Tenent Yet More Bloudy,* 4:170.
10. Emil Oberholzer Jr., *Delinquent Saints: Disciplinary Action in the Early Congregational Churches of Massachusetts* (New York: Columbia University Press, 1955), 230.
11. *The Complete Writings of Roger Williams, The Bloudy Tenent,* 3:226.
12. Ibid., 3:73.
13. Ibid.
14. John Winthrop, *Journal of John Winthrop,* ed. Richard Dunn, James Savage, and Laetitia Yeandle (Cambridge, MA: Belknap Press of Harvard University Press, 1996), 589; see Glenn LaFantasie, "Roger Williams and John Winthrop: The Rise and Fall of an Extraordinary Friendship," *Rhode Island History* 47 (August 1989): 85–95; see also Francis J. Bremer, *John Winthrop: America's Forgotten Founding Father* (New York: Oxford University Press, 2003), 364–365.
15. *Journal of John Winthrop,* 589; see LaFantasie, "Roger Williams and John Winthrop"; see also Bremer, *John Winthrop,* 364–365.
16. Oscar Straus, *Roger Williams: The Pioneer of Religious Liberty* (New York: Century Co., 1894), 154; James Ernst, *Roger Williams: New England Firebrand* (New York: Macmillan, 1932), 93.
17. Sargent Bush, *The Correspondence of John Cotton* (Chapel Hill: University of North Carolina Press, 2001), 245.
18. John Russell Bartlett, *Records of the Colony of Rhode Island and Providence Plantations, 1636–1792* (Providence, 1856–65), 1:112.
19. Quoted in Michael Mendle, *Henry Parker and the English Civil War: The Political Thought of the Public's "Privado"* (Cambridge: Cambridge University Press, 2003), passim, especially 85–87.
20. *The Complete Writings of Roger Williams, The Bloudy Tenent,* 3:249.
21. Ibid., 3:366.

22. Ibid., 3:398.
23. Ibid.
24. Ibid., 3:356.
25. Roger Williams to Major John Mason, June 22, 1670, in *The Correspondence of Roger Williams,* ed. Glenn W. LaFantasie (Hanover, NH, and London: Brown University Press, 1988), vol. 2.
26. *The Complete Writings of Roger Williams, The Bloudy Tenent,* 3:183.
27. Ibid., 3:202.

### Chapter 31

1. Bradford Swan, *Gregory Dexter of London and New England* (Rochester, NY: Leo Hart, 1949), 52.
2. Gordon Campbell and Thomas Corns, *John Milton: Life, Work, and Thought* (Oxford: Oxford University Press, 2008), 165.
3. Ibid.
4. Quoted in Ola Winslow, *Master Roger Williams: A Biography* (New York: Macmillan, 1957), 198.
5. Ibid., 200.
6. Robert Baillie, *Letters and Journals of Robert Baillie* (Edinburgh, 1882), 2:190.
7. Ibid., 1:231.
8. Ibid., 1:235.
9. John Milton, *The Reason for Church-Government,* 3; http://oll.libertyfund.org/?option=com_staticxt&staticfile=show.php%3Ftitle=1209&chapter=78007&layout=html&Itemid=27.
10. James Ernst, "Roger Williams and the English Revolution," *Collection of the Rhode Island Historical Society* 24 (January 1931): 1–58 and 118–128.
11. Ibid.
12. Ibid.
13. Harry Stout, "The Morphology of Remigration: New England University Men and Their Return to England, 1640–1660," *Journal of American Studies* 10, no. 2 (August 1976): 151–172.
14. John Winthrop, *Journal of John Winthrop,* eds. Richard Dunn, James Savage, and Laetitia Yeandle (Cambridge, MA: Belknap Press of Harvard University Press, 1996), 540–541.
15. Rev. William Hubbard, quoted in Howard Chapin, ed., *Documentary History of Rhode Island* (Providence: Preston and Rounds, 1916), 1:214.
16. Comment by Richard Scott; see ibid.
17. Stephen Foster, "New England and the Challenge of Heresy, 1630 to 1660: The Puritan Crisis in Transatlantic Perspective," *William and Mary Quarterly,* 3rd ser., 38, no. 4 (October 1981): 626.
18. Roger Williams, *The Complete Writings of Roger Williams* (New York: Russell and Russell, 1963), *The Bloudy Tenent Yet More Bloudy,* 4:30.

## PART VII: THE TEST

### Chapter 32

1. William Coddington to John Winthrop, August 5, 1644, in Samuel Eliot Morison, ed. *Winthrop Papers* (Boston: Massachusetts Historical Society, 1931), 4:489–491, reprinted in Howard Chapin, ed., *Documentary History of Rhode Island* (Providence: Preston and Rounds, 1916), 2:175–176.
2. Chapin, ed., *Documentary History of Rhode Island,* 2:224.
3. Ibid., 2:224–226.
4. John Winthrop, *Journal of John Winthrop,* eds. Richard Dunn, James Savage, and Laetitia Yeandle (Cambridge, MA: Belknap Press of Harvard University Press, 1996), 589; see Glenn LaFantasie, "Roger Williams and John Winthrop: The Rise and Fall of an Extraordinary Friendship," *Rhode Island History* 47 (August 1989): 85–95; see also Francis J. Bremer, *John Winthrop: America's Forgotten Founding Father* (New York: Oxford University Press, 1994), 364–365.
5. Roger Williams to John Winthrop, June 22, 1645, in *The Correspondence of Roger Williams,* ed. Glenn W. LaFantasie (Hanover, NH, and London: Brown University Press, 1988), vol. 1.
6. Letter to Roger Williams from Increase Nowell, Sc't, Boston, 27, 6 mo [August] 1645, in *Records of the Governor and Company of the Massachusetts Bay in New England,* ed. Nathaniel Shurtleff (Boston: Wm White, 1853), 3:49.
7. Roger Williams to Major John Mason [copy to Thomas Prence, governor of Plymouth], June 22, 1670, in *The Correspondence of Roger Williams,* vol. 2.

8. Roger Williams, *The Complete Writings of Roger Williams* (New York: Russell and Russell, 1963), 6:263.
9. Quoted in Samuel Brockunier, *The Irrepressible Democrat: Roger Williams* (New York: Ronald Press, 1940), 164
10. Ibid., 53.
11. Vernon Parrington, "Roger Williams, Seeker," from *Main Currents in American Thought* (New York: Harcourt Brace and Co., 1927), 1:49, 62.
12. *The Complete Writings of Roger Williams, The Bloudy Tenent Yet More Bloudy*, 4:471–472.
13. Ibid.
14. Town of Providence to the Governor and Council of Rhode Island, August 31, 1668, in *The Correspondence of Roger Williams*, 2:580.
15. For a review of this, see Roger Williams to Thomas Hickley and Special Court of Commissioners, June 18, 1678, in *The Correspondence of Roger Williams*, vol. 2.
16. John Russell Bartlett, *Records of the Colony of Rhode Island and Providence Plantations, 1636–1792* (Providence, 1856–65), 1:367–369.
17. Ibid., 1:147–208.
18. Ibid., 1:158–159.
19. Edward Winslow, *Hypocrisie Unmasked, a true Relation of the Proceedings of the Governor and Company of the Massachusetts against Samuel Gorton* (Providence: Club for Colonial Reprints, 1916), 82.
20. Arnold to Massachusetts, October 7, 1651, in Bartlett, *Records of the Colony of Rhode Island*, 1:234–235.
21. Ibid.
22. David Pulsifer, ed., *Acts of the Commissioners of the United Colonies of New England* (Boston: The Press of William White, 1859), 1:110.
23. Bartlett, *Records of the Colony of Rhode Island*, November 4, 1651, 1:233.
24. William Coddington to John Winthrop Jr., *Collection of the Massachusetts Historical Society*, 7:284, quoted in Brockunier, *The Irrepressible Democrat*, 217.
25. Quoted in Bradford Swan, *Gregory Dexter of London and New England* (Providence: Roger Williams Press, 1944), 72.
26. Bartlett, *Records of the Colony of Rhode Island*, 1:231.
27. John Clarke, *Ill Newes from New England* (1652), 56.
28. Quoted in Ola Winslow, *Master Roger Williams: A Biography* (New York: Macmillan, 1957), 232.
29. Bartlett, *Records of the Colony of Rhode Island*, May 23, 1652, 1:243.
30. Quoted in Raymond Stearns, *The Strenuous Puritan: Hugh Peter, 1598–1660* (Urbana: University of Illinois Press, 1954), 334.
31. John Milton, *The Prose Works of John Milton, with an Introductory Review by Robert Fletcher* (London: Wm Ball, 1838), 450.
32. Charles Carlton, *The Experience of the British Civil War* (London: Routledge, 1992), 211.
33. Roger Williams to towns of Providence and Warwick, April 1, 1653, in *The Correspondence of Roger Williams*, vol. 1.
34. Roger Williams to Anne Sadleir, ca. April 1652, in ibid.
35. Roger Williams to John Winthrop Jr., April 20, 1652, in ibid.
36. Quoted in *The Complete Writings of Roger Williams*, 7:17.
37. *The Complete Writings of Roger Williams*, 7:153, 164, 169.
38. Ibid., 7:164, 169.
39. Roger Williams to Gregory Dexter, October 7, 1652, in *The Correspondence of Roger Williams*, vol. 1.
40. Ibid.
41. Roger Williams to towns of Providence and Warwick, April 1, 1653, in ibid.
42. Ibid.
43. Ibid.
44. *British Civil War, Commonwealth and Protectorate 1638–60*, "The Rump Parliament (The Purged Parliament)," http://www.british-civil-wars.co.uk/glossary/rump-Parliament.htm.
45. Roger Williams to General Court of Massachusetts Bay, October 1654, in *The Correspondence of Roger Williams*, vol. 2.
46. Henry Vane to Providence Plantations, February 8, 1654, in ibid.
47. Chapin, ed., *Documentary History of Rhode Island*, 1:14; see also George Fox, *A New-England-firebrand quenched, . . .* , London, 1678, 2:247.
48. See editorial note, Williams to Winthrop, June 14, 1638, *The Correspondence of Roger Williams*, vol. 1.
49. Roger Williams to John Winthrop Jr., July 12, 1654, in ibid.

50. Oliver Cromwell to the President, Assistants, and Inhabitants of Rhode Island and Providence Plantations, March 29, 1655, in ibid.
51. Bartlett, *Records of the Colony of Rhode Island,* June 3 and 4, 1653, 1:270.
52. Henry Vane to Providence Plantations, February 8, 1654, in *The Correspondence of Roger Williams,* in ibid.
53. Roger Williams to town of Providence, April 1, 1653, in ibid.
54. Roger Williams to John Winthrop Jr., February 15, 1655, in ibid.
55. Ibid.
56. See editorial note, *The Correspondence of Roger Williams,* 419.
57. Roger Williams to town of Providence, ca. January 1654/55, in ibid.; reprinted from *Providence Gazette,* February 16, 1765.
58. Bartlett, *Records of the Colony of Rhode Island,* 1:327.

## Chapter 33

1. *Swarthmore Mss.*, Society of Friends Library, London, SW 1.66.239, quoted in Raymond L. Camp, *Roger Williams: God's Apostle of Advocacy* (Lewiston, NY: Edwin Mellen Press, 1989), 154.
2. *Records of the Governor and Company of the Massachusetts Bay in New England,* ed. Nathaniel Shurtleff (Boston: Wm White, 1853), 2:415–416.
3. Ibid.
4. Oscar Straus, *Roger Williams: The Pioneer of Religious Liberty* (New York: Century Co., 1894), 202.
5. Kai T. Erikson, *Wayward Puritans: A Study in the Sociology of Deviance* (New York: John Wiley and Sons, 1966), 122, quoted in Camp, *Roger Williams,* 160.
6. George Bishop, *New England Judged* (London, Robert Wilson, 1661), 430, quoted in Camp, *Roger Williams,* 161.
7. Quoted in Ola Winslow, *Master Roger Williams: A Biography* (New York: Macmillan, 1957), 259.
8. Roger Williams, *The Complete Writings of Roger Williams* (New York: Russell and Russell, 1963), 5:99–100.
9. Roger Williams to Massachusetts General Court, November 15, 1655, in *The Correspondence of Roger Williams,* ed. Glenn W. LaFantasie (Hanover, NH, and London: Brown University Press, 1988), vol. 2.
10. See for example Roger Williams to John Winthrop Jr., October 23, 1650, in ibid., vol 1, and February 15, 1655, in vol 2.
11. Roger Williams to Massachusetts General Court, November 15, 1655, in ibid., vol. 2.
12. John Russell Bartlett, *Records of the Colony of Rhode Island and Providence Plantations, 1636–1792* (Providence, 1856–65), May 21–23, 1656, 1:462.
13. See New England Historic Genealogical Society, *Historical and Genealogical Register* 8 (1854): 293; see also in *The Correspondence of Roger Williams,* 2:466.
14. *Records of the Governor and Company of the Massachusetts Bay,* May 23, 1650, 3:196, and May 22, 1651, 3:228.
15. Roger Williams to Arthur Fenner, February 24, 1657, in *The Correspondence of Roger Williams,* vol. 2.
16. *The Correspondence of Roger Williams,* 2:466.
17. *Records of the Governor and Company of the Massachusetts Bay,* May 6, 1657, 3:432.
18. Letter from Commissioners of the United Colonies to Rhode Island, Concerning the Quakers, September 12, 1657, in Bartlett, *Records of the Colony of Rhode Island,* 374.
19. Letter from Benedict Arnold to United Colonies, October 13, 1657, signed Benedict Arnold, president, in ibid., 376–78.
20. John Sanford to John Clarke, November 2, 1658, in ibid., 396–398. This letter recounts much of what happened in previous months.
21. Copy of letter from John Sanford to John Clarke, November 2, 1658, in ibid., 396.
22. General Assembly to Massachusetts (signed John Sanford, Clerk), March 13, 1658, in ibid., 478.
23. *The Complete Writings of Roger Williams, The Bloudy Tenent,* 3:13.

## Chapter 34

1. *The Speeches and Prayers of Major General Harison . . . Mr. Hugh Peters . . . Faithfully and Impartially Collected . . .* (London, 1660), 58–61, quoted in Raymond Stearns, *The Strenuous Puritan: Hugh Peter, 1598–1660* (Urbana: University of Illinois Press, 1954), 418.
2. *Mercurius Publicus,* October 15–22, 1660, quoted in ibid., 419.

3. Violet A. Rowe, *Sir Henry Vane the Younger: A Study in Political and Administrative History* (London: Athlone Press, 1970), 209.

4. Quoted in ibid., 241.

5. *The Diary of Sir Henry Pepys,* "Sir Henry Vane (younger)," http://www.pepysdiary.com/p/136.php; see also Rowe, *Sir Henry Vane the Younger,* 241.

6. The royal charter is reprinted in James Knowles, *Memoir of Roger Williams* (Boston: Lincoln and Edmands, 1834), 419–430; see also Appendix, No. XXI, *Collections of the Rhode Island Historical Society 4* (1838): 241–261.

7. Roger Williams to Major John Mason, June 22, 1670, in *The Correspondence of Roger Williams,* ed. Glenn W. LaFantasie (Hanover, NH, and London: Brown University Press, 1988), vol. 2.

8. Ibid.

9. Ibid.

10. Major John Mason to John Allyn et al., Aug 3, 1670, in John Russell Bartlett, ed., *Records of the Colony of Rhode Island and Providence Plantations, 1636–1792* (Providence, 1856–65), 2:348–350.

11. Roger Williams, *The Complete Writings of Roger Williams* (New York: Russell and Russell, 1963), vol. 5, *George Fox Digg'd Out of His Burrowes,* 26.

12. Ibid., vol. 3, *The Bloudy Tenent,* 3.

13. John Winthrop Jr. to Roger Williams, January 6, 1675, in *The Correspondence of Roger Williams,* vol. 2.

14. Richard Smith to John Winthrop Jr., June 25, 1673, in Daniel Berkeley Updike, *Richard Smith, First English Settler of the Narragansett Country* (Boston: Merrymount Press, 1937), 97.

15. Roger Williams to town of Providence, December 8, 1680, in *The Correspondence of Roger Williams,* vol. 2.

16. Roger Williams to town of Providence, January 15, 1682, in ibid.

17. Roger Williams to John Winthrop, October 24, 1636, in ibid., vol. 1.

18. Roger Williams to Robert Williams, April 1, 1676, in ibid., vol. 2. There is questionable provenance to this letter; while it clearly seems to contain authentic information, it is equally clear that the extant version was modified by someone who probably copied an original letter and changed it.

19. Ibid.

20. Providence Town Papers, June 5, 1676, 15:151.

21. Roger Williams to Governor Simon Bradstreet, May 6, 1682, in *The Correspondence of Roger Williams,* vol. 2.

22. Statement of Roger Williams, June 10, 1682, in *The Complete Writings of Roger Williams,* 6:407–408.

## Afterword

1. Memo of October 23, 2001, http://www.justice.gov/opa/documents/memomilitaryforcecombatus10232001.pdf.

2. *Collections of the Rhode Island Historical Society* 27:54.

3. William McLoughlin, *New England Dissent, 1630–1833: The Baptists and Separation of Church and State* (Cambridge, MA: Harvard University Press, 1971), 7.

4. Emil Oberholzer Jr., *Dominion and Civility: English Imperialism and Native America* (Ithaca, NY: Cornell University Press, 1999), 218.

5. Alan Simpson, "How Democratic Was Roger Williams?" *William and Mary Quarterly,* 3rd ser., 13 (February 1956): 53–67.

6. Perry Miller, *Roger Williams; His Contribution to the American Tradition* (Indianapolis: Bobbs-Merrill, 1953), 110.

7. Ibid.

8. Warren Chelline, "On the Relationship of Roger Williams and John Milton" (PhD thesis, University of Kansas, 1982), 114.

9. Vernon Parrington, "Roger Williams, Seeker," from *Main Currents in American Thought* (New York: Harcourt Brace and Co., 1927), 1:34, 36.

10. Ibid., 1:37.

11. Edmund Morgan, *Roger Williams: The Church and the State* (New York: Norton, 1967), 87.

12. Ibid., 99.

13. Georg Jellinek, *The Declaration of the Rights of Man and of Citizens,* translated by Max Farrand (New York, 1901), 77; see also Samuel Brockunier, *The Irrepressible Democrat: Roger Williams* (New York: Ronald Press, 1940), 101.

14. James Ernst, "Roger Williams and the English Revolution," *Collections of the Rhode Island Historical Society* 24 (January 1931): 1–58 and 118–128.

15. Jerome Merin, "The Supreme Court and Libel," *William and Mary Law Review* 11 (1969): 371–423.

16. Quoted in Edwin Gaustad, *Liberty of Conscience: Roger Williams in America* (Grand Rapids, MI: Erdmanns, 1991), 203.

17. Winthrop Hudson, "John Locke: Heir of Puritan Political Theorists," in George Hunt, ed., *Calvinism and the Political Order* (Philadelphia: Westminster Press, 1965), 117–118.

18. David Little, "Conscience, Theology, and the First Amendment," *Soundings* (Summer/Fall 1989).

19. W. K. Jordan, *The Development of Religious Toleration in England* (Cambridge, MA: Harvard University Press, 1932), 3:475.

20. George Bancroft, *History of the United States, from the Discovery of the Continent,* 10th ed. (Boston: Charles C. Little and James Brown, 1842), 1:375–376.

21. James Knowles, *Memoir of Roger Williams* (Boston: Lincoln and Edmands, 1834), xiii.

22. Quoted in Gaustad, *Liberty of Conscience,* 213.

23. Interview with Santorum. http://www.americanclarion.com/2012/02/15/rick-santorum-christian-faith.

24. Roger Williams, *The Complete Writings of Roger Williams* (New York: Russell and Russell, 1963), *The Bloudy Tenent,* 3:249.

# Bibliography

## PRIMARY AND CONTEMPORARY SOURCES

Bacon, Francis. *Personal History of Lord Bacon from Unpublished Papers.* Edited by William Dixon. Leipzig, 1861.

———. *The Works of Francis Bacon, Lord Chancellor of England.* Edited by Basil Montagu. Philadelphia: Carey and Hart, 1842.

Baillie, Robert. *A Dissuasive from the Errors of the Time.* 1645.

———. *Letters and Journals of Robert Baillie.* Edinburgh, 1882.

Barrington, Robert. "Letter of Robert Barrington to Lady Joan Barrington." *Collections of the Rhode Island Historical Society* 29:71.

*Barrington Family Letters.* Edited by Arthur Searle. London: Royal Historical Society, 1983.

Bartlett, John Russell, ed. *Records of the Colony of Rhode Island and Providence Plantations, 1636–1792.* Providence, 1856–65.

Bishop, George. *New England Judged.* London: Robert Wilson, 1661.

Bradford, William. *Of Plimoth Plantation.* Boston: Houghton Mifflin, 1912.

Brereton, John. "A Briefe and True Relation of the Discoverie of the North Part of Virginia." In Cotton and Cromwell letters in *The Hutchinson Papers,* edited by W. H. Whitmore and W. S. Appleton. 1865. Reprinted New York: Burt Franklin, 1967.

Callendar, John. *An Historical Discourse.* Boston, 1739.

Chapin, Howard, ed. *Documentary History of Rhode Island.* Providence: Preston and Rounds, 1916.

Clarke, John. *Ill Newes from New England.* 1652.

Clarke, William. *The Clarke Papers: Selections from the Papers of William Clarke, Secretary to the Council of the Army, 1647–1649, and to General Monck and Commmanders of the Army in Scotland, 1651–1660.* Edited by C. H. Firth. London: Camden Society, 1894.

Cobbet, Rev. Thomas. *The Civil Magistrates' Power in Matters of Religion Modestly Defined.* 1653.

Cobbett, William. *Cobbett's Complete Collection of State Trials and Proceedings for High Treason and Other Crimes and Misdemeanors from the Earliest Period to the Present Time.* Edited by Thomas Bayley Howell. London: T. C. Hansard, 1809.

Coke, Edward. *A Book of Entries.* 2nd ed. London: John Streater, 1671.

———. *The third part of the Institutes of the laws of England: concerning high treason, and other pleas of the crown.* London: W. Clarke, and sons, 1809.

———. *The Reports of Sir Edward Coke, Knt., in Thirteen Parts.* Edited by John Henry Thomas and John Farquar Fraser. London: Joseph Butterworth, 1826.

———. *The Selected Writings of Sir Edward Coke.* Edited by Steve Sheppard. Indianapolis: Liberty Fund, 2003. Available online at http://files.libertyfund.org/files/912/Coke_0462-02_EBk_v5.pdf.

*Commons Debates, 1621.* Edited by Wallace Notestein, Frances Helen Reif, and Hartley Simpson. New Haven, CT: Yale University Press, 1935.

*Commons Debates, 1628.* Edited by Robert Johnson, Mary Keeler, Maija Cole, and William Bidwell. New Haven, CT: Yale University Press, 1977.

Cotton, John. *Gods Promise to His Plantation . . . As it was delivered in a sermon.* London: Wm Jones & John Bellamy, 1630.

*Debates in the House of Commons in 1625.* Edited by Samuel Rawson Gardiner. London: Camden Society, 1878.

D'Ewes, Simonds. *The Autobiography and Correspondence of Sir Simonds D'Ewes.* Edited by J. O. Halliwell. London: Richard Bentley, 1845.

Emerson, Everett, ed. *Letters from New England: The Massachusetts Bay Colony, 1629–1638.* Amherst: University of Massachusetts Press, 1976.

Force, Peter, compiler. *Tracts and Other Papers, Relating Principally to the Origin, Settlement, and Progres of the Colonies in North America, from the Discovery of the Country to the Year 1776.* Washington, DC, 1836–46.

Fox, George. *A New-England-fire-brand quenched, . . .* [90-word title]. London, 1678.

Gardiner, Lion. "Leift Lion Gardiner His Relation of the Pequot Warres." *Collections of the Massachusetts Historical Society,* 3rd ser., 3 (1833).

———. "Relation of the Plott-Indian." *Collections of the Massachusetts Historical Society,* 3rd ser., 3 (1833): 161–164.

Gardiner, Samuel Rawson, ed. *The Constitutional Documents of the Puritan Revolution, 1625–1660.* Oxford, 1906.

Gookin, Daniel. *Historical Collections of the Indians of Massachusetts. Collections of the Massachusetts Historical Society.* 1792.

Hall, David, ed. *The Antinomian Controversy, 1636–1638: A Documentary History.* Durham, NC: Duke University Press, 1990.

Harris papers. *Collections of the Rhode Island Historical Society* 10 (1902).

Harris, William. *A Rhode Islander Reports on King Philip's War: The Second William Harris Letter.* Edited by Douglas Leach. Providence: Rhode Island Historical Society, 1963.

Hooker, Thomas. *Thomas Hooker: Writings in England and Holland, 1626–1633.* Edited by George H. Williams, Norman Pettit, and Sargent Bush. Cambridge, MA: Harvard University Press, 1975.

Hubbard, William. *General History of New England from the Discovery to MDCLXXX.* 1682.

———. *The History of the Indian Wars in New England.* 1677.

Johnson, Edward. *Wonder-Working Providence of Sion's Saviour in New-England.* Edited by J. Franklin Jameson. New York: Scribner, 1910. First published 1653.

Johnson, George, ed. *The Fairfax Correspondence: Memoirs of the Reign of Charles I.* London: Michael Bentley, 1848.

*Journal of the House of Commons,* vol. 1, *1547–1629.* 1802. http://www.british-history.ac.uk/report,aspx?pubid=14.

Laud, William. *The Autobiography of Dr. William Laud.* Oxford: John Henry Parker, 1839.

———. *The Works of the Most Reverend Father in God, William Laud, D.D.* London: R. Chitwell, 1694. Reprinted Oxford: John Henry Parker, 1843.

Lechford, Thomas. *Plain Dealing, or News from New England.* Introduction by Darrett Rutman. New York: Johnson Reprint Corporation, 1969.

Lutz, Donald, ed. *Documents of Political Foundations Written by Colonial Americans: From Covenant to Constitution.* Philadelphia: Institute for the Study of Human Issues, 1986.

Mason, John. *A Brief History of the Pequot War.* Boston, 1736.

Meacham, Jon. *American Gospel: God, the Founding Fathers and the Making of a Nation.* New York: Random House, 2007.

Mather, Cotton. *Magnalia Christi Americana.* Hartford, CT, 1855.

Milton, John. *An Apology for Smectymnuus with the Reason of Church-Government.* 1654. Available at Early English Books Online, http://eebo.chadwyck.com/home.

———. *Areopagitca: A Speech of John Milton for Vnlicensed Printing.* 1644. Available at Early English Books Online, http://eebo.chadwyck.com/home.

Morison, Samuel Eliot, ed. *Winthrop Papers.* Boston: Massachusetts Historical Society, 1931.

Morton, Nathaniel. *New Englands Memoriall.* 5th ed. Introduction by John Davis. Boston: Crocker and Brewster, 1826. First published 1669.

Morton, Thomas. *New-English Canaan.* 1637. Available at Early English Books Online, http://eebo.chadwyck.com/home.

Moses Brown papers. Misc. box 2, f 98, Rhode Island Historical Society.

Noble, John, ed. *Records of the Court of Assistants of the Massachusetts Bay, 1630–1692.* 1901.

Norton, John. *Abel Being Dead Yet Speaketh. . . .* London, 1658.

Pulsifer, David, ed. *Acts of the Commissioners of the United Colonies of New England.* Boston: The Press of William White, 1859.

*Records of the Governor and Company of the Massachusetts Bay in New England.* Edited by Nathaniel Shurtleff. Boston: Wm White, 1853.

Rogers, Richard. *Seven Treatises.* 1603. Available at Early English Books Online, http://eebo.chadwyck.com/home.

Rushworth, John. *Historical Collections of Private Passages of State, Weighty Matters in Law, Remarkable Proceedings in Five Parliaments.* London: Tho. Newcomb for George Thomason, 1659–1701.

Shepard, Thomas. "Autobiography of Thomas Shepard." *Collections of the Massachusetts Historical Society* 27 (1932).

Smith, John. *Travels and Work of Captain John Smith.* 1630 edition. Available at Early English Books Online, http://eebo.chadwyck.com/home.

Stock, Leo Francis, ed. *Proceedings and Debates of the British Parliaments Respecting North America.* Washington, DC: Carnegie Institution, 1924.

Stow, John. *A Survey of London.* Introduction by H. B. Wheatley. New York: E. P. Dutton, 1956. First published 1599.

Tanner, Joseph R., ed. *Constitutional Documents from the Reign of James I, 1603–1625.* London and New York: Cambridge University Press, 1960.

Underhill, John. *Newes from America . . . containing A Trve Relation of Their War-like Proceedings these two yeares last past.* London: Peter Cole, 1638. Available at Digital Commons, University of Nebraska–Lincoln, http://digitalcommons.unl.edu/. Edited by Paul Royster.

Ward, Nathaniel. *The Simple Cobbler of Agawam.* Edited by John Ward Dean. New York: Albert Munsell, 1868.

White, John. *The Planters Plea.* London, 1630.

Williams, Roger. *The Correspondence of Roger Williams.* Edited by Glenn W. LaFantasie. Hanover, NH, and London: Brown University Press, 1988.

———. *The Complete Writings of Roger Williams.* New York: Russell and Russell, 1963.

Winslow, Edward. *Good Newes from New England.* 1624. Available at Early English Books Online, http://eebo.chadwyck.com/home.

———. *Hypocrisie Unmasked, a true Relation of the Proceedings of the Governor and Company of the Massachusetts against Samuel Gorton.* Introduction by Howard Chapin. Providence: Club for Colonial Reprints, 1916.

Winthrop, John. *Journal of John Winthrop.* Edited by Richard Dunn, James Savage, and Laetitia Yeandle. Cambridge, MA: Belknap Press of Harvard University Press, 1996.

———. "The Short Story of the Rise, Reign, and Ruine of the Antinomians, Familists, and Libertines that Infected the Churches of New England." In Charles Francis Adams, *Antinomianism in Massachusetts* (Boston: The Prince Society, 1894).

Winthrop, Robert. *Life and Letters of John Winthrop.* Boston, 1889.

Wood, William. *New England's Prospect.* Edited by Alden Vaughan. Amherst, MA: University of Massachusetts Press, 1993. First published 1634.

Young, Alexander, ed. *Chronicles of the First Plantation of the Colony of Massachusetts Bay.* Boston: Little, Brown, 1846.

## SECONDARY SOURCES

### *Dissertations*

Bragdon, Kathleen. "'Another Tongue Brought In': An Ethnohistorical Study of Native Writings in Massachusetts." Brown University, 1981.

Calamandrei, Mauro. "Theology and Political Thought of Roger Williams." University of Chicago, 1953.

Ceci, Lynn. "The Effect of European Contact and Trade on Settlement Pattern of Indians in Coastal New York, 1524–1665." City University of New York, 1977.

Chelline, Warren. "On the Relationship of Roger Williams and John Milton." University of Kansas, 1982.

Hankins, Jeffery. "Local Government and Society in Early Modern England: Hertfordshire and Essex, c. 1590–1630." Louisiana State University, 2003.

Leach, Douglas E. "The Causes of King Philip's War." Harvard University, 1952.

McCarron, Robert L. "Some Considerations of Style and Rhetoric in the Writings of Roger Williams." Indiana University, 1980.

March, Kathleen. "Uncommon Civility: The Narragansetts and Roger Williams." University of Iowa, 1985.

Searles, Joan. "The Worlds of Roger Williams." Pennsylvania State University, 1971.

Skaggs, Donald. "Roger Williams: His Image in the American Mind." University of Southern California, 1972.

*Articles*

Axtell, James. "The Power of Print in the Eastern Woodlands." In *After Columbus: Essays in the Ethnohistory of Colonial North America*. New York: Oxford University Press, 1988.

Bentley, William. "A Description and History of Salem." *Collections of the Massachusetts Historical Society*, 1st ser., 6 (1800): 212–288.

Bercovitch, Sacvan. "Typology in Puritan New England: The Williams-Cotton Controversy Reassessed." *American Quarterly* 19 (1967): 166–191.

Bremer, Francis J. "In Defense of Regicide: John Cotton on the Execution of Charles I." *William and Mary Quarterly* 37 (1980): 110.

Bush, Sargent, Jr., "John Wheelwright's Forgotten *Apology*: The Last Word in the Antinomian Controversy." *New England Quarterly* 64 (1991): 22–45.

Calder, Isabel. "John Cotton's 'Moses His Judicials.'" *Publications of the Colonial Society of Massachusetts* 28 (1935): 86–94.

Callender, John. *Historical Discourse*. Boston, 1838. *Collections of the Rhode Island Historical Society* 4 (1838): 111.

Canny, Nicholas. "The Ideology of English Colonization: From Ireland to America." *William and Mary Quarterly*, 3rd ser., 30, no. 4 (1973): 575–598.

Cave, Alfred. "The Pequot Invasion of Southern New England: A Reassessment of the Evidence." *New England Quarterly* 62 (1989): 27–44.

———. "Who Killed John Stone? A Note on the Origins of the Pequot War." *William and Mary Quarterly* 49 (1992): 509–512.

Dawson, Hugh. "Christian Charitie as Colonial Discourse: Reading Winthrop's Sermon in its English Context." *Early American Literature* 33, no. 2 (1998): 117–148.

———. "John Winthrop's Rite of Passage: The Origins of the Christian Charity Discourse." *Early American Literature* 26, no. 3 (1991): 219–231.

Dexter, Henry. "As to Roger Williams, and his 'banishment' from the Massachusetts Plantation . . . : a monograph." Boston: Congregational Publishing Society, Franklin Press, 1876.

Dunn, Richard S. "John Winthrop Jr and the Narragansett Country." *William and Mary Quarterly*, 3rd ser., 13, no. 1 (January 1956): 68–86.

Easton, Emily. "Mary Bernard." *Collections of the Rhode Island Historical Society* 29 (1936): 65–80.

Ernst, James. "Roger Williams and the English Revolution." *Collections of the Rhode Island Historical Society* 24 (1931): 1–58, 118–128.

Felker, Christopher. "Roger Williams' Uses of Legal Discourse: Testing Authority in Early New England." *New England Quarterly* 63 (1990): 624–648.

Foster, Stephen. "New England and the Challenge of Heresy, 1630 to 1660: The Puritan Crisis in Transatlantic Perspective." *William and Mary Quarterly*, 3rd ser., 38, no. 4 (October 1981): 624–660.

Gray, Charles. "Reason, Authority, and Imagination: The Jurisprudence of Sir Edward Coke." In *Culture and Politics from Puritanism to the Enlightenment*, edited by Perez Zagorin. Berkeley: University of California Press, 1980.

Guggisberg, Hans. "Religious Freedom and the History of the Christian World in Roger Williams' Thought." *Early American Literature* 12, no. 1 (spring 1977): 36–49.

Gura, Philip. "'The Contagion of Corrupt Opinions' in Puritan Massachusetts: The Case of William Pynchon." *William and Mary Quarterly*, 3rd ser., 39, no. 3 (July 1982): 469.

———. "The Radical Thought and Ideology of Samuel Gorton: New Light on the Relation of English to American Puritanism." *William and Mary Quarterly*, 3rd ser., 36 (1979): 78–100.

———. "Samuel Gorton and Religious Radicalism in England." *William and Mary Quarterly*, 3rd ser., 40, no. 1 (January 1983): 121–124.

Healy, Simon. "Oh, What a Lovely War? War, Taxation, and Public Opinion in England, 1624–1629." *Canadian Journal of History* 38, no. 3 (December 2003): 439–465.

Heath, William. "Thomas Morton: From Merry Old England to New England." *Journal of American Studies* 41, no. 1 (2007): 135–168.

Hirsch, Adam. "The Collision of Military Cultures in Seventeenth-Century New England." *Journal of American History* 74 (1988): 1187–1212.

Hudson, Winthrop. "John Locke: Heir of Puritan Political Theorists." In *Calvinism and the Political Order*, edited by George Hunt. Philadelphia: Westminster Press, 1965.

———. "John Locke: Preparing the Way for the Revolution." *Journal of Presbyterian History* 42 (March 1964): 19–38.

James, Sydney. "Ecclesiastical Authority in the Land of Roger Williams." *New England Quarterly* 57 (1984): 323–346.

Jones, Howard Mumford. "The Colonial Impulse: An Analysis of the Promotion Literature of Colonization." *Proceedings of the American Philosophical Society* 90, no. 2 (May 1946): 131–161.

Keary, Anne. "Retelling the History of the Settlement of Providence: Speech, Writing, and Cultural Interactions on Narragansett Bay." *New England Quarterly* 64, no. 2 (June 1996): 250–286.

Kemp, John. "The Background of the Fifth Amendment in English Law: A Study of Its Historical Implications." *William and Mary Law Review* 1, no. 2 (1958): 247–286.

Kyle, Chris. "Prince Charles and the Parliaments of 1621 and 1624." *Historical Journal* 41, no. 3 (September 1998): 603–628.

LaFantasie, Glenn. "Murder of an Indian, 1638." *Rhode Island History* 38, no. 3 (1979): 67–77.

———. "Roger Williams and John Winthrop: The Rise and Fall of an Extraordinary Friendship." *Rhode Island History* 47 (August 1989): 85–95.

Leach, Douglas Edward. "A New View of the Declaration of War Against the Narragansetts, November 1675." *Rhode Island History* 15 (1956): 33–41.

Lowenherz, Robert J. "Roger Williams and the Great Quaker Debate." *American Quarterly* 11 (1959): 157–165.

Lucas, Paul. "Colony or Commonwealth: Massachusetts Bay, 1661–1666." *William and Mary Quarterly*, 3rd ser., 24, no. 1 (January 1967): 88–107.

McIlwain, C. H. "The House of Commons in 1621." *Journal of Modern History* 9, no. 2 (June 1937): 206–214.

McLoughlin, William G. "Isaac Backus and the Separation of Church and State in America." *American Historical Review* 73 (June 1968): 1392–1413.

McNear, James Fulton. "'The Heart of New England Rent': The Mystical Element in Early Puritan History." *Mississippi Valley Historical Review* 62 (1956): 621–652.

Maitland, F. W. "Elizabethan Gleanings: Defender of the Faith, and So Forth." *English Historical Review* 15, no. 57 (January 1900): 120–124.

Malone, Patrick. "Changing Military Technology Among the Indians of Southern New England, 1600–1677." *American Quarterly* 25 (1973).

Miller, Perry. "Roger Williams: An Essay in Interpretation." In *The Complete Writings of Roger Williams*, edited by Perry Miller. New York: Russell and Russell, 1963.

Moody, Robert Earle. "A Re-Examination of the Antecedents of the Massachusetts Bay Company's Charter of 1629." *Massachusetts Historical Society Publications*, 69 (1956): 56–80.

Morgan, Edmund. "The Puritans and Sex." *New England Quarterly* 15 (1952): 595–596.

———. "John Winthrop's 'Model of Christian Charity' in a Broader Context." *Huntington Library Quarterly* 50 (1987): 145–151.

Morrill, John. "The Religious Context of the English Civil War." *Transactions of the Royal Historical Society*, 5th ser., 34 (1984): 155–178.

Moynihan, Ruth Barnes. "The Patent and the Indians: The Problem of Jurisdiction in Seventeenth-Century New England." *American Indian Culture and Research Journal* 2, no. 1 (1977): 8–18.

Nelsen, Anne Kussener. "King Philip's War and the Hubbard-Mather Rivalry." *William and Mary Quarterly*, 3rd ser., 28 (1970): 615–629.

Parkes, H. B. "Morals and Law Enforcement in Colonial New England." *New England Quarterly* 5 (July 1932): 445–467.

Perley, Sidney. "Where Roger Williams Lived in Salem." *Essex Institute Historical Collections* 52 (1916): 97–111.

Pestana, Carla Gardina. "The City upon a Hill under Siege: The Puritan Perception of the Quaker Threat to Massachusetts Bay, 1656–1661." *New England Quarterly* 56 (1983): 323–353.

Porter, Kenneth. "Samuell Gorton: New England Firebrand." *New England Quarterly* 7 (1934): 405–444.

Potter, George. "Roger Williams and John Milton." *Collection of the Rhode Island Historical Society* 13, no. 4 (1920): 113–129.

Pursell, Brennan. "James I, Gondomar and the Dissolution of the Parliament of 1621." *History* 85, no. 279 (July 2000): 428–445.

Reinitz, Richard. "The Separatist Background of Roger Williams' Argument for Religious Toleration." In *Typology and Early American Literature*, edited by Sacvan Bercovitch. Amherst: University of Massachusetts Press, 1972.

———. "The Typological Argument for Religious Toleration: The Separatist Tradition and Roger Williams." *Early American Literature* 5, no. 4 (1970): 74–111.

Sachse, William. "The Migration of New Englanders to England, 1640–1660." *American Historical Review* 53 (1947): 251–279.

Sainsbury, John. "Miantonomo's Death and New England Politics, 1630–1645." *Rhode Island History* 30 (1971): 111–123.

Sandler, S. Gerald. "Lockean Ideas in Thomas Jefferson's Bill for Establishing Religious Freedom." *Journal of the History of Ideas* 21, no. 1 (1960): 110–116.

Scholz, Robert. "Clerical Consociation in Massachusetts Bay: Reassessing the New England Way and Its Origins," *William and Mary Quarterly* 29 (1972): 391–414.

Sehr, Timothy. "Nionigret's Tactics of Accommodation: Indian Diplomacy in New England, 1637–1675." *Rhode Island History* 36 (1977): 44–53.

Simmons, William. "Cultural Bias in the New England Puritans' Perception of Indians." *William and Mary Quarterly* 38 (1981): 56–72.

Simpson, Alan. "How Democratic Was Roger Williams?" *William and Mary Quarterly,* 3rd ser., 13 (February 1956): 53–67.

Smolinski, Reiner. "Israel Revivus: The Eschatological Limits of Puritan Typology in New England." *New England Quarterly* 63 (1990): 357–396.

Snyder, David. "John Locke and the Freedom of Belief." *Journal of Church and State* 30, no. 2 (Spring 1988): 227–243.

Springer, James Warren. "American Indians and the Law of Real Property in Colonial New England." *American Journal of Legal History* 30, no. 1 (1986): 25–58.

Stearns, Raymond. "The Weld-Peter Mission to England." *Publications of the Colonial Society of Massachusetts* 32 (1934): 188–246.

Stout, Harry. "The Morphology of Remigration: New England University Men and Their Return to England, 1640–1660." *Journal of American Studies* 10, no. 2 (August 1976): 151–172.

Teunissen, John J., and Evelyn J. Hinz. "Roger Williams, Thomas More, and the Narragansett Utopia." *Early American Literature* 2 (1976–1977): 281–295.

Underdown, David. "John White Revisited." http://www.dorchesteranglican.info/stpeters/johnwhite/jww/JWRevisited.pdf.

Usher, Roland. "James I and Edward Coke." *English Historical Review* 18, no. 72 (1903): 664–675.

Vaughan, Alden T. "From White Man to Redskin: Changing Anglo-American Perceptions of the American Indian." In *Roots of American Racism: Essays on the Colonial Experience.* New York: Oxford University Press, 1995; also in *American Historical Review* 86 (1982): 917–953.

Vaughan, Alden T., and Virginia Mason Vaughan. "England's 'Others' in the Old and New World." In *The World of John Winthrop: Essays on England and New England, 1588–1649,* edited by Francis Bremer and Lynn Botelho. *Massachusetts Historical Society Studies in American History and Culture* 9. Boston: Massachusetts Historical Society, 2005.

Waite, P. B. "The Struggle of Prerogative and Common Law in the Reign of James I." *Canadian Journal of Economics and Political Science* 25, no. 2 (May 1959): 144–152.

Warren, Elizabeth. "Roger Williams' Landmarks, Memorabilia, Writings, Memorials, Selected References." *Collections of the Rhode Island Historical Society,* July 1968, typescript.

Whiting, Samuel. "Concerning the Life of the Famous Mr. Cotton." In *Chronicles of the First Planters of the Colony of Massachusetts Bay, from 1623 to 1636,* edited by Alexander Young. Boston: Little, Brown, 1846.

Winship, Michael. "'The Most Glorious Church in the World': The Unity of the Godly in Boston, Massachusetts, in the 1630s." *Journal of British Studies* 39 (2000): 71–98.

Wroth, Lawrence. "Roger Williams." The Marshall Woods Lecture, October 26, 1936. Pamphlet. Providence: Brown University, 1937.

Ziff, Larzer. "The Salem Puritans in the 'Free Aire of a New World.'" *Huntington Library Quarterly* 20, no. 4 (1957): 373–384.

Zuckerman, Michael. "Pilgrims in the Wilderness: Community, Modernity, and the Maypole at Merrymount." *New England Quarterly* 50, no. 2 (1977): 255–277.

## Books

Achinstein, Sharon, and Elizabeth Sauer, eds. *Milton and Toleration.* New York: Oxford University Press, 2007.

Andrews, Charles. *The Colonial Period in American History,* vol. 1, *The Settlements.* New Haven, CT: Yale University Press, 1964.

Andrews, K. R., N. P. Canny, and P. E. H. Hair, eds. *The Westward Enterprise: English Activities in Ireland, the Atlantic, and America, 1480–1650*. Detroit: Wayne State University Press, 1979.

Axtell, James. *After Columbus: Essays in the Ethnohistory of Colonial North America*. New York: Oxford University Press, 1988.

———. *The Invasion Within: The Context of Cultures in Colonial America*. New York: Oxford University Press, 1985.

Backus, Isaac. *History of New England with Particular Reference to the Baptists*. New York: Arno Press, 1969. First published 1776.

Battis, Emery. *Saints and Sectaries: Anne Hutchinson and the Antinomian Crisis in Massachusetts Bay Colony*. Chapel Hill: University of North Carolina Press, 1962.

Bearcroft, Philip. *An Historical Account of Thomas Sutton, Esq., and of his Foundation in Charterhouse*. London: E. Owen, 1737.

Benedict, David. *A General History of the Baptist Denomination in America*. Boston: Lincoln & Edmonds, 1813.

Bercovitch, Sacvan. *The Puritan Origins of the American Self*. New Haven, CT: Yale University Press, 1975.

———, ed. *Typology and Early American Literature*. Amherst, MA: University of Massachusetts Press, 1972.

Bicknell, Thomas. *The Story of Dr. John Clarke*. Providence, 1915.

Black, Robert C. *The Younger John Winthrop*. New York: Columbia University Press, 1966.

Bonomi, Patricia. *Under the Cape of Heaven: Religion, Society, and Politics in Colonial America*. New York: Oxford University Press, 1986.

Bowen, Catherine Drinker. *The Lion and the Throne: The Life and Times of Sir Edward Coke, 1552–1634*. New York: Little, Brown, 1990. First published 1957.

Boyer, Allen D. *Sir Edward Coke and the Elizabethan Age*. Stanford, CA: Stanford University Press, 2003.

Bozeman, Theodore Dwight. *To Live Ancient Lives: The Primitivist Dimension in Puritans*. Chapel Hill: University of North Carolina Press, 1998.

Bragdon, Kathleen. *Native People of Southern New England*. Norman: University of Oklahoma Press, 1996.

Braithwaite, William C. *The Beginnings of Quakerism*. London: Macmillan, 1912.

Breen, Louise. *Transgressing the Bounds: Subversive Enterprises Among the Puritan Elite in Massachusetts, 1630-1692*. New York: Oxford University Press, 2001.

Breen, Timothy. *The Character of a Good Ruler: A Study of Puritan Political Ideas*. New Haven, CT: Yale University Press, 1970.

Bremer, Francis J. *Congregational Communion: Clerical Friendship in the Anglo-American Puritan Community*. Boston: Northeastern University Press, 1994.

———. *John Winthrop: America's Forgotten Founding Father*. New York: Oxford University Press, 2003.

Bremer, Francis J., and Tom Webster. *Puritans and Puritanism in Europe and America: A Comprehensive Encyclopedia*. Santa Barbara, CA: ABC-Clio, 2006.

Brockunier, Samuel. *The Irrepressible Democrat: Roger Williams*. New York: Ronald Press, 1940.

Brook, Benjamin. *Lives of the Puritans*. London: J. Black, 1813.

Bross, Kristina. *Dry Bones and Indian Sermons: Praying Indians and Colonial American Identity*. New York: Cornell, 2004.

Bush, Sargent. *The Correspondence of John Cotton*. Chapel Hill: University of North Carolina Press, 2001.

Butler, Jon. *Awash in a Sea of Faith: Christianizing the American People*. Cambridge, MA: Harvard University Press, 1990.

Cady, John. *Civic Architectural Development of Providence, 1636–1650*. Providence: The Book Shop, 1957.

Caldwell, Patricia. *The Puritan Conversion Narrative: The Beginnings of American Expression*. New York: Cambridge University Press, 1983.

Camp, Raymond L. *Roger Williams: God's Apostle of Advocacy*. Lewiston, NY: Edwin Mellen Press, 1989.

Campbell, Gordon, and Thomas Corns. *John Milton: Life, Work, and Thought*. Oxford: Oxford University Press, 2008.

Carpenter, Edmund. *Roger Williams: A Study of the Life, Times, and Character of a Political Pioneer*. New York: Grafton Press, 1909.

Cave, Alfred. *The Pequot War*. Amherst: University of Massachusetts Press, 1996.

Chapin, Howard Millar. *Roger Williams and the King's Colors*. Providence: Rhode Island Historical Society / E. L. Freeman, 1928.

———. *The Trading Post of Roger Williams, with Those of John Wilcox and Richard Smith*. Providence: Rhode Island Historical Society / E.A. Johnson, 1933.

Chroust, Anton. *The Rise of the Legal Profession in America.* Norman: University of Oklahoma Press, 1965.

Chupack, Henry. *Roger Williams.* New York: Twayne, 1969.

Cogley, Richard. *John Eliot's Mission to the Indians Before King Philip's War.* Cambridge, MA: Harvard University Press, 1999.

Cohen, Charles. *God's Caress: The Psychology of Puritan Religious Experience.* New York: Oxford University Press, 1986.

Crawford, Patricia. *Women and Religion in New England, 1500–1720.* London: Routledge, 1996.

Cressy, David. *Coming Over: Migration and Communication Between England and New England in the Seventeenth Century.* New York: Cambridge University Press, 1987.

Croft, Pauline. *King James.* London: Palgrave Macmillan, 2003.

Cromartie, Alan. *The Constitutionalist Revolution: An Essay on the History of England, 1450–1642.* New York: Cambridge University Press, 2006.

Cronon, William. *Changes in the Land: Indians, Colonists, and the Ecology of New England.* New York: Hill and Wang, 1983.

Daniels, Bruce. *Dissent and Conformity on Narragansett Bay: The Colonial Rhode Island Town.* Middletown: CT: Wesleyan University Press, 1983.

Davies, D. W. *Dutch Influence on English Culture, 1558–1625.* Washington, DC: Folger Books, 1964.

Delbanco, Andrew. *The Puritan Ordeal.* Cambridge, MA: Harvard University Press, 1989.

Demos, John. *Entertaining Satan: Witchcraft and the Culture of Early New England.* New York: Oxford University Press, 1982.

Donnelly, Marian Card. *The New England Meeting Houses of the Seventeenth Century.* Middletown, CT: Wesleyan University Press, 1968.

Dunn, Richard. *Puritans and Yankees: The Winthrop Dynasty of New England, 1630–1717.* Princeton, NJ: Princeton University Press, 1962.

Durant, Will. *The Age of Reason Begins.* New York: MJF Books, 1997.

*Ecclesiastical Records of the State of New York.* Edited by Hugh Hastings et al. Albany, NY, 1901–16.

Emerson, Everett. *John Cotton.* Revised edition. Boston: Twayne, 1990.

Erikson, Kai T. *Wayward Puritans: A Study in the Sociology of Deviance.* New York: John Wiley and Sons, 1966.

Ernst, James. *The Political Thought of Roger Williams.* Seattle: University of Washington Press, 1929.

———. *Roger Williams: New England Firebrand.* New York: Macmillan, 1932.

Felt, Joseph. *Annals of Salem.* Salem: W. & S. B. Ives / Boston: J. Munroe, 1827.

Field, Jonathan Beecher. *Errands into the Metropolis: New England Dissidents in Revolutionary London.* Hanover, NH: Dartmouth College Press, 2009.

Fischer, David Hackett. *Albion's Seed: Four British Folkways in America.* New York: Oxford University Press, 1989.

Fletcher, Harris. *The Intellectual Development of John Milton.* Urbana: University of Illinois Press, 1956–61.

Forster, John. *Sir John Eliot: A Biography.* London: Chapman and Hall, 1872.

Foster, Stephen. *The Long Argument: English Puritanism and the Shaping of New England Culture, 1500–1700.* Chapel Hill: University of North Carolina Press, 1991.

Foxe, John. *Acts and Monuments of Martyrs.* http://www.hrionline.ac.uk/johnfoxe/.

Fuller, Thomas. *Church History of Britain.* Book X. 1655.

Games, Allison. *Migration and the Origins of the English Atlantic World.* Cambridge, MA: Harvard University Press, 1999.

Gardiner, Samuel Rawson. *History of the Commonwealth and the Protectorate.* New York: Longmans, Green, and Co., 1903.

Garrett, John. *Roger Williams: Witness Beyond Christendom.* New York: Macmillan, 1970.

Gaustad, Edwin. *Baptist Piety: Last Will and Testament of Obadiah Holmes.* Grand Rapids, MI: Erdmanns, 1978.

———. *Liberty of Conscience: Roger Williams in America.* Grand Rapids, MI: Erdmanns, 1991.

Gildrie, Richard. *Salem, Massachusetts, 1626–1683: A Covenant Community.* Charlottesville: University of Virginia Press, 1975.

Gilpin, W. Clark. *The Millenarian Piety of Roger Williams.* Chicago: University of Chicago Press, 1979.

Greaves, Richard. *Society and Religion in Elizabethan England.* Minneapolis: University of Minnesota Press, 1981.

Greene, Theodore P. *Roger Williams and the Massachusetts Magistrates.* Boston: D. C. Heath, 1964.

Gura, Philip. *A Glimpse of Sion's Glory: Puritan Radicalism in New England, 1620–1660.* Middletown, CT: Wesleyan University Press, 1984.

Hall, David D. *The Antinomian Controversy, 1636–1638: A Documentary History.* Durham, NC: Duke University Press, 1990.

———. *The Faithful Shepherd: A History of the New England Ministry in the Seventeenth Century.* Chapel Hill: University of North Carolina Press, 1972.

———. *Worlds of Wonders, Days of Judgment: Popular Religious Belief in Early New England.* Cambridge, MA: Harvard University Press, 1989.

Hall, David D., and David Allen, eds. *Seventeenth-Century New England.* Boston: Colonial Society of Massachusetts, publication no. 63, 1984.

Hall, David D., John Murrin, and Thad Tate, eds. *Saints and Revolutionaries: Essays on Early American History.* New York and London: W. W. Norton, 1984.

Hall, Timothy. *Separating Church and State: Roger Williams and Religious Liberty.* Champaign: University of Illinois Press, 1998.

Halliday, Paul. *Habeas Corpus: From England to Empire.* Cambridge, MA: Harvard University Press, 2010.

Haskins, George. *Law and Authority in Early Massachusetts.* New York: Macmillan, 1960.

Hauptman, Laurence, and James Wherry, eds. *The Pequots in Southern New England: The Fall and Rise of an American Indian Nation.* Norman: Oklahoma University Press, 1990.

Hibbard, Caroline. *Charles I and the Popish Plot.* Chapel Hill: University of North Carolina Press, 1983.

Hill, Christopher. *Milton and the English Revolution.* New York: Viking, 1978.

Hosmer, James Kendall. *The Life of Young Sir Henry Vane, Governor of Massachusetts Bay and Leader of the Long Parliament.* New York: Houghton Mifflin, 1888.

Hostettler, John. *Sir Edward Coke: A Force for Freedom.* Chichester, UK: Barry Rose Law Publishers, 1997.

Howe, Mark DeWolfe. *The Garden and the Wilderness: Religion and Government in American Constitutional History.* Chicago: University of Chicago Press, 1967.

Hunt, George Laird, and John McNeill, eds. *Calvinism and the Political Order.* Philadelphia: Westminster Press, 1965.

Hunt, William. *The Puritan Moment: The Coming of Revolution in an English County.* Cambridge, MA: Harvard University Press, 1983.

Ireland, W. W. *The Life of Sir Henry Vane the Younger.* London: E. Nash, 1905.

James, Sydney. *Colonial Rhode Island: A History.* New York: Scribner, 1975.

———. *John Clarke and His Legacies: Religion and Law in Colonial Rhode Island, 1638–1750.* University Park: Pennsylvania State University Press, 1999.

Jennings, Francis. *The Invasion of America: Indians, Colonialism, and the Cant of Conquest.* Chapel Hill: University of North Carolina Press, 1975.

Jones, Mary Jeanne Anderson. *Congregational Commonwealth: Connecticut, 1636–1662.* Middletown, CT: Wesleyan University Press, 1968.

Jordan, W. K. *The Development of Religious Toleration in England.* Cambridge, MA: Harvard University Press, 1932.

Kamensky, Jane. *Governing the Tongue: The Politics of Speech in Early New England.* New York: Oxford University Press, 1997.

Kawashima, Yasuhide. *Puritan Justice and the Indian: White Man's Law in Massachusetts, 1630–1763.* Middletown, CT: Wesleyan University Press, 1986.

Kishlansky, Mark. *A Monarchy Transformed: Britain, 1603–1714.* New York: Penguin, 1997.

Knowles, James. *Memoir of Roger Williams.* Boston: Lincoln and Edmands, 1834.

Kupperman, Karen Ordahl. *Indians and English: Facing Off in Early America.* Ithaca, NY: Cornell University Press, 2000.

———. *The Jamestown Project.* Cambridge, MA: Belknap Press of Harvard University, 2007.

Kyle, Chris, and Jason Peacey, eds. *Parliament at Work: Parliamentary Committees, Political Power, and Public Access in Early Modern England.* Woodbridge, UK: Boydell Press, 2002.

Langdon, George D. *Pilgrim Colony: A History of New Plymouth, 1620–1692.* New Haven, CT: Yale University Press, 1966.

Laplante, Eve. *American Jezebel: The Uncommon Life of Anne Hutchinson, the Woman Who Defied the Puritans.* San Francisco: Harper San Francisco, 2003.

Lauber, Almon Wheeler. *Indian Slavery in Colonial Times Within the Present Limits of the United States.* New York: Edward Braddock, 1913.

Law, Ernest. *History of Hampton Court Palace.* London: Bell and Sons, 1888.

Leach, Douglas Edward. *Flintlock and Tomahawk: New England in King Philip's War.* New York: Norton, 1966. First published 1958.

Lepore, Jill. *The Name of War: King Philip's War and the Origins of American Identity.* New York: Knopf, 1998.

Levermore, Charles Herbert. *Forerunners and Competitors of the Pilgrims and Puritans.* Brooklyn, NY: New England Society of Brooklyn, 1912.

Levy, Leonard. *Emergence of a Free Press.* New York: Oxford University Press, 1985.

———. *The Establishment Clause: Religion and the First Amendment.* Chapel Hill: University of North Carolina Press, 1986.

———. *Origins of the Bill of Rights.* New Haven, CT: Yale University Press, 1999.

Lewalski, Barbara. *The Life of John Milton: A Critical Biography.* Malden, MA: Blackwell, 2000.

Lindeboom, Johannes. *Austin Friars: History of the Dutch Reformed Church in London, 1550–1950.* The Hague: M. Nijhoff, 1950.

Liu, Tai, et al. *Discord in Zion: The Puritan Divines and the Puritan Revolution, 1640–1660.* New York: Brill Academic, 1973.

Lockyer, Roger. *Buckingham: The Life and Political Career of George Villiers, First Duke of Buckingham, 1592–1628.* London and New York: Longman, 1981.

———. *The Early Stuarts: A Political History of England, 1603–1642.* New York: Longman, 1989.

Lutz, Donald, ed. *Origins of American Constitutionalism.* Baton Rouge: Louisiana State University Press, 1988.

MacCulloch, Diarmaid. *The Later Reformation in England.* New York: St. Martin's Press, 2001.

Mack, Phyllis. *Visionary Women.* Berkeley and Los Angeles: University of California Press, 1992.

McLoughlin, William G. *New England Dissent, 1630–1833: The Baptists and the Separation of Church and State.* Cambridge, MA: Harvard University Press, 1971.

———. *Soul Liberty: The Baptist Struggle in New England, 1630–1833.* Hanover, NH: Brown University Press / University Press of New England, 1991.

Main, Gloria L. *Peoples of a Spacious Land: Families and Cultures in Colonial New England.* Oxford: Oxford University Press, 1986.

Maitland, F. W. *The Constitutional History of England.* Cambridge: Cambridge University Press, 1968. First published 1908.

Malone, Patrick. *The Skulking Way of War: Technology and Tactics Among the New England Indians.* Lanham, MD: Madison Books, 1991.

Mann, Charles. *1491: New Revelations of the Americas Before Columbus.* New York: Alfred A. Knopf, 2005.

March, Kathleen. *Uncommon Civility: The Narragansetts and Roger Williams.* Iowa City: University of Iowa Press, 1985.

Martin, John Frederick. *Profits in the Wilderness: Entrepreneurship and the Founding of New England Towns in the Seventeenth Century.* Chapel Hill: University of North Carolina Press, 1991.

Masson, David. *The Life of Milton: Narrated in Connexion with the Political, Ecclesiastical, and Literary History of His Time* (7 vols.). New York: Peter Smith, 1946. (Originally published 1877–1896.)

Mayo, Lawrence. *John Endecott: A Biography.* Cambridge, MA: Harvard University Press, 1971. First published 1936.

Mendle, Michael. *Henry Parker and the English Civil War: The Political Thought of the Public's "Privado."* Cambridge: Cambridge University Press, 2003.

Miller, Perry. *Errand into the Wilderness.* Cambridge, MA: Belknap Press of Harvard University Press, 1956.

———. *The New England Mind: The Seventeenth Century.* Cambridge, MA: Harvard University Press, 1982 edition.

———. *Orthodoxy in Massachusetts, 1630–1650.* Charlottesville: University of Virginia Press, 2007.

———. *Roger Williams: His Contribution to the American Tradition.* Indianapolis: Bobbs-Merrill, 1953.

Moore, Susan. *Pilgrim: New World Settlers and the Call Home.* New Haven, CT: Yale University Press, 2007.

Morgan, Edmund. *Inventing the People: The Rise of Popular Sovereignty in England and America.* New York: Norton, 1988.

———. *The Puritan Dilemma: The Story of John Winthrop.* New York: Little, Brown, 1958.

———. *The Puritan Family: Religious and Domestic Relations in Seventeenth-Century New England.* 3rd ed. New York: Harper and Row, 1966.

———, ed. *Puritan Political Ideas.* New York: Bobbs-Merrill, 1965.

———. *Roger Williams: The Church and the State.* New York: Norton, 1967.

———. *Visible Saints: The History of a Puritan Idea.* New York: New York University Press, 1963.

Morison, Samuel Eliot. *Builders of the Bay Colony.* Whitefish, MT: Kessinger, 2004.

————. *The European Discovery of America: The Northern Voyages, 500–1600*. New York: Oxford University Press, 1971.

————. *The Founding of Harvard College*. Cambridge, MA: Harvard University Press, 1935.

————. *Harvard College in the Seventeenth Century*. Cambridge, MA: Harvard University Press, 1936.

————. *The Puritan Pronaos: Studies in the Intellectual Life of New England in the Seventeenth Century*. New York: New York University Press, 1936.

Moseley, James. *John Winthrop's World*. Madison: University of Wisconsin Press, 1992.

Neal, Daniel. *The History of the Puritans*. New York: Harper, 1844.

Neale, J. E. *Elizabeth I and Her Parliaments, 1548–1601*. New York: St. Martin's Press, 1958.

Norton, Mary Beth. *Founding Mothers and Fathers: Gendered Power and the Forming of American Society*. New York: Knopf, 1996.

————. *In the Devil's Snare: The Salem Witchcraft Crisis of 1692*. New York: Knopf, 2002.

Oberg, Michael Leroy. *Dominion and Civility: English Imperialism and Native America*. Ithaca, NY: Cornell University Press, 1999.

Oberholzer, Emil, Jr., *Delinquent Saints: Disciplinary Action in the Early Congregational Churches of Massachusetts*. New York: Columbia University Press, 1955.

Osgood, Herbert. *The American Colonies in the Seventeenth Century*. New York: Columbia University Press, 1904–1907.

Pagden, Anthony. *Lords of All the World: Ideologies of Empire in Spain, Britain, and France, c. 1500–c. 1800*. New Haven, CT: Yale University Press, 1995.

Palfrey, John Gorham. *History of New England*. Boston: Little, Brown, 1876.

Parker, William Riley. *Milton: A Biography*. New York: Oxford University Press, 1968.

Parrington, Vernon. *Main Currents in American Thought*. New York: Harcourt Brace and Co., 1927.

Perley, Sidney. *The History of Salem Massachusetts*. Salem: Sidney Perley, 1926.

Pestana, Carla. *Liberty of Conscience and the Growth of Religious Diversity in Early America*. Providence, RI: John Carter Brown Library, 1986.

Peterson, Merrill D., and Robert C. Vaughan, eds. *The Virginia Statute for Religious Freedom: Its Evolution and Consequences in American History*, Cambridge: Cambridge University Press, 1988.

Philbrick, Nathan. *Mayflower: A Study of Courage, Community, and War*. New York: Viking, 2006.

Polishook, Irwin H. *Roger Williams, John Cotton, and Religious Freedom: A Controversy in New and Old England*. Englewood Cliffs, NJ: Prentice Hall, 1967.

Powell, Sumner. *Puritan Village: The Formation of a New Engand Town*. Garden City, NY: Anchor, 1965.

Price, David. *Love and Hate in Jamestown: John Smith, Pocahontas, and the Heart of a New Nation*. New York: Knopf, 2003.

Rappaport, Steven. *World Within Worlds: The Structure of Life in Sixteenth-Century London*. Cambridge: Cambridge University Press, 1988.

Rath, Richard. *How Early America Sounded*. Ithaca, NY: Cornell University Press, 2003.

Read, David. *New World, Known World: Shaping Knowledge in Early Anglo-American Writing*. Columbia: University of Missouri Press, 2005.

Richman, Irving. *Rhode Island: A History*. Boston and New York: Houghton Mifflin, 1905.

Rowe, Violet A. *Sir Henry Vane the Younger: A Study in Political and Administrative History*. London: Athlone Press, 1970.

Rubertone, Patricia. *Grave Undertakings: An Archaeology of Roger Williams and the Narragansett Indians*. Washington, DC: Smithsonian Institution Press, 2003.

Russell, Conrad. *The Crisis of Parliaments*. Oxford: Oxford University Press, 1971.

————. *Parliaments and English Politics, 1621–1629*. New York: Oxford University Press, 1979.

————. *Unrevolutionary England, 1603–1642*. London: Hambledon Press, 1990.

Rutman, Darrett B. *John Winthrop's Decision for America, 1629*. Philadelphia: Lippincott, 1975.

————. *Winthrop's Boston: A Portrait of a Puritan Town, 1630–1649*. Chapel Hill: University of North Carolina Press, 1965.

Salisbury, Neal. *Manitou and Providence: Indians, Europeans, and the Making of New England, 1500–1643*. New York: Oxford University Press, 1982.

Scheffer, J. De Hoop. *History of the Free Churchmen Called the Brownists, Pilgrim Fathers, and Baptists in the Dutch Republic, 1581–1701*. Ithaca, NY: Andrus and Church, 1922.

Schochet, George, ed. *Religion, Resistance, and Civil War*. Washington, DC: Folger Institute, 1990.

Scott, Jonathan. *England's Troubles: Seventeenth-Century English Political Thought in European Context*. Cambridge: Cambridge University Press, 2000.

Searle, Arthur, ed. *Barrington Family Letters*. London: Royal Historical Society, 1983.

Simpson, Alan. *Puritanism in Old and New England*. Chicago: University of Chicago Press, 1955.

Skaggs, Donald. *Roger Williams' Dream for America*. New York: Peter Lang, 1993. American University Studies, Series 9, History, vol. 129.

Slotkin, Richard, and James Folsom, eds. *So Dreadfull a Judgment: Puritan Responses to King Phillip's War, 1676–1677*. Middletown, CT: Wesleyan University Press, 1978.

Smith, James, ed. *Seventeenth-Century America: Essays in Colonial History*. Chapel Hill: University of North Carolina Press, 1980.

Stearns, Raymond. *The Strenuous Puritan: Hugh Peter, 1598–1660*. Urbana: University of Illinois Press, 1954.

Stewart, Alan. *The Cradle King: James VI & I, the First Monarch of a United Great Britain*. New York: St. Martin's Press, 2003.

Straus, Oscar. *Roger Williams: The Pioneer of Religious Liberty*. New York: Century Co., 1894.

Stubbs, William. *The Constitutional History of England*. Oxford: Oxford University Press, 1897.

Swan, Bradford. *The Case of Richard Chasmore alias Long Dick*. Providence: Roger Williams Press, 1944.

———. *Gregory Dexter of London and New England*. Rochester, NY: Leo Hart, 1949.

Taylor, Alan. *American Colonies: The Settling of North America*. New York: Viking Penguin, 2001.

Trevor-Roper, Hugh. *Archbishop Laud, 1573–1645*. 2nd ed. London: Macmillan, 1940.

Torbet, Robert. *A History of the Baptists*. Valley Forge, PA: Judson Press, 1969.

Underdown, David. *Fire from Heaven: Life in an English Town in the Seventeenth Century*. New Haven, CT: Yale University Press, 1992.

Updike, Daniel Berkeley. *Richard Smith, First English Settler of the Narragansett Country*. Boston: Merrymount Press, 1937.

Van der Zee, Henri, and Barbara van der Zee. *A Sweet and Alien Land: The Story of Dutch New York*. New York: Viking, 1978.

Vaughan, Alden. *The New England Frontier: Puritans and Indians, 1620–1675*. New York: W. W. Norton, 1979.

Vaughan, Alden, and Francis Bremer, eds. *Puritan New England: Essays on Religion, Society, and Culture*. New York: St. Martin's Press, 1977.

Wall, Robert Emmett, Jr. *Massachusetts Bay: The Crucial Decade, 1640–1650*. New Haven, CT: Yale University Press, 1972.

Ward, Harry. *The United Colonies of New England, 1643–1690*. New York: Vantage, 1961.

Weisman, Richard. *Witchcraft, Magic, and Religion in Seventeenth-Century Massachusetts*. Amherst: University of Massachusetts Press, 1984.

White, Stephen D. *Sir Edward Coke and "The Grievances of the Commonwealth," 1621–1628*. Chapel Hill: University of North Carolina Press, 1979.

Wilson, Lisa. *Ye Heart of a Man: The Domestic Life of Men in Colonial New England*. New Haven, CT: Yale University Press, 1999.

Winship, Michael. *Making Heretics: Militant Protestantism and Free Grace in Massachusetts, 1636–1641*. Princeton, NJ: Princeton University Press, 2002.

Winslow, Ola. *John Eliot: Apostle to the Indians*. Boston: Houghton Mifflin, 1968.

———. *Master Roger Williams: A Biography*. New York: Macmillan, 1957.

Winsor, Justin. *Narrative and Critical History of America*. Vol. 3. Boston: Houghton Mifflin, 1884.

Worth, Lawrence. *The Voyages of Giovanni da Verrazzano, 1524–1529*. New Haven, CT: Yale University Press, 1970.

Zagorin, Perez. *Francis Bacon*. Princeton, NJ: Princeton University Press, 1998.

———. *How the Idea of Religious Toleration Came to the West*. Princeton, NJ: Princeton University Press, 2003.

———, ed. *Culture and Politics from Puritanism to the Enlightenment*. Berkeley: University of California Press, 1980.

Zaller, Robert. *The Discourse of Legitimacy in Early Modern England*. Stanford, CA: Stanford University Press, 2007.

Ziff, Larzer. *The Career of John Cotton: Puritanism and the American Experience*. Princeton, NJ: Princeton University Press, 1962.

———. *John Cotton on the Churches of New England*. Cambridge, MA: Belknap Press of Harvard University Press, 1968.

# Index

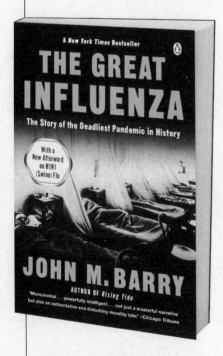